As Time Goes By in Argentina

DIRECTIONS IN DEVELOPMENT
Human Development

As Time Goes By in Argentina

*Economic Opportunities and Challenges
of the Demographic Transition*

Michele Gragnolati, Rafael Rofman, Ignacio Apella, and Sara Troiano

WORLD BANK GROUP

Contents

**Chapter 10   The Argentine Labor Market in a Context of
Demographic Transition   259**
Ignacio Apella and Sara Troiano

**Chapter 11   Argentine Labor Force Productivity in a Context of
Demographic Aging   285**
Ignacio Apella and Sara Troiano

**Chapter 12   Demographics and Macroeconomics: Opportunities
and Risks in Dividend-Era Argentina   305**
José María Fanelli

Tables

Abbreviations

ADL	activity of daily living
AFJP	Administradora de Fondos de Jubilaciones y Pensiones (Retirement and Pension Fund Administrators)
ANSES	Administración Nacional de la Seguridad Social (National Social Security Administration)
AUH	Asignación Universal por Hijo (Universal Child Allowance)
BCRA	Banco Central de la República de Argentina (Central Bank of Argentina)
BGR	benefit generosity ratio
CABA	Ciudad Autonoma de Buenos Aires (Autonomous City of Buenos Aires)
CELADE	Centro Latinoamericano y del Caribe de Demografía (Latin American and Caribbean Demographic Centre)
CV	coefficient of variation
–DC	less developed countries
+DC	more developed countries
DD	demographic dividend
DiNIECE	Dirección Nacional de Información y Evaluación de la Calidad Educativa (National Department of Information and Evaluation of the Quality of Education)
DNCN	Dirección Nacional de Cuentas Nacionales (National Directorate of National Accounts)
DWO	demographic window of opportunity
EAP	economically active population
ECNT	enfermedades crónicas no transmisibles (noncommunicable chronic disease)
EGB	Educación General Básica (General Basic Education)
ENDI	Encuesta Nacional de Personas con Discapacidad (National Disability Survey)
EPH	Encuesta Permanente de Hogares (Continuous Household Survey)

EST	education, science, and technology
FD	first demographic dividend
GDP	gross domestic product
IADL	instrumental activity of daily living
ILO	International Labour Organization
IMSS	Instituto Mexicano de Seguridad Social (Mexican Institute of Social Insurance)
INDEC	Instituto Nacional de Estadística y Censos (National Institute of Statistics and Censuses)
INSSJyP	Instituto Nacional de Seguridad Social para el Jubilado y Pensionado (National Institute of Social Services for Retirees and Pensioners)
LAC	Latin America and the Caribbean
LCD	life-cycle deficit
LE	life expectancy
LEB	life expectancy at birth
LEN	Ley Nacional de Educación (National Education Law)
LFE	Ley de Financiamiento Educativo (Education Funding Law)
LW	life-cycle wealth
MTEySS	Ministerio de Trabajo, Empleo y Seguridad Social (Ministry of Labor and Social Security)
NCD	noncommunicable disease
NTA	National Transfer Accounts
OECD	Organisation for Economic Co-operation and Development
ONE	Oficina Nacional de Evaluación (National Evaluation Operation)
OSN	Obra Social Nacional (national employer-based health plans)
OSP	Obra Social Provincial (provincial employer-based health plans)
PACBI	*prestaciones de alto costo y baja incidencia* (high-cost services and low-incidence ailments)
PAMI	Programa de Asistencia Médica Integral (Comprehensive Medical Assistance Program)
PCLD	per capita life-cycle deficit
PISA	Programme for International Student Assessment
PMO	Programa Médico Obligatorio (Compulsory Medical Program)
PPP	purchasing power parity
PROFE	Programa Federal de Salud (Federal Health Care Program)
SD	standard deviation; second growth dividend
SENAMA	Servicio Nacional del Adulto Mayor (National Service for the Elderly)

SIJP	Sistema Integrado de Jubilaciones y Pensiones (Integrated Retirement and Pension System)
SMRA	standardized mortality ratio by age
TDR	total dependency ratio
TFR	total fertility rate
UN	United Nations
WHO	World Health Organization

Preface

This book was written as part of a World Bank project coordinated by Michele Gragnolati, Rafael Rofman, Ignacio Apella, and Sara Troiano, who are also the volume editors and coauthors of the opening chapter. The book follows the line of research initiated by Daniel Cotlear on population ageing in Latin America.

This book's development benefitted from valuable contributions and comments from Daniel Heymann, Fabio Bertranou, Maria Eugenia Bonilla-Chacin, Cristina Massa, Marta Novick, Jorge Paz, and Axel Rivas, received during a preliminary results workshop in Buenos Aires, May 27–28, 2013. In addition this book was enhanced by comments and suggestions from Diego Ambasz, Penelope Brook, Daniel Cotlear, Rafael de Hoyos, Ariel Fiszbein, Roberta Gatti, Joana Godinho, Margaret Grosh, Sabine Hader, Peter Holland, Christine Lao Pena, Anibal Lopez, Eugenia Marinova, Zafer Mustafaoglu, Luis Perez, Hannah Sybille Nielsen, and Cassio Turra.

The authors extend special thanks to the team at the National Transfer Accounts project, led by Ronald Lee and Tim Miller, for their support and cooperation in the development of the projection methodology used for the majority of this book, as well as their suggestions on how to use the information generated by the project.

This book consists of 12 chapters that discuss and analyze the potential economic impact of the demographic transition in Argentina. The first chapter summarizes the book's findings. Chapter 2 presents Argentina's demographic forecasts up to 2100. Chapter 3 estimates national transfer accounts and consumption profiles and labor income by age. Chapter 4 presents a basic forecast model for social spending on education, health care, and pensions from 2010 to 2100. Chapters 5, 6, 7, and 8 analyze the potential impact of the demographic transition on the pension, health care, long-term care, and education systems, respectively, according to different public policy options. Chapter 9 analyzes the fiscal impact of the demographic transition and the trade-offs among social sectors. Chapters 10 and 11 study the dynamics of the labor market in the context of ageing and the potential impact on global labor force productivity. All of these analyses are performed considering different public policy tools. Chapter 12 studies Argentina's macroeconomic performance in relation to international experiences and the challenges and opportunities created by the demographic transition.

The authors hope that your reading this book will not only open up space for ideas and public policy debates, but that it will also be enjoyable.

CHAPTER 1

Introduction

Michele Gragnolati, Rafael Rofman, Ignacio Apella, and Sara Troiano

Motivation

Argentina is in the middle of a profound socioeconomic transformation driven by demographic change. Overall population size increased from 17 million in 1950 to 41 million in 2010 with a 1.4 percent average annual growth rate, which has been decreasing over time. (It decreased from an average of 1.6 percent during the first three decades to 1.2 percent during the last three.) Population size is expected to increase to 54 million in 2050 and 59 million in 2100 with an average 0.4 percent annual growth rate (with decreasing rates of 0.8 percent, 0.3 percent, and 0.1 percent during each of the three decades between 2010 and 2100). As can be seen in figure 1.1, the population age structure is gradually changing over time because different age groups grow at different speeds: Between 2010 and 2100, the growth rate will be zero for those under age 15, 0.3 percent for those between 15 and 64, and 1.4 percent for those older than 64.

As a result, the elderly population, which represented 4.2 percent and 10.4 percent of the total population in 1950 and 2010, respectively, will represent 19.3 percent of the total population in 2050 and 24.7 percent in 2100, in a process of convergence with the "old continent" of Europe—where the average proportion is currently at 24 percent. In absolute numbers, the elderly population increased from 0.7 million in 1950 to 4.2 million in 2010 and will further increase to 10 million in 2050. Moreover, the proportion of the working-age population—between 15 and 64 years—compared with total population will start declining around 2040, and, after that, population growth in Argentina will be mainly due to increases in the older population.

Although the demographic transition started much earlier in Argentina and is more advanced compared with other Latin American countries, Argentina is still relatively young compared to Organisation for Economic Co-operation and Development (OECD) countries. Interestingly, the recent pace of both fertility and mortality decline in Argentina has been slower than in many

Figure 1.1 Population Size, by Age Group, Argentina, 1950–2100

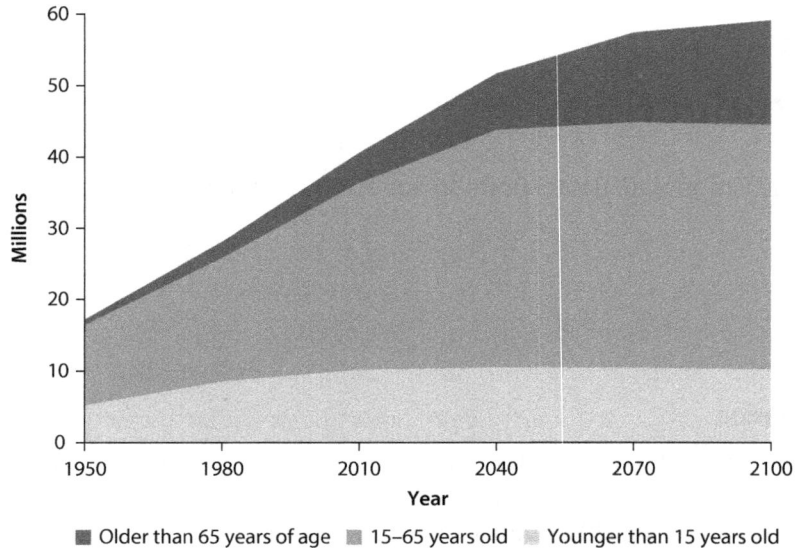

■ Older than 65 years of age   ▨ 15–65 years old   ▨ Younger than 15 years old

other Latin American countries so that differences have been reduced substantially during the past three decades. Nevertheless, the prospect of population aging in Argentina, as for most middle-income (and even more so for most low-income) countries, is a source of concern for two reasons: (a) it may hinder further economic growth, and (b) it may put a strain on existing institutions as they adjust to respond to changing needs and demands. On the first point, achieving high-income status may be more difficult for countries with large elderly populations. Developed countries, by and large, first became rich and then became old. Argentina and other emerging countries at a similar stage of socioeconomic development are becoming older at a much faster rate. On the second point, meeting the needs of a large elderly population requires rethinking the economic and social institutions and policies that are needed to realize income security and provide adequate health care and other services for an aging society. Take the change in the relative size of the population of elderly adults and working-age persons as an example of how changes in Argentina's population age structure are going to affect the financing of the pay-as-you-go pension system and the partially payroll contribution–financed health care system. Although in 2010 there were almost six people of working age for every elderly person, the same ratio is projected to decline to three in 2050 and to two in 2100.

Moreover, a certain urgency is seen in putting in place the right institutional and policy frameworks. This is for two reasons: (a) institutions are slow to change, and (b) those who will be part of the elderly population in 2050 and beyond are already entering the workforce today, and the rules of the current system are affecting their choices. Decisions they make over their entire adult lives will be framed by the social and economic institutions, actual and expected, that influence economic security in old age. In addition, political realities typically impose a long transition period until a new regulatory framework is fully implemented. The longer a reform is postponed, the greater the need for one, and the more drastic it will need to be. As a result, the cost of existing programs (relative to gross domestic product [GDP]) may continue to rise for a number of years during the transition period before the stabilizing effects of a reform are felt.

Consider the reforms that European countries have undertaken to make their pensions systems more affordable as an example. Postponing the retirement age to increase the economic and financial contributions of the working-age population and reduce the pressure on social security is proving very hard to do. Recent experiences in Europe are not encouraging. In France, a proposal to increase the statutory retirement age by two years faced very strong political opposition in 2010, including massive strikes and demonstrations, and was reversed in 2012. In Italy, a similar reform was enacted in 2012 that will make the minimum retirement age 66 years for both men and women by 2018. This proposal was also received with strong resistance, but was approved in the context of a critical economic situation. On the other hand, data from Uruguay's pension system indicate that workers are slowly delaying their retirement, responding to incentives in terms of expected benefits, but also to the fact that they perceive themselves as able to continue working beyond the statutory retirement age of 60 years. In any case, for this option to be feasible it is imperative to ensure that the future cohorts of older people will grow older in good health—and remain healthy for many years beyond the 60 or 65 "old age" landmark.

The crucial bottom line is that Argentina cannot afford simply to emulate the policies adopted by richer countries that have aged over a much longer period and within a context of relative wealth and that, themselves, are still struggling to address the same issues. Solutions will have to be developed from within Argentine society. Certainly, the experiences of other countries need to be observed—particularly those of other developing countries that have experienced faster population aging during the past half century, especially in East Asia—but the devised solutions need to be coherent with the country's individual history, culture, resources, and values.

Only a few articles have analyzed demographic trends and their implications on several dimensions of the Argentine economy, welfare system, public policy, and society. At the same time, no report has yet presented these questions in a comprehensive and systematic way that captures the broad complexity of issues, from economic growth to poverty, from public financing of social services and transfers to savings, from employment to health and long-term care, and their interrelations. This study aims to fill this gap by providing an overview of past and future demographic dynamics, analyzing their effect on social and economic development in Argentina. It identifies opportunities and challenges associated with population aging, highlighting those topics and sectors that will require policy changes. The aim of the study is not to provide policy prescriptions or detailed indications on how to reform each sector specifically, but to stimulate an analytical discussion of the possible policy options that could take advantage of the demographic opportunities and be sustainable in the medium to long term.[1] Finally, the study compares Argentina to other countries that have experienced or are currently in the middle of a demographic transition and offers examples of their experiences in addressing similar policy issues.

This initial section introduces the main issues associated with population aging, many of which will be investigated in detail in the following chapters. The second section describes the demographic transformation that Argentina has been experiencing and highlights its specific features, including very advanced demographic behavior in the 1950s and a slowdown observed during the past three decades with respect to other countries in Latin America. The third section presents the main economic framework behind this work—the life-cycle theory, according to which individuals' economic behavior varies according to their age. In the fourth section, we introduce the first and second demographic dividends associated with the changing population age structure that accompanies the demographic transition of any country. In the fifth, we investigate how public expenditures in the social sectors have changed during the past two decades and how they vary across age groups. The sixth section explores how poverty is linked to the life cycle in Argentina and the role played by public transfers in reducing poverty among different age groups. In the seventh section, we present the main findings of the report, and in the eighth, we present a short description of the chapters, which analyze the questions presented in this chapter in much more depth.

Demographic Change in Argentina

The discussion about aging in Argentina in this book is grounded in population projections, prepared by one of the contributing authors, from 2010 to 2100. Although it is clear that the robustness of assumptions used to develop these projections more than 85 years into the future may be arguable, we found that this time horizon is more effective for discussing long-term trends than the traditional 2050 threshold, which is now only 35 years away, and although it is still far into the future in regard to any individual lifetime, it represents the short to medium term in the context of demographic change. Prolonging the time reference to 2100 allows highlighting trends that would not be manifest if the projections were to stop 50 years earlier.

For Argentina, the 2010 census was used as the baseline data. To run the 2010–2100 population projections, life expectancy (LE) at birth (LE_0) is assumed to increase by an average of 0.15 years per year between 2010 and 2040 and 0.08 years per year between 2040 and 2100. We see that LE_0 will reach 85 years in 2100 (82 years for men and 89 for women). The total fertility rate (TFR), the average number of children per woman, is assumed to decrease gradually and monotonically to 2.0 in 2100. The 2013 population projections of the Population Division of the United Nations (United Nations 2013) were used for the countries used as comparators.

The population projections presented in this study, in line with INDEC (2004) and ECLAC (2011), assume a null net impact of migration starting from 2010. Although migration historically played a significant role in Argentina, especially in the first three decades of the twentieth century, its role has been much less significant since 1930. In particular, toward the end of the century, the net migration rate has moved progressively closer to zero, as modest immigration by neighboring countries has been compensated for by emigration of Argentineans. More information can be found in chapter 2.

Demographic patterns in Argentina are characterized by four main features: (a) the demographic transition started much earlier and is advanced compared with other Latin American countries, but Argentina is still a relatively young country compared with OECD countries; (b) the recent pace of both fertility and mortality decline in Argentina has been slower than in many other Latin American countries, and the differences have been reduced substantially during the past three decades; (c) the population age structure has been changing significantly and will keep doing so in the decades to come; and (d) Argentina has just started its 30-year period of most favorable age structure, which is potentially conducive to higher economic growth. It will stop at the end of the 2040s.

First, Argentina is at an advanced phase of the demographic transition (compared with other Latin American countries) but is not as advanced as most European and other OECD countries, where mortality and, most important, fertility decline started much earlier (figure 1.2a). Although the average number of children per Argentine woman 2010 (2.3) is very close to the average number of children in Latin America (2.4), it is higher than the corresponding number for the average European woman (1.5) and in the more developed neighboring countries: Brazil (1.9), Chile (1.9), and Uruguay (2.1). The lowest TFR in the world is found in the Republic of Korea (1.2). At the same time, life expectancy at birth of the average Argentine an in 2010 is higher than that of the average Latin American (75.2 and 73.4 years, respectively) and much lower than that observed in Japan, where currently people live longer (almost 83 years). As expected in such a large and heterogeneous country, demographic indicators in Argentina vary considerably across geographic areas (figure 1.2b). For example, the TFR in 2004 was 1.4 in the Autonomous City of Buenos Aires (CABA) and 3.1 in Misiones, and LE was 76 years in the CABA and 70 in Chaco.

Second, although in the 1950s Argentina's fertility and mortality levels were similar to those of more developed regions,[2] and, with the exception of Uruguay, much more advanced than in the rest of Latin America, the pace of change has not kept up with that observed in European countries nor with that observed in comparator Latin American countries (Brazil, Chile, Mexico, and Uruguay). The consequence is that the fertility and mortality gaps have increased between Argentina and European countries and have decreased to almost zero (and in some cases reversed) between Argentina and the four

Figure 1.2 Life Expectancy at Birth and Total Fertility Rate, 2010 and 2004

a. Argentina and comparator countries and regions, 2010

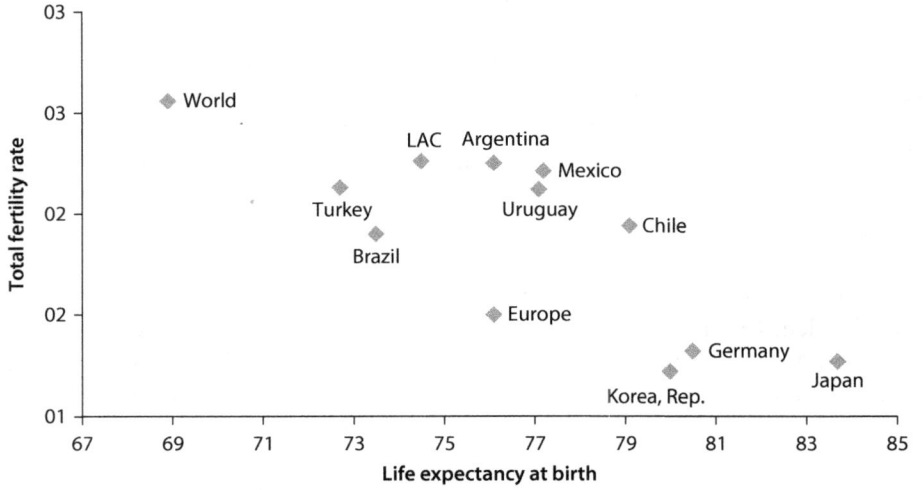

Scatter plot. Y-axis: Total fertility rate (03 to 01). X-axis: Life expectancy at birth (67 to 85). Points: World, LAC, Argentina, Mexico, Turkey, Uruguay, Brazil, Chile, Europe, Germany, Korea, Rep., Japan.

Note: LAC = Latin America and the Caribbean.

b. Argentine provinces, 2004

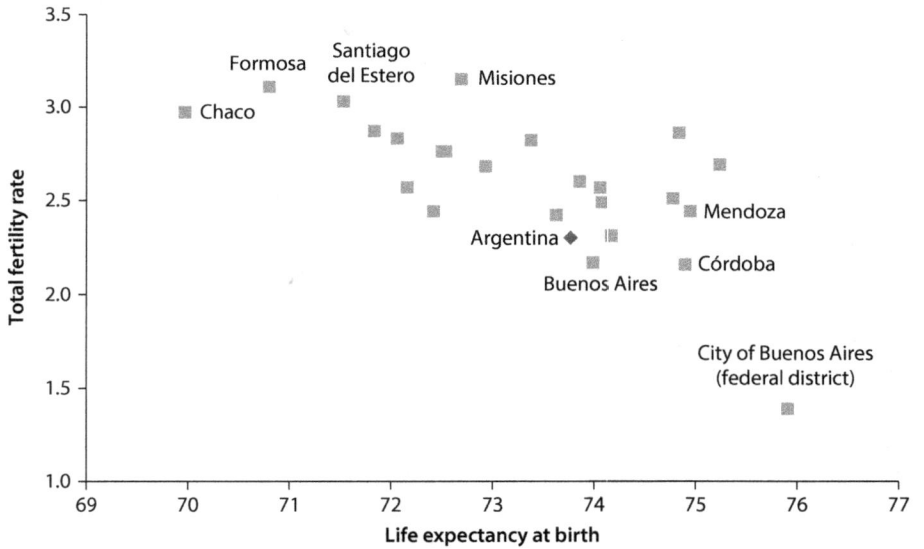

Scatter plot. Y-axis: Total fertility rate (1.0 to 3.5). X-axis: Life expectancy at birth (69 to 77). Points labeled: Formosa, Santiago del Estero, Misiones, Chaco, Argentina, Buenos Aires, Mendoza, Córdoba, City of Buenos Aires (federal district).

Source: United Nations 2011.

Latin American comparators. In 2010 Argentine women have the same average number of children as the average Latin American woman (figure 1.3), and the average person in Argentina lives only one year longer than the average Latin American (figure 1.4).

Third, the population age structure has been changing significantly. Each stage in the transition corresponds to a pyramid shape indicative of the population distribution: Countries in the early stages of the transition display an age-sex distribution as a large-base pyramid with a narrow top. As countries advance in the transition process, the base (young population) narrows and the top (elderly population) increases. In the later stages, countries would display a pillar-shaped age-sex distribution. The whole progression is called from pyramid-to-pillar and is shown in figure 1.5 for Argentina.

It is clear on examination of these figures that the Argentine population will experience, as is the case for most of the already aged world, a feminization of aging with many more women than men living longer. This has important health and long-term care as well as employment policy implications. The longer lives of these women are often marked by poor health and frailty. They are particularly prone to nonfatal but debilitating conditions. Added to this is loneliness, as they more often than not survive their male partners, ending their lives in widowhood, which is commonly accompanied by poverty. At the same time, although a substantial increase has been seen in female labor force participation since at least

Figure 1.3 Total Fertility Rate, 1950–2010

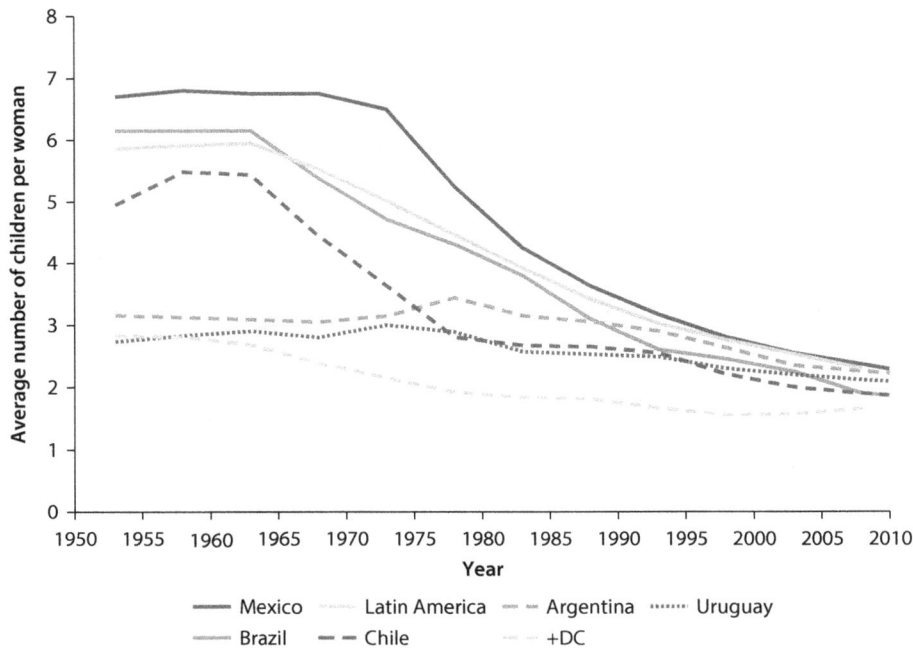

Note: +DC = more developed countries.

Figure 1.4 Life Expectancy, 1950–2100
Years of age

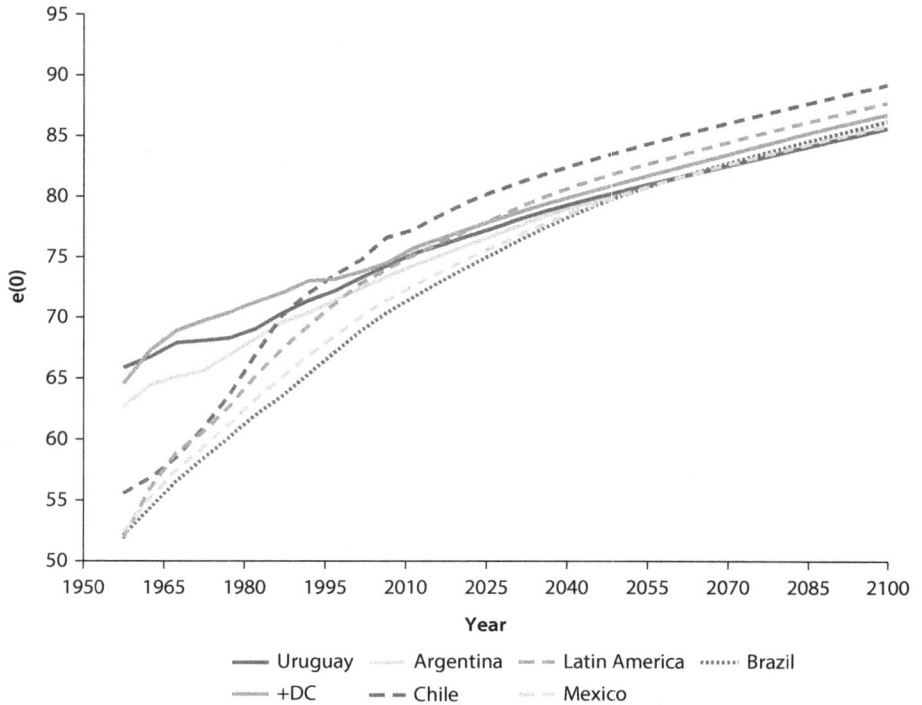

Note: +DC = More Development Countries.

the early 1980s, underemployment and early retirement are still common among women. This has important consequences for economic production, duration of life after retirement, and cost and financing of pension benefits. These issues are investigated in chapters 6 and 9.

Fourth, Argentina is currently enjoying a very favorable age structure with the largest share of its population in working ages. This is often referred to as a demographic bonus. During the demographic transition, not only for Argentina but for all countries, there is a period when the proportion of people of potentially productive age grows steadily in relation to potentially inactive ages. During that period, when the dependency ratio—which relates the number of people in dependent age groups (children younger than 15 years of age and adults older than 64 years of age, in this study) to that of people in the working-age group (ages 15–64)—drops to record lows, the situation is particularly conducive to development, because there are more possibilities for savings and investment, leading to capital accumulation and economic growth, while there is also reduced pressure on spending on education and other programs targeted at families with children, such as conditional cash transfers and family allowances. In Argentina, the dependency ratio reached its nadir in 2010 and will remain close to that level until 2040. After that, it will keep increasing (see figure 1.6).

As Time Goes By in Argentina • http://dx.doi.org/10.1596/978-1-4648-0530-1

Figure 1.5 Population Age Structure, by Sex, Argentina, 1950–2100

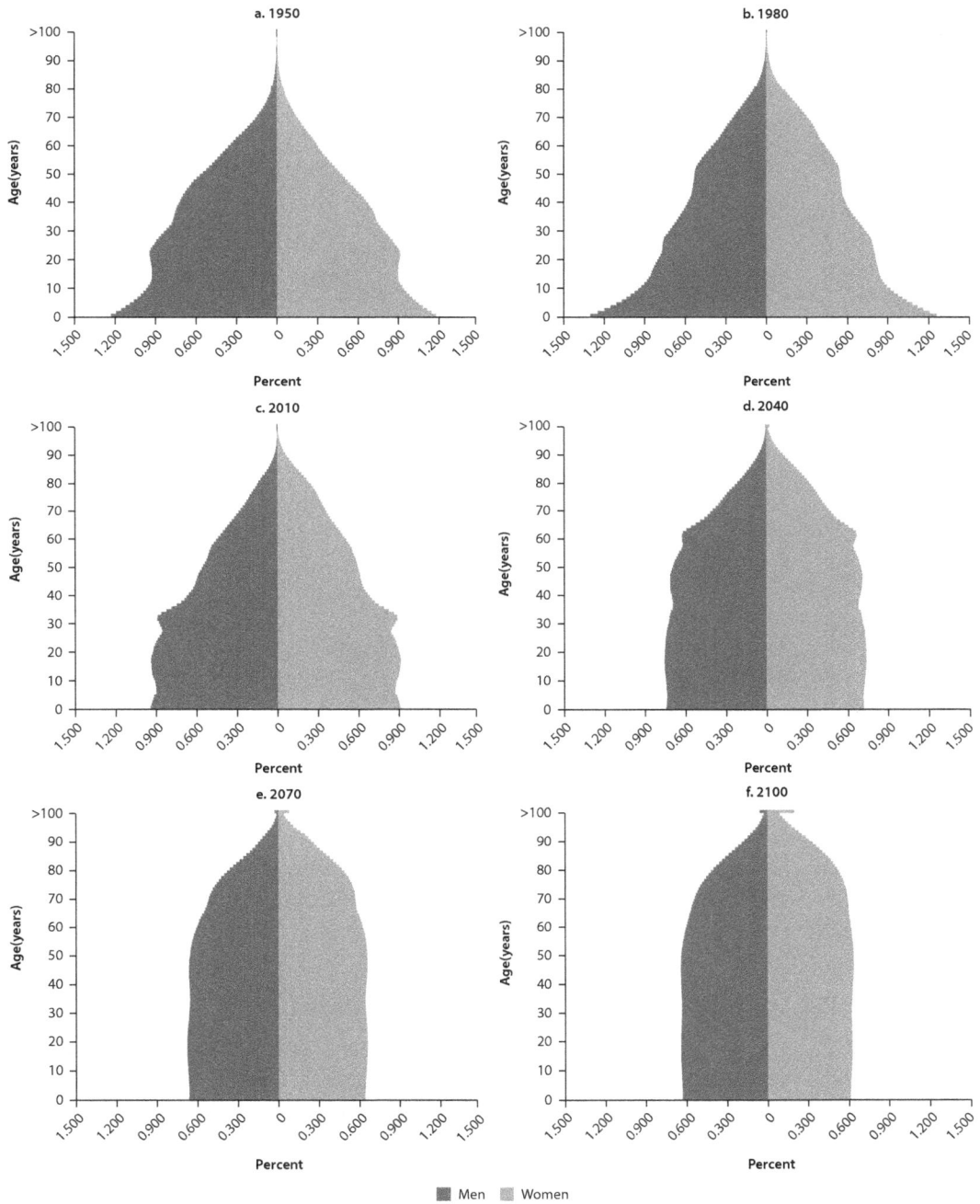

Men   Women

Figure 1.6 Total Dependency Ratio, Argentina, 1950–2100

Percent

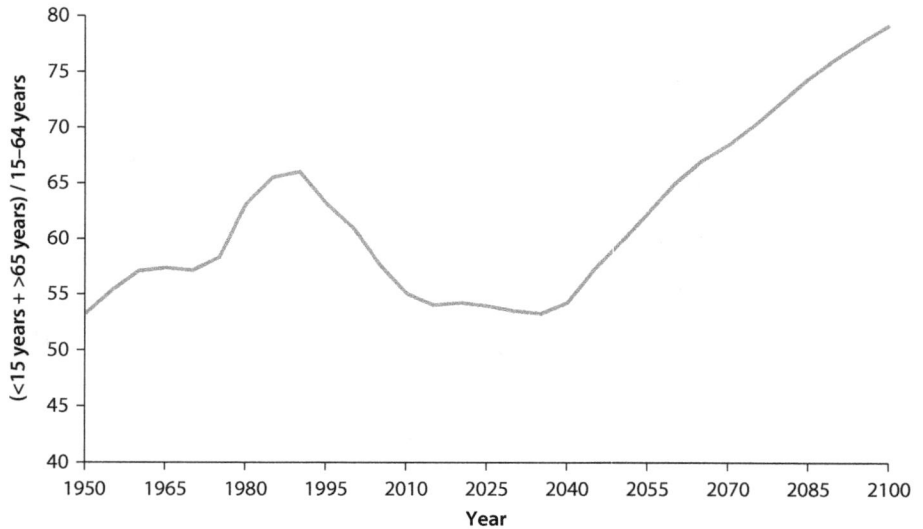

It is important that significant differences exist in regard to the distribution of elderly in Argentina. As an example, in 2010 the average proportion of residents aged 65+ years was 10 percent but ranged from 4 percent in Tierra del Fuego to 16 percent in CABA. This heterogeneity derives mainly from significant variations in fertility and to a lesser extent from mortality, as described above. However, the last three decades have been a period of demographic convergence, mainly because TFR and LE are progressively getting closer to their hypothetical asymptotic values. This reduction of win-country demographic heterogeneity is expected to continue in the future.

The Economic Life Cycle

Changes in the population age distribution matter because individuals vary their economic behavior according to their age. The life-cycle theory helps to understand labor income, consumption, and saving patterns of individuals across their life span. The simple idea is that people make choices about how much to spend on the basis of their permanent lifetime rather than current income (Modigliani and Brumberg 1954; Modigliani 1988). Indeed, individuals start consuming at the moment they are born and never cease to do so. However, they start working only later in life and at some point may have to, or decide to, stop. Indeed, the life cycle can be divided into three stages: (a) pre-work, (b) work, and (c) post-work.

As Time Goes By in Argentina • http://dx.doi.org/10.1596/978-1-4648-0530-1

During the first and last stages, individuals consume more than they produce, whereas in the second stage they produce more than they consume. The length of each stage differs across individuals and is affected by many factors beyond biology, for example, the economic structure of society, educational opportunities, family needs and expectations, and health. The existence of public programs, the level of wealth, the availability of financial institutions, and cultural expectations are all important drivers of the leisure-work trade-off. Likewise, the relative level of consumption across the life cycle combines biological needs, living arrangements, public programs for children and for elderly adults, fertility rates among the poor and the nonpoor, and the like (Cotlear 2011).

Private consumption and labor income have a standard relationship in Argentina; consumption is increasing and is relatively smooth over time, whereas labor income has a steep increase as young adults enter the labor market and a much slower reduction as the elderly population starts exiting it (figure 1.7). As discussed in box 1.1, during the first and last stages, individuals have a "life-cycle deficit," as their consumption is higher than their labor income. During these periods, consumption is mainly financed by private or public transfers. Indeed, intergenerational transfers play a major role in redistributing resources from people of working ages to children and elderly adults. Whereas the elderly

Figure 1.7 Private Consumption and Labor Income, 30–49-Year-Old Adults, 2010

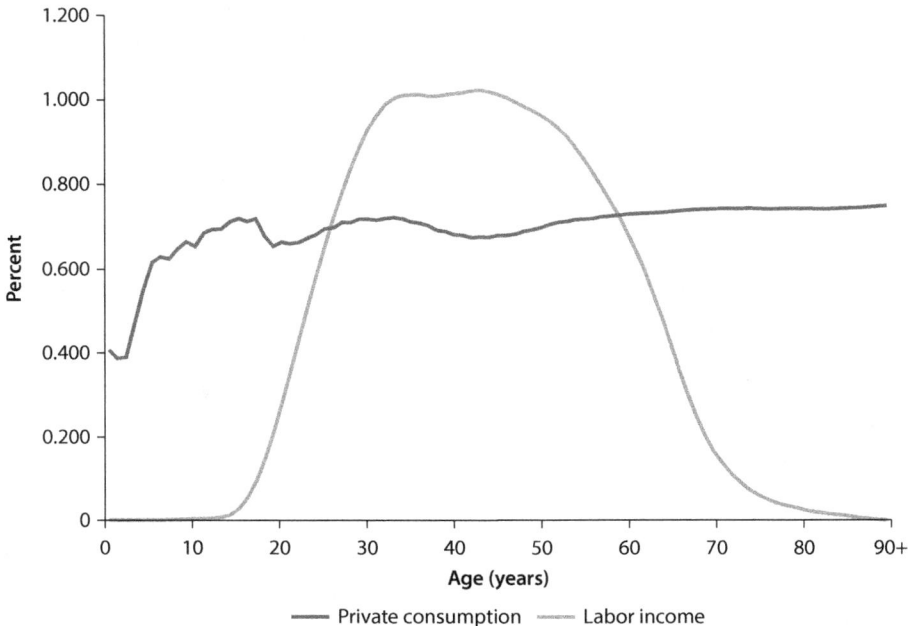

Source: Chapter 12.

As Time Goes By in Argentina • http://dx.doi.org/10.1596/978-1-4648-0530-1

Box 1.1 National Transfer Accounts

In all societies, intergenerational transfers are large and have an important influence on inequality and growth. The development of each generation of youth depends on the resources that it receives from productive members of society for health, education, and sustenance. The well-being of the elderly population depends on familial support and a variety of social programs. The National Transfer Accounts (NTA) project provides a comprehensive approach to measuring all reallocations of income across age and time at the aggregate level. It encompasses reallocations achieved through capital accumulation and transfers, distinguishing those mediated by public institutions from those relying on private institutions (Mason and Lee 2010).

NTA is a system for measuring economic flows across age at the aggregate level in a manner consistent with national income and product accounts. These flows arise primarily because of a fundamental feature of the economic life cycle—that children and elderly adults consume more than they produce through their labor. NTA provides estimates of the components of the economic life cycle and the interage flows that inevitably arise. The accounts distinguish the economic form of flows, transfers, asset-based flows, and institutions that mediate the flows (government and private institutions). Currently, 33 countries from the Americas (10), Europe (9), Asia and the Pacific (9), and Africa (5) are participating in the project.[a]

The NTA data for Argentina are presented in chapter 3. Firsthand data from public accounts compiled by official sources (Treasury, Ministry of Economy and Public Finance, Ministry of Education, Social Security Agency, among others) serve as a basis for computing macrocontrols of public and private consumption, that is, estimates of aggregate public and private consumption in each social sector, as well as the total wage bill. From there, total consumption is divided among single-age groups based on information from either specific national surveys, such as the Survey of Household Expenditures (ENGHO), or ad-hoc sectoral studies. In this way, the NTA methodology allows profiles for Argentina of public and private expenditure as well as of labor earnings by single ages.

a. Detailed methodology and other information can be found at www.ntaccounts.org.

---

generally receive substantial support through social insurance programs, family transfers are the main support for children (Lee 2003).

In Argentina, the average labor income of earners begins to exceed average consumption around age 26 years, and then around age 58 years, it decreases. Withdrawal from the labor market is slow, and there is no complete exit; labor income remains significant even at age 75 years and older. The average adult age 60 years of age earns a little less than two-thirds of what the average adult age 30–49 years earns, and the average adult 70 years of age earns slightly less than 20 percent of what prime-age adults earn. Evidence presented in chapter 10 suggests that low earnings among the elderly population are for the most part explained by a higher proportion of lifetime poor who continue working when they are old, rather than a reduction in the hours worked at older ages.

Public transfers play a major role in financing the life-cycle deficit at older ages (about 90 percent) and share almost evenly with families the financing of consumption at younger ages.

The relationship between labor income and consumption differs across countries. Figure 1.8 shows the ratio of labor income and private consumption in Argentina, Brazil, China, Chile, and Korea. When the value of the ratio is greater than 1, it means that the specific age cohort is contributing to a life-cycle surplus, because its labor income is higher than its private consumption, and savings are positive. For ages when the value is less than 1, there is a life-cycle *deficit*, and labor income is not enough to finance private consumption. The selected high-growth Asian countries show a pattern of private consumption that is much lower than in the selected Latin American countries. The ratio is much greater than in China and Korea; in China it even exceeds 2. In particular, figure 1.8 reveals a much lower tendency to limit consumption for primary savers (30–49) in Argentina. The same is true for Brazil and Chile. As discussed in depth in chapter 12 and summarized later in this chapter, this is not a favorable economic behavior able to take advantage of the demographic bonus.

It is very important to keep in mind that the previous analysis does not account for the stock of people in each stage. In other words, the aggregate deficit will

Figure 1.8 Ratio of Labor Income and Private Consumption in Argentina (2010) and Other National Transfer Accounts Countries

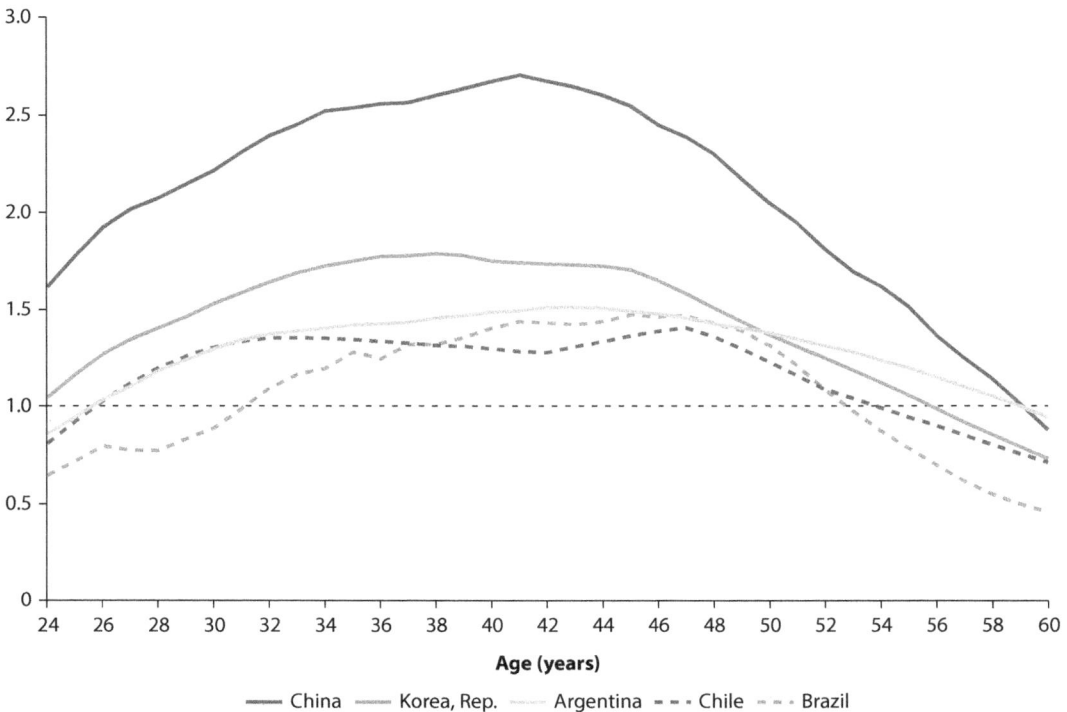

depend on the proportion of individuals at each stage of the life cycle, which will change with changes in the population age structure associated with the demographic transition. For example, for a given relation between labor income and consumption, such as the one in figure 1.7, the stock of people in each stage may be very different across countries and points in time. The stock is what determines the total "deficit" or total "surplus" faced by the economy. With an aging population, we would expect a higher number of individuals in the third stage. Chapter 12 describes the life-cycle concepts and estimates for Argentina in detail.

The Implications of Demographic Change on Economic Growth

Changes in age structure tend to have a major impact on economic outcomes because people's economic behavior changes throughout the life cycle. As noted, Argentina currently has a very favorable age structure with a large share of the population of working age, that is, with a positive life-cycle surplus. However, the dependency ratio will reach its lowest value in 2020 and then will rise rapidly, resulting in an increasing number of people at any given point in time living in a "life-cycle deficit" stage with important consequences to public finance (especially for transfers and services for elderly adults), economic growth, and poverty.

Initially, the declining dependency ratio will free up resources for private and public investment in human and physical capital. The ensuing economic growth is the *first demographic dividend*. Hence, the GDP growth generated by the additional workers is the measure for the first dividend. More workers generate more output, *ceteris paribus*, and the same workers generate more savings. To the extent that saving is converted into domestic investment, more capital (human and physical) will be accumulated. As a result, each worker will have more capital to work with in the future, and production will rise on account of that, giving rise to the *second demographic dividend*. As the aging population in Argentina can expect to live longer, they need to finance a longer period of retirement, and, thus, saving and capital accumulation might increase even further, enhancing the second demographic dividend.

The first dividend typically lasts for decades, but it is transitory in nature. A rise in the share of the working-age population is likely to lead to an increase in output per capita, as the labor force used in production simply grows faster than the population as a whole. The first dividend arises to the extent that the economy is able to create productive jobs for the increasingly larger working-age population. It will then turn negative as total population growth outstrips growth in the productive labor force. However, the same demographic forces that put an end to the first dividend may lead to a second demographic dividend. The second dividend is not, unlike the first dividend, transitory in nature, because aging may produce a permanent increase in capital per worker and, thus, in per capita income, and is very likely to increase further in proportion to increases in life expectancy. The second dividend arises to the extent that the institutional and policy frameworks induce individuals, firms, and governments to accumulate capital.

The dividends are not automatic but depend on institutions and policies to transform changes in population age structure into economic growth. Thus, the dividend period is a window of opportunity rather than a guarantee of improved standards of living. In particular, when policies are designed to deal with the economic growth and public finance implications of population aging, it is crucial to consider the effects such policies might have on economic behavior. How exactly might demographic change lead to these two demographic dividends, and what is the implication of alternative policy responses?

In Argentina, the first dividend per se has a relatively modest effect on growth. In particular, estimates presented in this book (chapter 2) suggest that Argentina's first dividend will be both shorter in terms of the period of time in which the country will experience a favorable ratio between dependent and working-age population and less deep in terms of the magnitude of the decrease in this ratio. Therefore, it would probably be more profitable for policy to focus on the second dividend, which has greater potential to increase productivity via boosting savings and investment. If this were to be accomplished, a higher human and capital accumulation in the remaining years of the demographic window of opportunity would result in higher productivity growth and would allow the country to be prepared for an older society in the long run.

Chapter 12 analyzes in details all these issues and discusses how Argentina macroeconomic conditions interact with its demographic transition, focusing on the country's opportunity to gain a maximum advantage from the two dividends. Currently Argentina has a relatively low saving rate and a quite excessive life-cycle deficit with respect to labor income, especially when compared with other countries that have been successful in creating the right conditions to seize the benefits of the first and second dividend. In particular, a high tax burden on primary savers reduces disposable income and may eventually hinder the propensity to save of private investors.

It is noteworthy that during the window of demographic opportunity, the tax rate has a positive multiplicative effect on the fiscal space available to the government, because the increase in the proportion of working-age population results in an increase in the tax base. Therefore, this is the perfect period to implement policies to boost human capital accumulation and public investment. In this sense, a trade-off emerges between spending by the social security system and the availability of resources for investment in infrastructure and their relative weight in the public budget.

A crucial point related to the creation of a second demographic dividend is associated with the level of development and efficiency of the financial sector. This aspect is often disregarded in the models of economic growth, because they assume that savings are equal to investment. However, a poor financial sector may affect the efficiency in the intermediation of savings from an increased pool of primary savers to productive investment, thus reducing the scope for a second demographic dividend. Argentina will have to improve its financial system if it wants to take full advantage of the ongoing demographic change to boost economic growth.

The Implications of Demographic Change on the Welfare State

Demographic change also matters because the demand and type of social services and associated financing needs in countries vary with population age structure. This section describes the evolution and characteristics of public expenditures in the social sectors with special attention placed on their age profiles.

Expenditures on Education, Health, and Social Protection

The origin of Argentina's current welfare system dates back to the late nineteenth and early twentieth centuries. The Argentine social security system has been modified a number of times since its creation in 1904. The originally fragmented, occupation-specific pension funds evolved over time, and, by 1945, a national scheme with clear intervention from the state was in place. The system's underlying financial problems led the government to undertake an integral reform of its social security program in 1993, in a context of serious concerns about fiscal sustainability in the medium and long term, particularly in the context of a population-aging process. The new system adjusted several parameters and also introduced a funded scheme that transferred the risk linked to longevity from the state to system participants. While this reform limited the fiscal pressure produced by the pension system, it did not improve the level of coverage, which continued to slowly decline. In the mid-2000s an indirect reform (Moratoria Previsional) granted access to pension benefits to most elderly, even if they had not contributed to the system in the past, and in December 2008, the funded scheme was terminated, and its members and beneficiaries were transferred to the pay-as-you-go scheme.

The modern health system of Argentina was developed during 1945–55, a period of economic growth characterized by industrialization, rapid urbanization, and activist labor organizations. During the ensuing years, it evolved into three sectors: public, social security, and private, with separate services, population coverage, and funding. During the 1980s and 1990s, the health system experienced further transformations, as neoliberal policies took hold in the country and resulted in a reduction of state involvement in social services in favor of privatization and decentralization of health care. Note that Argentina is the only country in Latin America and the Caribbean with a dedicated institution for elderly adults (Programa de Asistencia Médica Integral, PAMI, discussed in chapter 6). The National Education System was created in 1884 and established the state's obligation to provide public universal, compulsory, free, and secular education to children of school age. As with health, education is also a responsibility of the provincial governments.

Public expenditures in Argentina, measured as a percentage of GDP, saw sharp variations in recent years. Although in the 1980s and 1990s they amounted to slightly more than 30 percent, the 2001 crisis led to a decline that fell to minimum of 28.7 percent of GDP in 2004. Expenditures began to grow after that, and by 2009 they represented 43 percent of GDP. Within these parameters, social expenditures have been very stable, representing approximately 65 percent of total spending since the early 1990s. Spending in the three main social sectors has also shown a rapid increase in the last decade. The education sector, which amounted to just more than 2.5 percent of GDP in the 1980s and 3.5 percent in the 1990s, was by 2009 close to the Education Financing Law target, at 5.6 percent.[3] In the case of health, total expenditures also grew consistently since the 1980s and explained almost 6 percent of GDP by 2009. Finally, the social protection system (which includes social security, social assistance, and employment programs) saw a sharp increase in the 1980s and 1990s (from 6.7 percent to 9.9 percent of GDP) and again in the first decade of the 2000s, when it reached 12.9 percent of GDP. Part of this change can be explained by the adoption of a much stronger social assistance strategy (resulting in a doubling of expenditures from the late 1990s to the late 2000s), but, given its relative weight, the pension system explains most of the increase, particularly due to the expansion in coverage seen since 2006 with the Moratoria program (see figure 1.9).

Figure 1.9 Public Spending on Education, Health, and Social Security in Argentina, 1980–2009
Percentage of GDP

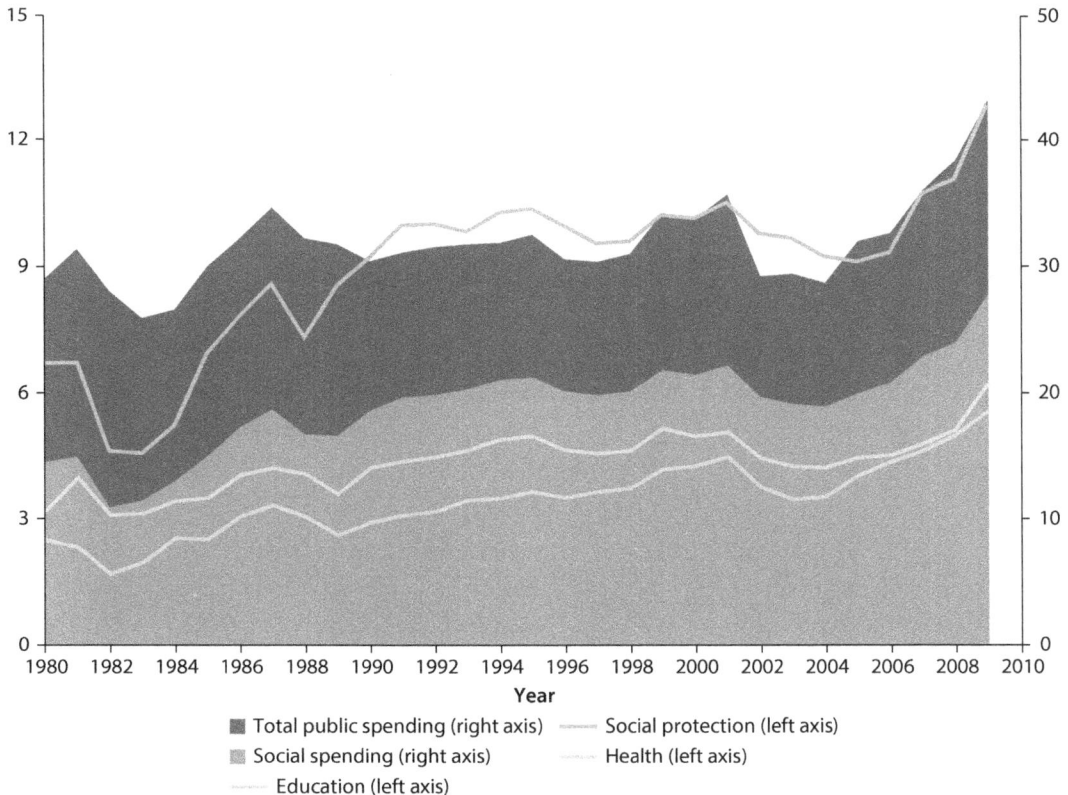

Source: Ministry of Economy and Public Finances 2010.

As Time Goes By in Argentina • http://dx.doi.org/10.1596/978-1-4648-0530-1

Table 1.1 presents data on total spending on education, health, and pensions for 30 countries (OECD plus Argentina) in 2010.

Figure 1.10 (a through c) presents spending for each type of expenditure as a proportion of GDP and GDP per capita (in 2009 purchasing power parity [PPP]) of each of the countries in the sample. The last chart (d) shows the total of social spending. All graphs also present the ordinary-least-squares regression line. Argentina has higher (in the case of education and health care) or equal (in the case of pensions) spending than the average country in the sample when income levels are controlled for.

Table 1.1 Public Expenditures on Education, Health, and Pensions as Proportion of GDP, 2010

	Education	Health	Old-age and survival pensions	Total	GDP per capita PPP
France	5.9	9.0	14.1	29.0	34,689
Italy	4.7	7.4	15.6	27.7	31,909
Denmark	8.7	9.5	8.2	26.4	36,763
Sweden	7.3	7.7	10.7	25.7	37,905
Portugal	5.8	7.1	12.3	25.2	24,021
Germany	5.1	8.8	11.2	25.1	36,449
Belgium	6.6	7.9	10.1	24.6	36,048
Finland	6.8	6.7	11.1	24.6	34,652
Japan	3.8	7.4	11.8	23.0	32,443
Norway	7.3	8.0	7.4	22.7	55,672
Netherlands	5.9	10.3	6.0	22.2	40,715
Spain	5.0	7.1	9.8	21.9	32,545
Poland	5.1	5.0	11.5	21.6	19,059
United States	5.7	8.5	6.9	21.1	46,436
Hungary	5.1	5.0	10.4	20.6	19,765
New Zealand	7.2	8.4	4.7	20.3	28,722
United Kingdom	5.4	8.0	6.8	20.2	36,496
Czech Republic	4.4	6.3	8.5	19.1	25,232
Ireland	5.8	6.4	5.6	17.8	41,282
Canada	5.0	8.1	4.5	17.6	37,945
Argentina	5.8	5.3	6.4	17.5	11,452
Slovak Republic	4.1	5.8	7.3	17.2	22,357
Brazil	5.6	4.2	6.6	16.4	10,427
Turkey	2.6	5.0	6.9	14.5	13,904
Chile	4.2	3.8	3.6	11.6	14,331
Korea, Rep.	5.0	4.1	2.4	11.5	27,169
Mexico	5.3	3.1	1.7	10.1	14,337
Average	6.0	7.9	10.5	24.3	35,665

Sources: Data on education: UNESCO statistics. Data on health: WHO. Data on social security: OECD 2011. World Bank for Per Capita PPP 2009.
Note: PPP = purchasing power parity.

Figure 1.10 Expenditures on Education, Health, Social Security and Total, as a Percentage of GDP Per Capita, 2000s

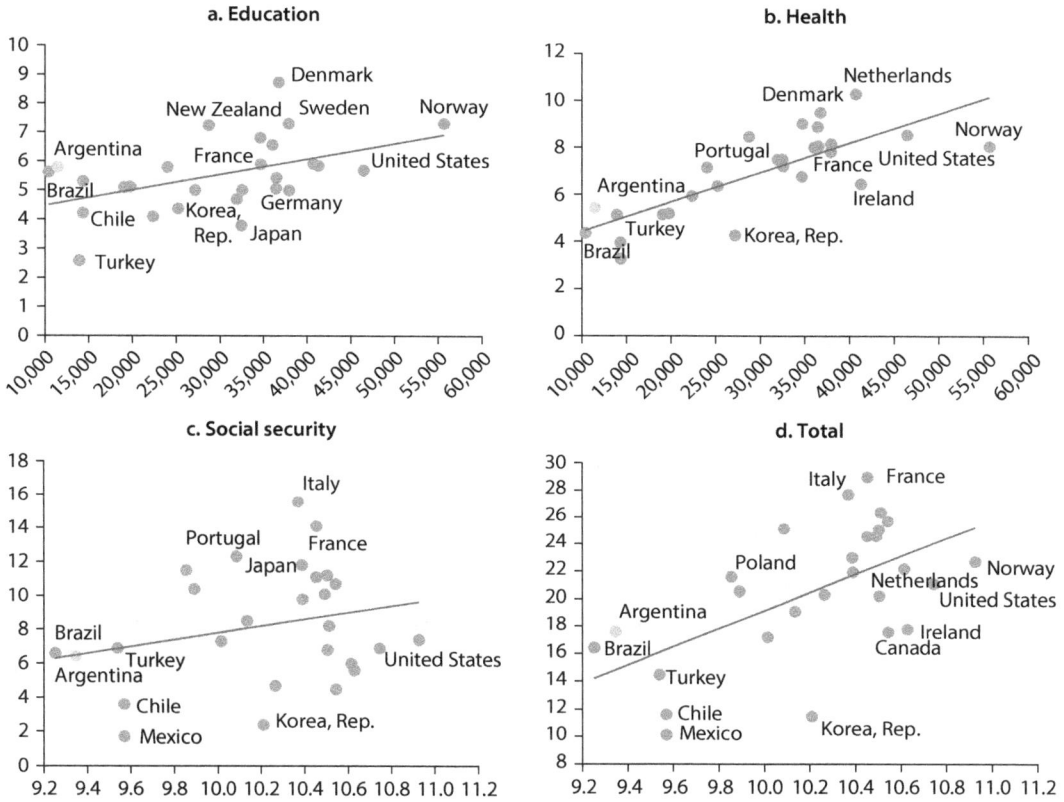

Sources: Data on education: UNESCO statistics. Data on health: WHO. Data on pensions: OECD 2011. World Bank for Per Capita PPP (2009).

Public Expenditures across Age Groups

Age Profiles of Public Spending on Education, Health, and Social Protection

In every country, individual and aggregate public spending in the social sectors varies by age. In Argentina, the per capita profiles have a small bulge among children and young adults and then fall to grow steeply at around age 50 (figure 1.11). The overall per capita profile also reflects the weight of pensions; public spending on an individual elderly person is several times higher than public spending on an individual child. When the overall distribution of the population is taken into account, the aggregate public expenditures on elderly adults and the young remains biased toward the elderly population in Argentina despite a still-young population age structure (figure 1.12).

Age-Normalized Public Spending on Education, Health, and Pensions

The share of economic output directed toward education, health care, and pensions through the public sector can be broken down into two

Figure 1.11 Age Profile of Per Capita Public Expenditures on Education, Health, and Pensions, Argentina, 2010

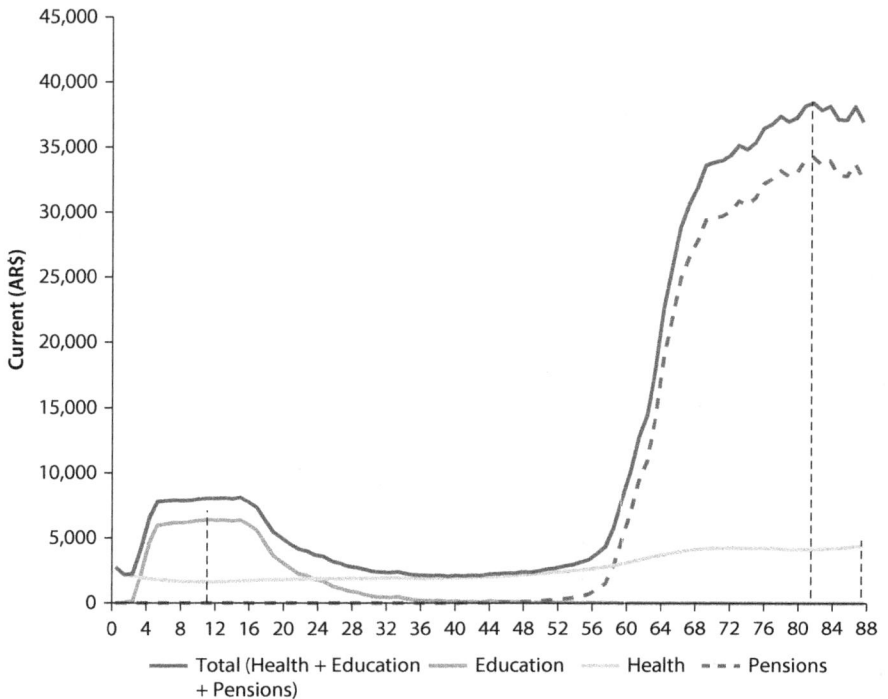

Total (Health + Education + Pensions) —— Education —— Health - - - Pensions

multiplicative components: a demographic factor and an economic factor. The demographic factor measures the size of the demand for a specific benefit (education, health, or pension) relative to the working-age population. The economic factor measures the average benefit received, which is measured in terms of the proportion of the economic output of the average primary-age worker that goes to each eligible individual (such as school-age children in the case of education and elderly adults in the case of pensions). Table 1.2 compares Argentina's public sector spending in 2005 and 2010 to that of six wealthy OECD countries in 2010.[4] A few patterns are worth noting.

First, as we have seen before, Argentina's public spending (measured as a proportion of GDP) between 2005 and 2010 increased significantly for all social sectors. Second, given that the sector dependency ratios varied little between 2005 and 2010, this resulted in a significant increase of average benefits in all sectors. Third, in 2010, the situation of Argentina is different from that in the comparator OECD countries in the three sectors. For education, despite a slightly higher overall public spending as a percentage of GDP, the younger population age structure translates into smaller benefits per school-age population in Argentina. For pensions, the situation is the opposite.

Figure 1.12 Age Profile of Aggregate Public Expenditures on Education, Health, and Pensions, Argentina, 2010

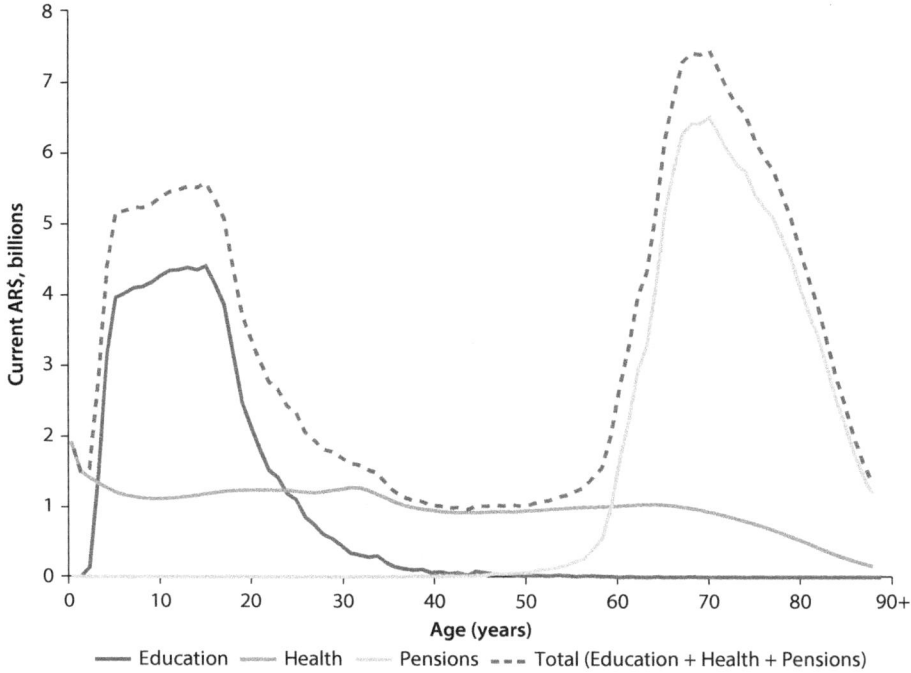

Table 1.2 Summary of Argentina and High-Income Countries, Public Spending

Percent

	Argentina (2005)	Argentina (2010)	Average high-income, OECD (2010)
Education			
Aggregate spending	4.5	5.8	5.7
Sector dependency rate	41.6	38.7	23.4
Benefit generosity	10.8	14.9	24.1
Pensions			
Aggregate spending	5.6[a]	9.1[a]	11.4
Sector dependency rate	16.0	16.4	28.5
Benefit generosity	35.0	55.4	40.1
Health care			
Aggregate spending	4.5	5.3	7.7
Sector dependency rate	12.7	12.4	15.1
Benefit generosity	35.4	42.7	51.1

Source: Calculations based on various data sources: population data (UN Population Division); expenditure data on public education (UNESCO), expenditure data on public pensions (OECD and Ministry of Labor and Social Security); expenditure data on public health care (WHO).
a. Includes provincial spending.

The younger population age structure translates into average benefits in Argentina that are higher than those observed in OECD countries despite the larger share of GDP that is spent on public pensions in the OECD states. For health, the lower aggregate public spending is only partially compensated by the younger population age structure, and average benefits remain lower in Argentina.

Chapter 4 presents a detailed description of the methodology used to estimate the benefit generosity structure of Argentina and comparator OECD countries.

Preference toward Public Spending on Elderly Adults

It is instructive to compare the situation of Argentina with that of other countries. In general terms, the reallocation system in Argentina is very similar to that in other countries represented in the NTA project. But elderly adults in Argentina receive higher per capita public transfers than children do. Figure 1.13, which compares the ratio of net per capita public transfers for elderly adults (ages 65+ years) to net per capita public transfers for children (ages 0–15 years), shows that the ratio in Argentina of 4.2 is higher than anywhere else with the exception of Brazil.

This pattern suggests a society in Argentina where the public sector is responsible for the sustenance of elderly adults and where families remain responsible for the sustenance of children. Is this perhaps a "normal" pattern found in other regions of the world? To answer this question, it is possible to use data from

Figure 1.13 Ratio of Net Per Capita Public Transfers (Elderly Adults to Children), Selected Countries

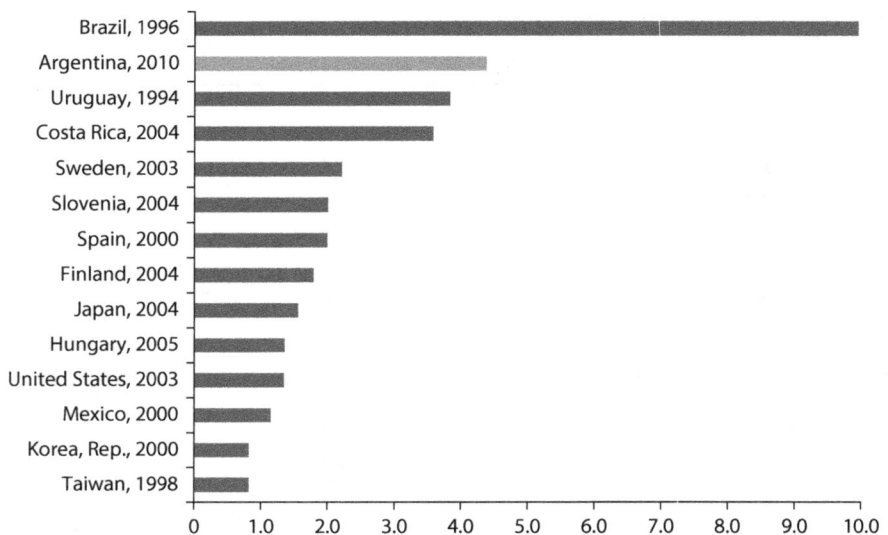

Source: Turra, Lanza, and Rios-Neto 2012.

the NTA project to compare the importance of public transfers as a proportion of the consumption of elderly adults and of children; these data are shown in figure 1.14.[5]

The importance of public transfers in financing the consumption of the young and elderly is found to vary widely across countries and regions. Figure 1.14a shows that in Europe, a full two-thirds of elderly consumption is financed from public transfers. At the other end of the spectrum, public transfers to elderly adults are very small in Korea and Taiwan, China (under Asia). Japan is in the middle of the spectrum, with about half of the consumption of the elderly financed by public pensions. Data are available for five countries in Latin America and the Caribbean (LAC): Chile, Costa Rica, and Uruguay are in the middle of the spectrum, as is Japan, while Argentina and Brazil stand out in LAC and the world, with pension benefits equivalent to more than 90 percent of the consumption of the elderly—more than in Europe.

Figure 1.14b shows that public transfers also finance a significant fraction of children's consumption through cash transfers and through the in-kind

Figure 1.14 Public Transfers as a Percentage of Total Consumption, 2000s

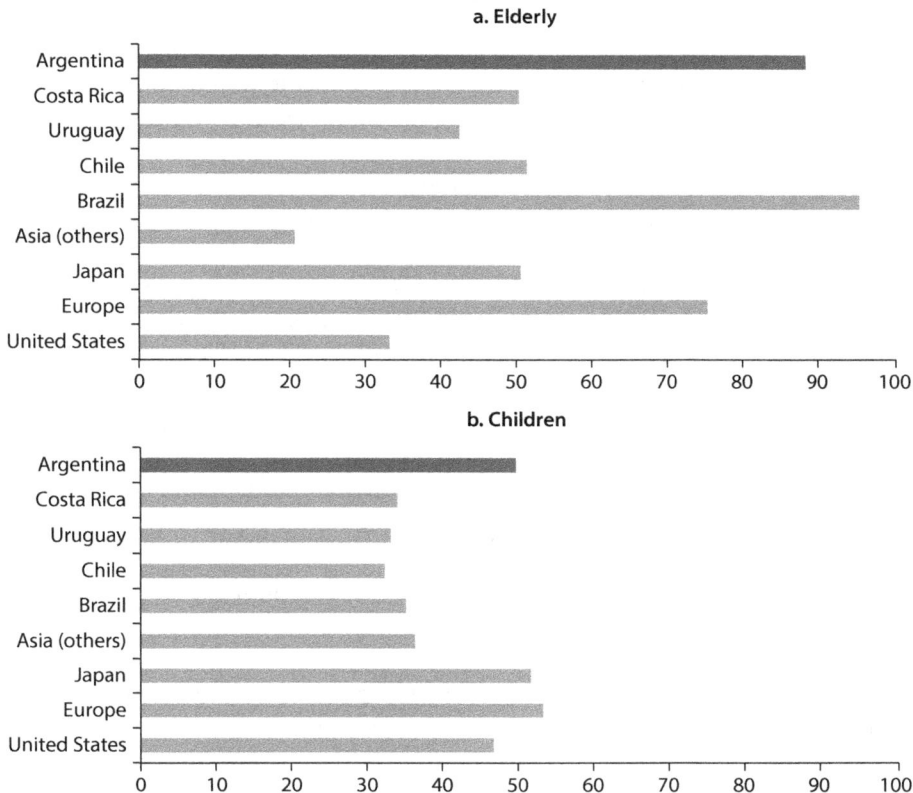

Sources: Turra and Holz 2010.

provision of services, such as education and health. Public financing for children is highest in Europe, followed by Japan and Argentina, where it constitutes more than half of children's total consumption. In other LAC and Asia (other) countries, it is smaller but not insignificant, at about a third of children's total consumption.

Poverty across the Life Cycle and the Role of Public Transfers

Significant progress was attained in reducing poverty and inequality during the last decade,[6] following the severe crisis in 2001–02.[7] Poverty declined from the post-2001 crisis peak of 45.5 percent in 2002 to 11.8 percent in 2012, according to the Socio-Economic Database for Latin America and the Caribbean, and unemployment declined from 17.8 percent to 7.2 percent in the same period. The inequality measured by the Gini coefficient declined from 50.4 in 2000 to 42.3 in 2012. The middle class, defined as persons having an income between US$10 PPP per day and US$50 PPP per day, increased by 22 percent during 2003–09.[8]

Cotlear and Tornarolli (2009) compared poverty rates with and without pensions for two large age groups—60 and older and 15 and younger—across several Latin American countries (see table 1.3). Argentina, together with Brazil, Chile, and Uruguay, are "pro-aging" countries, that is, countries with large and generous pension systems that have a relatively greater impact on poverty rates among the elderly (65+ years). In Argentina, the poverty headcount ratio declined in 2008, from 46.5 percent to 3.7 percent, after pensions were taken into account. However, not surprisingly, the authors found that the effect of pensions on poverty among children (<15) in Argentina was much smaller (the poverty headcount ratio in 2008 declined from 21.9 percent to only 19.2 percent after pensions were taken into account).

To better understand the role of public transfers in reducing poverty among different age groups in Argentina, figure 1.5 compares poverty rates by age for 1998 and 2012. Poverty rates are estimated with and without public transfers, including contributory and noncontributory retirement benefits, such as the Moratoria program, unemployment insurance, family allowances, and conditional cash transfers from the Universal Child Allowance program. Data from EPH-INDEC are used (a national representative household survey from Argentina) are used to measure the percentage of the population living in poverty.[9]

Figure 1.15 presents the proportion of the population living in poor households living in poverty by age group before and after receiving the different public transfers. In 1998 the poverty rate was 36.7 percent and would have increased to 43.4 percent without transfers. The program with the largest impact is the contributory pensions, with its largest impact on elderly adults. In 2012 the overall poverty rate was substantially lower (18.8 percent). Without public transfers, the poverty rate would have been 29.7 percent. Although the impact on poverty remains largest among the elderly, the expansion of the noncontributory

Table 1.3 Headcount Ratio, by Age and Region Poverty Line, US$2.50 a Day (PPP)

Country	All		60 + years		0–59 years		65+ years		0–64 years		0–14 years		15–24 years		25–59 years	
	With	Without	With	Without	With	Without	With	Without	With	Without	With	Without	With	Without	With	Without
Argentina	11.0	18.6	4.9	40.0	12.0	15.1	3.7	46.5	11.8	15.4	19.2	21.9	11.6	15.1	8.0	11.1
Bolivia	35.0	38.1	26.6	48.6	35.8	37.1	25.3	52.8	35.6	37.1	44.5	45.6	28.4	30.1	30.7	31.9
Brazil	18.2	29.2	4.2	49.3	19.8	26.8	3.5	54.9	19.3	27.1	31.8	38.0	18.3	25.5	13.8	21.0
Chile	5.2	9.2	2.5	18.0	5.7	7.9	2.3	20.7	5.5	8.1	8.6	10.7	5.5	8.0	4.2	6.5
Colombia	37.8	40.6	42.2	52.0	37.3	39.2	44.3	54.2	37.3	39.5	46.3	47.5	36.3	38.5	31.0	33.4
Costa Rica	11.6	15.2	17.2	39.0	11.0	12.8	18.7	44.3	11.1	13.2	16.7	18.1	8.7	10.7	8.5	10.5
Dominican Republic	18.7	19.5	16.0	18.6	19.0	19.6	15.6	18.6	18.9	19.6	26.8	27.4	16.6	17.5	14.0	14.6
Ecuador	17.6	19.1	16.2	23.6	17.7	18.5	17.2	26.3	17.6	18.5	24.0	24.7	15.1	15.8	13.8	14.7
El Salvador	27.1	27.9	20.3	23.9	27.8	28.4	20.7	24.6	27.5	28.2	35.2	35.6	24.9	25.6	22.4	23.1
Guatemala	33.9	36.1	28.2	34.9	34.4	36.2	29.1	37.1	34.2	36.0	42.4	44.0	28.4	30.1	27.6	29.8
Honduras	36.9	37.3	35.6	37.4	37.0	37.2	37.0	38.9	36.9	37.2	45.7	45.8	30.1	30.4	31.3	31.6
Mexico	13.9	15.9	19.9	30.1	13.3	14.5	21.9	33.0	13.3	14.8	18.2	19.1	11.8	13.0	10.2	11.8
Nicaragua	42.7	43.2	32.5	34.5	43.5	43.9	32.5	34.8	43.2	43.7	53.2	53.7	38.5	38.8	36.6	37.1
Panama	22.3	27.9	16.9	36.0	22.9	26.9	18.1	39.3	22.7	27.0	32.4	36.5	21.8	25.6	16.6	20.5
Paraguay	21.4	22.1	16.9	20.4	21.8	22.2	17.2	21.2	21.7	22.1	29.7	30.0	18.1	18.5	16.5	17.0
Peru	21.0	22.0	19.9	23.1	21.2	21.8	20.4	24.2	21.0	21.7	28.9	29.4	21.6	22.3	20.5	21.1
Uruguay	6.7	14.8	1.1	23.5	8.1	12.6	0.9	26.4	7.7	12.7	14.6	19.6	7.2	12.2	4.8	9.0
Venezuela, RB	38.7	41.4	32.9	44.6	39.1	41.2	34.1	46.9	38.9	41.1	49.7	51.1	36.0	38.3	32.2	34.6
LAC average (unweighted)	23.3	26.6	19.7	33.2	23.7	25.7	20.1	35.8	23.6	25.7	31.5	33.3	21.1	23.1	19.0	21.1

Source: Cotlear and Tornarolli 2009.

Note: LAC = Latin America and the Caribbean; PPP = purchasing power parity.

Figure 1.15 Poverty Rates by Age, with and without Transfers, Argentina, 1998 and 2012

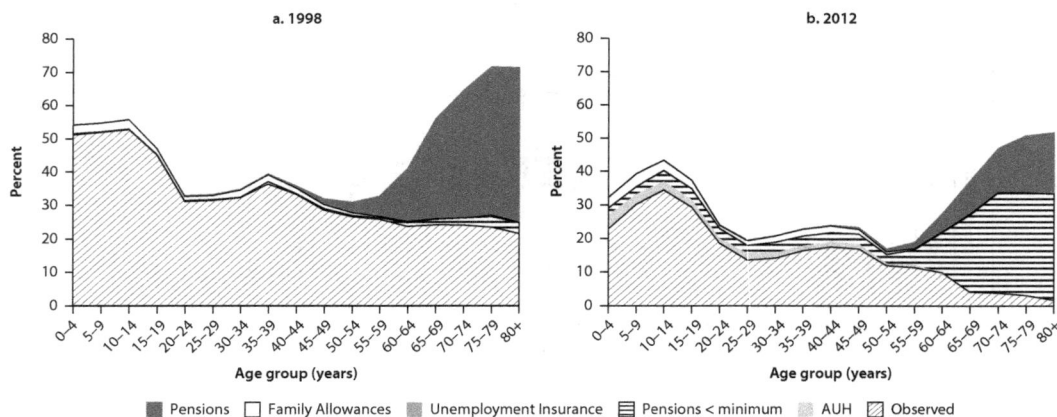

| ■ Pensions | ☐ Family Allowances | ▨ Unemployment Insurance | ▤ Pensions < minimum | ▨ AUH | ▨ Observed |

social protection programs did have a big impact on poverty among the non-elderly as well.

It is important to note that public transfers in Argentina have been very effective in reducing poverty among the elderly. Poverty levels for this group are very low by international standards when, instead, they would be very high in the absence of public transfers. Unfortunately, poverty incidence remained substantial in 2012 among children despite the positive impact of the Family Allowance program and, most important, the more recent Universal Child Allowance program. Detailed information on the social protection system in Argentina and its impact on poverty is found in chapter 5.

Cross-Cutting Issues and Main Conclusions

Demographic change is one of the most important forces shaping the outcome of social and economic policy, but it cannot be observed in the short term. In the following chapters, this report analyzes the socioeconomic and macroeconomic impacts of demographic change in Argentina from a long-term perspective. The main findings are presented in subsequent sections.

Labor Force, Productivity, and Economic Growth

The size and composition of the workforce in Argentina is changing as a consequence of the demographic transition. In particular, the share of the working-age population reached its highest level in 2010 and will remain approximately at this level until 2035. Argentina is experiencing a demographic window of opportunity during which a large working-age population results into more people in the labor force, which, in turn, all else remaining equal, results in more wealth being generated. This phenomenon of a large working-age population is referred to as a *demographic bonus*.

Moreover, Argentina is currently experiencing a very favorable age structure of its working-age population. Although the share of the mature labor force (aged 25–65 years) is expected to continue growing until the late 2030s, the share of the junior labor force (15 to 24 years of age) has already started declining. As the mature workforce has higher overall economic activity and usually generates most of a country's wealth, Argentina has a great opportunity to increase growth, savings, and government revenues.

Argentina needs to seize the current opportunity and prepare for the structural changes it will face over the next decades and beyond. The first demographic dividend measures the economic output associated with a larger share of the population being of working age. Chapter 12 shows that in Argentina, despite a relatively long window of opportunity, the impact of the first dividend is going to be relatively small because the average age period in which labor income is higher than consumption is relatively short (from 26 to 58 years in 2010), and the difference during this period is also relatively small.

To take advantage of the first dividend Argentina needs to reduce further the economic dependency rate and increase the productivity of the workforce. With respect to the first issue, in Argentina there are three types of behavior that can have impact on the economic dependency ratio. The first one is associated with youth having access to the labor market. The more delayed the entry into the labor market by youth, the lower the rate of activity within this population group. The trend, observed between 1974 and 2012, suggests relatively constant growth in the rate of schooling of young people in all age brackets. This suggests not only an expansion of formal education, but also an increase in the number of years of schooling. Although this creates a larger youth dependency ratio, it also implies greater accumulation of human capital and thus a potential increase in the productivity of the future workforce. The second one is associated with increasing the economic participation of women. Although Argentina has seen women's participation in the labor force growing rapidly in recent decades, the gap with respect to men is still very significant (almost 30 percentage points in 2012). The third one is associated with sustaining the economic activity of senior workers. In this case, Argentina already exhibits higher participation rates of the elderly with respect to other countries in the region.

With respect to productivity, it is important that the large work force employed in the next few decades has high productivity jobs. In 2012 the overall employment rate was 93 percent; however, 45 percent of the employed population was working in the informal sector. To boost the productivity potential of future generations, Argentina needs to invest in better public education, as well as incentives and means for the education and retraining of mature workers. The changing structure of the workforce will also have implications in terms of the average productivity of the economy. An older workforce is at risk of being a less productive workforce in the absence of proper measures. Increased women's participation will require rethinking gender-related employment policies. Among the active population, women suffer much more severe problems than men in terms of unemployment or underemployment and informality. Finally, workers older than 65 years of age usually have access to poor-quality jobs, and their choice of remaining in the labor market is mostly due to perverse incentives of the social security system rather than labor market conditions. The implications of the demographic change on the share of working-age population and productivity are discussed in chapters 9 and 10, respectively.

Over the medium term, however, the expected changes in the labor force composition resulting from the aging of the population will pose challenges to economic growth in Argentina. After the late 2030s, the growth rate of the 15–64 age group will turn negative. A shrinking labor force means that Argentina will have to rely more on productivity growth than on new entrants in the labor market to sustain aggregate output growth. Fortunately, the period of the first dividend creates the conditions for a second demographic dividend by increasing the share of primary savers, that is, the individuals with a higher propensity to save because of their higher income relative to their consumption—those aged 20–39. The larger the share of this group, the larger will be the average propensity to save of the economy. At present, the share of primary savers in Argentina is rising, and it will reach its maximum value between 2025 and 2030. Also, as life expectancy continues increasing, the stock of assets needed to finance a longer retirement period will also increase, and this will stimulate more savings. The main objective of saving during this period is to finance capital accumulation necessary to increase productivity in the period when the workforce is smaller, and through this, sustain the level of production of the economy.

It is indeed the temporary nature of the demographic bonus and the first dividend that makes it urgent to create the conditions to produce a large second demographic dividend. Chapter 12 shows, however, that Argentina currently has a higher life-cycle deficit relative to labor income and lower savings compared with countries such as China, Japan, and Korea, which have been able to take advantage of the opportunities offered by demographic change in the past. Policy focus should be placed on strengthening the institutions and policies needed to stimulate saving and its proper use to increase the capital/labor ratio, productivity, and economic growth in the future when the age structure of the population will have become less favorable.

Public Finance and Service Delivery

The impact of population aging becomes readily apparent in long-term projections of public spending on education, health care, and pension, which is the product of the average generosity of the benefits received by each individual and the age structure of the population. Each social sector will face different challenges and opportunities. Projecting all three expenditure paths with a comparable methodology provides insight into the interconnections and trade-offs available to Argentine policymakers. Too often, policy reforms of pension, health care, and education systems are debated, analyzed, and implemented in isolation from each other, without considering the links among these systems. Such projections are presented in chapters 4, 5, 6, and 7. If no change is introduced to the current structure and generosity of social spending, the shift in population age structure projected for the next decades is going to lead to substantial additional fiscal pressures on publicly financed health care and pensions, along with some reduction in fiscal pressures for publicly financed education.[10]

In 2010, total public spending on education, pensions, and health care amounted to approximately 20 percent of Argentina's GDP. Although forecasts of both demographic and benefit change have to be interpreted with caveats, a few robust conclusions emerge. The status quo scenario in which current benefits (for education and pension) and expenditures by age (for health care) remain the same as in 2010 would result in an increase in total social spending to almost 27 percentage points of GDP in 2050 and 34 percentage points of GDP in 2100. With regard to *education*, the increasingly smaller size of the school-age population provides a unique opportunity to increase per student investment to high-income countries' levels without adding much burden on public finance. An expansion of educational spending to reach these levels of investment per student within a decade would require keeping aggregate spending at the 2010 level until 2030. After that, the share of GDP devoted to education would gradually decline in concert with the decline in the school-aged population—while maintaining investment levels per student at those of more developed countries. However, this strategy implies a trade-off with other sectors that will, on the other hand, see a rising demand for services as the population ages and would therefore benefit from fiscal resources freed up by the education sector.

One of the key findings is that the demographic change alone would imply a modest increase in *health care* expenditures in Argentina. We project an increase of slightly more than 1 percentage point of GDP in 2100, mainly because of the peculiar profile of public health expenditure by age in the country, with relatively high spending for younger ages. Nevertheless, as discussed in chapters 4 and 6, international experience shows that this spending profile is likely to change as the country grows richer, because of both epidemiological changes and changes in consumers' preferences. Finally, the level of health expenditure is likely to increase overall because of changes in medical technology (Kumar 2011). When combined with the demographic transition, these transformations are projected to cause an increase to almost 7 percent of GDP in 2050, and 9 percent in 2100.

In terms of *pensions*, even if the recent expansion of coverage associated with the *Moratoria* reform were not sustained in the future, public spending would decline, starting at 9 percent of GDP in 2010 to 8 percent in 2035, and would rise again after that, to 11 percent and 20 percent of GDP in 2050 and 2100, respectively, because of the mere increase in the number of eligible pensioners associated with population aging. If it were to be sustained, aggregate spending would increase to almost 15 percent and 22 percent of GDP in 2050 and 2100.

Clearly the old support system would be very difficult to afford. In an alternative scenario, we forecast a series of reforms that gradually would bring Argentina's pension benefits in line with those of high-income countries. Even in this optimistic scenario, pension expenditures would increase to 13 percent and 17 percent of GDP in 2050 and 2100 and would still dominate the fiscal outlook for Argentina.

So what policy actions can be taken to help mitigate the unavoidable tension toward increasing social expenditures that is driven by population aging in Argentina? First, as more resources per student become available in Argentina as the demographic structure changes, it is important to invest those funds in an effective and strategic way to improve the education system. The European countries, Japan, Korea, and the United States used declines in student numbers to shift resources toward quality. The simulations presented in this report (chapter 7) show that the decline in the school-age dependency rate offers room for tackling specific problems of the Argentine education system, and at the same time reducing public spending on education as a percentage of GDP. In particular, the lower youth demographic burden will allow expanding coverage, fostering inclusion of the poorest segments of the population, and reducing overage rates, while still allowing for a progressive decrease in public education spending.

Nevertheless, international comparisons highlight how the current level of spending per student in Argentina is significantly lower when compared with OECD countries. Although spending per student is not necessarily an indicator per se of the quality of the education system, still it is associated with more resources available for financing teacher training and salaries, infrastructure, information and communication technologies, and other crucial inputs for educational achievement. In this sense, if Argentina were to increase spending per student to OECD levels, the decrease in the school-age dependency rate would not be sufficient to overcompensate the increase in spending per pupil, meaning that public expenditure on education as a percentage of GDP would not decrease even in the very long run (2100). Chapter 5 concludes by describing the differences in terms of the allocation of resources per school level (pre-primary, primary, secondary) that exists within the Argentine educational system and the potential implications that these would have for achieving policy objectives at each educational level.

Second, the pension system design will have to be revised to ensure that it provides adequate income protection to the elderly. The pension system currently extends benefit coverage to most of the old-age population and provides protection to the poorest segments of society. However, this has been through a temporary policy (the 2004 *Moratoria* program, which extended coverage under a one-time exceptional regime to more than 2.7 million beneficiaries), and its effects will decline over time unless new reforms are introduced. At the same time, Argentina will have to be careful in designing a social security system that is sustainable in the medium and long term when an older population age structure will put increasing stress on public resources needed to provide comprehensive old-age pension coverage. Increasing formal employment and thereby increasing contribution-based financing, fostering a healthier and more productive workforce at older ages, gradually readjusting benefit levels, and incentivizing workers to retire later are options Argentina could consider to plan for its increasingly older population.

Third, it is urgent that the organization of the health care system also adapts to the different demographic and epidemiological profile of the increasing older population in Argentina. Despite Argentina's passage through the advanced stages of the epidemiological transition, its health system, especially for those who do not have social security health care coverage, is still designed to address maternal and child health issues and communicable diseases. As noncommunicable diseases (NCDs) emerge as the leading cause of morbidity, disability, and mortality, effective programs must be implemented to address their main risk factors: smoking, physical inactivity, alcohol consumption, and unhealthy diet.

Indeed, the Argentine government has made important progress in its NCD strategy. In particular, Argentina's experience with the promotion of healthy living and particularly efforts to reduce sodium and trans fat consumption has been exemplary in Latin America. In the case of sodium, the government has reached agreements with the food industry for the reduction of sodium in processed food, including artisanal breads. In the case of trans fats, the national Food Code was amended to limit the amount of trans fats in processed foods. At the same time, despite not having ratified the Framework Convention on Tobacco Control, the Ministry of Health has also put much effort into tobacco control, and tobacco use prevalence among adults has decreased significantly in the last few years.[11] Moreover, the Ministry of Health has strengthened its surveillance system to better monitor NCDs and their risk factors. The country has a series of risk factor surveys, tobacco use surveys, and school health surveys and is currently developing a telephone surveillance system. Finally, the government has recently added to its maternal and child public insurance scheme (Plan Nacer) some interventions to prevent and control chronic conditions, creating a new scheme known as Plan Sumar. At the same time, it is striving to strengthen the public health care delivery system to deliver better prevention and control of NCDs by ensuring both early detection of these conditions and their risk factors and programmed and continued care for patients with NCDs.

The magnitude of the increase of health expenditures associated with an older population will depend crucially on whether longer life spans mean more healthy years or added years of illness and dependency. Prevention and postponement of disease and disability and maintenance of health, independence, and mobility in an aging population will continue to remain the major health-related challenges of population aging.[12] Recently, a life course framework was proposed to design policies addressing the needs of the elderly

(Aboderin et al. 2002). Central to the life course approach to aging is the notion of functional capacity—that is, that individuals reach the peak of their physical functional capacity early in adulthood and then progressively experience a decline throughout the life course that is a natural result of the aging process. Importantly, however, this is not necessarily a problem. Provided that at, say, age 85 one continues to be independent and capable of performing the activities of daily living, the individual will remain a resource to their family, their community, their society, and the economy. Thus, good policies on aging are those policies that will help individuals to remain above the disability threshold as they age.

It is anticipated that the number of elderly people generating a demand for formal long-term care will increase because of two factors. First, the number of very old adults (80+ years of age) in Argentina will increase significantly in the twenty-first century (from 2.6 percent in 2010 to 5.4 percent in 2050 and to 12.3 percent in 2100), and this will result in larger numbers of frail elderly adults at any given point in time, even if a decrease in the proportion of this group is expected as a result of improvements in health prevention and postponement and better administration of disabilities. Second, the changing status of women and family and social values will continue to impact the availability of family caregivers.

Structure of the Report

The rest of the book is organized as follows. Chapter 2 describes the long-term dynamics of demographic factors in Argentina, presenting historical trends and projecting their future evolution. Chapter 3 describes more in detail the NTA approach and how it was applied to Argentina to estimate age-specific labor earnings, public transfers, and spending profiles. Chapter 4 uses NTA profiles for Argentina to highlight the potential impact that demographic change alone will have on social expenditure and public finances, by projecting the evolution of social spending as the number of potential beneficiaries by age change over time. Chapters 5, 6, 7, and 8 describe the recent evolution of social policies in Argentina in terms of social protection, health, long-term care, and education, respectively. These chapters discuss likely implications of current social policies in a changing demographic context and propose alternative policy options to mitigate potential challenges and take advantage of eventual opportunities arising from the demographic transition. Chapter 9 brings the three social sectors together to highlight fiscal trade-offs between among them and how these will change as the age structure of the population changes. In chapters 10 and 11, the focus shifts from the expenditure side to revenue. These chapters discuss if and how the demographic transition will alter the production capacity of Argentina by introducing modifications in the age composition of the labor force and in its productivity. Finally, chapter 12 puts these conclusions into a macroeconomic context and discusses implications in terms of the country's future savings level and GDP growth.

As Time Goes By in Argentina • http://dx.doi.org/10.1596/978-1-4648-0530-1

Notes

1. The analysis of this book does not deepen the political economy implications of the policy options analyzed, which of course are a relevant dimension to be considered at the moment of designing specific policies. One aspect of particular interest within the framework developed here is that, in many cases, policies that can be seen as positive and feasible in the long term are politically difficult in the short term; hence one of the main challenges for policy makers is to find the right balance between the long-term and short-term trade-offs.

2. According to the definition used by the UN Population Division, more developed regions include the countries in Europe and, North America along with Australia, New Zealand, and Japan.

3. This law, passed in 2005, established that consolidated public spending in education (including federal and provincial governments) should reach 6 percent of GDP by 2010.

4. The OECD countries included as comparators are Austria, Finland, Germany, Japan, Spain, and Sweden. The choice of these countries is arbitrary and was limited by availability of NTA estimates. Nevertheless, cross-checking with official spending data for the set of high-income OECD countries indicated very similar figures.

5. "Consumption" is defined to include in-kind services in education and health care and private consumption of goods and services purchased by the household.

6. This subsection draws heavily on chapter 5.

7. In 2005, GDP per capita and poverty rates returned to precrisis levels, and poverty has been declining since then.

8. The World Bank LAC Regional Flagship Study "Economic Mobility and the Rise of the Latin American Middle Class" defines the middle class as households with an income per capita above US$10 PPP a day (or US$3,650 per person per year), and less than US$50 PPP a day. In this regard, middle-class status is defined as the income level that allows sufficient resilience to shocks as to result in a low probability of falling into poverty.

9. Poverty is calculated as a function of income per equivalent adult measured by INDEC. The poverty headcount is estimated using the official 1998 poverty line and an extrapolation of the 2006 official basket and the inflation rate reported by the province of Santa Fe.

10. Note that these projections do not take into account behavioral responses, which are very likely to change over the medium to long run.

11. From 29.7 percent of adults older than 18 in 2005 (National Risk Factors Survey 2005) to 21.4 percent in 2012 (Global Adult Tobacco Survey 2012).

12. The compression of morbidity paradigm, introduced in 1980, maintains that if the average age of first infirmity, disability, or other morbidity is postponed, and if this postponement is greater than increases in life expectancy, then cumulative lifetime morbidity will decrease—compressed between a later onset and the time of death. The National Long-Term Care Survey, the National Health Interview Survey, and other data have documented declining disability trends beginning in 1982 and recent acceleration. The decline is about 2 percent per year, contrasted with a decline in mortality rates of about 1 percent per year, thereby documenting compression of morbidity in the United States at the population level (Fries 2003).

More recent studies confirm compression of morbidity from stroke in the United States, where it remains one of the major causes of death and long-term disability (Mitnitski and Gubitz 2010).

References

Aboderin, I., A. Kalache, Y. Ben-Shlomo, J. W. Lynch, C. S. Yajnik, D. Kuh, and D. Yach. 2002. *Life Course Perspectives on Coronary Heart Disease, Stroke and Diabetes: Key Issues and Implications for Policy and Research.* Geneva: World Health Organization.

Cotlear, D., ed. 2011. *Population Aging: Is Latin America Ready?* Washington, DC: World Bank.

Cotlear, D., and L. Tornarolli. 2009. "Poverty, the Aging and the Life Cycle in LAC." Paper presented at authors' workshop for the Regional Study on Demographic Change and Social Policy in LAC, World Bank, Washington, DC, July 14–15.

ECLAC (Economic Commission for Latin America and the Caribbean). 2011. *Proyecciones de población a largo plazo.* Observatorio Demográfico 11. Santiago de Chile.

Fries, J. F. 2003. "Measuring and Monitoring Success in Compressing Morbidity." *Annals of Internal Medicine* 139: 455–59.

INDEC-CELADE (Instituto Nacional de Estadística y Censos–Centro Latinoamericano y del Caribe de Demografía). 2004. "Estimaciones y proyecciones de población. Total del país, 1950 –2015." Serie Análisis Demográfico no. 30, INDEC, Buenos Aires.

Kumar, R. K. 2011. "Technology and Health care Costs." *Annals of Pediatric Cardiology* 4 (1): 84–86.

Lee, R. 2003. "Demographic Change, Welfare, and Intergenerational Transfers: A Global Overview." *Genus* 49 (3–4): 43–70.

Mason, A., and R. Lee. 2010. "Introducing Age into National Accounts." NTA Working Paper. http://www.ntaccounts.org/web/nta/show/WP10-02.

Ministry of Economy and Public Finances. 2010. "Social Public Expenditure." http://www .mecon.gov.ar.

Mitnitski, A. B., and G. J. Gubitz. 2010. "Trends in Survival and Recovery from Stroke and Compression of Morbidity." *Stroke* 41: 415–16.

Modigliani, F. 1988. "The Role of Intergenerational Transfers and Life Cycle Saving in the Accumulation of Wealth." *Journal of Economic Perspectives* 2 (2): 15–40.

Modigliani, F., and R. Brumberg. 1954. "Utility Analysis and the Consumption Function: An Interpretation of Cross-Section Data." In *Post-Keynesian Economics*, edited by Kenneth K. Kurihara, 388–436. New Brunswick, NJ: Rutgers University Press.

OECD (Organisation for Economic Co-operation and Development). 2011. Social Expenditure Database. http://oberon.sourceoecd.org/vl=2355160/cl=17/nw=1/rpsv /ij/oecdstats/1608117x/v135n1/s1/p1.

Turra, C. M., and M. Holz. 2010. "Who Benefits from Public Transfers? Incidence across Income Groups and across Generations." Paper presented at authors' workshop for Demographic Change and Social Policy: A LAC Regional Study, World Bank, Washington, DC, July 14–15.

Turra, C. M, B. Q. Lanza, and E. Rios-Neto. 2012. "Idiosyncrasies of Intergenerational Transfers in Brazil". NTA project 1st Book. http://www.ntaccounts.org/doc/repository /BR.pdf.

United Nations. 2011. *World Population Prospects: The 2010 Revision*. Population Division, Department of Economic and Social Affairs, United Nations Secretariat, New York.

————. 2013. *World Population Prospects: The 2012 Revision*. Population Division, Department of Economic and Social Affairs, United Nations Secretariat, New York. http://esa.un.org/wpp.

CHAPTER 2

Demographic Panorama in Argentina

Carlos Grushka

Introduction

Long-term planning for various public policies must begin with estimates of population, its structure by age and gender, and its determinant variables (birth rate, mortality rate, and migration). In general, this information is available from official statistics,[1] but in this chapter we choose to offer our own estimates, concerning gender and age, covering the period of analysis to cover each calendar year from 2010 to 2100. Compared with the most recent projections from the United Nations (2013), the total estimated population from our estimate is similar to the middle of the century but then differs by up to 20 percent in the second half of the twenty-first century. As we will explain, the difference is mainly the result of the methodological decision to make different assumptions regarding the evolution of fertility.[2]

The following section analyzes the trends (1950–2010) and future expectations (2010–2100) for the Argentine population, emphasizing that it is made up of large age groups. The third section studies the evolution of the determinant demographic variables (fertility, mortality, and, to a lesser extent because of its low impact, migration). Finally, the fourth section discusses the implications for the dependency ratio and the demographic dividend (DD) and their international comparisons over the medium and long term.

Trends and Prospects for the Argentine Population

The total Argentine population grew from 17 million in 1950 to 41 million in 2010, an average annual growth rate of 1.4 percent, which has been decreasing gradually, from 1.6 percent in the first three decades to 1.2 percent in the last three. The population will increase to 54 million people by 2050 and to 59 million by 2100,[3] growing at a rate of 0.4 percent annually, representing decreasing growth rates of 0.8 percent, 0.3 percent, and 0.1 percent for each three-decade period considered (see figure 2.1).

Over time, the age structure of the Argentine population has gradually changed as different age groups have grown at different rates: during the period

Figure 2.1 Prospects for the Population, by Major Age Group, 1950–2100

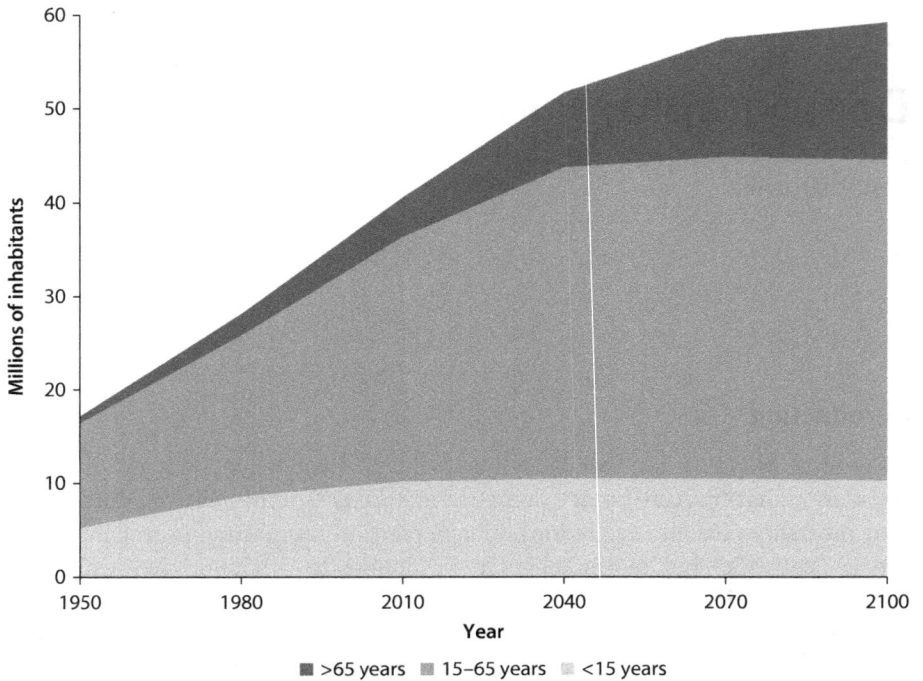

Source: Based on INDEC 2004 and United Nations 2011.

2010–2100 the growth rate will have been null (0 percent) for individuals 20 years of age and younger, 0.3 percent for those 20–65 years of age, and 1.4 percent for adults older than 65 years of age.

The elderly (over age 65) population's growing weight relative to the rest of the population is known as population aging and has been widely discussed in the literature (INDEC 2003; UNFPA-ECLAC 2009; UNFPA 2010; ECLAC 2011b), occasionally from a critical perspective (Sanderson and Sherbov 2007; d'Albis and Collard 2013). This group was 4 percent of the population in Argentina in 1950; it grew to 11 percent in 2010 and will reach 19 percent in 2050 and 25 percent in 2100.

The aging phenomenon is primarily the product of a significant decrease in fertility, and to a lesser extent, a decrease in mortality. In the future, we expect that the fertility rate will have a more gradual impact, whereas the impact from mortality will be more significant, which is detailed here. In these predictions (the same as with the official predictions prepared by INDEC 2004 and ECLAC 2011a), the assumption is that migration will have no net effect on population after 2010. This assumption differs from United Nations (2013) projections, which show a gradual decrease in the negative net migration rates recorded at the beginning of the twenty-first century.

Figure 2.2 Population Structure, by Age and Gender, 1950–2100

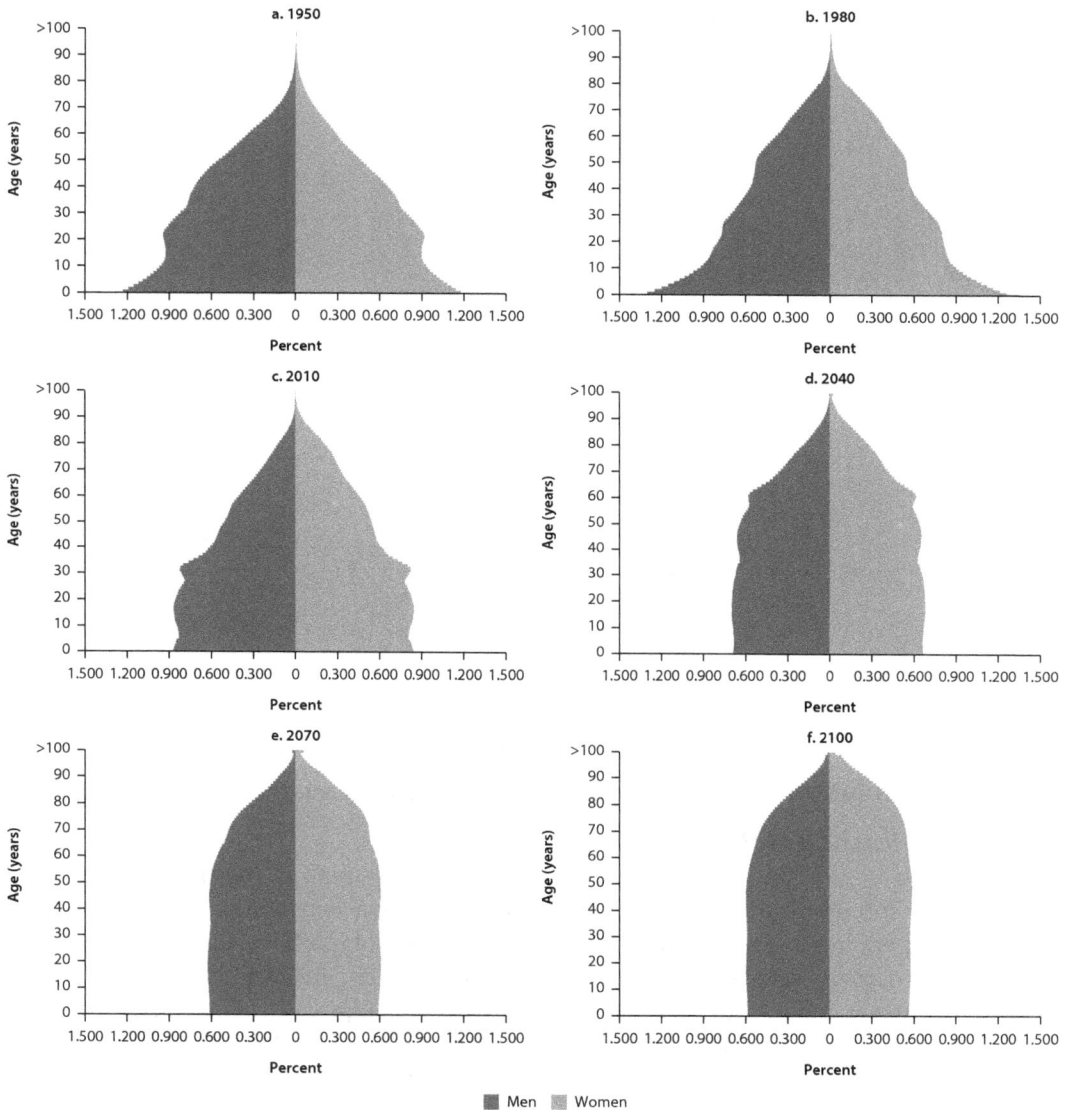

Source: World Bank elaboration.

Frequently, the process of changes to the population structure in terms of age and gender is summarized in "population pyramids," whose shape gradually shifts from a "triangle" until the lower age groups narrow so that the figure resembles a "funeral urn" (as the middle age groups widen) and eventually resembles a "rectangle" (except for the oldest age groups, which exhibit decreasing numbers and a clear advantage for women based on the mortality effect). A synthesis of this process for Argentina is presented in figure 2.2. In general terms, the aging process is showed in figure 2.3, where one observes an increase among the elderly over time.

As Time Goes By in Argentina • http://dx.doi.org/10.1596/978-1-4648-0530-1

Figure 2.3 Population by Age over Time, 1950–2100

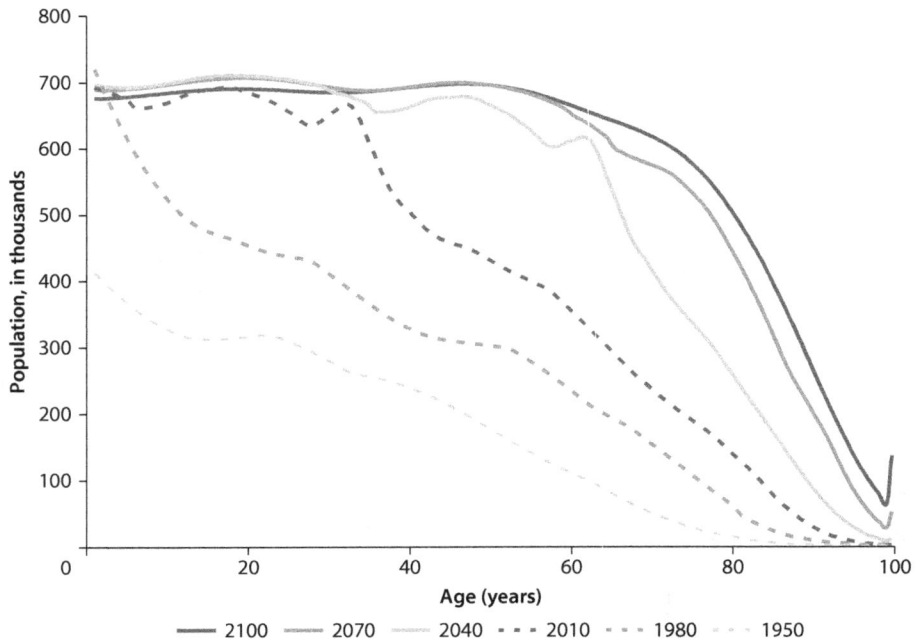

Source: World Bank elaboration.

Evolution of the Determinant Demographic Variables in Argentina

Historical Evolution and Mortality Trends

It is customary to begin any analysis of the evolution of mortality by using the mortality rate, which is available for Argentina beginning with the five-year period encompassing 1870–74.[4] The high level of mortality and variability of the mortality rates at the end of the nineteenth century are attributable to epidemics from illnesses, such as yellow fever (1871), smallpox (1874), cholera (1886–87 and 1894–95), and bubonic plague (1899–1900), in addition to the impact of dysentery and typhoid fever.

A more appropriate indicator for describing the changes in general mortality over time is life expectancy at birth (e_0 or LEB), which is a mortality indicator that is not affected by changes to the population's age structure.

Since the end of the nineteenth century, the LEB has shown a nearly linear increasing trend. From 1883 (the midpoint of the first intercensus period, 1869–95) until the two-year period comprising 2000–01, the LEB increased from 33 to 74 years, an absolute increase of 41 years, equivalent to 0.35 years gained during each calendar year. After a moderate increase until the middle of the twentieth century, the growth produced between the first and second decades of the century stands out, with a gain of almost one year of life for each calendar year. In the years that followed, the growth continued, but at a slower

As Time Goes By in Argentina • http://dx.doi.org/10.1596/978-1-4648-0530-1

pace, until reaching an LEB of around 74 years in 2000–01. This behavior is consistent with the expected reduction in LEB gains as the mortality rate decreases, which has led several authors to propose a logarithmic evolution.

In terms of the international context, it is evident that the reduction in the mortality rate in Argentina began earlier than in the majority of both Latin American countries and less developed countries DC.[5] In contrast to the latter countries, the reduction in Argentina was initially a response to improvements in general living conditions associated with socioeconomic development more than a product of advances in knowledge and medical technologies or specific efforts aimed at directly combating infectious diseases (Lattes 1975). In this sense, although mortality in Argentina was initially at a higher level, the fall in mortality is similar in part to the process experienced by more developed countries (+DC)[6] and differs from the majority of the countries in the rest of Latin America (figure 2.4).

Argentine society's early modernization relative to almost all the other countries in the region, its high level of urbanization, and the expansion of formal education stand out as the main factors that contributed to the country's early, yet sustained, decrease in mortality. While many countries in the region were taking their first steps in the epidemiological transition in the 1950s, Argentina had already completed a significant portion of this process (see figure 2.5).

Figure 2.4 Life Expectancy at Birth (Years), World and Regions with Different Levels of Development, 1950–2100

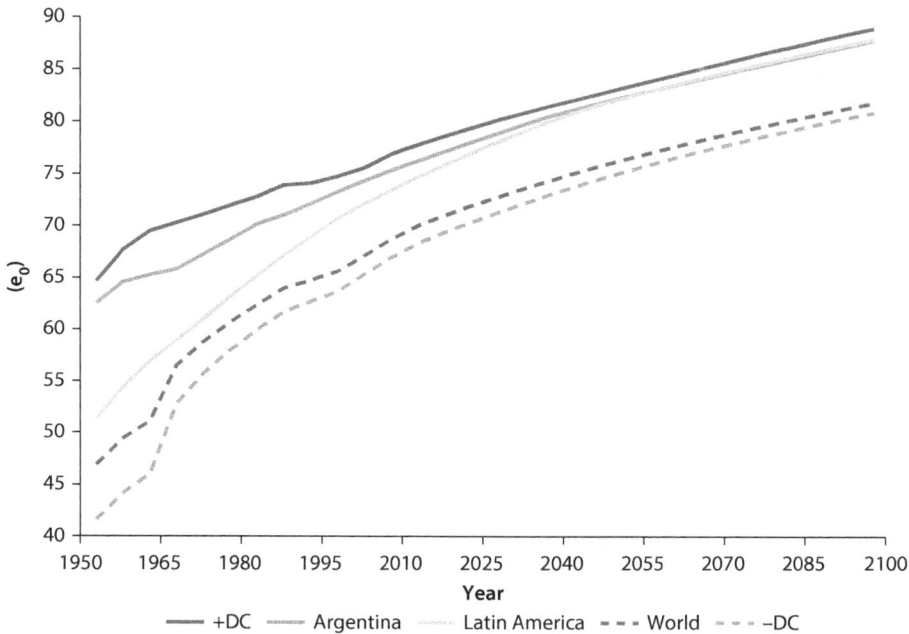

Source: World Bank elaboration based on United Nations 2013.
Note: +DC = more developed countries; −DC = less developed countries.

Figure 2.5 Life Expectancy at Birth (Years), Selected Latin American Countries, 1950–2100

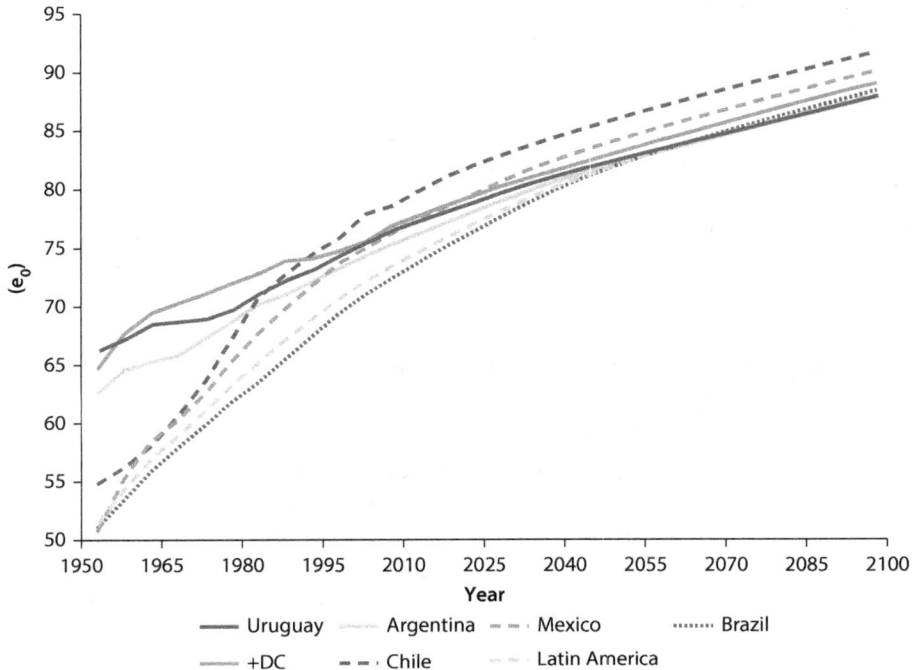

Source: World Bank elaboration based on United Nations 2013.
Note: +DC = more developed countries.

Mortality, as with many demographic phenomena, behaves differently according to age. The risk of death is high during the early years of life, especially in the first year, and decreases substantially between ages 5 and 15. As an individual ages, mortality increases slightly until around age 40, subsequently increasing more rapidly until again reaching elevated levels during old age.

In turn, reductions in mortality are not achieved at the same pace among all age groups: as mortality decreases, the quickest reduction occurs at younger ages. At the same time that age increases, the dispersion of the values for the distinct periods analyzed decreases. This process has given rise to the typical transformation of the mortality age structure, which changes from a U-shaped distribution (with similar intensity of mortality for younger and older age groups) to a more J-shaped distribution.

Even though mortality decreased among all age groups during the twentieth century, the reductions varied significantly among different age groups. The largest relative reductions between the periods 1869–95 and 2000–01 belonged to the 35–60 age groups (decreases that range from 70 percent to 90 percent). Finally, from age 60 upward, the relative improvements began to decrease (ranging from 50 percent to 70 percent). During all the periods analyzed, this pattern of relative reductions remained the same.

As Time Goes By in Argentina • http://dx.doi.org/10.1596/978-1-4648-0530-1

Furthermore, mortality affects men and women differently. As a result of bio-logical, socioeconomic, and cultural factors, men exhibit higher mortality than women. For all of the years analyzed, LEB for women was higher than that for men. The difference between men's and women's LEBs was less than one year only during the 1869–95 period, and it increased rapidly and significantly until 1970. However, since 1970 the gains experienced by men have been similar to or greater than those experienced by women. As a result, during the last two decades, men's higher mortality began to decrease and stabilize around a gap of slightly more than seven years. This difference between men and women is among the highest by international standards, as detailed in table 2A.1.

The so-called epidemiological transition describes the empirical process of decreasing mortality and the transformation of the structure of the causes of death that accompanies it. In general terms, the decrease in mortality is, at the beginning, a product of the reduction in the incidence of transmittable diseases (both infectious and parasite borne), giving rise to an increase in the relative importance of circulatory illnesses, tumors, and traumatic injuries. Once trans-missible diseases have been controlled, decreases in mortality occur more slowly because of the greater difficulty in controlling the remaining causes of death.

According to Pantelides (1983), Argentina began to experience significant changes in its epidemiological profile near the end of the 1930s. From this period on, mortality from transmissible diseases decreased at a faster pace than overall mortality, reducing its relative significance because of medical advances (espe-cially with the introduction of penicillin and sulphonamides), progress toward the provision of potable water, and social and health policies that included social awareness of hygienic standards in child care (Carbonetti and Celton 2007).

Moreover, the distribution of deaths according to causes is also affected by changes in the age structure of the population. An analysis of overall indicators (not standardized by age) shows that the changes observed after 1945 exhibit a decrease in the risk of death from infectious diseases, but this gross reduction is also the product of the relative decrease in the proportion of younger age groups in the population, because they exhibit higher mortality. As a result, the correct method of analyzing changes in mortality risk associated with different causes of death is not based on the distribution of deaths, but rather by comparing the mortality rates (specific to each cause) standardized by age (SMRA, standardized mortality ratio by age). Grushka (2010) presents SMRAs by cause, grouped in to five large categories for 1960 and 2007. In almost half a century, the general mortality level decreased 43 percent; the lowest relative reduction belonged to deaths from violence or external causes (35 percent), and the highest belonged to infectious diseases (with a decrease of 74 percent), whose relative weight continued to decrease in terms of all causes of death.

To estimate mortality, INDEC used the hypothesis of change based on stan-dard UN criteria, which allows for the determination of expected values for LEB for each five-year period of the prediction until 2045–50 and according to a decreasing median gain (in years of life) (INDEC 2004). In addition, given that the difference between genders in the level of mortality is the highest in all of

Latin America, the estimate uses a constant difference of seven years in favor of women.

According to these estimates (figure 2.6), during the next four decades the LEB for Argentina will increase from 75.2 years for the 2005–10 period to 80.7 for the 2045–50 period, or 0.14 years per calendar year (0.16 during the first two decades and 0.12 during the following two decades).

Toward the end of the projection presented in this chapter (and extended until 2100), criteria are used that are very similar to those cited and adopted by the United Nations (2011), with average improvements of 0.15 years per calendar year during the first three decades (from 2010 to 2040) and of 0.08 years during the following six decades (from 2040 to 2100), reaching an LEB of 85 years (82 for men and 89 for women). Nonetheless, the assumptions adopted by the United Nations (2013) result in more rapid growth, with LEB for the period 2095–2100 reaching 87.8 years.

With the goal of predicting the age structure of mortality, the analysis uses an interpolation of the initial mortality by gender tables (2000–01) and the so-called limit tables, keeping in mind that the resulting mortality probability by age values should be consistent with the previously estimated mortality levels (LEB).

Moreover, the United Nations (2004) published very long-term projections that reached 2300, with details at the global, regional, and country levels.

Figure 2.6 Life Expectancy at Birth (e_0) Argentina, 1950–2100

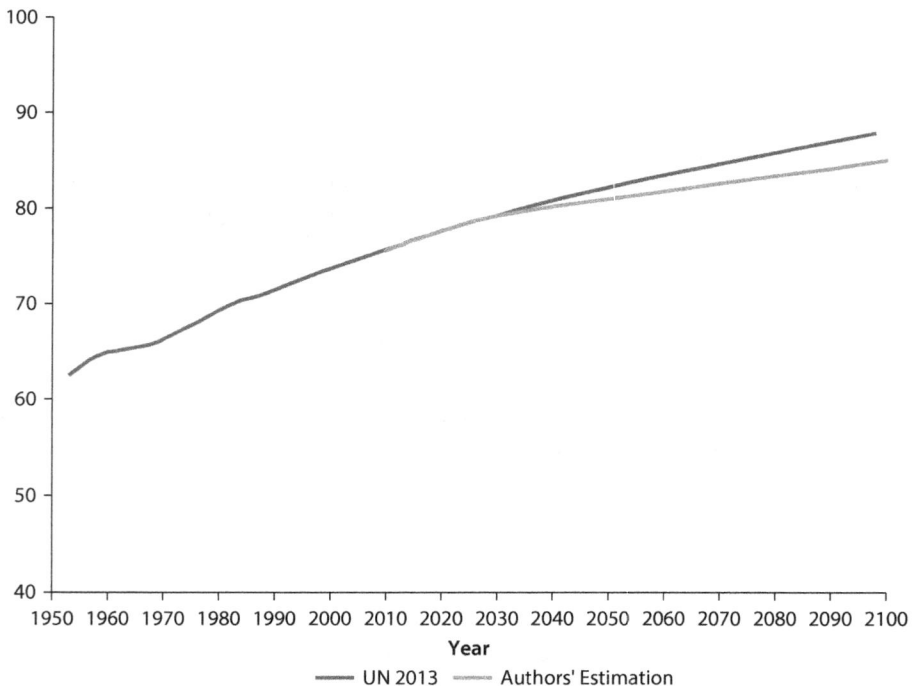

Source: Based on United Nations 2013.

The estimated LEB for Argentina in 2300 is nearly 100 years, with an average 0.08 year increase per calendar year between 2050 and 2300.

One of the most relevant implications of having long-term estimates available is related to the field of social security. Social security system estimates in Argentina have been performed based on the mortality rates of the entire population (Rofman, Stirparo, and Lattes 1997; Grushka 2002, 2010), even though there are clear indicators that social security beneficiaries constitute a select group that exhibits lower mortality (Rofman 1994; Lacasta 2008). With the goal of making precise local estimates and evaluating and checking alternative hypotheses, it is necessary to overcome the severe data limitations and undertake more research, including various interdisciplinary focuses on longevity (Grushka 2010).

Historical Evolution and Trends in Fertility

In terms of historical context, the panorama that emerges upon analysis of the period from 1869 to 1947 is not very clear, but three discoveries stand out, as summarized by Pantelides (2006):

(a) The available series of total fertility rates (TFR) shows a decline in the levels of fertility beginning at the end of the 1880s.

(b) The fertility rates organized by age and the measurements that are based on them (TFR), which are only available for census years and are rare, are not very useful for tracing the path of this decline. The TFR was around 3.2 (children per woman at the end of her reproductive period) in 1947 and probably around 7.0 in 1895. For the intervening years, only one estimate, of unknown quality, exists: 5.3 in 1914. Before 1895, the estimate of TFR at 5.1 in 1869 is probably very low; the estimate of 6.8 appears to be more appropriate.

(c) The analysis of the structure by parity and of the median number of children born based on the censuses of 1895, 1914, and 1947 provides some patterns that reveal that the decline in total fertility could have begun before 1914, although probably not before 1895.

From 1950 on, the data are more reliable, and the downward trend shows a clear reversal between 1970 and 1980, later resuming the century-old downward trend to arrive at 2010 with a TFR of 2.25.

The increase in the TFR between 1970 and 1980 was a product of the increase in the fertility rates among almost all age groups, but most notably among adolescents and young adults between 20 and 24 years old (Pantelides and Moreno 2009). In addition, the most significant increases occurred in jurisdictions that had previously exhibited levels below the average (Pantelides 1989). The high level of births in the 1970s is responsible for the peculiar age distribution of the population in 2010 (with a surge in the 30–40-year-old age group, as detailed earlier).

Argentina represents a unique situation in Latin America because its fertility rate began to fall earlier (figures 2.7 and 2.8). The largest part of the decrease

Figure 2.7 Total Fertility Rate (Children per Woman), World and Regions with Different Levels of Development, 1950–2100

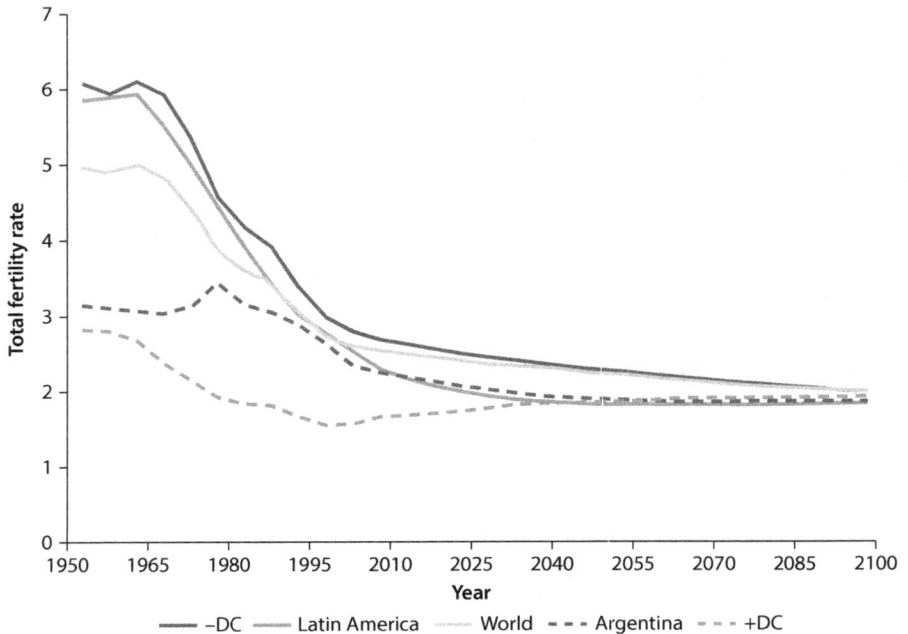

Source: United Nations 2013.
Note: +DC = more developed countries; –DC = less developed countries.

took place during the first four decades of the twentieth century and later exhibited a much slower pace with temporary plateaus (Pantelides and Moreno 2009). Up until the end of the 1990s, Argentina still exhibited fertility rates below the regional average, but since then its TFRs have been equal or just slightly lower than the regional median of 2.4 for the 2005–10 period (ECLAC 2008).

When INDEC made its fertility estimates, it adhered to the change hypothesis based on the standard United Nations criteria, which allowed it to determine the expected values for TFR for each projected five-year period until 2045–50, with a decline that asymptotically nears a preestablished lower limit (Pujol 1995; INDEC 2004).

According to these estimates, during the next four decades the TFR will decrease from 2.25 during the 2005–10 period to 1.85 in the 2045–50 period (ECLAC 2008). It should be mentioned that in previous estimations made by the same institution, some years earlier, the chosen asymptote was a TFR of 2.1, equal to the replacement rate. For its part, the United Nations (2013) tends to adopt the same parameters experienced in European countries with a greater decrease and a subsequent recovery, combining two logarithmic curves and two asymptotic limits (of 1.85 for 2050 and 2.1 over the longer term), which creates some unexpected intersections.

Figure 2.8 Total Fertility Rate (Children per Woman), Selected Latin American Countries, 1950–2010

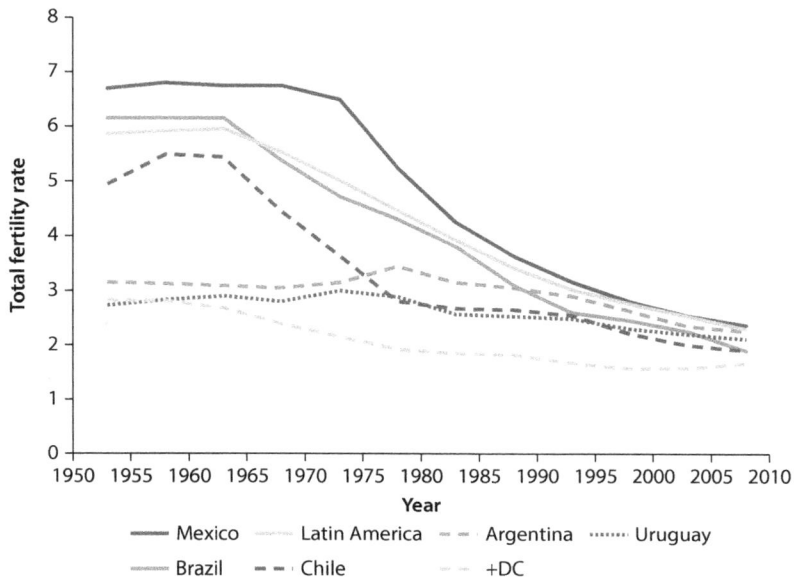

Source: United Nations 2013.
Note: +DC = more developed countries.

At the end of the prediction period used in this document (extended until 2100), we follow criteria similar to those that have been mentioned, although we prioritize a more gradual and continuous decrease. As a result, to predict the TFR, we adopt a value of 2.0 as the only lower asymptotic limit (figure 2.9).

Historical Evolution and Trends in International Migration

Although international migration is a very relevant factor for many countries, in the case of Argentina this variable played a fundamental role at the end of the nineteenth century and the first half of the twentieth century, but its demographic impact has been practically null since then.[7]

As figure 2.10 illustrates, Argentina's total population growth experienced very pronounced increases and decreases, mainly during the first three decades of the past century as a consequence of large waves of immigration. After 1930, immigration notably declined provoking a decrease in the population growth rate and in the difference between total growth and the natural increase.[8]

Following European migration in the post–World War II period, net migration tended to decrease and by the end of the century was practically null, as a result of a lower rate of external immigration, mainly from neighboring countries, which was offset by the growing emigration of Argentinians.

At the end of the 1960s, two new phenomena began to emerge: a shift in the composition of external migration (which changed to be almost exclusively

Figure 2.9 Total Fertility Rate, Argentina, 1950–2100

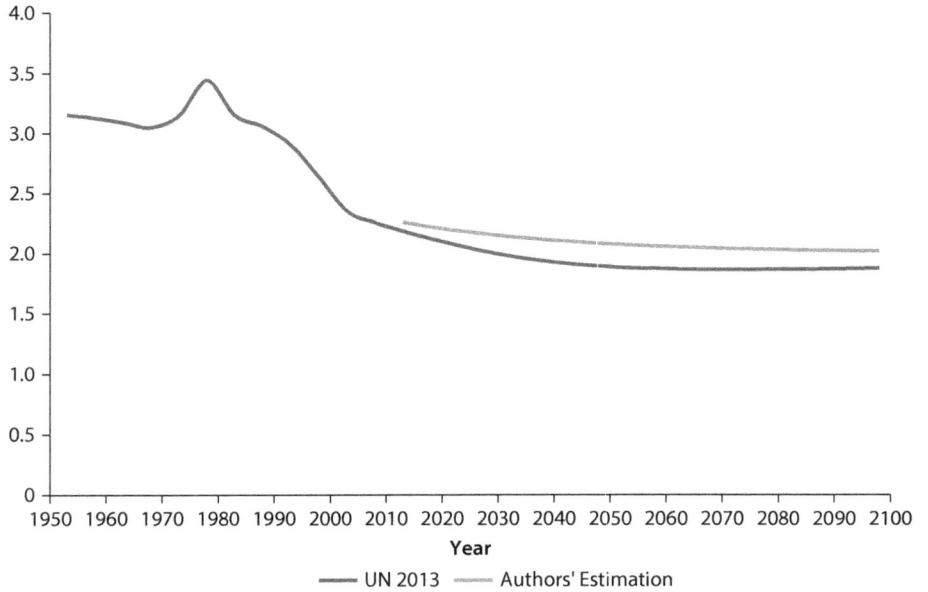

Source: World Bank elaboration and United Nations 2013.

Figure 2.10 Total Migration-Based and Natural Growth, by Five-Year Period, Argentina, 1870–2010

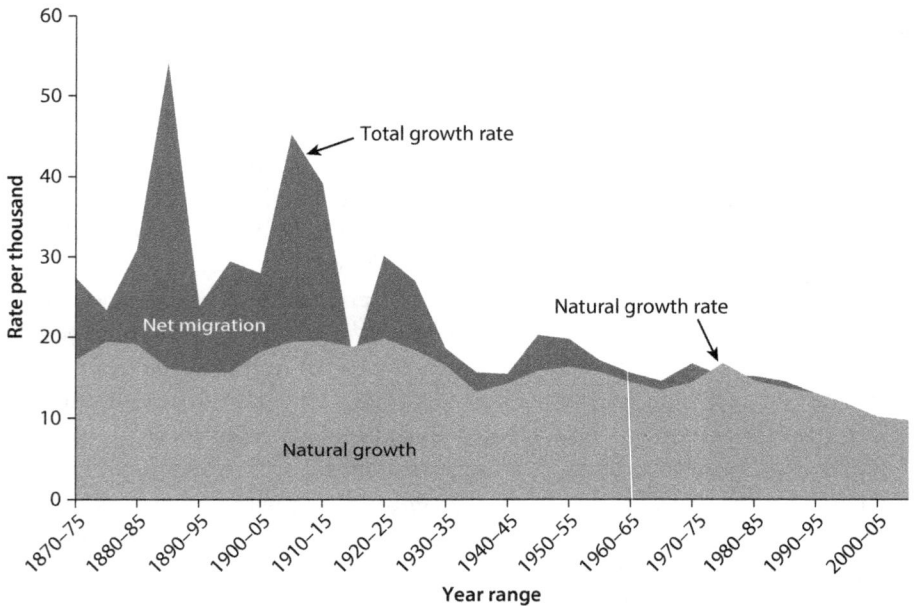

Source: World Bank elaboration based on Lattes 1975 and United Nations 2013.

from neighboring countries) and the emigration of Argentinians (who mostly emigrated to the United States and, following the crisis at the beginning of the twenty-first century, to Europe, to Spain in particular).

In this way, Argentina has become the heart of a regional migration subsystem in the Southern Cone and a country that discharges members of its population. This dual condition constitutes a peculiar aspect of a society that still perceives itself as the product of European immigration. The movements of people from neighboring countries have a long historical tradition: For many years these movements took place in integrated transborder areas. However, after the 1960s the migratory flows from neighboring countries were directed toward the metropolitan area of Buenos Aires, which is now the primary destination and forms the center of the Southern Cone migratory subsystem in Latin America.

Following the period of mass immigration, the immigration flows became more modest and mainly from neighboring countries.[9] Currently, with the largest number of immigrants in the region, Argentina continues to be the epicenter of migration in South America. The changes in immigrants' origins and the migratory dynamic have had an impact on the characteristics of the foreigners who reside in the country.

As a result of the aging and mortality of older transatlantic immigration cohorts, the total proportion of foreigners has decreased over the decades (from 29.9 percent in 1914 to 4.2 percent in 2001—with a slight recovery in 2010 to 4.5 percent as observed in figure 2.11).[10]

Figure 2.11 Proportion of Foreigners in the Argentine Population, 1869–2010

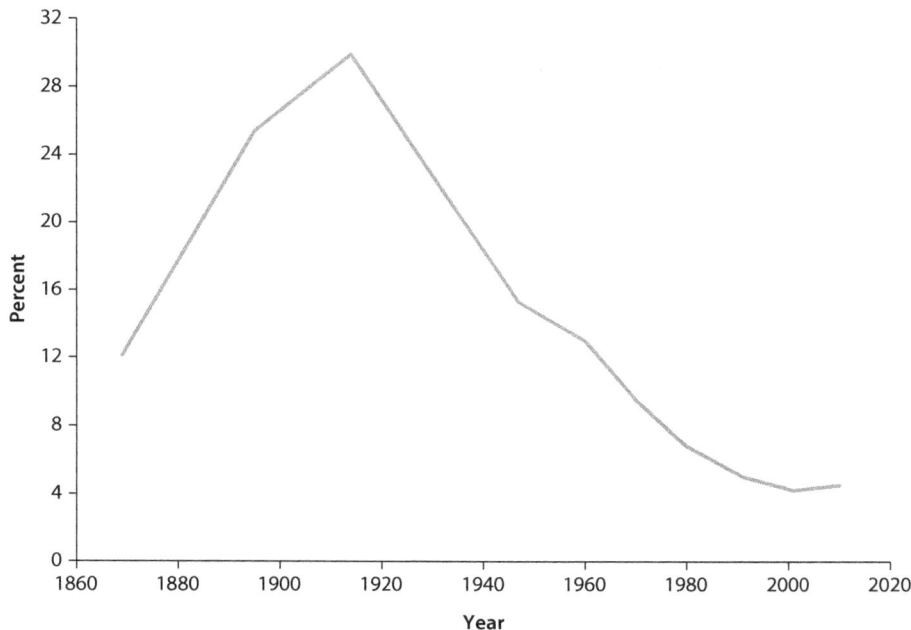

Source: Elaboration based on INDEC 2013.

In contrast, and as an effect of the increase and the continuous entry of immigrants from neighboring countries, foreigners' numbers have increased, growing from 800,000 in 1980 to 1 million in 2001 and to 1.8 million in 2010, with a significant change in the origin of their flows. Economic and social factors in countries of origin, along with changes in Argentina's attractiveness, changed both South Americans' emigratory propensity as well as their preferred destination. Thus, for example, the propensity of Chileans to emigrate decreased, probably as a result of the improvement of social and economic conditions in their country: The proportion of Chilean immigrants in Argentina increased slightly between 1980 and 1991, but subsequently decreased significantly a decade later.[11] Uruguayan citizens present a different case. Even though they continued emigrating, they no longer migrated toward Argentina in the same numbers, but rather they preferred developed countries, such as the United States and Spain (Cabella and Pellegrino 2005; Pellegrino and Vigorito 2005).

In contrast, since 1980, and with growing intensity in the 1990s, immigration from Bolivia, Paraguay, and Peru has grown significantly. Immigration from Bolivia grew systematically beginning in the 1980s: The country's difficult economic conditions, combined with the possibility of entering the labor force in Argentina, led to the intensification of a relatively continuous flow, which was promoted by extensive social networks among migrants (Benencia 1997, 2005).

The Peruvian case is the more obvious recent example of regional immigration in Argentina. The flow of migrants from Peru during the last two decades has been very significant. Even though the number of persons born in Peru that live in Argentina is less than the number of immigrants from three of the countries with which Argentina shares a border,[12] the growth in relative terms has been notable: Between 1991 and 2010, it grew by almost 10 times, from 16,000 to 158,000.[13]

On the basis of information from the Continuous Household Survey (Encuesta Permanente de Hogares, EPH), during the early years of the twenty-first century immigration stalled as a consequence of the 2001 crisis, regaining its momentum after 2004, particularly among immigrants from Bolivia and Paraguay. In the same vein, the registration of undocumented immigrants under the Grand Homeland (Patria Grande) program that began in 2006 stands out as a milestone in the history of Argentine migration policy.[14]

In terms of the emerging patterns of international emigration, the most noticeable changes began in the 1990s and appear to have intensified at the beginning of the millennium. One component is that not only did the rate of growth increase, but destinations like Spain and other European countries also established themselves as alternatives to the long-established destination of the United States. Another component is the growing diversification of the migrant population.

Until the middle of the 1970s, the extra-regional flows were mainly made up of highly educated professionals and experts; later, political exiles joined this group. From the mid-1990s on, consistent economic decline and its effects on the labor market not only contributed to an increase in the volume of these emigration flows, but also to making them more heterogeneous in terms of social makeup.[15]

As mentioned earlier, for purposes of the projections presented in this work, as well as in the official estimates by INDEC (2004) and ECLAC (2011a), we assume a net migration balance of zero from 2010 onward. Nonetheless, in the United Nations (2013) estimates, the net negative balances estimated at the beginning of the century (180,000 net emigrants for 2000–05 and 200,000 for 2005–10) will gradually decrease to 100,000 for 2010–15 and 2015–20, to 50,000 in each five-year period from 2020 to 2050, and linearly (with decreases of 5,000 per five-year period) until reaching 0 during 2095–2100. The criteria adopted by the United Nations do not appear to account for the strong economic recovery and the specific policies adopted during the last decade, which would make it more appropriate to make a conservative assumption (but not overly pessimistic) of null net balances in the long term.

Demographic Heterogeneity and Differences by Area

Even though the previous sections have analyzed the demographic evolution of Argentina as a whole, we recognize both the presence and the influence of significant differences within the country. For example, in 2010 the proportion of the population older than 65 years of age averaged 10 percent nationally, ranging

---

Box 2.1 Methodological Summary of the Estimates Made and Comparison to United Nations

Base population as of June 30, 2010: Estimates based on the correction of the 2001 national census (INDEC 2004), similar to UN estimates.

Mortality: Gradual growth of LEB, from 75 years for 2005–2010 to 85 or 2095–2100, more moderate than UN estimates, which will reach 88 years.

Fertility: Gradual decline of TFR until it settles around 2.0. UN estimates assume a larger decrease and a subsequent recovery, combined with two logarithmic curves and two asymptotic limits (of 1.85 for 2050 and 2.1 for the longer term).

Migrations: Null balance during the entire estimate period, different from UN estimates, in which the net negative balances estimated at the beginning of the century decrease very gradually.

Total population: On the basis of the assumptions adopted, grows from 41 million in 2010 to 54 million in 2050 and 59 million in 2100. The UN estimate reaches 51 million in 2050 and remains stable.

Aging (proportion of the population of adults older than 65 years of age); Increases from 11 percent in 2010 to 19 percent in 2050 and 25 percent in 2100. For the second half of the century, the UN estimate grows at a faster pace (based on earlier lower fertility), reaching 29 percent in 2100.

Source: United Nations 2013.

---

from 4 percent in Tierra del Fuego to 16 percent in the Autonomous City of Buenos Aires (CABA). This heterogeneity is associated with significant variations in fertility (principally) and mortality, with TFRs ranging from 1.8 children per woman (CABA) to 3.1 (Santa Cruz) and LEBs from 72.9 years (Chaco) to 77.3 (Neuquén).

During the last three decades, the gaps among regions have decreased in terms of the three variables considered for the three indicators of heterogeneity available: range (distance between the maximum and minimum values), standard deviation (SD), and coefficient of variation (CV, ratio of the SD to the mean), which are presented in table 2.1.[16]

Between 1980 and 2010, the range of values for the percentage of adults older than 65 years of age decreased from 12.7 to 12.6, the SD from 2.6 to 2.5, and the CV from 19 percent to 12 percent. As for LEB, its range decreased from 8.5 to 4.4, SD from 2.2 to 1.0, and CV from 3.2 percent to 1.4 percent.

This process of homogenization, of both LEB as well as TFR, can be explained in part because the values are nearing the supposed asymptotic limits and by the phenomenon known as regression to the mean: The regions with larger increases/decreases are those that begin from lower/higher levels. In both cases,

Table 2.1 Demographic Variables and Heterogeneity, by Region in Argentina, 1980–2010

	1980	1991	2001	2010
Percentage of the population older than 65 years of age				
Mean	6.17	6.69	7.74	8.50
Maximum	14.83	16.31	17.23	16.40
Minimum	2.09	1.56	2.93	3.82
Range	12.74	14.75	14.30	12.58
Standard deviation	2.61	2.86	2.82	2.52
Coefficient of variation (%)	42.20	42.80	36.50	29.70
Total fertility rate (TFR)				
Mean	4.05	3.44	2.88	2.29
Maximum	5.21	4.77	3.67	3.14
Minimum	2.16	1.81	1.75	1.85
Range	3.05	2.96	1.91	1.29
Standard deviation	0.78	0.60	0.42	0.27
Coefficient of variation (%)	19.30	17.40	14.60	11.60
Life expectancy at birth by region (LEB)				
Mean	67.19	70.76	73.30	75.41
Maximum	72.23	72.79	75.91	77.29
Minimum	63.77	68.37	69.97	72.85
Range	8.46	4.42	5.94	4.44
Standard deviation	2.16	1.22	1.46	1.05
Coefficient of variation (%)	3.20	1.70	2.0	1.40

Source: Percentage > 65 based on INDEC: National census of 1980, 1991, 2001, and 2010. TFR: based on INDEC data.
LEB: based on INDEC data.
Note: The data for LEB correspond to the periods 1980–81, 1990–92, 2000–01, and 2008–10.

the linear relationship between the variation for 1980–2010 and the 1980 level is significant with an R^2 coefficient around 0.8.[17]

In the specific case of the percentage of the population of adults older than 65 years of age, the relationship is much reduced ($R^2 = 0.1$), because the values are still far from the predictable limits, and possibly due in part to the lag in the impact of the changes in fertility and mortality and to the different weight of internal migration by region.

Implications of the Demographic Evolution on "Dependency" and "Dividends"

The process of change in a population's age structure has an important impact from a social and economic point of view, because it implies changes in the weight of the age groups that make up the potentially dependent population, relative to those that belong to age groups considered potentially active or productive.

The aging process is just one part of the change in the age structure of a population.[18] During certain periods, the growth of the older age groups is compensated for by a (relative) decrease among younger age groups (also economically dependent). As Chackiel (2004) points out, in general, a low demographic dependency ratio is considered positive for a society because this means that there are proportionally fewer persons that are a "burden" that must be supported by the economically active population.

At the beginning of a demographic transition, the dependency ratio is high because of the elevated percentage of children. The subsequent decrease in fertility brings about a period (that can last several decades) in which the population is made up of a greater proportion of intermediate age groups and is called the demographic dividend or window of opportunity. This period is referred to in this way because the demographic situation means that society can access savings that can be turned into productive investments or reassigned to social benefits that were not easily provided before this point. Because the savings are the result of the reduced demand for resources from children (this population is practically static), a restructuring of social spending is proposed, mainly to focus on the quality of education and reforms in the health care sector to deal with the change in the epidemiological profile. The period is considered an opportunity to undertake reforms and investments that will prepare countries for the moment when the dependency ratio returns to elevated levels again as the relative weight of the elderly population increases.

Even though the presence of low dependency ratios is positive, certain reservations have been expressed to avoid the error of unmeasured optimism: For a truly favorable dependency ratio to exist, society must successfully meet the growing economically active population's demand for jobs. A country with a significant unemployed population will lead to an elevated real dependency ratio, and the favorable demographic structure will be dependent on the labor market's capacity to meet the growing demand for jobs.

As Time Goes By in Argentina • http://dx.doi.org/10.1596/978-1-4648-0530-1

Another point to consider is what happens within countries where the DD is especially beneficial to middle– and upper– class households that have experienced a greater decrease in fertility. Meanwhile, for poorer sectors to benefit (and adopt the new demographic behaviors), the government must implement income redistribution policies that ensure that the entire society benefits from the freeing up of resources that the low dependency ratio brings about (Chackiel 2004).[19]

The total dependency ratio (TDR), which measures the ratio of children/ adolescents and the elderly (younger than age 15 and older than 65) relative to the population at economically active ages (between 15 and 65 years), is used to determine the period of the DD. The TDR in Argentina grew from 53 percent in 1950 to 66 percent in 1990, reversed this trend, falling to 55 percent in 2010, and will remain relatively stable until 2040. After that, it will restart its upward trend, reaching 61 percent in 2050 and possibly 72 percent in 2100 (figure 2.12).

If we arbitrarily establish a maximum TDR of 60 percent (six persons in the inactive age groups per 10 persons in the economically active age range), the demographic window of opportunity (DWO) will include the four decades from 2005 to 2045.

Alternatively, if we adopt a maximum TDR of 66 percent (two persons in the inactive age groups per three persons in the economically active age range), the DWO (when the TDR is below this level) would include the seven decades from 1990 to 2060.

Figure 2.12 The Demographic Dividend: Total Dependency Ratio, 1950–2100

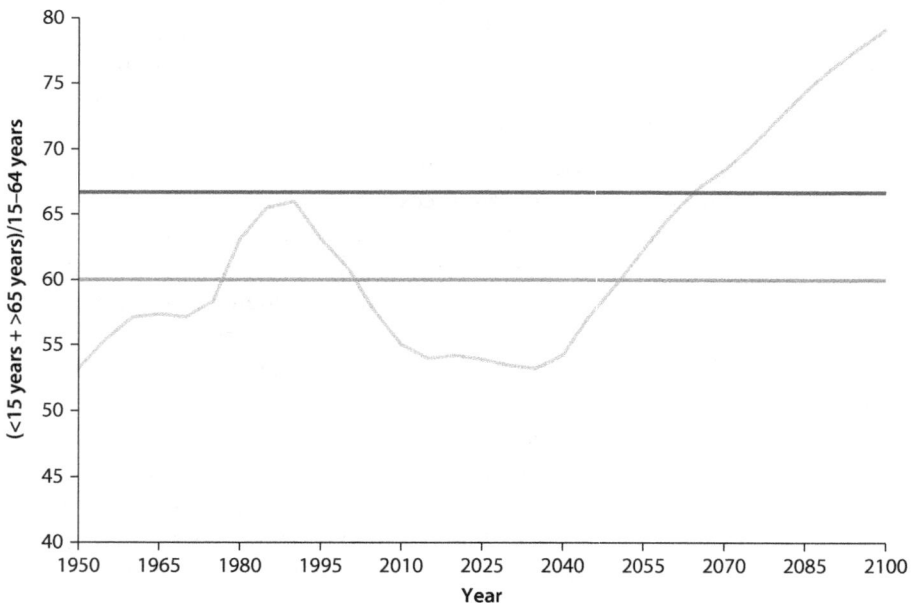

Source: World Bank elaboration.

We also estimate the evolution of the TDR considering alternative age groups for the economically active population:

(a) From age 20 to 65 years [(<20 + >65)/20–64], the values are higher but with the same trend: The ratio remains near 75 between 2010 and 2040, subsequently growing gradually until reaching 92 in 2100.

(b) From age 15 to 60 years [(<15 + >60)/15–59], the values are intermediate (closer to the base case) but with the same trend: the ratio remains near 65 between 2010 and 2030, subsequently growing gradually until reaching 91 in 2100.[20]

In the literature, it is common to refer to the DD and the DWO as synonyms. However, recognizing that there is not an exact measurement of the beginning and the end of the DD, Gragnolati and colleagues (2011), following the work of ECLAC (2008), consider that the DD begins with the decline of the TDR until it reaches the arbitrarily chosen level, subsequently continuing with the predefined DWO. In this vision, the DD can be divided in three stages: the decline of the TDR until reaching the arbitrarily chosen level, the decline of the TDR below the chosen level, and, finally, the increase of the TDR while it is still below the chosen level.

The comparison of the Argentine demographic process with other international experiences that we will set forth in the following sections with three groups of selected countries—from the region (Brazil, Chile Mexico, and Uruguay), some more developed (Germany, Italy, Japan, and Spain), and some less developed (China, the Republic of Korea, and Thailand)—will highlight the differences and similarities as well as the limitations of the established indicator. The analysis centers on the evolution of the TDR [(<15 + >65)/15–64] and the subsequent appearance of the DD, although in all of the cases, this evolution depends on combinations of past trends and estimates of mortality, fertility, and international migration that are not dealt with in detail here.[21] For the comparison, we consider three variables: the beginning year, the duration of each stage, and the "depth" (maximum distance achieved from the TDR value at the moment it begins to decline or the limit established in 60 percent to the minimum value achieved).[22]

In the Latin American context, the Argentine case is very similar to the Uruguayan case (both show early fertility declines), with a delayed DD, a shorter duration, and not as deep as Chile and Brazil, while Mexico remains in an intermediate situation (as a result of its more rapid and delayed decline in fertility, with large deficits before and after) (figure 2.13).

In the context of more developed countries (+DC), the Argentine case is different, with a more delayed DD of lesser duration and depth. The TDR values gradually near the +DC group, but they maintain significant distance from the three selected European countries (Germany, Spain, and Italy), which behave similarly to each other, having achieved much lower levels of fertility that are projected to recover gradually. Argentina's TDR values are even

Figure 2.13 Total Dependency Ratio, Selected Latin American Countries, 1950–2100
Percent

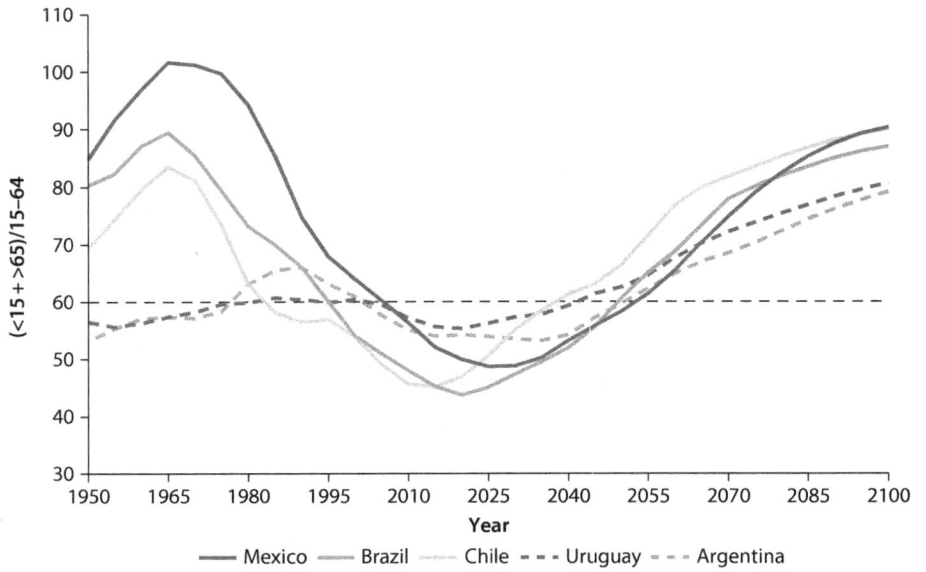

Source: World Bank elaboration based on United Nations 2013.

Figure 2.14 Total Dependency Ratio, Selected More Developed Countries, 1950–2100
Percent

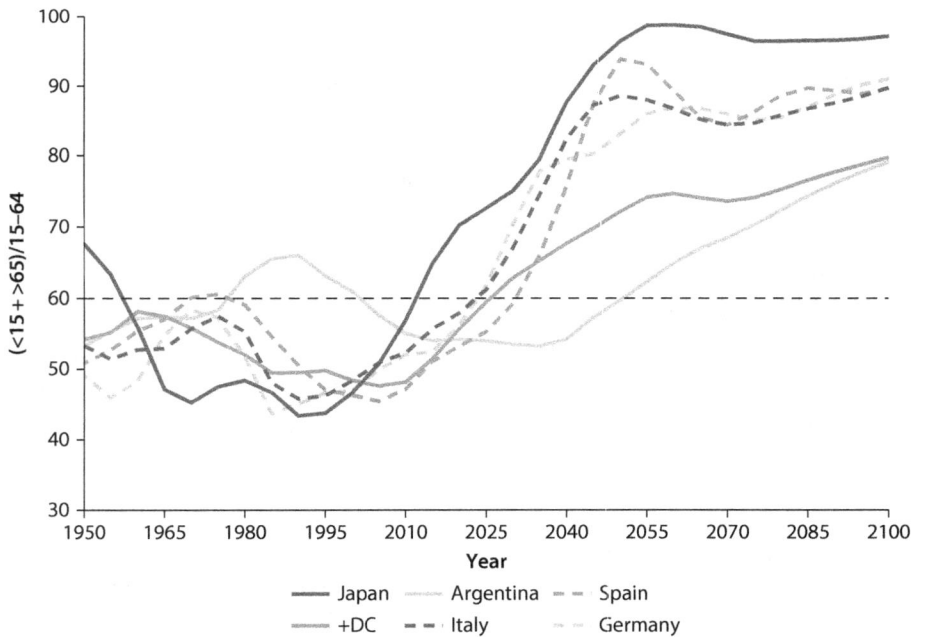

Source: World Bank elaboration based on United Nations 2013.
Note: +DC = more developed countries.

Figure 2.15 Total Dependency Ratio, Selected Less Developed Countries, 1950–2100
Percent

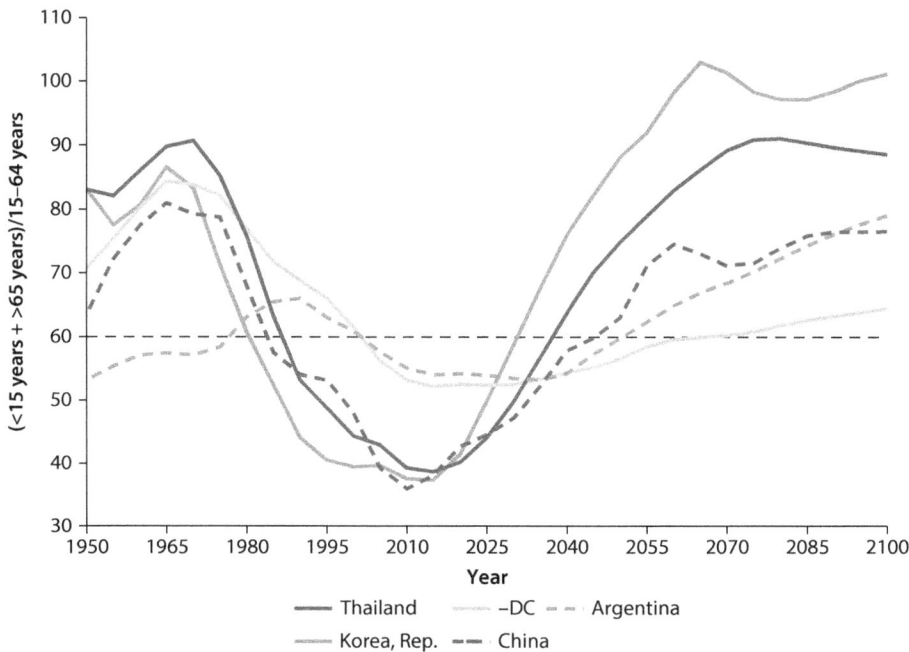

Source: Elaboration based on United Nations 2011.
Note: -DC = less developed countries.

further from Japan's, whose TDR at mid-century will reach values near 100 percent (figure 2.14).

In the context of less developed countries (–DC), the evolution of the Argentine TDR from 1990 on is similar to the –DC group (accompanying the gradual decrease of fertility), although the DD has a shorter duration. Compared with the selected emerging Asian countries (China, Korea, and Thailand), the DD is much less significant (deep) and occurs two decades later (figure 2.15).

Summarizing the international comparison, Argentina has maintained a very gradual evolution of TDR, with a window of opportunity and a DD character-ized (in general) by a later start, a lesser or equal duration, and less depth, above all when compared with more developed countries or with selected emerging countries in Asia and Latin America. Table 2A.3 summarizes the international comparison.

Annex 2A

Table 2A.1 Gender Differences in Life Expectancy at Birth, World and Regions with Different Levels of Development, 1950–2010

Five-year period	LEB (in years), women					LEB (in years), men					LEB difference (Women–Men)				
	Argentina	World	+DC	–DC	Latin America	Argentina	World	+DC	–DC	Latin America	Argentina	World	+DC	–DC	Latin America
1950–55	65.1	47.9	67.2	42.0	53.1	60.4	45.9	62.1	41.3	49.7	4.7	2.0	5.1	0.8	3.4
1955–60	67.4	50.7	70.4	44.8	56.3	62.1	48.1	64.8	43.5	52.5	5.3	2.6	5.6	1.3	3.8
1960–65	68.6	53.0	72.4	47.4	59.0	62.5	49.2	66.3	44.8	54.9	6.2	3.7	6.1	2.6	4.1
1965–70	69.3	57.9	73.6	53.4	61.1	62.8	55.1	66.9	52.2	56.8	6.6	2.8	6.7	1.3	4.3
1970–75	70.8	60.7	74.5	56.9	63.5	64.1	56.9	67.5	54.6	58.7	6.7	3.8	7.1	2.3	4.9
1975–80	72.2	62.8	75.6	59.4	65.9	65.4	58.6	68.2	56.7	60.6	6.8	4.2	7.4	2.8	5.3
1980–85	73.7	64.7	76.5	61.6	68.5	66.8	60.2	69.0	58.4	62.1	6.9	4.5	7.5	3.2	6.3
1985–90	74.6	66.2	77.4	63.4	70.5	67.6	61.8	70.2	60.2	64.0	7.0	4.4	7.2	3.2	6.6
1990–95	75.8	67.1	78.0	64.5	72.4	68.6	62.5	70.2	61.1	65.6	7.2	4.6	7.8	3.4	6.8
1995–00	77.0	68.0	78.5	65.5	74.0	69.7	63.4	71.0	62.0	67.4	7.3	4.6	7.6	3.5	6.6
2000–05	78.1	69.3	79.3	67.1	75.5	70.6	64.9	71.8	63.7	68.9	7.5	4.4	7.4	3.4	6.6
2005–10	79.1	71.0	80.4	68.8	76.7	71.6	66.5	73.4	65.2	70.2	7.5	4.5	7.0	3.6	6.5

Source: Elaboration based on United Nations 2013.

Table 2A.2 Total Foreign-Born Population, by Place of Birth, Gender, and Age Groups, Argentina, 2010

Place of birth	Total foreign population	Gender and age group							
		Men				Women			
		Total	0–14 years	15–64 years	65 years and older	Total	0–14 years	15–64 years	65 years and older
Total	1,805,957	831,696	70,314	599,536	161,846	974,261	69,998	690,003	214,260
America	1,471,399	681,585	63,971	538,371	79,243	789,814	63,885	629,246	96,683
Neighboring countries	1,245,054	577,654	50,662	451,693	75,299	667,400	50,610	524,200	92,590
Bolivia	345,272	171,493	18,518	137,699	15,276	173,779	18,552	139,926	15,301
Brazil	41,330	17,423	1,717	12,816	2,890	23,907	1,782	17,704	4,421
Chile	191,147	88,973	2,457	65,668	20,848	102,174	2,363	76,500	23,311
Paraguay	550,713	244,279	26,112	190,172	27,995	306,434	26,083	243,263	37,088
Uruguay	116,592	55,486	1,858	45,338	8,290	61,106	1,830	46,807	12,469
Non neighboring countries (America)	226,345	103,931	13,309	86,678	3,944	122,414	13,275	105,046	4,093
Peru	157,514	70,899	6,860	61,393	2,646	86,615	7,058	77,060	2,497
Rest of America	68,831	33,032	6,449	25,285	1,298	35,799	6,217	27,986	1,596
Europe	299,394	131,577	5,424	46,332	79,821	167,817	5,200	48,163	114,454
Germany	8,416	3,889	293	2,082	1,514	4,527	272	2,070	2,185
Spain	94,030	40,437	3,041	12,702	24,694	53,593	2,843	13,506	37,244
France	6,995	3,513	322	2,386	805	3,482	302	2,098	1,082
Italy	147,499	65,021	966	20,226	43,829	82,478	1,011	21,597	59,870
Rest of Europe	42,454	18,717	802	8,936	8,979	23,737	772	8,892	14,073
Asia	31,001	15,997	747	12,757	2,493	15,004	779	11,444	2,781
China	8,929	4,897	124	4,635	138	4,032	116	3,817	99
Korea, Rep.	7,321	3,671	113	2,989	569	3,650	132	2,999	519
Japan	4,036	1,944	122	973	849	2,092	129	946	1,017
Lebanon	933	441	4	195	242	492	4	154	334
Syrian Arab Republic	1,337	701	4	389	308	636	8	274	354
Taiwan, China	2,875	1,435	22	1,280	133	1,440	11	1,308	121
Rest of Asia	5,570	2,908	358	2,296	254	2,662	379	1,946	337
Africa	2,738	1,825	74	1,514	237	913	45	593	275
Oceana	1,425	712	98	562	52	713	89	557	67

Source: INDEC 2013.
Note: The total population includes persons living on the street.

Figure 2A.1 Total Population, Argentina, 1950–2100

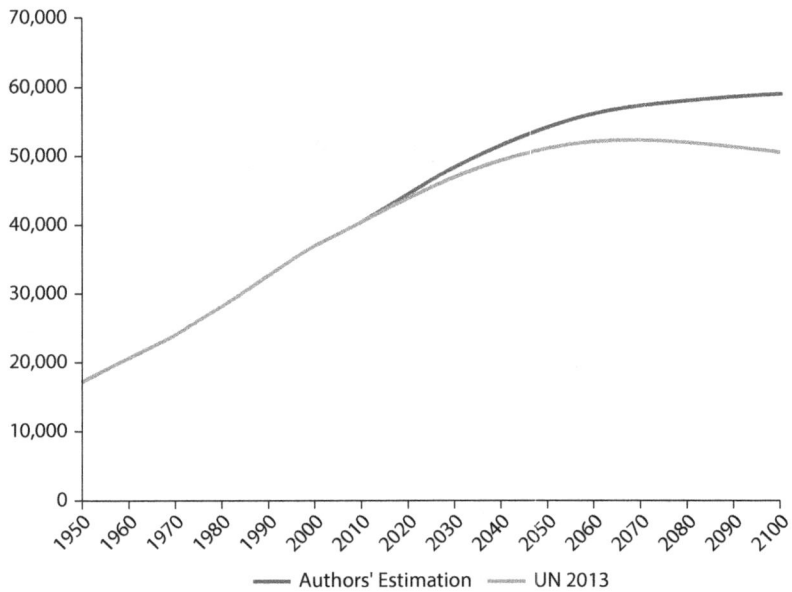

Source: United Nations 2013.

Table 2A.3 Summary: Evolution of the Total Dependency Ratio, Window of Opportunity, and Demographic Dividend

Country/ region	Beginning year stage 1 (TDR declining)	Beginning year stage 2 (TDR <60% and declining)	Beginning year stage 3 (TDR <60% and growing)	Final year	Duration (years)			DWO (stages 2 + 3)	DD (stages 1 to 3)	Minimum TDR value
					Stage 1	Stage 2	Stage 3			
Argentina	1990	2005	2035	2050	15	30	15	45	60	53
Latin America	1965	2005	2020	2050	40	15	30	45	85	50
Brazil	1965	1995	2020	2045	30	25	25	50	80	44
Chile	1965	1985	2015	2035	20	30	20	50	70	45
Mexico	1965	2010	2025	2050	45	15	25	40	85	49
Uruguay	1985	2005	2020	2040	20	15	20	35	55	55
C+D	1960	1965	2005	2025	5	40	20	60	65	48
Germany	1970	1975	1985	2020	5	10	35	45	50	44
Spain	1975	1980	2005	2030	5	25	25	50	55	45
Italy	1975	1980	1990	2020	5	10	30	40	45	46
Japan	1950	1960	1990	2010	10	30	20	50	60	43
C–D	1965	2005	2015	2065	40	10	50	60	100	52
China	1965	1985	2010	2045	20	25	35	60	80	36
Korea, Rep.	1965	1985	2000	2030	20	15	30	45	65	37
Thailand	1970	1990	2015	2035	20	25	20	45	65	39

Source: Elaboration based on United Nations 2013.
Note: +DC = more developed countries; –DC = less developed countries.

Figure 2A.2 Percentage of the Population over Age 65 by Province, 1980–2010

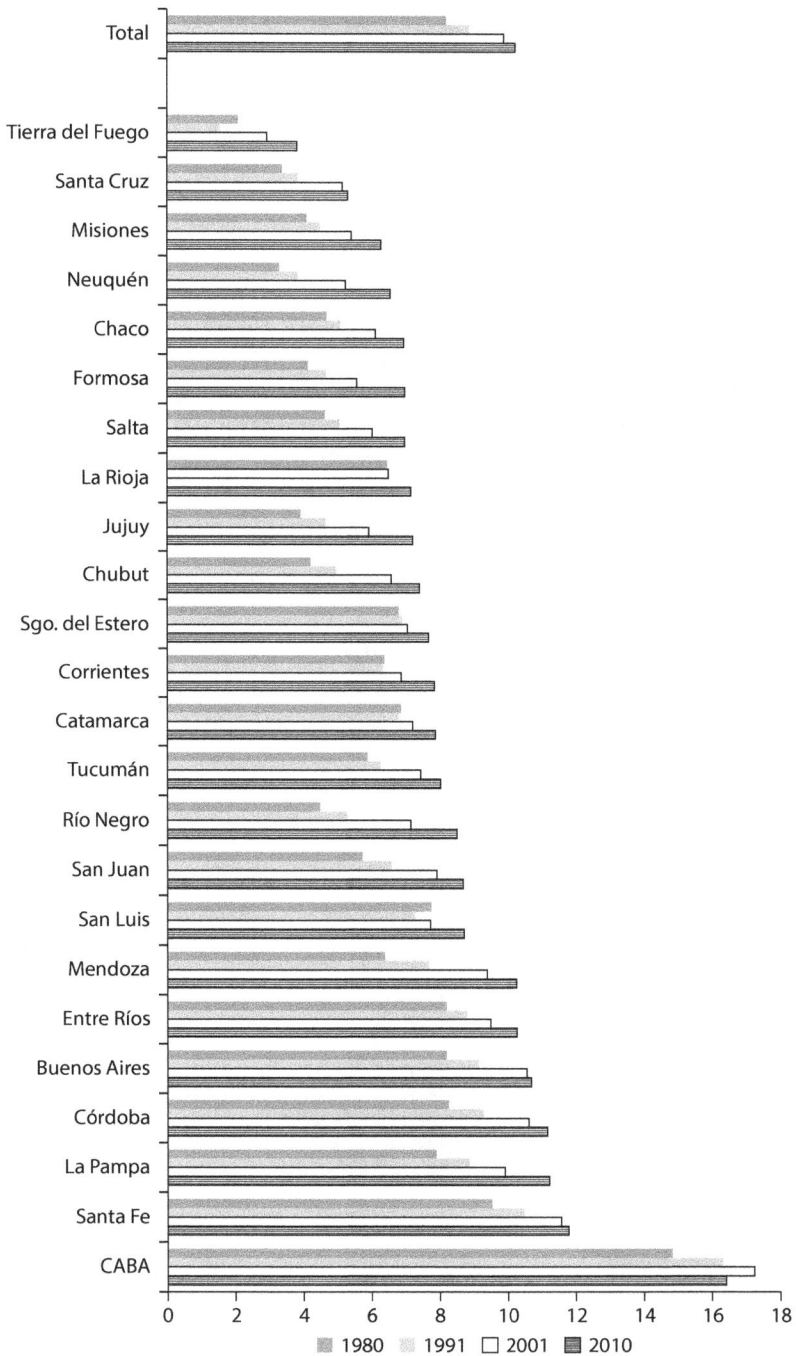

Source: Based on INDEC 2013.

Figure 2A.3 Total Fertility Rate, by Province, 1980–2010

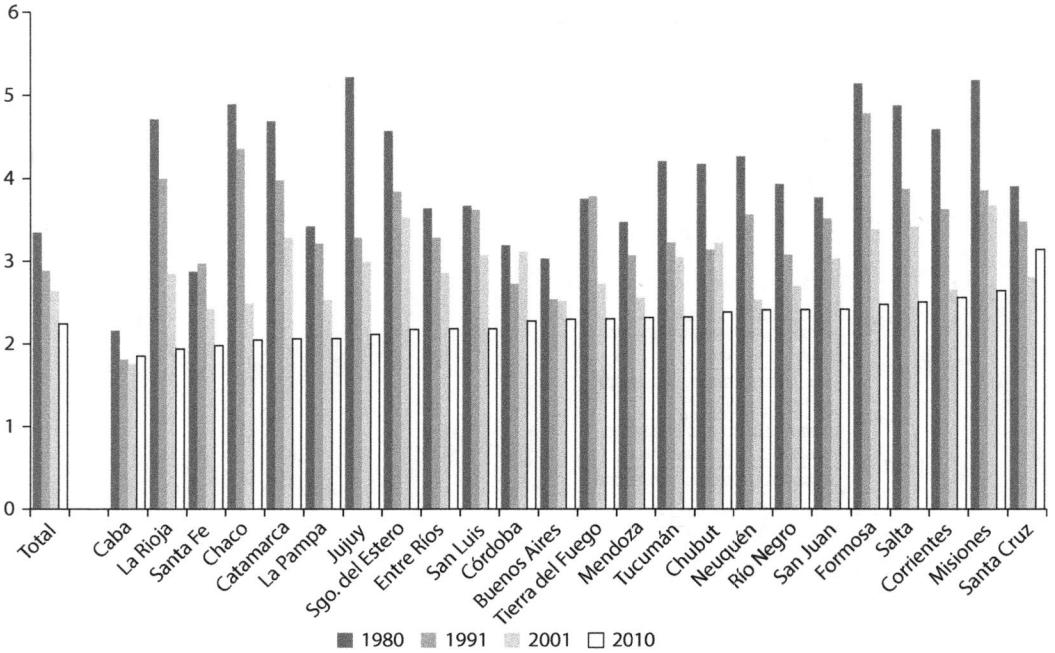

Source: Based on INDEC 2013.

Figure 2A.4 Life Expectancy at Birth, by Province, 1980–2010

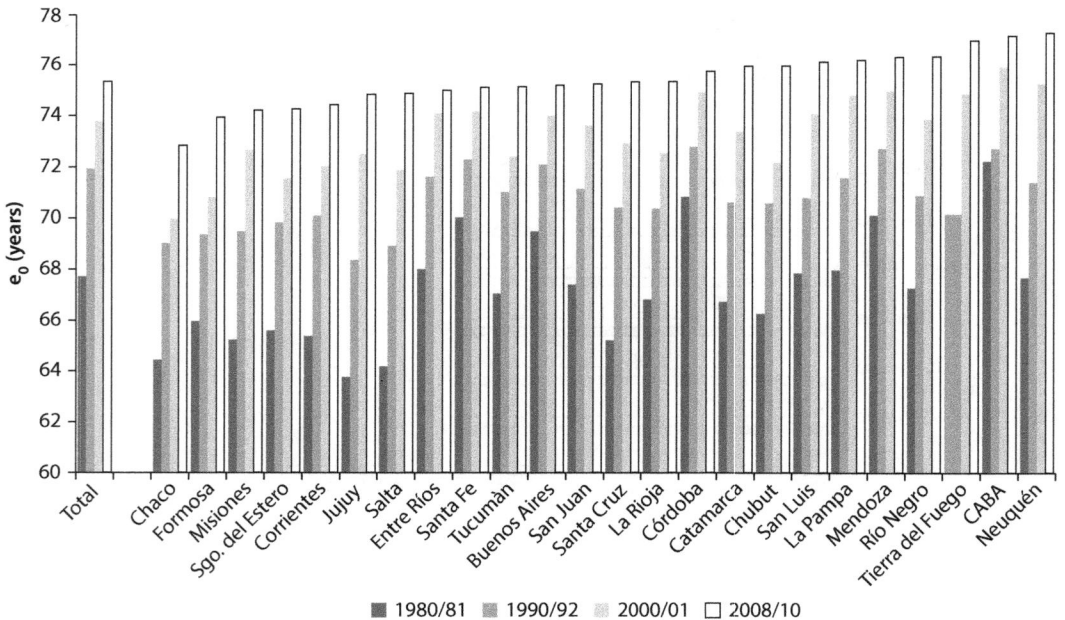

Source: Based on INDEC data.

Figure 2A.5 Reduction of the Total Fertility Rate, by Province, by Initial Level, 1980–2010

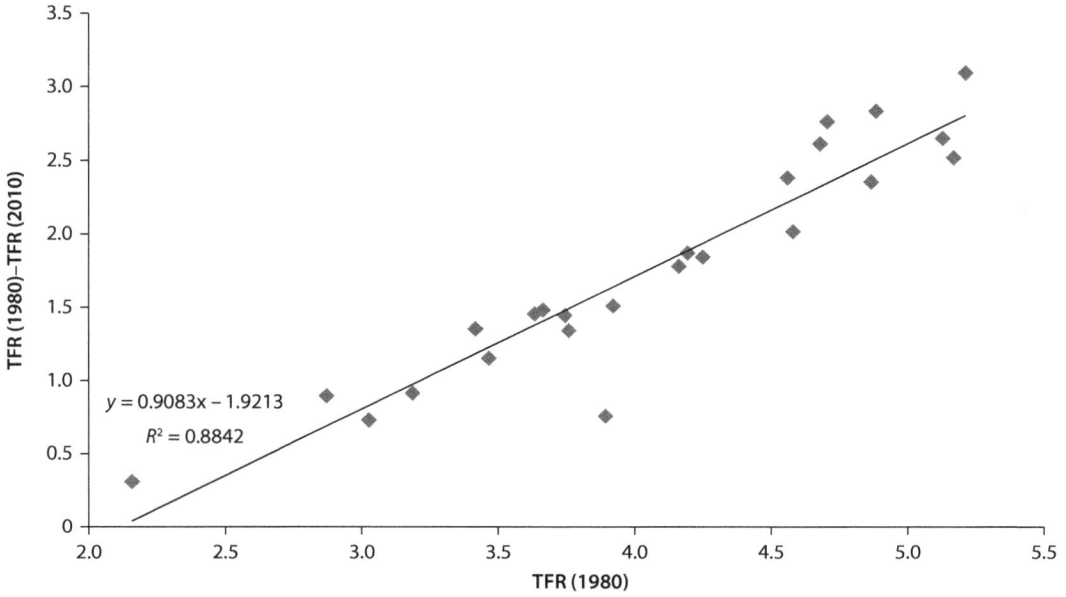

$y = 0.9083x - 1.9213$

$R^2 = 0.8842$

Source: Based on INDEC 2013.

Figure 2A.6 Gain in Life Expectancy, by Province by Initial Level, 1980–2010

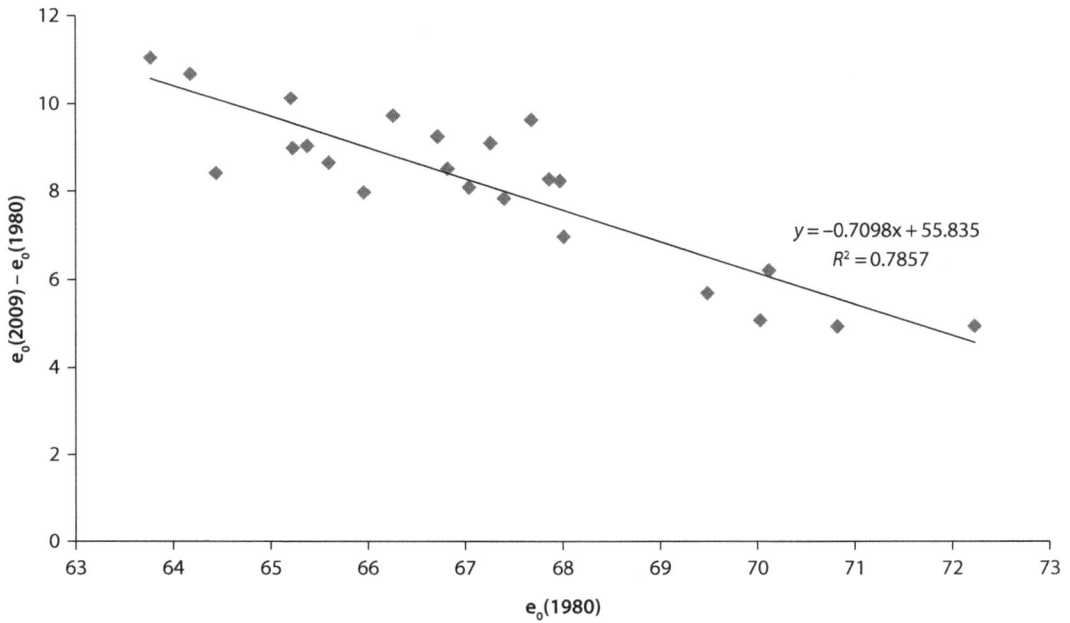

$y = -0.7098x + 55.835$

$R^2 = 0.7857$

Source: Based on INDEC 1988 and 2013.

As Time Goes By in Argentina • http://dx.doi.org/10.1596/978-1-4648-0530-1

Figure 2A.7 Proportion of the Population over Age 65, World and Regions with Different Levels of Development, 1950–2100

Percent

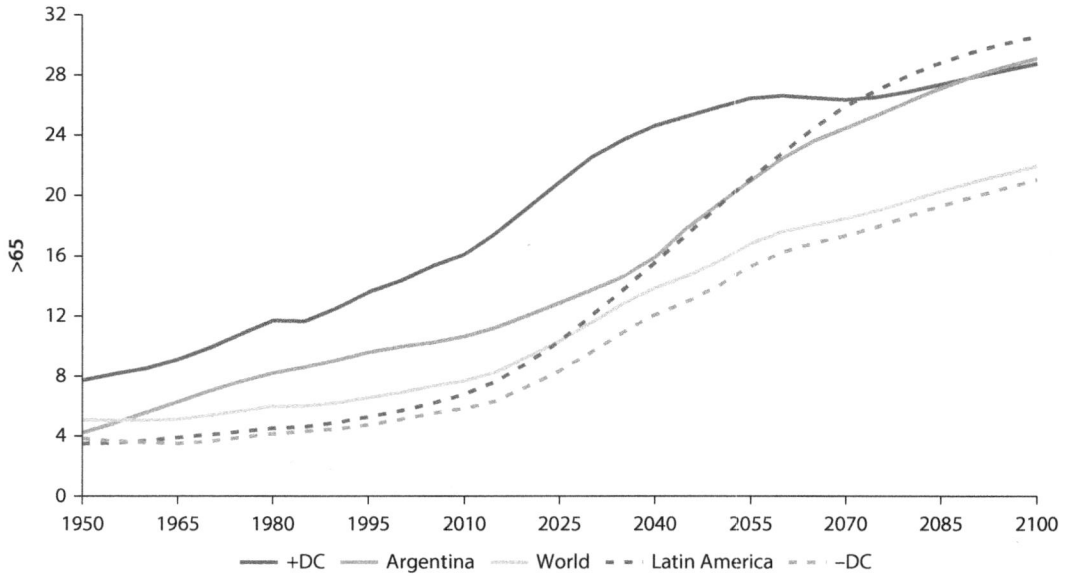

Source: Based on United Nations 2013.
Note: +DC = more developed countries; –DC = less developed countries.

Figure 2A.8 Total Dependency Ratio, 1950–2100, Population <15 Years and >65 Years/15–64 Years

Percent

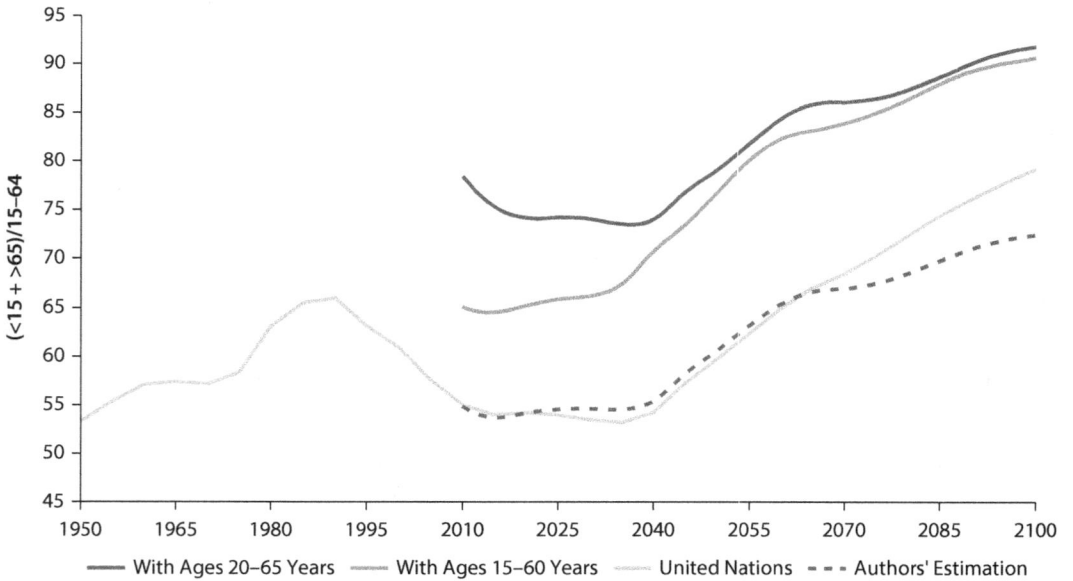

Source: Based on United Nations 2013.

Notes

1. The most recent official projections were prepared jointly by the National Institute of Statistics and Censuses (Instituto Nacional de Estadística y Censos, INDEC) and the Population Division of the Latin American and Caribbean Demographic Centre (Centro Latinoamericano y del Caribe de Demografía, CELADE), although the criteria differ because CELADE (2004) has continued the practice of publishing information up to 2050, whereas INDEC (2004) goes only up to 2015 (for more details, see Rofman 2007).

2. For more details, see box 2.1. The decrease in mortality is slower, and the migration estimates imply no net change, instead of a slightly negative effect.

3. According to United Nations (2013). In contrast, the Argentine population will reach 51 million people in 2050 and will remain relatively stable according to the data provided below. See figure 2A.1.

4. This section is primarily based on Grushka (2010).

5. According to United Nations (2013) criteria, the less developed regions include Africa, Asia (except for Japan), Latin America and the Caribbean, and Melanesia, the Federated States of Micronesia, and Polynesia (the rest of Oceania).

6. The more developed regions include Europe, North America, Australia and New Zealand, and Japan.

7. This section is primarily based on Pantelides and Moreno (2009) and INDEC (2013).

8. The predominance of working–age population among immigrants created a demographic dividend that will not be considered in this work.

9. It should be pointed out that immigration from neighboring countries to Argentina dates back many years. In 1869, these immigrants represented 20 percent of foreigners. This share fell to its lowest level in 1914 (8.6 percent). Since 1947, the relative importance of immigrants from neighboring countries among all foreign residents has increased continuously (Ceva 2006).

10. For example, between 1980 and 2010, immigrants of Italian origin, who historically made up the largest group in Argentina, decreased from 488,000 to 147,000, and those of Spanish origin (the second-largest group) fell from 374,000 to 94,000. The makeup of the foreign population in 2010 is presented in table 2A.2.

11. During the 1990s, Chile began to receive regional immigrants, especially from Peru (Martínez Pizarro 2005).

12. In 2010, the number of Peruvians residing in Argentina was equal to 29 percent of the immigrants from Paraguay, 46 percent of those from Bolivia, and 82 percent of those from Chile, as well as 11 percent of the total foreign-born population from the American continent.

13. Argentina was one of several migrant destinations during the so-called Peruvian exodus that took place during the 1990s. Peru's economic and social situation, and especially the political violence experienced during the 1980s, were key drivers of this massive emigration (Cerrutti 2005).

14. Since this program was implemented, any citizen of a MERCOSUR country or associated state (Brazil, Bolivia, Chile, Colombia, Ecuador, Paraguay, Peru, República Bolivariana de Venezuela, and Uruguay) can obtain legal residency in Argentina by just proving his or her nationality and possessing a clean criminal record. At the end of 2007, 566,000 individuals had registered, of whom 442,000 were already living in

Argentina on April 17, 2006, when the program began. Sixty percent of those who began the process were from Paraguay, who along with Bolivians and Peruvians make up 95 percent of the total.

15. For greater detail, see Maguid and Martinez (2008).

16. For greater detail, see figures 2A.2–2A.4.

17. For more details, see figures 2A.5 and 2A.6.

18. For more details, see figure 2A.7.

19. Recall the significant differences by region in Argentina presented above.

20. See figure 2A.8.

21. To achieve greater comparability, the TDR values for Argentina are from United Nations (2013) and do not strictly match those presented previously.

22. For numerical details, see table 2A.3.

References

Benencia, R. 1997. "De peones a patrones quinteros. Movilidad social de familias bolivianas en la periferia bonaerense." *Estudios Migratorios Latinoamericanos* 12 (35): 63–102.

———. 2005. "Migración limítrofe y mercado de trabajo rural en la Argentina. Estrategias de familias bolivianas en la conformación de comunidades transnacionales." *Revista Latinoamericana de Estudios del Trabajo* 10 (17): 5–30.

Cabella, W., and A. Pellegrino. 2005. "Una estimación de la emigración internacional uruguaya entre 1963 y 2004." Documento de Trabajo 70, Facultad de Ciencias Sociales, Unidad Multidisciplinaria, Universidad de la República, Montevideo.

Carbonetti, A., and D. Celton. 2007. "La transición epidemiológica." In *Población y bienestar en la Argentina del Primero al Segundo Centenario. Una historia social del siglo XX*, edited by S. Torrado. Buenos Aires: Edhasa.

CELADE (Centro Latinoamericano y del Caribe de Demografía). 2004. "América Latina y el Caribe. Estimaciones y proyecciones de población, 1950–2050." Boletín demográfico 73, CELADE, Santiago de Chile.

Cerrutti, M. 2005. "La migración peruana a la Ciudad de Buenos Aires. Su evolución y características." *Revista Población de Buenos Aires* 2 (2): 7–28.

Ceva, M. 2006. "La migración limítrofe hacia Argentina en la larga duración." In *Migraciones regionales hacia la Argentina. Diferencia, desigualdad y derechos*, edited by A. Grimson and E. Jelin. Buenos Aires: Prometeo.

Chackiel, J. 2004. "La dinámica demográfica de América Latina." Serie Población y desarrollo 52, ECLAC, Santiago de Chile.

d'Albis, H., and F. Collard. 2013. "Age Groups and the Measure of Population Aging." *Demographic Research* 29 (23): 617–40.

ECLAC (Economic Commission for Latin America and the Caribbean). 2008. "Fecundidad." Observatorio Demográfico 5, ECLAC, Santiago de Chile.

———. 2010. "Mortalidad." Observatorio Demográfico 9, ECLAC, Santiago de Chile.

———. 2011a. "Proyecciones de población a largo plazo." Observatorio Demográfico 11, ECLAC, Santiago de Chile.

———. 2011b. "Envejecimiento poblacional." Observatorio Demográfico 12, ECLAC, Santiago de Chile.

Gragnolati, M., O. H. Jorgensen, R. Rocha, and A. Fruttero, eds. 2011. *Growing Old in an Older Brazil: Implications of Population Aging on Growth, Poverty, Public Finance, and Service Delivery*. Washington, DC: World Bank.

Grushka, C. 2002. "Proyecciones previsionales de largo plazo. Argentina, 2000–2050." Estudio Especial 14, SAFJP, Buenos Aires.

———. 2010. "¿Cuánto vivimos? ¿Cuánto viviremos?" In *Dinámica de una ciudad. Buenos Aires*, 1810–2010, edited by A. Lattes. Buenos Aires: Dirección General de Estadística y Censos, Gobierno de la Ciudad Autónoma de Buenos Aires.

INDEC (Instituto Nacional de Estadística y Censos). 2003. "Características de los adultos mayores en un país que envejece. Aquí se cuenta." Revista informativa del Censo 2001 no. 9, INDEC, Buenos Aires.

———. 2004. "Estimaciones y proyecciones de población. Total del país, 1950–2015." Serie Análisis Demográfico no. 30, INDEC, Buenos Aires.

INDEC. 1988. "Tablas de Mortalidad, 1980–1981, Total y Jurisdicciones." Serie Estudios INDEC 4, Buenos Aires.

INDEC. 2013. "Estimaciones y Proyecciones de Población 2010–2040: Total del País," Serie Análisis Demográfico 35, Buenos Aires.

Lacasta, L. 2008. *Estudio de la mortalidad en el SIJP, 2002–2006*. Ministerio de Trabajo, Empleo y Seguridad Social, Buenos Aires.

Lattes, A. 1975. "El crecimiento de la población y sus componentes demográficos entre 1870 y 1970." In *La población de Argentina, Buenos Aires*, edited by Z. Recchini de Lattes and A. Lattes. Buenos Aires: CICRED Series.

Maguid, A., and R. Martinez. 2008. "La emigración reciente de sudamericanos a Estados Unidos y a España. El caso de los argentinos." Document presented at III Congress of the Latin American Population Association, Córdoba, Argentina, September 25.

Martínez Pizarro, J. 2005. "Magnitud y dinámica de la inmigración en Chile según el censo del 2002." *Papeles de Población* 44: 109–47.

Pantelides, E. A. 1983. "La transición demográfica argentina. Un modelo no ortodoxo." *Desarrollo Económico* 22 (88): 511–34.

———. 1989. "La fecundidad Argentina desde mediados del siglo XX." Cuaderno del CENEP 41, Centro de Estudios de Población, Buenos Aires.

———. 2006. "La transición de la fecundidad en la Argentina, 1869–1947." Cuaderno del CENEP 54, Centro de Estudios de Población, Buenos Aires.

Pantelides, E. A., and M. J. Moreno, coords. 2009. *Situación de la población en Argentina*. Buenos Aires: United Nations Development Programme.

Pellegrino, A., and A. Vigorito. 2005. "Emigration and Economic Crisis: Recent Evidence from Uruguay." *Revista Migraciones Internacionales* 8: 57–81.

Pujol, J. M. 1995. "La metodología utilizada por el CELADE para la proyección de la mortalidad." Workshop Evolución futura de la mortalidad, CELADE-Escuela de Salud Pública, Santiago de Chile, November 22–24.

Rofman, R. 1994. "Diferenciales de mortalidad adulta en Argentina." *Notas de Población* 22 (59), ECLAC-CELADE.

———. 2007. "Perspectivas de la población en el siglo XXI. L segundos doscientos Años." In *Población y bienestar en la Argentina del primer al segundo Centenario: Una historia social del siglo XX*, vol. 2, compiled by S. Torrado, 603–41. Buenos Aires: Edhasa.

Rofman, R., G. Stirparo, and P. Lattes. 1997. "Proyecciones del sistema integrado de jubilaciones y pensiones 1995–2050." Estudio Especial 12, SAFJP, Buenos Aires.

Sanderson, W., and S. Sherbov. 2007. "A New Perspective on Population Aging." *Demographic Research* 16 (2): 27– 58.

UNFPA (United Nations Population Fund). 2010. *Estado de la población mundial. Desde conflictos y crisis hacia la renovación: generaciones de cambio.* Fondo de Población de las Naciones Unidas (UNFPA). http://www.unfpa.org.

UNFPA-ECLAC (United Nations Population Fund–Economic Commission for Latin America and the Caribbean). 2009. *El envejecimiento y las personas de edad. Indicadores sociodemográficos para América latina y el Caribe.* UNFPA-ECLAC, Santiago de Chile. www.unfpa.org.

United Nations. 2004. *World Population to 2300.* ST/ESA/SER.A/236. New York: United Nations.

———. 2011. *World Population Prospects: The 2010 Revision.* New York: Population Division, Department of Economic and Social Affairs, United Nations Secretariat.

———. 2013. *World Population Prospects: The 2012 Revision.* New York: Population Division, Department of Economic and Social Affairs, United Nations Secretariat.

CHAPTER 3

National Transfer Accounts in Argentina

Pablo Comelatto

Introduction

Demographic change, understood as the change in the size and composition of a certain population, is the direct result of the joint evolution of fertility, mortality, and migration. The demographic dynamic constitutes a process of transformation with potential socioeconomic consequences in the medium and long term that is worthy of study.

Although the size of the population, especially relative to the availability of natural resources, is a significant factor, the change in the age structure, understood as the variation in the relative sizes of individual age groups, is more important, because throughout a person's life, behavior patterns and exposure to different types of risks fluctuate in ways that are more or less known. In this sense, fertility, mortality, marriage, migration, economic participation, and savings and consumption levels, among other relevant socioeconomic phenomena, present characteristic profiles that mean that the increase or decrease of the relative size of a certain age group will have consequences for the aggregate level of the phenomenon in question. For example, population aging, defined as the increase in the relative size of the population group older than a certain age (usually 65 years), results in a reduction in the gross birth rate, an increase in the gross mortality ratio, and a reduction in the relative size of the labor force (or an increase in the levels of economic dependency). Simultaneously, this dynamic is more complex because of the existence of flows of transfers of resources between different age groups, whether between private parties or intermediated by the public sector.

Population aging is on the international agenda because of its potential consequences for the size of the labor force, as well as for the sustainability of transfer programs to the elderly (pension programs). However, from a comprehensive life-cycle perspective, the elderly are not the only age group that is, on average, economically dependent. In fact, children are also economically dependent, and the same demographic forces that drive aging affect the relative size of the group of dependents in childhood. As a result, phenomena such as population aging should be examined in light of the entire set of resource transfers that take place in a certain society, both "upward" (to the elderly) as well as "downward" (to children).

During the last decade, notable advances in the development of a research agenda focused on the comprehensive analysis of the economic consequences of demographic change have been achieved, with a special emphasis on the analysis of the transfers that take place between age groups or, similarly, between generations (Mason and Lee 2011). The development of the National Transfer Accounts (NTA) project is a global effort to apply a consistent accounting methodology across a set of countries to obtain comparable results directed toward analysis of the impact of demographic change in these countries.

This chapter presents a brief introduction to the NTA methodology and its estimates for the case of Argentina. The following section presents the basic motivation for the analysis of the NTA project and introduces the concept of *life-cycle deficit* (LCD). The third section introduces the basic concepts of NTAs. The fourth section discusses the results of an estimate of the principal components of NTAs in Argentina, in 2010, with special attention paid to the public component of consumption and transfers, and its comparison with 1997 and comparable data from other selected countries. The fifth section analyzes the public expenditure composition in 2010. Finally, the sixth section contains reflections on the results obtained.

Why Estimate National Transfer Accounts?

The study of intergenerational transfers comprises the analysis of the intersection between the economy and demographics, as the evolution of the latter impacts the former through a set of institutions and social arrangements that mobilize economic resources between different generations or age groups. The starting point of the analysis of intergenerational transfers lies in the nearly universal situation that during individuals' life cycles consumption and production evolve differently. This disparate evolution gives rise to stages of the life cycle in which individuals' consumption outstrips their production (particularly during childhood and old age) and periods during which the opposite occurs. On the whole, the cumulative result of these deficit and surplus stages is the LCD.

From the individual point of view, the LCD pattern creates the need to find a way to fund consumption during the deficit stages and save in the surplus stages. From the perspective of society as a whole, it implies the existence, at any given time, of population groups that need to fund their consumption and of others with surpluses. Although at the individual level consumption and production are the reference points that determine one's surplus and deficit stages, at the population level the relative size of the deficit and surplus groups is determined by the population's age structure. Given that the demographic change in the population's age structure is a consequence of the evolution of basic demographic variables (fertility, mortality, and, to a lesser extent, migration), knowing how these variables will change over time is important for understanding the current situation and the expected future evolution of the LCD.

Historically, and in different societies, paying for consumption during deficit periods has been resolved through the coexistence of private (familial) and public agreements for resource transfers. The specific combination of the different types of agreements at any given time is the result of the historical evolution of each society, as well as the individual and collective decisions that people make daily to face the challenges and take advantage of the opportunities that demographic change presents.

Currently, developing countries, with relatively young, fast-growing populations, face different challenges than developed countries, with older, slow-growing populations (or even negative growth). The process of demographic transition, which affects nearly all developing countries, creates declining levels of fertility and mortality and aging populations, which as a result must face the specific challenges of changing from public and private systems more focused on and supportive of children to the implementation of arrangements that support the elderly age groups' consumption.

The institutions that mediate the reallocation of resources from the surplus age groups to the deficit groups are made up of the family, markets, and the public sector. These institutions channel significant volumes of resources between age groups, making it possible to satisfy the consumption needs of the deficit groups. Traditionally, families have stood out fundamentally because they meet children's consumption needs and, to a lesser extent, those of the elderly. Financial markets, on the other hand, facilitate the existence of credit and savings operations through which individuals can finance their own deficit years. Finally, the public sector funds consumption by deficit groups or directly provides goods and services to them, from tax resources or debt.

The balance among the different institutions that fund consumption by age varies from one society to another, reflecting the particular historical evolution of each country, as well as the common attitudes regarding the role of family, the state, and individual self-sufficiency. In addition, the different relative weights of the institutional support arrangements for deficit age groups in different countries are associated with the relative importance of the groups themselves. In this sense, the programs that attend to children make up the most significant component of resource flows in countries with young, fast-growing populations. Conversely, support programs for the elderly receive the majority of resources in societies with populations in a more advanced stage of aging.

The flow of resources between age groups can be understood as a flow between generations, inasmuch as the current age structure of any population is the result of the birth, in the past, of the successive generations that make it up today. In this sense, the concept of *intergenerational transfers* represents the set of resource movements that fund the deficit periods of the life cycle, through resources that come from the surplus period.

Intergenerational transfers are a way of meeting the material consumption needs of two age groups that generally present the greatest risk of vulnerability because they are dependents. The transfers directed toward children, even though they sustain their consumption, are also an investment in the human capital of future generations of workers, forming the foundation for wealth generation. On the other hand, caring for the elderly in populations undergoing the aging process creates challenges that must be dealt with by managing the different alternatives available to fund this care. In effect, the use of family arrangements, public pay-as-you-go pension programs, or collective or individual savings in pension funds are alternatives that can substitute for or complement one another. The sustainability over time of each of these institutional arrangements cannot be ensured without an analysis of the expected evolution of the age structure of the population.

These considerations highlight the importance of incorporating the *generational* dimension into the study of the economy. In this sense, the development of the NTA project represents an effort to structure a comprehensive analysis of all aspects of the workings of the economy that are susceptible to changes in the age structure of the population. A group of contributions to the economic literature highlighted early on the importance of the generational economy (Samuelson 1958; Diamond 1965; Willis 1988). Lee (1994) made one of the first attempts to construct a formal framework for studying the interaction between the demographic dynamic and intergenerational transfers. A significant portion of the development of the NTA project is based on this work. The goal of the project is to "provide a systematic and comprehensive focus on the measurement of economic flows from a generational perspective" (Mason et al. 2009). In this sense, the NTA project is based on and complements the System of National Accounts (Mason and Lee 2011), by incorporating the age dimension into some of the basic aggregates of national accounts.

National Transfer Accounts Project: Basic Concepts

Estimating NTAs revolves around the basic concept of the LCD. This is understood as the difference between the level of consumption and production via work throughout an individual's life cycle. It is a nearly universal constant (Lee 1994) that individuals experience two deficit periods (during childhood and old age) and one surplus period (during middle age).

The existence of the LCD is subject to the different age profiles for consumption and production. These profiles, meanwhile, respond to both biological factors as well as behavior patterns that can change over time and from one society to another. The physical and intellectual capacity to perform work, the customs and institutions that regulate when one enters and leaves the labor force, individual productivity, and the incidence of unemployment are some of the factors that determine the existence of different levels of *production* for different age groups. In turn, physiological requirements, individual preferences, and habits are some of the factors that define the *consumption* profile for different age groups.

These individual profiles, combined with the relative size of each age group, determine the aggregate LCD. Therefore, the LCD is a reflection as much of the determinants of individual profiles as of the specific age structure of the population at any given time. With stable consumption and production patterns at the individual level, demographic change by itself is sufficient to provoke considerable changes in the aggregate LCD and, therefore, in the need to adapt the existing institutional agreements to the funding needs for different age groups' consumption.

The LCD's existence is feasible only to the extent that various institutional agreements allow for the transfer of resources from surplus groups to deficit groups. These agreements reflect a complex combination of private and public commitments. The specific combination scheme between these agreements in each society is the result, among other things, of customary practices, policy decisions, advances, and setbacks in terms of public intervention, as well as changes in the structure and makeup of households and families. Over time, customary practices of supporting children and the elderly have changed to reflect new political and demographic realities, such as the rise of social security plans to protect the elderly, which substituted traditional practices by which adult children supported their parents, or the development of mechanisms of individual savings that reduce dependency on public programs of resource transfers.

The NTA project distinguishes between two basic types of resource reassignment between age groups: *transfers* and *capital reallocations*. The former are resource transfers that do not assume an exchange or the expectation of future repayment. *Private transfers* are essentially voluntary, or their implicitly compulsory character is based on customs and practices that for the most part are not open to debate (not excluding the possibility of changes over time). *Public transfers*, in turn, are compulsory because they are tax-based without any expectations of a quid pro quo above and beyond those related to belonging to a society in general, and they are the delivery of benefits in the form of cash payments and provision of goods and services that are the result of the political decision-making process.

Capital reallocations, meanwhile, reflect the accumulation and disaccumulation of assets, as well as the capital income resulting from the past accumulation of assets. Through these operations, individuals and societies as a whole are capable of transferring resources to or from the future, helping to fund the deficit periods of the LCD.

The NTA project constitutes an accounting framework that identifies and quantifies these flows. As such, it seeks to reflect the patterns of consumption and production by age as they occur, without identifying the motives that define them. Understood as an accounting scheme, the project does not make assumptions about individual behavior, although its estimates require considerable assumptions about the nature of the operations recorded.

The economic resource reallocation operations between generations create a flow of goods and services and monetary transfers to the individuals in each age group (*inflows*) and a flow of resources from individuals to fund this consumption and transfers (*outflows*). *Inflows* are separated into several main components: education, health care, retirement and pensions, other in-kind consumption, and other monetary transfers. In cases in which specific taxes are directed to fund a particular public program (typically contributions to social security), these *outflows* are specific to the corresponding program. In cases in which a program is funded from general revenues, the profile of the general taxes is identified as a profile of the corresponding *outflow*.

Consumption profiles record spending on final consumption, both by the government (public consumption) as well as by households and nonprofit institutions that serve households (private consumption). These profiles of public and private consumption exclude investment spending because they constitute asset accumulation operations that permit the financing of deferred consumption. The production profile, in turn, is operationalized in the NTA as labor income, comprising payment for salaried work; income from self-employed workers is estimated assigning them two-thirds of the *mixed gross income*. This arbitrary proportion is an attempt to separate the portion of income that corresponds to returns on labor from that which corresponds to returns on capital.

One of the most interesting applications of the NTA project consists of the analysis of the generational dimension of transfers mediated by the public sector, that is, the study of the different age profiles of tax income and the benefits paid by the public sector. Different public programs are targeted at specific age groups by their own design. Children tend to benefit from public education programs, health care services, and monetary transfers specific to childhood. Similarly, pension programs are directed to individuals that are older than the retirement age. On the other hand, public programs can be identified that may not have clearly defined targeting criteria but by their very nature have a different age profile that reflects the specific characteristics of the benefit provided and how different age groups make use of these benefits. In this way, for example, public health care programs that do not have an age component specified will still treat different age groups differently based on their health care requirements.

From the point of view of tax income, different age groups contribute varying amounts to the generation of these resources. Although it is not common for tax systems to have a component that accounts for the age of the taxpayer, the transactions or assets that are taxed usually affect specific age groups. As an example, different age groups face consumption taxes on goods and services based on their levels of consumption, while property taxes affect different groups based on their ownership of taxable properties.

The NTAs in Argentina, 2010

Estimating NTAs requires processing multiple sources of information to calculate the age profiles for the different components, as well as the *macrocontrols*, which consist of aggregate values that are largely consistent with the corresponding accounts in the National Accounts System. In the annex, we detail the sources of information used and the major methodological assumptions.

Each macrocontrol is assigned a corresponding age profile. The labor income profile was obtained from the Continuous Household Survey (Encuesta Permanente de Hogares [EPH]; income amount from the primary occupation, total income amount from other occupations, and income amount for independent workers).

Box 3.1 Estimating the Macrocontrols and Age Profiles

Constructing the NTAs requires that we estimate two datasets: the macrocontrols and the age profiles. The former seek to guarantee consistency between the aggregate values and the corresponding items in the national accounts. On the basis of data published by the National Directorate of National Accounts, we obtained totals for the following variables: *consumption, gross internal fixed investment, net exports, wages for salaried labor, gross operating surplus, gross mixed income,* and *taxes on goods.* The distinction between the public and private components of consumption was made based on an estimate of public consumption consistent with the *Savings-Investment-Financing Account* of the nonfinancial public sector, presented in chapter 9 of this book. The details of the components in health and education, meanwhile, were constructed based on the estimates discussed in chapters 6 and 8, respectively, and the amount assigned to other consumption is calculated as a residual value.

Other variables require that we make assumptions or apply ad hoc estimation techniques usually outlined in the NTAs Project methodology (United Nations 2013). The public and private consumption profiles result from the sum of the respective profiles for *education, health care,* and *other consumption.* The education profiles are based on the attendance rates for educational institutions (public or private, respectively) by age calculated based on the EPH. The public consumption profile in health care is estimated based on three components: social Insurance (excluding the National Institute of Social Services for Retirees and Pensioners' Comprehensive Medical Assistance Program, INSSJyP-PAMI), INSSJyP-PAMI, and public health care. Employer-based health insurance coverage was estimated based on the EPH, excluding members of the INSSJyP-PAMI whose age profile was obtained based on data from the Institute. The age profile of individuals without health coverage (employer-based coverage or private insurance) that used the public health care system could only be estimated based on data from 1997. The private consumption profile in health care was estimated with data from the National Household Expenditure Survey 2004–05, using a regression analysis of expenditure per household in the health sector, using ages of the household members as regressors along with other control variables. Finally, the profile corresponding to *other consumption* is uniform by age group (in the case of public consumption) or follows an ad hoc structure (private consumption).

For monetary transfers from the public sector (pensions, unemployment insurance, family allowances, and the Universal Child Allowance [Asignación Universal por Hijo, AUH]), specific profiles were estimated based on the EPH and other administrative data (for the AUH). Finally, faced with a lack of specific data to calculate the age profiles for each tax, an estimate was made based on the asset profiles or transactions that are subject to taxation.

Figure 3.1 presents the components of the Argentine LCD in 2010. Panel a shows the LCD in per capita terms, presenting the two deficit periods, from birth

Figure 3.1 Life-Cycle Deficit: Consumption and Labor Income, in Per Capita Terms and Aggregate, Argentina, 2010

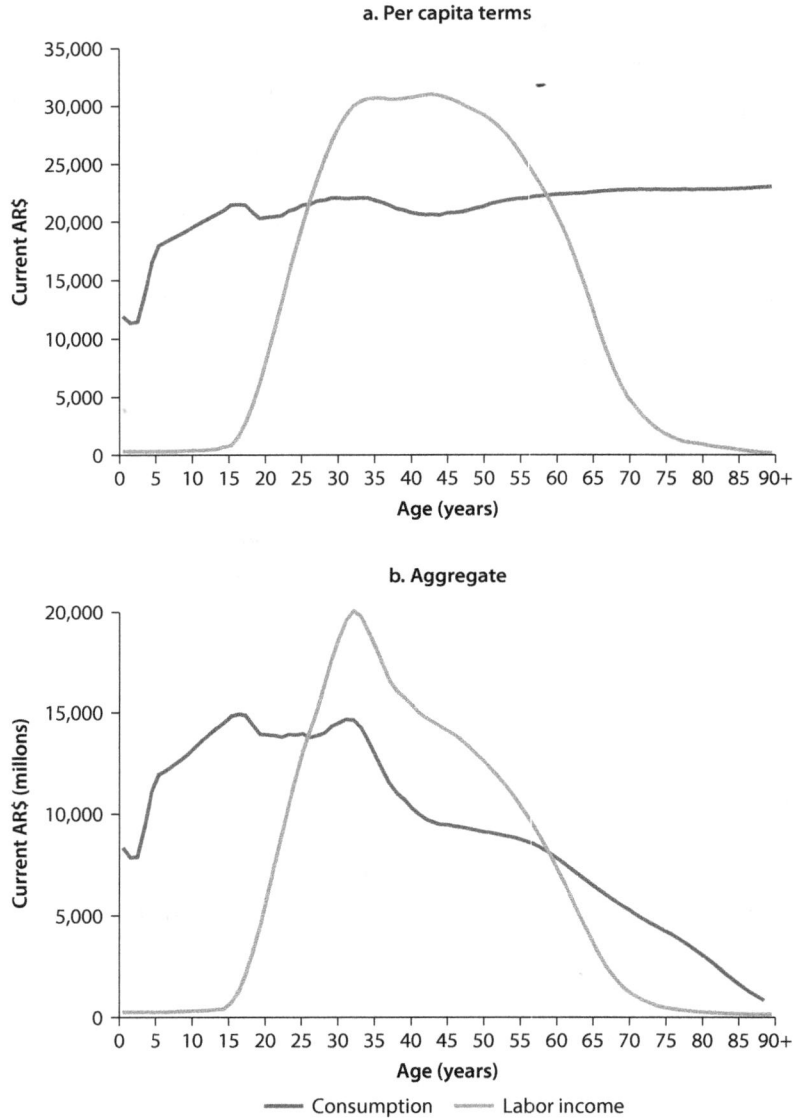

a. Per capita terms

b. Aggregate

— Consumption   — Labor income

Source: World Bank elaboration.

until age 25 years and after age 59 years, and a surplus period between ages 26 and 58 years. Panel b shows the LCD in aggregate terms; in addition to the individual patterns observed in panel a, panel b shows the specific age structure of the Argentine population in 2010.

Panel a shows the specific consumption and production patterns for an average individual, suggesting entry and exit and productivity trends in the labor force and consumption habits. As a result of these profiles, the LCD is slightly larger at older ages than the funding needed for children's consumption.

In contrast, the right panel allows one to observe how the age structure of the Argentine population combines with the individual profiles to produce a panorama that is completely different from the point of view of the aggregate funding needs for the deficit age groups. Whereas the combined deficit for children and the elderly is equivalent to 57.7 percent of aggregate labor income, the deficit for children is 3.1 times greater than the corresponding amount for the elderly.

Figure 3.2 presents the LCDs in Argentina for children in 2010 and 1997 together. This 13-year period spans profound changes in the conditions of the macroeconomic workings of the country as well as in the social policies and programs implemented. In macroeconomic terms, the fundamental change was the variation in the external commercial balance, which improved from a deficit equal to 2.2 percent of gross domestic product (GDP) in 1997 to a surplus equal to 3.3 percent GDP in 2010. This accumulated change of 5.5 percent of GDP is reflected in figure 3.2 as a much larger surplus area in 2010 (the aforementioned 26–58 age group) compared with 1997 (surplus between ages 30 and 52). Nonetheless, it must be pointed out that the deficit for children in 2010 is greater than that exhibited in 1997, contrary to the effects observed among all other age groups.

The right panel of figure 3.2 shows the aggregate LCD for these two years, again evidencing the larger deficit accumulated in 1997, but also reflecting the demographic changes and consumption patterns that occurred in the interim. On one hand, the two deficit periods grew shorter as the surplus ages grew by 10 years (30–52 years in 1997 versus 26–58 in 2010). On the other hand, the relative number of the elderly grew more than the number of children, reflecting the standstill in the number of births during the period and the increase in the proportion of the elderly in the population. Finally, this trend is counteracted by the increase in the children's deficit (evidenced by the levels of LCD per capita). As a result of the combined effect of the two changes mentioned, the accumulated deficit for children grew from 2.5 times that of the elderly in 1997 to 3.1 times larger in 2010. Finally, the aggregate LCD allows one to appreciate the increase in the working-age population. This stage, during which this population group makes up the largest proportion of the overall population, is known as the *demographic dividend*.

The changes observed in the behavior of the LCD are the result of the changes in the consumption profiles observed between 1997 and 2010. The results presented in the left panel of figure 3.3 suggest that the lower relative levels of consumption after age 18 explain the observed change in the LCD in figure 3.2. In a context of lower private consumption and higher public consumption, the weight of public education spending sustained childhood consumption, while the levels of consumption for all the other groups fell.

The Argentine LCD follows a universal pattern prevalent in all contemporary societies, even though each LCD reflects the specific nature of a society's

Figure 3.2 Life–Cycle Deficit, in Per Capita Terms and Aggregate, Argentina, 1997 and 2010

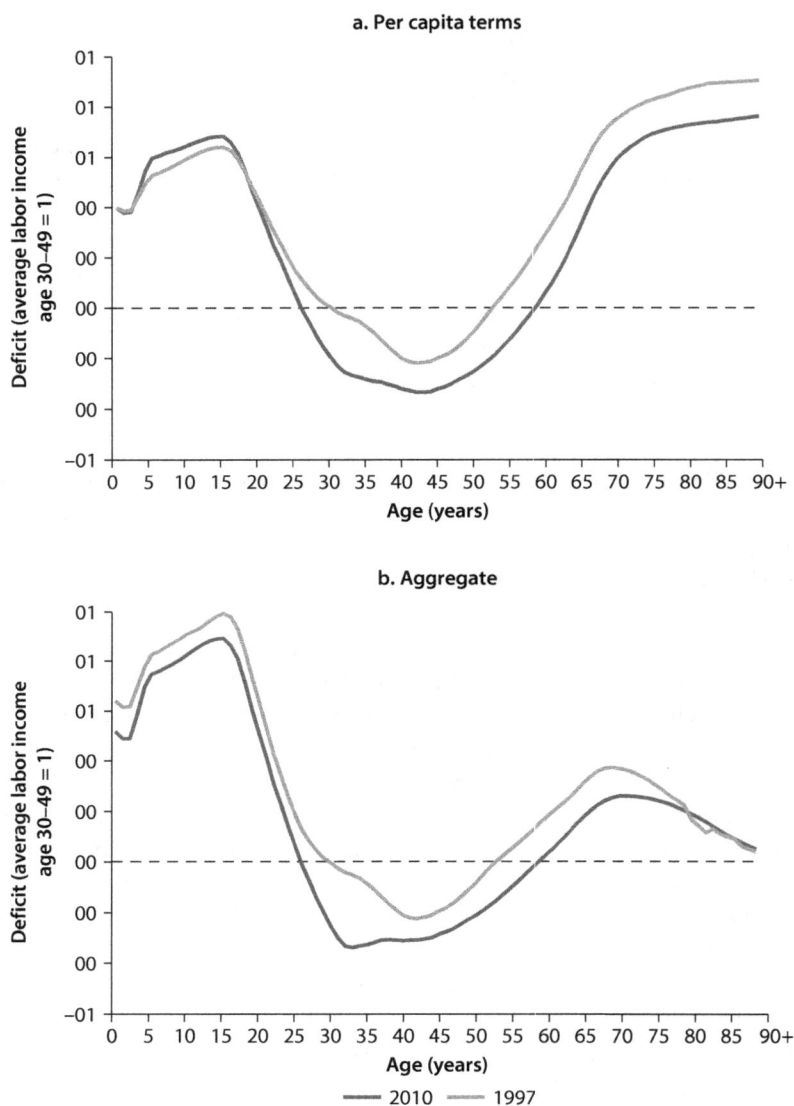

a. Per capita terms

b. Aggregate

━━ 2010 ━━ 1997

Source: Elaboration based on EPH, Encuesta Nacional de Gato de los Hogares, and data from the National Accounts. See the annex for details on the sources used.

transfer systems and consumption and production patterns. Figure 3.4 compares Argentine LCD with a select group of countries for which NTA estimates are available.[1]

In this comparative international context, the Argentina LCD in 1997 stands out based on its pronounced deficit levels, which required significant external financing to sustain consumption levels. The LCD in 2010, on the other hand, is

Figure 3.3 Consumption Profiles and Labor Income, in Per Capita Terms, Argentina, 1997 and 2010

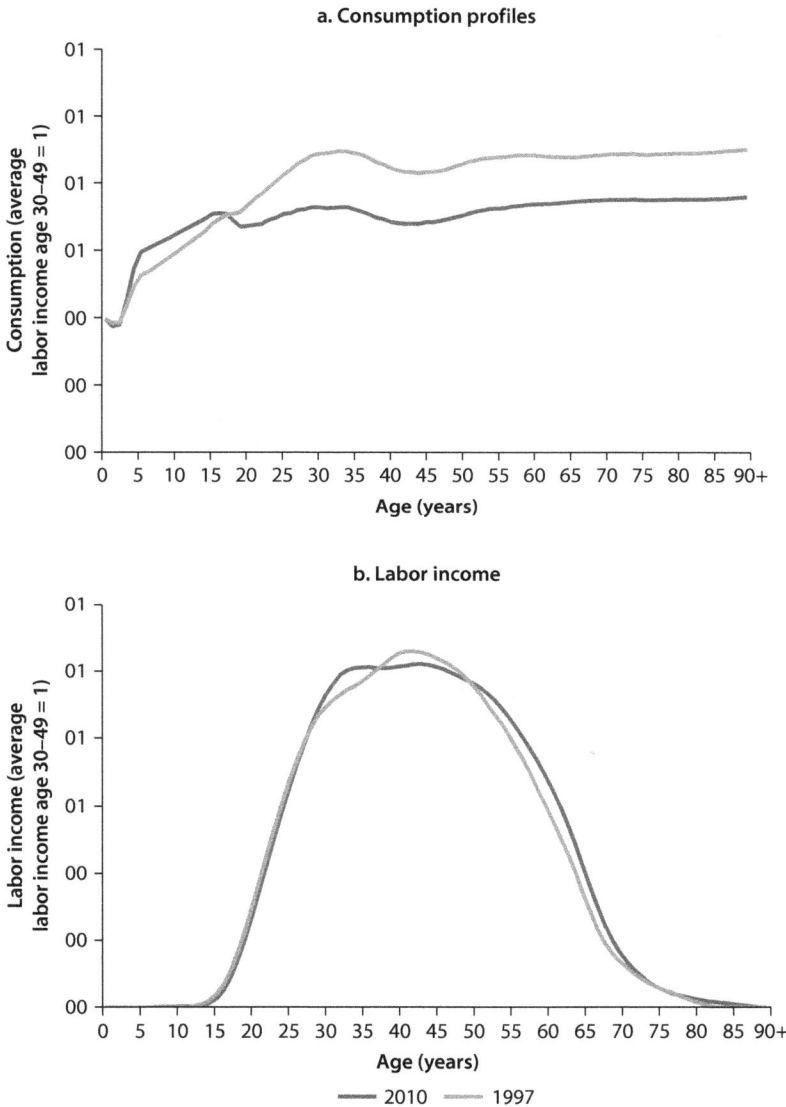

a. Consumption profiles

b. Labor income

2010   1997

Source: Based on EPH, Encuesta Nacional de Gato de los Hogares, and data from the National Accounts. See the annex for details on the sources used.

more in line with the levels observed in other countries, although the significant childhood deficit stands out in the comparison.

The existence of deficits during childhood and old age begs the question regarding the source of funding for these deficits and, more specifically, the role played by public transfers in this funding. Figure 3.5 shows the percentage of the deficit financed through public transfers in a group of selected countries during

Figure 3.4 Normalized Life-Cycle Deficit in Argentina, 1997 and 2010, versus Other NTA Countries, 2003

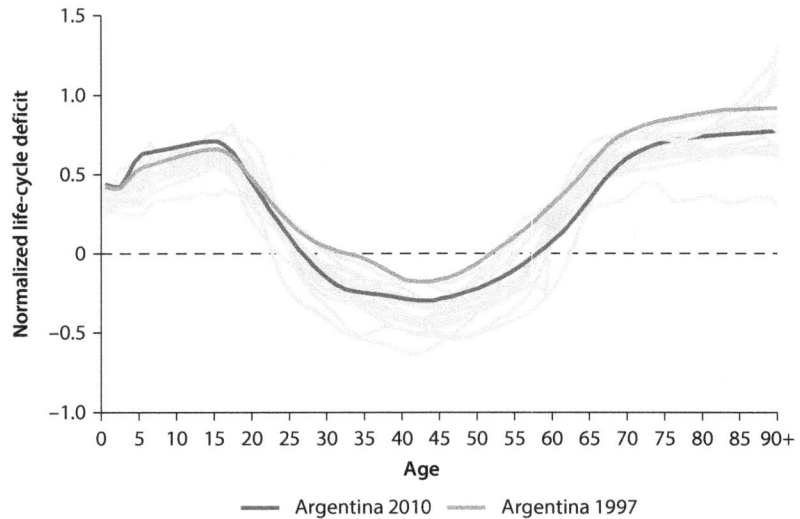

Source: World Bank elaboration (Argentina) and http://ntaccounts.org (rest of the countries).

childhood (left panel) and old age (right panel). In all cases, public transfers fund a greater proportion of the deficit during old age than during childhood, with public transfers reaching levels of more than 100 percent of the old-age deficit in some cases (Brazil and Sweden). In the Argentine case, one observes that the transfers played a limited role in 1997, but with the growth of public spending during the first decade of this century, transfers grew significantly, such that in 2010 Argentina was among the top five countries with the greatest proportion of the LCD funded by transfers, both among youth as well as the elderly. In this sense, 40 percent of the childhood deficit and 91 percent of the old age deficit were funded via public sector transfers in 2010.

The information presented in figure 3.5 outlines how public transfer programs impacted deficit groups in each country. As a result of the design of these programs and the relative size of the respective deficit groups, figure 3.6 presents the relationship between the public transfers per capita to the elderly (population older than 65 years of age) and to children (age 0–14 years). Aside from the case of Brazil, which stands out with a factor of 10 in favor of the elderly in 1996 (before the introduction of the Bolsa Família program), Argentina in 1997 is also one of the countries that is most generous to elderly age groups relative to children. The per capita value of transfers to the elderly is six times greater than those to children. The strong growth of spending on transfers recorded since then has been biased toward younger age groups, while the increase in tax charges that accompanied this process has fallen more heavily on adults in general (because they make up the primary tax base), including the elderly. As a result of the combination of these two effects, the per capita net transfer balance to adults

Figure 3.5 Proportion of the Life-Cycle Deficit Funded via Public Transfers

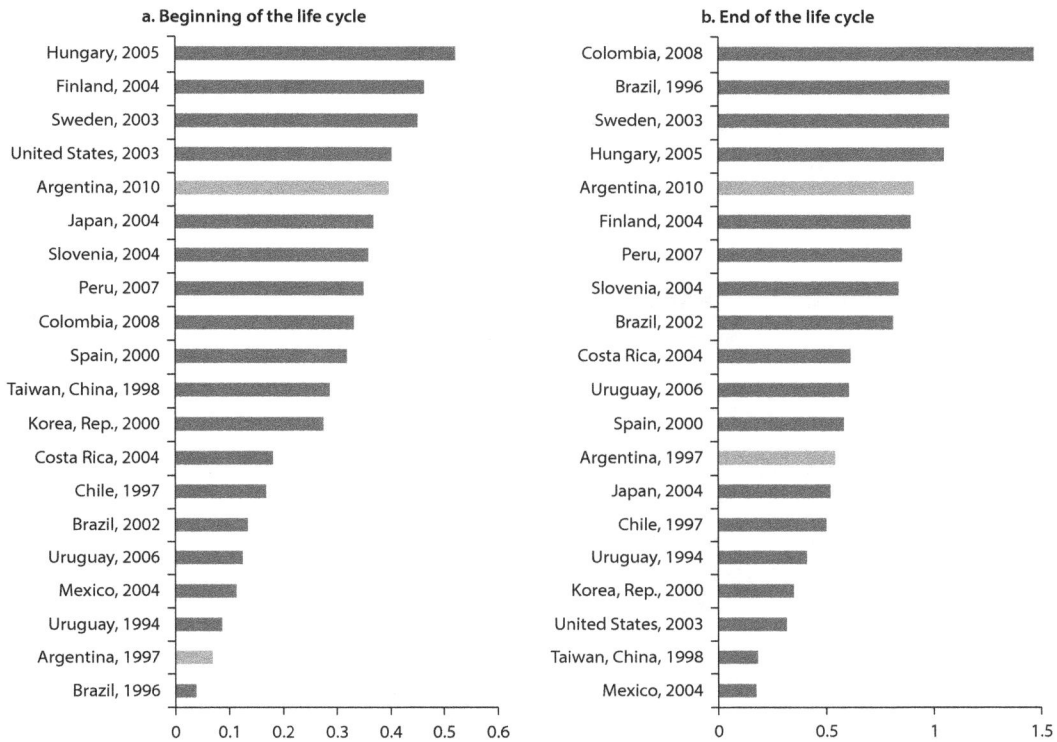

Source: World Bank elaboration (Argentina) and http://ntaccounts.org (rest of the countries).
Note: For each country, the beginning and end of the life cycle is defined as the deficit ages. These age limits can vary from case to case.

older than 65 years of age and youth younger than 15 years of age changed significantly, falling to nearly 2.3 in 2010.

Age Profile of Public Transfers and Their Components, 2010

Figure 3.7 presents total consumption according to its public and private components. At the aggregate level, public consumption represented 42.9 percent of total consumption, although its level fluctuates depending on age from a minimum of 32 percent at age 36 years to a maximum of 66 percent at age 5 years.

In addition to consumption directly financed by the public sector (education, health care, and other in-kind spending), the public sector actively participates in monetary transfer programs with a strong age component, among which retirement and pensions, as well as transfers to youth, stand out. In this way, public spending can be classified as *social spending*, which includes public consumption of education, health care, retirement and pensions, and other social protection programs,[2] and *other spending*, which includes basically all other

Figure 3.6 Relationship between Net Public Transfers Per Capita to the Elderly and Children

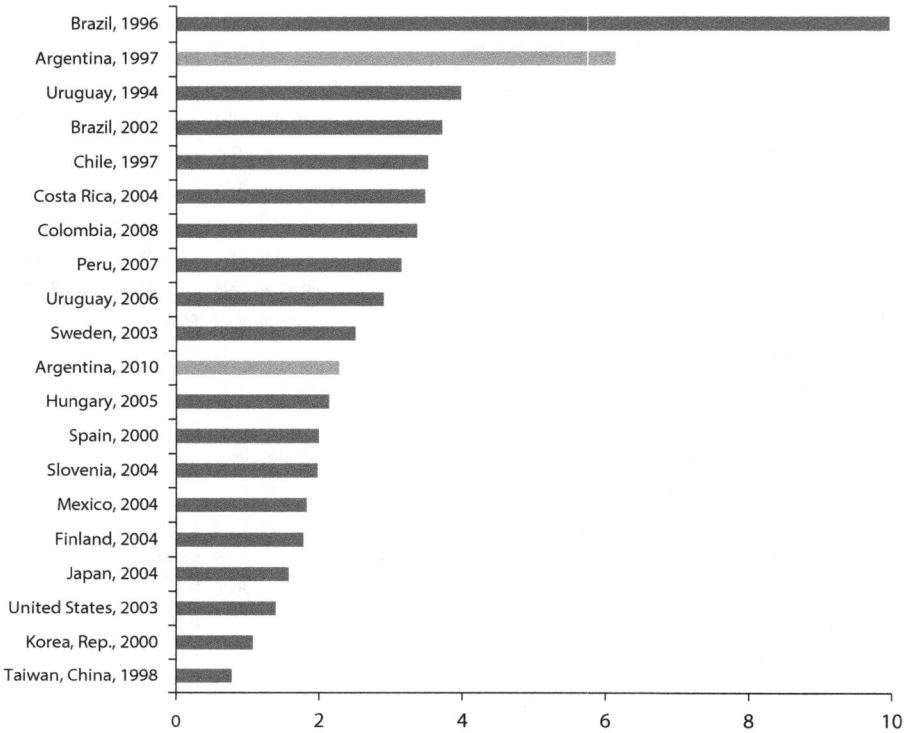

Brazil, 1996					
Argentina, 1997					
Uruguay, 1994					
Brazil, 2002					
Chile, 1997					
Costa Rica, 2004					
Colombia, 2008					
Peru, 2007					
Uruguay, 2006					
Sweden, 2003					
Argentina, 2010					
Hungary, 2005					
Spain, 2000					
Slovenia, 2004					
Mexico, 2004					
Finland, 2004					
Japan, 2004					
United States, 2003					
Korea, Rep., 2000					
Taiwan, China, 1998					
	0	2	4	6	8 10

Source: World Bank elaboration (Argentina) and http://ntaccounts.org (rest of the countries).

Figure 3.7 Public and Private Consumption, in Per Capita Terms and Aggregate, Argentina, 2010

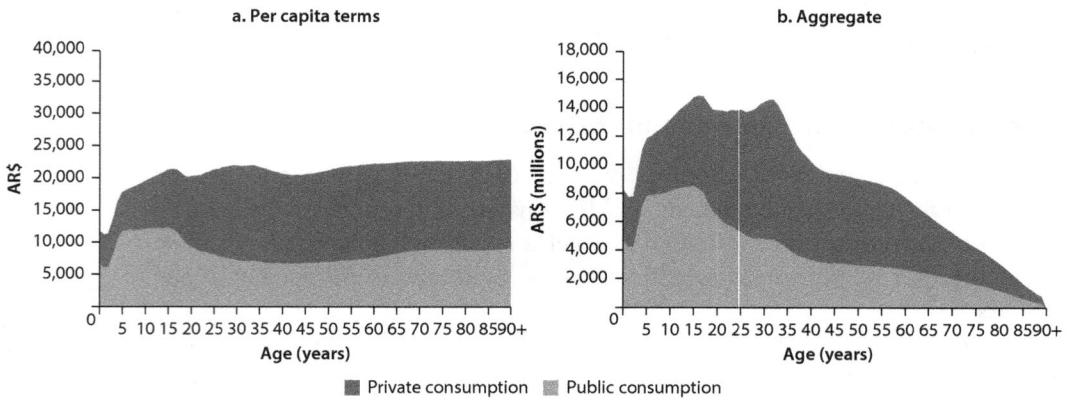

a. Per capita terms

b. Aggregate

Private consumption   Public consumption

Source: World Bank elaboration.

spending associated with the functioning of the public sector, the provision of goods and services not included in health care and education, and other transfers to the private sector not included in social protection.

Figure 3.8 presents the total amount of transfers received by individuals (*inflows*), categorized as *social spending* and *other spending*. Social spending stands out because of its marked age profile, resulting from the particular characteristics of the programs that make it up, with the most significant programs being public education among children and youth, and retirement and pensions among the elderly. In turn, the spending categorized as "other" exhibits a nearly constant profile because it is composed of consumption and transfers that do not demonstrate a marked age profile.[3] The right panel of figure 3.8 shows the age profile of tax income that the public sector obtained from taxpayers (*outflows*, from the point of view of these individuals).[4]

The profiles presented in figure 3.8, however, are not a reflection of the relative weight that each program has in the aggregate. In effect, the benefit for each age group must be weighed considering the relative size of the corresponding age group within the total population. Thus, in figure 3.9 we can appreciate that the transfers that flow toward children and youth acquire a much more significant volume, as a consequence of the weight that these age groups have in the total population. In the same way, the importance of middle-aged adults in the generation of tax income can be seen in the right panel.

The components of *social spending* are presented in figure 3.10, and figure 3.11 shows the breakdown of the components of *other social protection*. The right panel of figure 3.10 shows evidence of the bimodal aspect of public transfers in social spending. Essentially, the per capita generosity of retirement and pension payments, relative to the average benefit received by children, is offset in the aggregate by the relative size of the children and youth age group.

Figure 3.8 Public Transfer Flows: Inflows and Outflows, in Per Capita Terms, Argentina, 2010

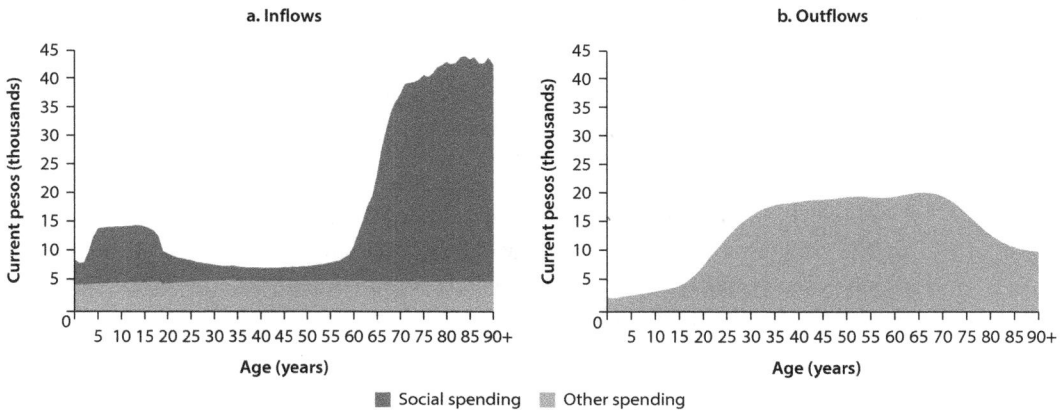

Source: World Bank elaboration.
Note: Social spending includes education, health care, retirement, and other social protection. Other spending includes rest of in-kind public spending and other transfers to the private sector.

Figure 3.9 Public Transfer Flows: Inflows and Outflows, in Aggregate Terms, Argentina, 2010

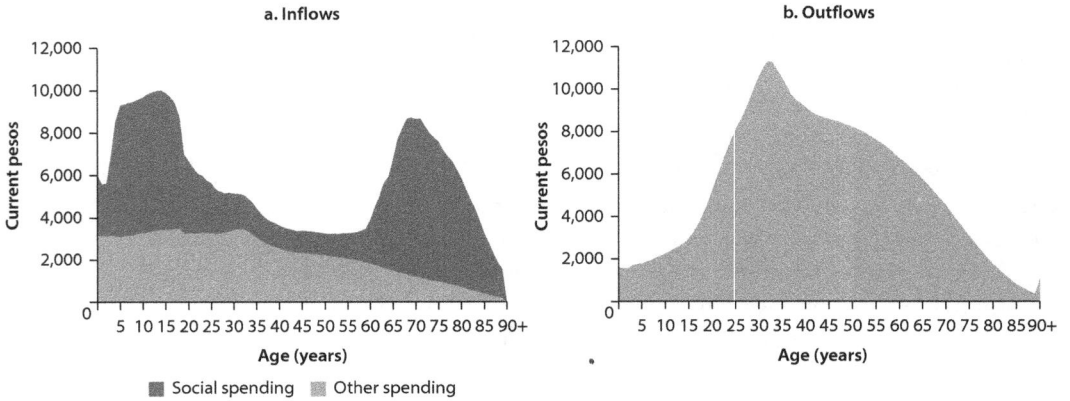

Source: World Bank elaboration.
Note: Social spending: Education, health care, retirement, and other social protection. Other spending: Rest of in-kind public spending and other transfers to the private sector.

Figure 3.10 Public Transfers: Social Spending, by Program, in Per Capita Terms and Aggregate, Argentina, 2010

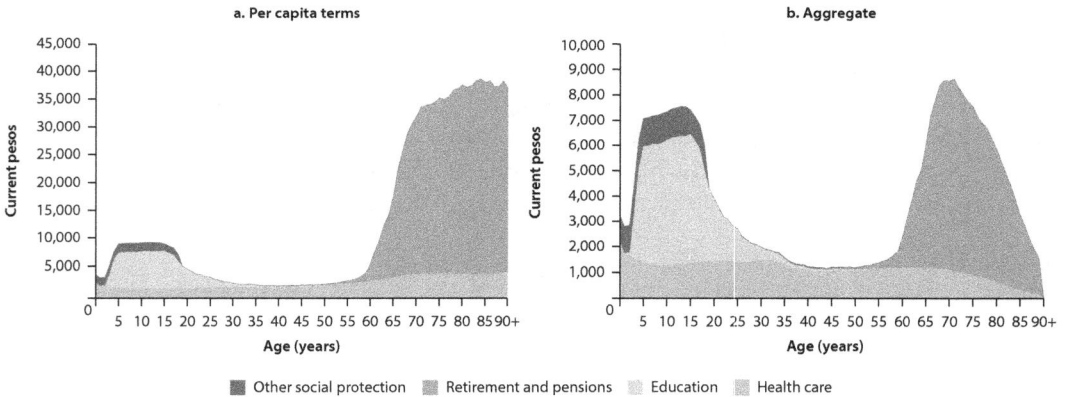

Source: World Bank elaboration.
Note: Other social protection: Unemployment insurance, family allowances, and Universal Child Allowance.

A synthetic way of presenting the different age profiles of the individual public programs consists of calculating the median age at which an individual receives the benefit, and the age at which an individual pays the taxes that fund these benefits. Table 3.1 allows us to categorize the programs as a function of whether their transfer flows are directed "upward" (when the median *inflow* age is greater than the median *outflow* age) or "downward" in the opposite case.

As a whole, social spending in Argentina is upward, with a median taxpayer age of 42.4 years old and a median beneficiary age of 44 years old. Of course, these average levels hide significant differences among individual programs,

Figure 3.11 Public Transfers: Breakdown of Other Social Protection, by Type, in Per Capita Terms, Argentina, 2010

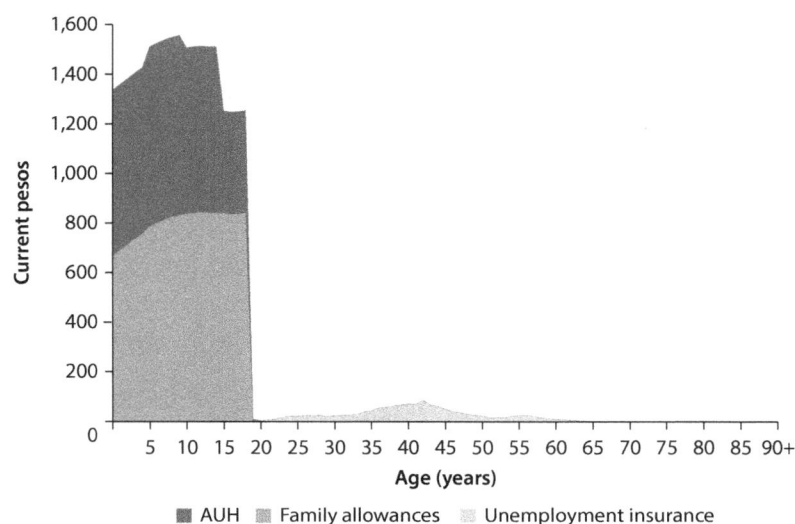

Source: World Bank elaboration.
Note: AUH = Asignación Universal por Hijo (Universal Child Allowance).

Table 3.1 Average Age of Inflow and Outflow Transfers, by Program Type, Argentina, 2010

	Average age (years)	
	Inflows	Outflows
Education	13.9	42.7
Health care	38.5	41.3
Retirement and pensions	73.9	39.6
Other social protection	10.0	42.7
Total social spending	44.0	42.4

Source: Based on EPH, ENGHO, and National Accounts data. See the annex for details on the sources used.

depending on the group that is targeted and the primary source of funding. Basically, average *inflow* ages reflect the specific target of each program, ranging from 10.0 years old for the beneficiaries of the family allowances and AUH and an average of 13.9 years old for education to 73.9 years old for retirement and pensions, with intermediate values for health care (38.5 years).

The average *outflow* age for pensions corresponds to the social security contributions age profile, producing an average contribution age of 39.6 years, while the average *outflow* age for public health care is the result of the combination of contributions to the employer-based health care system and the general taxes that cover public health care, with an average value of 41.3 years old. The *outflows* for education and other social protection programs correspond to the joint profile for tax income, excluding social contributions and contributions to employer-based health insurance, with an average age of 42.7 years.

Final Reflections

Upon primary inspection, the results of the NTA estimates for Argentina exhibit a changing LCD pattern between 1997 and 2010, which shrunk from representing 72.4 percent of total labor income in 1997 to 57.7 percent in 2010. This reduction is the result of a drop in the level of general consumption, private consumption more specifically, which was only partially offset by an increase in public consumption. In this context of falling consumption, public expenditures on education sustained children's consumption levels.

As a result of the decline in consumption, the most noticeable change in the behavior of the LCD was the growth of the surplus period from 22 years in 1997 (between age 30 and 52) to 32 years in 2010 (between age 26 and 58), which, combined with the increase of the relative size of the surplus group, reduced the need for funding for the LCD in the aggregate.

Moreover, one must note the importance of public sector intervention for funding consumption in the deficit stages of the life cycle and the increase that took place between 1997 and 2010. Although Argentina did not stand out for the significance of its public transfers in 1997, this context had changed markedly by 2010, as the levels of public transfers increased for both children and the elderly. In effect, by 2010 public transfers directed to the elderly funded approximately 90 percent of this group's deficit, and transfers to children funded some 40 percent of their deficit (although transfers to this group began from a relatively lower base in 1997).

In 2010 Argentina presented a pattern more similar to some European countries than to other countries in the region. Although Colombia (2008) and Brazil (1996) stand out in international rankings for the size of public transfers to the elderly (figure 3.5), these countries rank lower in terms of transfers to children. Inversely, countries such as the United States (2003) and Japan (2004) stand out for the size of public transfers to children, while exhibiting relatively low levels in terms of funding the deficit during old age. In the case of Argentina (2010), which is similar to that of Sweden (2003) and Hungary (2005), public transfers to both children and the elderly place the country near the top of the ranking presented in figure 3.5. Thus, in contrast to Brazil, where the generosity of the system of transfers to the elderly is well known (Turra, Queiroz, and Rios-Neto 2011), the Argentine situation in 2010 stands out for the greater relative significance of public transfers at both extremes of the life cycle. As a result, Argentina places near the middle of the distribution of countries ranked by the ratio of transfers to the elderly to transfers to children.

Finally, the age component turns out to be relevant in the allocation of public social spending, which means that the programs that make up this spending are exposed to the influence of the demographic change in the coming decades. In particular, the expected evolution of Argentina's demographics opens up the possibility of facilitating the funding of investment in the human capital children and youth, which will be a fundamental requirement for taking advantage of the demographic dividend that Argentina is currently experiencing and will facilitate the ability to pay for elderly consumption.

The analysis of the NTAs thus allows us to contextualize the well-known process of population aging, highlighting not only the challenges but also the opportunities that this process offers.

Annex 3A

Macrocontrols

Public consumption (in-kind) was disaggregated into its component parts: education, health care, and other in-kind consumption (including private consumption financed by transfers or specifically allocated subsidies).

The total values of public consumption (as well as private) come from the series published by the National Directorate of National Accounts (DNCN). Following the NTA methodology, we proceeded to reclassify private consumption funded with government transfers and subsidies as public in-kind consumption, specifically transfers to private schools and fiduciary funds and transfers to private firms to fund household consumption.

As a whole, total public consumption, transfers to and from the private sector, and tax income was calculated in such a way as to maintain the level of detail of the Savings-Investment-Financing Account of the nonfinancial Argentine public sector, published by the Ministry of Economy and Public Finance. Thus, for example, the value for total consumption from the national accounts was compared to consumption and operating spending from the Savings-Investment-Financing Account for consistency. The remaining sources mentioned below were used to open up components in cases when the specified table did not provide all of the information required, combining in part the details provided by the 1997 Product Input Matrix (MIP97), components of health care consumption presented in Ministerio de Economía (2001), and the Consolidated Public Spending series (from the three levels of government), from the Directorate of Public Spending and Social Programs analysis at the Secretariat of Economic Policy.

In terms of public consumption in education and health care, we used the values provided by the MIP97 and Ministerio de Economía (2001) as a baseline, calculating their value for 2010 according to the temporal evolution of the Consolidated Public Spending series for each component.

Within public consumption of education, we separated basic education and higher and university education, by their division in the Consolidated Public Spending series, as well as transfers to private establishments, estimated based on data from the General Coordination Office for the Study of Educational System Costs.

Public consumption of health care is separated into public health care (individual final consumption provided by the government and government transfers), transfers to employer-based health plans, and transfers to the INSSJyP. This division followed the evolution of the Consolidated Public Spending series between 1997 and 2010, based on the final consumption components presented in Ministerio de Economía (2001). The other public in-kind consumption component was estimated as the difference between total public consumption and consumption in health care and education.

The transfers comprise three main categories: retirement and pensions, other social protection, and other transfers. The first includes the estimate of the retirement and pension benefits paid by the Argentine Integrated Social Security System and the Provincial Pension Systems as a component of the social security benefits and transfers from social security to the private sector presented in the Savings-Investment-Financing Account.

The other social protection category includes family allowances, the Universal Child Allowance, employment programs, unemployment insurance, and other public social assistance and promotion programs.

Private consumption from the consumption series published by the DNCN was disaggregated among the same components (education, health care, and other consumption) based on data from the MIP97, and a growth factor was applied that accounts for the change in health care and education consumption recorded between 1997 and 2005 by the National Household Expenditure Survey.

Age Profiles

The age profiles applied to the respective macrocontrols mainly come from estimates based on the 2010 Continuous Household Survey (EPH2010) and the 2004–05 National Household Expenditure Survey (ENGHO2004–05).

On one hand, the labor income profile was obtained from the EPH2010 considering income from the primary occupation of salaried workers and that from other occupations and independent workers' income separately.

In terms of consumption, the values corresponding to consumption profiles in education, both public and private, were estimated from the EPH2010, using the attendance rates for educational institutions in both categories. In the case of public institutions, we also separated consumption according to the educational level: basic (including secondary) and higher or university, given that disaggregated information for the corresponding macrocontrols was available. In the case of private consumption, because macrocontrols for each level were not available, we calculated attendance rates by age without distinguishing between levels.

In the case of health care, the public consumption profile was divided into three categories: insured in employer-based plans, insured by PAMI, and uninsured direct users of the public sector system. For those insured in employer-based plans, we created a profile based on the type of health coverage stated in the EPH2010 and adjusted it based on the estimated per capita age groups in Cetrángolo (2004). The age profile for those insured by PAMI was estimated based on the "Salud en la Argentina Atención del Adulto Mayor" ("Health Care in Argentina Elderly Care") report. Finally, for uninsured direct users of the public sector system, we estimated the population profile that stated they visited a public health clinic in the ENGHO1996–97 whether they were uninsured or had employer-based coverage.

Private health care consumption was estimated using the methodology suggested in the NTAs manual, via a regression analysis that allocated household health care spending as measured in the ENHO2004–05 to each household member based on their age.

Finally, the consumption profile for the rest of public consumption was allocated uniformly to all age groups, assuming that this consumption did not have a specific age profile, while the remaining private consumption was allocated using the NTAs methodology based on an equivalency scale that allocates consumption for children up to age 4 as 40 percent of the consumption of adults older than 20 years of age and adjusts this proportion on a linear scale from age 5 to 20 years.

The transfer profiles were estimated from the EPH2010, distinguishing among retirement and pension income, unemployment insurance income, family allowances, and subsidies or social assistance income. Finally, the profile for the Universal Child Allowance program was obtained from ANSES (2011).

Notes

1. Austria (2005), Brazil (2002), Chile (1997), China (2002), Colombia (2008), Costa Rica (2004), Finland (2004), Germany (2003), Hungary (2005), India (2004), Japan (2004), Peru (2007), Slovenia (2004), Spain (2000), Sweden (2003), Taiwan, China (2003), the United States (2003), and Uruguay (2006).

2. Other social protection programs include family allowances, the Universal Child Allowance, and unemployment insurance.

3. In effect, faced with a lack of information that would allow us to assign this spending based on some differential age-based criteria, as we constructed the NTAs presented in this chapter we assumed that their age distribution was uniform.

4. Social security contributions and contributions to employer-based health care are included in these outflows.

References

ANSES (Administración Nacional de la Seguridad Social). 2011. "Asignación universal por hijo para protección social: una política de inclusión para los más vulnerables." Observatorio de la Seguridad Social.

Cetrángolo, O. 2004. "Introducción de ajustes por riesgos en el subsidio automático nominativo a las obras sociales (SANO)." Draft.

Diamond, P. 1965. "National Debt in a Neoclassical Growth Model." *American Economic Review* 55: 1126–50.

Lee, R. D. 1994. "The Formal Demography of Population Aging, Transfers, and the Economic Life Cycle." In *Demography of Aging*, edited by L. G. Martin and S. H. Preston, 8–49. Washington, DC: National Academy Press.

Mason, A., and R. Lee. 2011. "Introducing Age into National Accounts." In *Population Aging and the Generational Economy: A Global Perspective*, edited by A. Mason and R. Lee, 55–78. Cheltenham, UK: Edward Elgar.

Mason, A., R. Lee, G. Donehower, S.-H. Lee, T. Miller, A.-C. Tung, and A. Chawla. 2009. "National Transfer Accounts Manual." NTA Working Papers, vol. 09–08. http://www .ntaccounts.org/web/nta/show/Working%20Papers.

Ministerio de Economía. 2001. "Estimaciones de gasto y financiamiento del sector salud en Argentina año 1997 y proyecciones, 1997–2000." Ministerio de Economía-Secretaría de Política Económica and Ministerio de Salud-Secretaría de Políticas y Regulación Sanitaria, Buenos Aires.

Salud en la Argentina Atención del Adulto Mayor. w.d. http://www.ciss.org.mx/cadam /pdf/es/Salud_en_Argentina_Atencion_del_AM.pdf.

Samuelson, P. 1958. "An Exact Consumption Loan Model of Interest with or without the Social Contrivance of Money." *Journal of Political Economy* 66: 467–82.

Turra, C., L. Queiroz, and E. Rios-Neto. 2011. "Idiosyncrasies of Intergenerational Transfers in Brazil." In *Population Aging and the Generational Economy: A Global Perspective*, edited by A. Mason and R. Lee, 394–407. Cheltenham, UK: Edward Elgar.

United Nations. 2013. "National Transfer Accounts Manual: Measuring and Analysing the Generational Economy." Population Division, Department of Economic and Social Affairs, United Nations, New York.

Willis, R. J. 1988. "Life Cycles, Institutions and Population Growth: A Theory of the Equilibrium Interest Rate in an Overlapping-Generations Model." In *Economics of Changing Age Distributions in Developed Countries*, edited by R. D. Lee, W. B. Arthur, and G. Rodgers, 106–38. Oxford: Oxford University Press.

CHAPTER 4

Public Finance Implications of Population Aging in Argentina: 2010, 2050, 2100

Michele Gragnolati and Sara Troiano

Introduction

As shown in chapter 2, Argentina is currently enjoying a window of demographic opportunity that translates into a favorable ratio in terms of the working-age to dependent population. Nevertheless, the country will experience significant changes in its population age structure in the near future. After having reached a peak in 1990, with roughly 10.3 million people ages 0–19 years, the proportion of the youngest over total population has started declining steadily. In contrast, t percentage of adults aging 65+ will double in the next 50 years. Whereas in 2010 there were almost six people of working age for every elderly adult, the same ratio is projected to decrease to 3 in 2050 and to 2 in 2100. This chapter draws attention on the likely fiscal implications of this aging of the population by projecting the evolution of social expenditures for in the period 2010–2100.

We focus on three key areas of public spending: education, pensions, and health care. Our projections are based on a simple model in which aggregate public expenditures are driven by changes in the age structure of Argentina's population as well as changes in the average public transfers received by the population at each age. Although this exercise may seem overly simplistic, it gives a good idea of the magnitude that demographic changes only will have on social policy. If future economic and political context may be hard to foresee, especially in a country such as Argentina, demographic trends are much more certain. This exercise does not aim at estimating a number for Argentina social spending in 2100, but rather at proving the utility of taking into consideration a predictable factor such as demographic transition when designing and projecting the impact of public policy.

In particular, the gradual changes in age structure unfolding in the coming decades will present different challenges and opportunities to education, health, and pension programs. Projecting all three expenditure paths with a comparable methodology will provide insights into the interconnections and trade-offs available to national policy makers. Too often, policy reforms of pension, health care, and education systems are debated, analyzed, and implemented in isolation from each other without considering the fiscal links among these systems.

Finally, comparing the projections of Argentina with those of other countries that are built using the same methodology will permit identifying and understanding possible alternative scenarios and ultimately discussing advantages and suitability of different policy options. Understanding the fiscal implications of population aging in the period considered allows anticipating the potential impact that policies of today will have tomorrow in a different demographic context, which, in turn, could eliminate the need to make urgent, disruptive adjustments at huge political, social, and economic costs.

Methodology: Age Structure and the Generosity of Public Benefits

Theoretical Model

Public spending on education, pensions, and health care is the product of the average generosity of the benefits received by each individual and the age structure of the population.[1] The share of economic output directed toward consumption of education, health care, and pensions through the public sector can be decomposed into two multiplicative components. Equation 1 shows an example of public spending on education:[2]

$$\frac{B_t}{Y_t} = \frac{B_t/P_t}{Y_t/P_{20-64,t}} \times \frac{P_t}{P_{20-64,t}}, \tag{1}$$

where B_t = aggregate benefits, P_t = eligible population (by sector), and $P_{20-64,t}$ = working age population.

Let us take the example of aggregate public spending on education. Assume that all public education benefits are targeted to individuals between the ages of 5 and 20 and further that these benefits do not vary by age. In this case, aggregate public expenditure on education as a share of gross domestic product (GDP) is simply the product of two scalar factors: one economic and the other demographic. The economic factor measures the average educational benefit received per school-age person (ages 5–20). The demographic factor measures the size of the school-age population relative to the working-age population.[3]

In equation 1, the economic factor is represented by the first scalar quantity. Following Miller et al. (2009), we call this factor the education benefit generosity ratio? (BGR), which measures the generosity of average educational benefits relative to GDP per working-age adult. Standardizing by economic output per working-age adult is useful for making international comparisons of benefits as well as for projecting future expenditures, as will be discussed later.

The second scalar quantity, $P(5–20,t)/P(20–64,t)$, is the education dependency ratio and measures the size of the school-age population relative to the working-age population. By definition, the product of these two terms yields aggregate educational spending as a share of GDP.

Note that a higher BGR does not necessarily imply a more generous transfer per beneficiary. It is important to keep in mind that this variable captures social spending in terms of both monetary level of benefits and coverage, that is, the actual quantity of people of the eligible population that actually benefit of public social program in each sector. To keep education as an example, a higher BGR in one country may indicate either a higher level of public investment per pupil or higher coverage of public education or both. Equation 2 illustrates this decomposition, with E_t being the actual number of beneficiaries. As shown in this equation, the BGR equals the benefit per eligible person when policy coverage (education in this case), is universal, that is, equal to one:

$$\frac{B_t}{Y_t} = \frac{\dfrac{B_t}{P_t}}{\dfrac{Y_t}{P_{20-64,t}}} \times \frac{P_t}{P_{20-64,t}} = \frac{\dfrac{B_t}{E_t}}{\dfrac{Y_t}{P_{20-64,t}}} \times \frac{E_t}{P_t} \times \frac{P_t}{P_{20-64,t}}. \tag{2}$$

Benefit per eligible person

| Benefit generosity ratio | Dependency ratio | Average benefit per beneficiary (normalized by output per worker) | Coverage | Dependency ratio |

Projection Scenarios

Our projections of public spending are based on forecast of the population age structure and age-specific benefits. The population forecasts are described in chapter 2. Estimations are based on the cohort component method in which single trends in mortality rates, fertility rates, and migration rates are combined to generate a forecast of the age structure of the population.

Age-specific profiles of public expenditure in each social sector have been calculated in chapter 3 using the National Transfer Accounts (NTA) methodology. As described in chapter 3, these figures draw directly from national firsthand data. As such, they may differ from numbers presented in international databases because of different criteria applied when analyzing the sources and in defining social spending categories. In particular, in the attempt to attribute each part of the spending to a specific age group, NTA figures focus on public consumption (i.e., consumption financed by public transfers), disregarding fixed-capital investment. If figures from international databases are best suited for cross-country comparisons, NTA estimates on the other hand reduce potential bias when projecting Argentina's social public expenditures for the period 2010–2100 by better considering the country-specific context and allowing for a more precise age-specific profile of public spending. In terms of the theoretical model just described, NTA figures normalized by output per worker are equivalent to the BGR. As such, NTA estimates of spending per person by single age take into account coverage rates.[4]

In terms of average benefit and aggregate spending, we consider three scenarios for each sector. In the first (status quo) we leave spending per person constant at its 2010 level and allow aggregate public spending to change as the age structure of the population changes. In the second (convergence), we set the more ambitious goal of reaching high-income countries' levels of investment per capita within two decades, by 2030. Finally, as a reference, we show the scenario in which aggregate public spending is maintained at its current level until 2100.

How realistic are these scenarios? The status quo scenario, in which age-specific benefits are kept constant throughout the period considered, reflects the impact of demographic pressure under the assumption that current policy remains unchanged. In the case of education and health care, these sorts of forecasts ignore likely policy changes, such as increases in school enrollment rates and increases in utilization of health services by the elderly. Hence, those forecasts are likely to understate the likely fiscal impacts of population change in these sectors and represent a lower bound in the estimation.

In some ways, constant aggregate public spending may represent a more likely scenario in some cases. Both literature and empirical evidence show that social spending in each sector, as a percentage of GDP, suffers from some inertia in most developed countries (Carsten 2007). Once a certain threshold is reached, social public expenditure is likely to stabilize at a certain level. However, historical evidence and recent developments show that this has not been the case in Argentina. The country has gone through a major shift in paradigm in terms of its welfare system, and it seems to be still in the process of finding the right balance between coverage, average benefit, and aggregate spending. This scenario will hence be included just as a reference point.

Convergence toward current high-income countries' average benefits seems the most plausible case for emerging economies. The pace at which this convergence will occur is highly uncertain. We opted for an optimistic scenario and assumed this process to be completed in the next two decades. However, the trend in social spending that we will observe in Argentina in the future is going to crucially depend on the policies the country chooses to adopt. The specific policy options for each sector are discussed in details in the following chapters. Here our aim is to present some baseline projections to highlight why, and to what magnitude, changes in sectoral policies will be needed to ensure social programs that are both effective and fiscally sustainable in the context of the unavoidable demographic change ahead.

Projections of Social Spending for Argentina and Comparator Countries

Where Do We Stand? Social Expenditure in Argentina Compared with Other Countries

Before projecting the future fiscal impacts of population aging, it is useful to begin with a discussion of where Argentina stands today. In table 4.1 we show Argentina's public sector spending in 2005 and 2010 relative to two middle-income countries in the same region (Brazil and Mexico) and a group of high-income Organisation for Economic Co-operation and Development (OECD) countries,[5] based on figures on social expenditures from international databases. The effort made by Argentina between 2005 and 2010 is remarkable. In 2005 levels of social spending and relative generosity in Argentina were pretty much in line with those of comparable developing countries. On the other hand, in 2010 the structure of the social system in Argentina was much more similar to that of high-income countries. The progressive shift in the welfare state paradigm has been reflected by a significant increase in aggregate expenditure in social sectors.

Note that similar levels of aggregate spending in education, health, and social security in different countries translate into very different benefits levels for citizens in those economies, because of the different sizes of the eligible populations in such countries. Using data from UNESCO on aggregate spending and data from the UN Population Division for the education dependency ratio, we calculate the BGR as a residual for a large set of countries in the world that differ in terms of both population age structure and income per capita, among other factors. Results are shown in figure 4.1.

Table 4.1 Summary of Argentina's Spending in International Context
Percent

	Mexico, 2010	Brazil, 2010	Argentina, 2005	Argentina, 2010	OECD, 2010
Public education					
Aggregate spending	5.3	4.4	4.5	5.8	5.7
Sector dependency rate	44.9	50.5	41.6	38.7	23.4
Benefit generosity	11.8	8.7	10.8	14.9	24.1
Public pensions					
Aggregate spending	1.7	6.6	4.2	6.4	11.4
Sector dependency rate	9.8	10.8	16.0	16.4	28.5
Benefit generosity	17.3	61.1	26.3	39.0	40.1
Public health care					
Aggregate spending	3.1	3.3	4.5	5.3	7.7
Sector dependency rate	8.0	11.0	12.7	12.4	15.1
Benefit generosity	38.7	30.0	35.4	42.7	51.1

Sources: Based on various data sources: population data from the UN Population Division; expenditure data on public education (UNESCO), public pensions (OECD and Ministry of Labor and Social Security of Argentina), and public health care (WHO).

Figure 4.1 School-Age Population and Public Education Spending per Young Person, Argentina, Austria, and Senegal, 2010

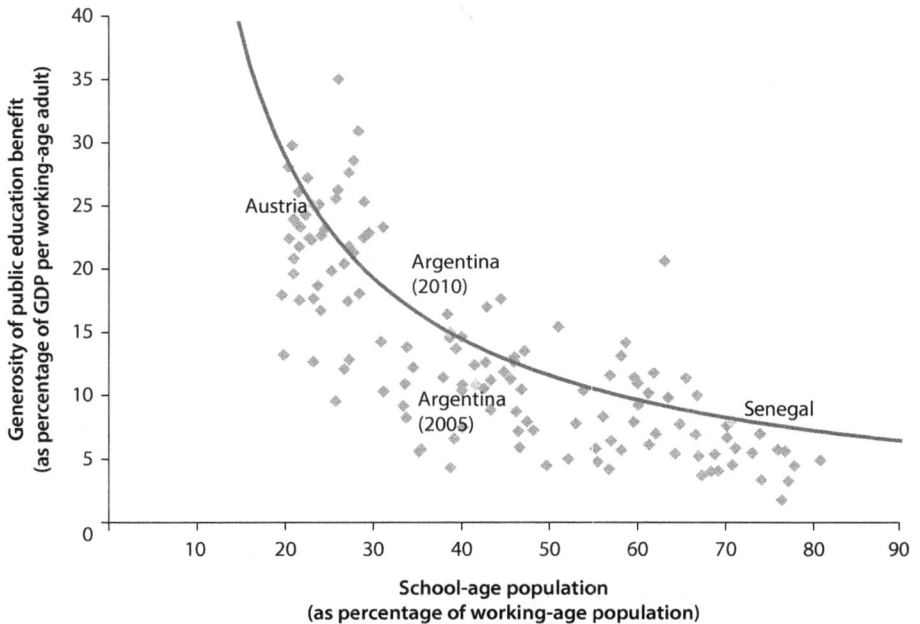

Source: Based on population data from UN Population Division for 2010 and expenditure data from UNESCO 2012.

In Senegal, there is nearly one school-age child for every 1.5 working-age person in the population. Public investment in education is approximately 5.8 percent of GDP. Hence, the average public investment per school-age child in Senegal accounts for just 7.9 percent of the average annual salary,[6] as reflected by the BGR. This low level of investment may reflect both low participation rates and low investment per student.

Austria lies at the other extreme. Total public spending on education as a percentage of GDP approaches very much that of Senegal. Nevertheless, this results in vastly more public investment per youth. The more favorable age structure in Austria allows for much higher investment in youth at the same levels of aggregate spending. In Austria, there are more than four working-age persons for every school-age child. Public investments per youth are 25 percent of the average annual salary—more than triple the investment in Senegal.

Argentina, which similarly to Senegal and Austria devotes approximately 5.8 percent of GDP to public investments in education, lies between those two countries. In Argentina, there are approximately three working-age adults for every school-age child. Public investment per youth in Argentina is about 15 percent of the average wage or a lifetime educational investment of about two and a half years of annual wages. The governments of all three countries are investing approximately the same relative amounts in educating the next generation—roughly 5.8 percent of GDP—but with very different investments per youth on account of the difference in the age structure of their populations. On the basis of this cross-national sample for 2010, it appears that if there is very little variation in aggregate public spending in response to the size of the youth population, educational investments per student are inversely related to population size.

In terms of expenditure on pensions, we observe a significant change in Argentina's positioning relative to other countries. If in 2005 the proportion of GDP devoted to pensions was just 4.2 percent, in 2010 the level of expenditure on this sector was much more comparable to richer OECD countries. The country seems to have a quite balanced position in terms of sustainability of public pensions with respect to its demographic structure, as opposed to Brazil, where the level of average benefit is clearly unsustainable.

As the old-age dependency ratio approaches the European level, Argentina may have to rethink its approach to pensions. We have recently observed how Italy and Spain, for instance, as well as other several European countries had to reorganize their pensions system following the 2008–09 economic downturn. The high political cost of this maneuver may be even higher if such changes are introduced as an urgent exit strategy. Last-minute reforms are rarely accompanied by careful design, poverty considerations, and long-term planning, and as such may be extremely risky from both a political and an economic point of view. An international analysis of the relationship between age structure and pensions system could help Argentina in understanding which model it might want to adopt in the future and how to get there. Figure 4.2 shows the relationship between the age structure of the population and the generosity of the pensions system.

In the case of education and pensions, there is a clearly defined demographic group to which benefits are directed. In the case of health spending, it is difficult to define which dependency ratio we should consider and what age groups are included. Therefore, the decomposition of spending into demographic and economic scalar values works less well than in the case of education or pensions. In keeping with the simple decomposition method of equation 1, we look for a best approximation by considering that group for which most health care spending is directed: the population close to death.

To estimate the number of persons close to death in the population, we use estimates and projections of the number of deaths over the next decade in the original cohort using population estimates and projections from the UN Population Division. This is an approximation of the number of people who are likely to use a high proportion of all health care services consumed within the year, at least in developed countries. Many studies of OECD countries have shown that most health costs for individuals occur in the final decade of life, and in that decade, in the final year of life (Lee and Miller 2001; McGrail et al. 2000; Zweifel et al. 1999). That is, most health systems devote a large

Figure 4.2 Elderly Population and Public Pension Spending per Older Adult, Argentina, Brazil, and Spain, 2010

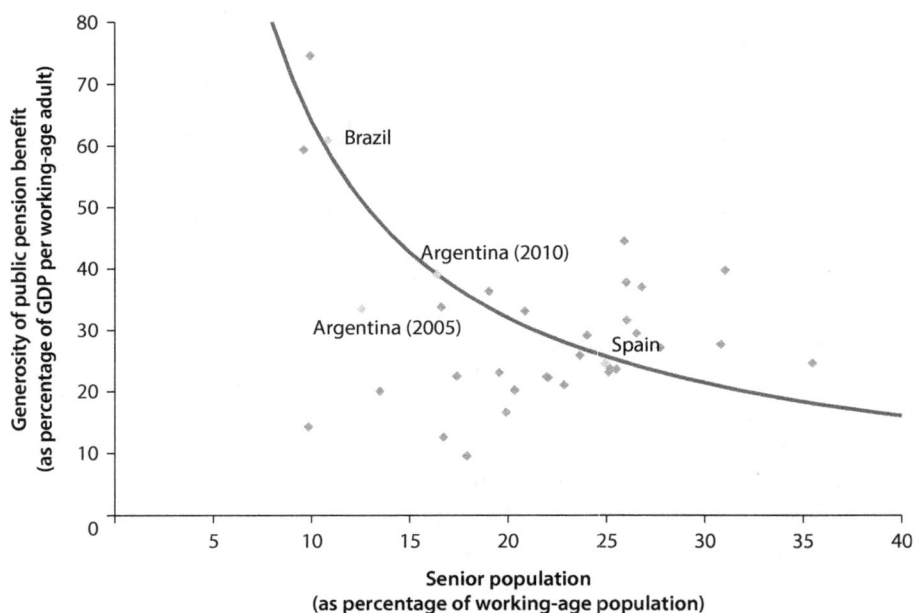

Source: Based on population data from the UN Population Division; expenditure data from NTA and OECD.

percentage of their resources to curative and palliative services rather than preventive services.

Using World Health Organization (WHO) data on public expenditures on health as a percentage of GDP,[7] we divide by the health dependency ratio (the near-death population as a proportion of the working-age population) to derive the generosity ratio for public health benefits.

Figure 4.3 presents estimates of the near-death population and the generosity of public health benefits around the world. Again, we see that countries that are very different in terms of both income and age structure of the population might nonetheless devote the same percentage of GDP to public health services. Argentina, Hungary, and Turkey present a similar level of public expenditures in the health sector. Life expectancy differs considerably among these three countries, so we can expect them to face different shares of the population likely to need health services in the future. On one hand, we have a country such as Turkey, in which the number of people who will die within the next decade is nearly 9 percent of the size of its working-age population. At the other extreme, Hungary is likely to lose almost 20 percent of its working-age population in the next decade. Still, these two countries devote approximately 5 percent of GDP to finance public health services—roughly the same percentage invested by Argentina—resulting in very different degrees of generosity of the health sector for the population in need.

Figure 4.3 Near-Death Population and Public Health Spending Per Capita, Argentina, Hungary, and Turkey, 2010

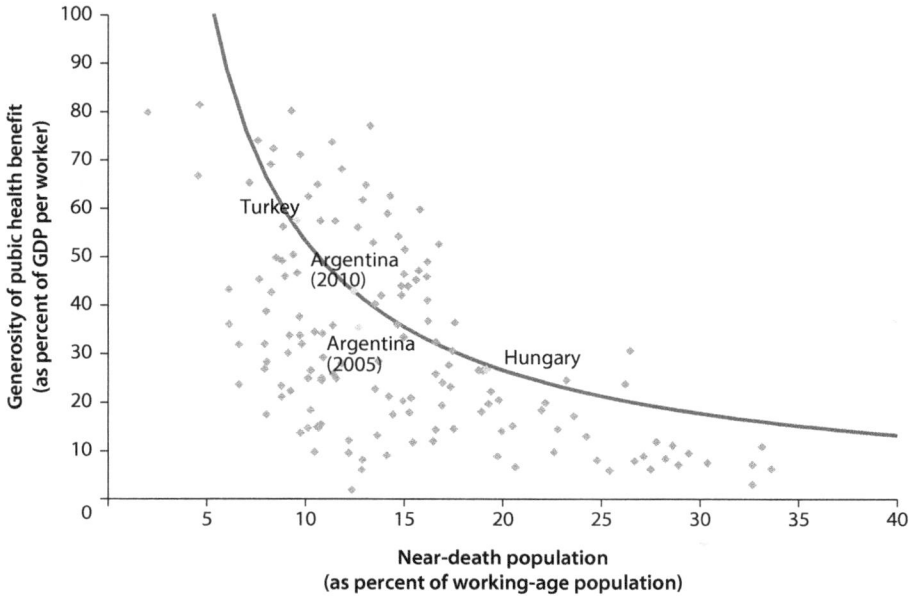

Sources: Based on population data from UN Population Division 2010, and expenditures data from WHO 2010.

Demographic Changes and Their Effects on Social Spending

Our projections are based on changes in the age profile of the population and the profile of public benefits by single age, estimated using NTA methodology.[8] Equation 3, which is used for our projections on spending, is simply the vector version of equation 1, which was used for our international cross-sectional comparisons. The share of GDP devoted to education is the sum over all ages of these two vectors: (1) an economic factor reflecting average education benefits received by age and (2) a demographic factor, the age structure of the population:

$$\frac{B_t}{Y_t} = \sum_x \left(b_{t,x} \cdot \frac{P_{t,x}}{P_{t,15-64}} \right), \tag{3}$$

where $b_{t,x}$ = average education benefits received at age x in year t relative to economic output per working-age adult in year t = B(t)/P(t)/Y(t)/P(20–64,t). Here P(x,t) = population at age x in year t and P(15–64,t) = working-age population (ages 15–64) in year t.

Education

With the slow but constant decline in fertility in Argentina over the past few decades, the size of the school-age population has continuously declined as shown in figure 4.4. The baby boom in the 1980s resulted in a peak in 1990,

Figure 4.4 School-Age Population Relative to Working-Age Population, Austria, Argentina, and Senegal, 1950–2100

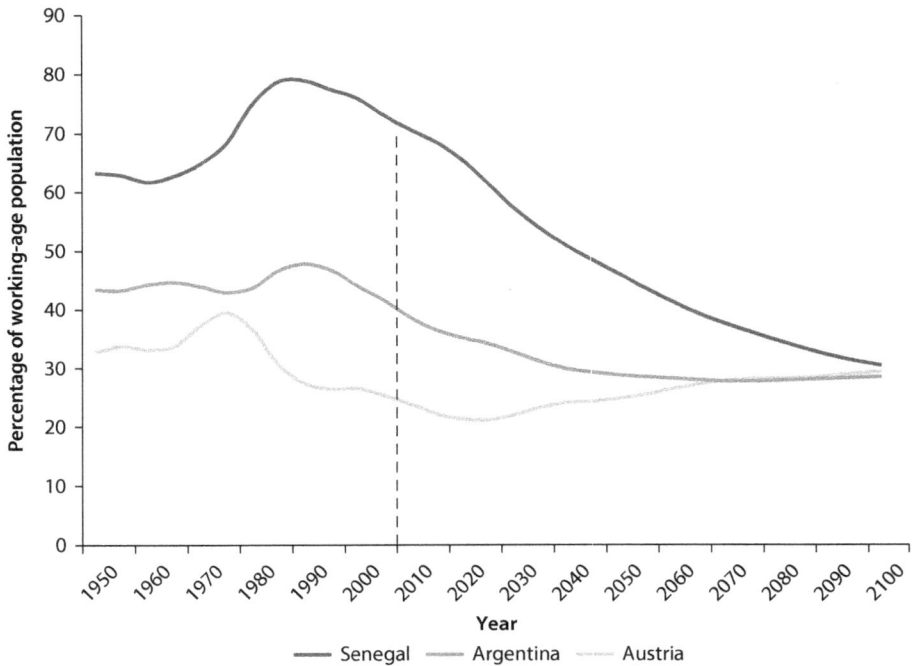

Source: Based on population data from UN Population Division 2010.

with the school-age population being 48 percent as large as the working-age population. By 2010, the proportion of the school-age population over the working-age population had fallen by 10 percentage points. Given the faster decline in fertility that we expect Argentina to experience in the following decades, the country will see a school-age dependency ratio of roughly 28 percent in 2050, similar to the one observed in richer countries: Denmark, Norway, and even Austria. This reduction in the demographic pressure in the education sector offers an exclusive range of opportunities in terms of per capita educational investment and development of human capital.

We present three scenarios for projecting future public spending on education in figure 4.5, using NTA estimates of education public consumption as the reference for public spending. The straight line represents our starting point, with aggregate spending in education at 5.6 percent of GDP. Giving the decline in fertility and the favorable demographic transition in this sector, keeping aggregate spending constant would imply a rise in the level of benefits, although without ever reaching high-income OECD levels.

Let us now turn at the status quo scenario, in which the government opts to maintain constant current levels of average investment per student. As the population of students declines over time, aggregate spending can be reduced to roughly 4.6 percent of GDP in 2030—18 percent less than the current level in

Figure 4.5 Public Spending on Education as a Percentage of GDP, Argentina, 2010–2100

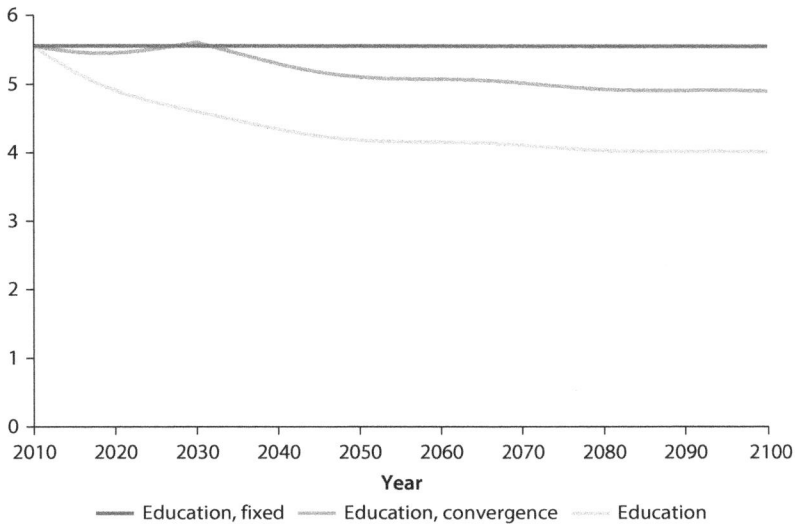

Source: Based on fiscal projection model.

just two decades. Although the option seems appealing from a fiscal point of view, its advantages in terms of educational policy and human capital development may be questionable.

Finally, let us suppose that Argentina decides to gradually increase investment per student in order to reach the level of high-income, OECD countries by 2030. As shown in figure 4.3, this would imply keeping aggregate spending almost constant for the next two decades. After this period, the change in the demographic structure will allow the country to enjoy both higher investment per student and lower aggregate expenditure as a percentage of GDP. Hence, by investing an additional 0.05 percent of GDP up to 2030, the government could make sure to take full advantage of the first demographic dividend to sustain long-term investment in human capital.

Such an ambitious increase in educational investment per student would likely have profound implications for both economic growth and inequality in Argentina. Indeed, Lee and Mason (2010) present simulation results that suggest that such investments in human capital can offset the costs of population aging.

Pensions

Argentina introduced major reforms in the pension sector in the last decade, that allowed the country to improve the generosity of the system both in terms of benefits and coverage. This large expansion of the public pension system, however, took place under moderate demographic pressure. This will all change significantly in the coming decades as seen in figure 4.6. In 2005 the elderly

Figure 4.6 Elderly Population Relative to Working-Age Population, Spain, Argentina, and Brazil, 1950–2100

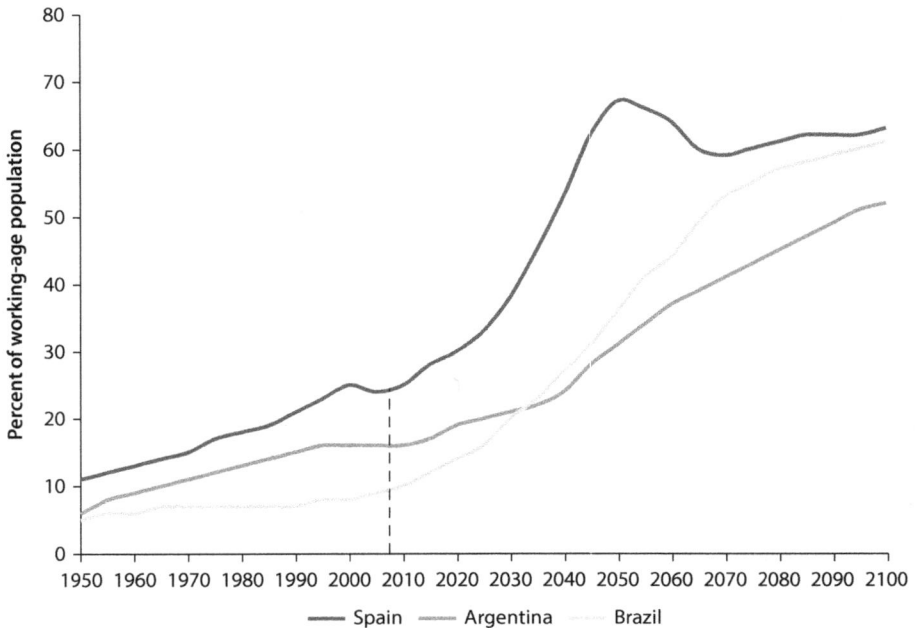

Source: Calculation based on population data from UN Population Division 2010.

population in Argentina was about 18 percent the size of the working-age population. In less than 50 years, this ratio will more than double—with the elderly population in Argentina at about 36 percent of the size of the working-age population.

As discussed above, we present the same scenarios for future public spending on pensions, using NTA estimates of public financing of social security (figure 4.7). The first scenario (status quo) assumes no change in the current generosity of pensions. In this case, the rapid increase in the ratio of older adults to working-age adults directly translates into dramatic and unsustainable increases in public spending; spending on pensions would almost double, from 9.1 percent of GDP in 2010 to roughly 11.1 percent in 2030 and 15.5 percent by 2050, up to an astounding 22.3 percent of GDP by 2100.

To put these figures into context, consider that those pensions systems in high-income OECD countries that are currently considered fiscally unsustainable, and going through major reforms, spend overall between 10 and 15 percent of GDP. Typical examples include France and Italy, whose population age structure looks very much like the one Argentina will experience in 2050. On the other hand, by lowering benefit generosity to the levels of benefits these richer countries are currently granting, Argentina would be able to save roughly 5 points of GDP by 2100 compared with the status quo scenario. In either case,

Figure 4.7 Public Spending on Pensions as a Percentage of GDP, Argentina, 2010–2100

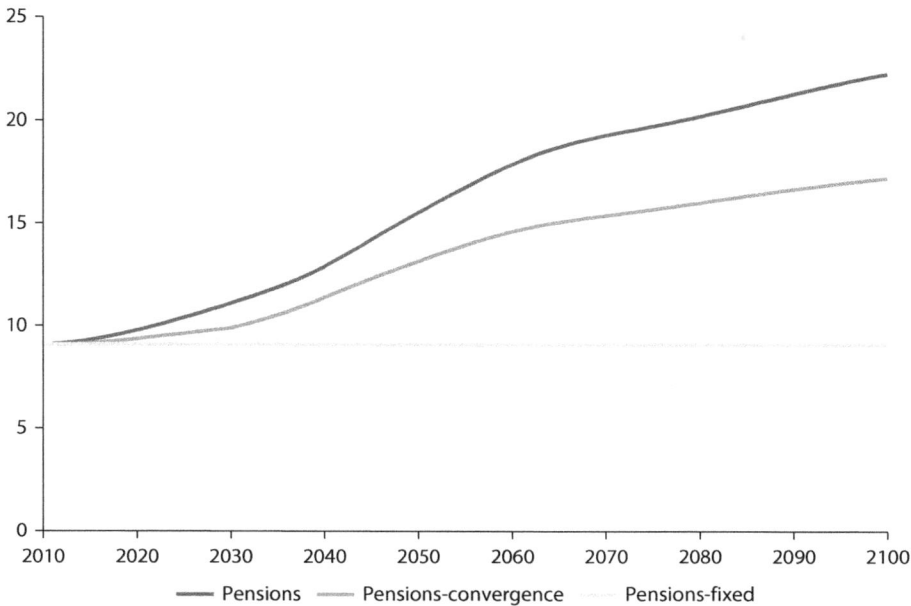

Source: Based on fiscal projection model.

it is evident that the demographic factor will have a huge impact on the sustainability of the pension system not only in the long run, for example, 2100, but even in in the near-term future.

Health
As countries move through the demographic transition, the health sector dependency ratio follows a U-shaped curve. Initially, declines in mortality rates lead to declines in the proportion of the population near death. As is evident in the case of Turkey as shown in figure 4.8, such declines can be quite rapid and substantial. The near-death population was more than 40 percent the size of the working-age population in 1950 in Turkey. Over five decades, the near-death population declined to about one-tenth the size of the working-age population. Eventually, as the demographic transition proceeds, the age structure of the population shifts substantially toward older persons, and the near-death population begins to increase relative to the working-age population.

In virtually all Latin American and Caribbean countries, the population near death will grow more quickly than the population of working-age adults, and this will tend to increase the financial burden associated with financing health care. In the case of Argentina, the near-death population has been declining since 1965, when it was about 15 percent of the working-age population. It will reach its nadir of about 12 percent of the working-age population in 2015 and is projected to reverse the trend and start increasing that year. After decades of

Figure 4.8 Near-Death Population Relative to Working-Age Population, Argentina, Hungary, and Turkey, 1950–2100

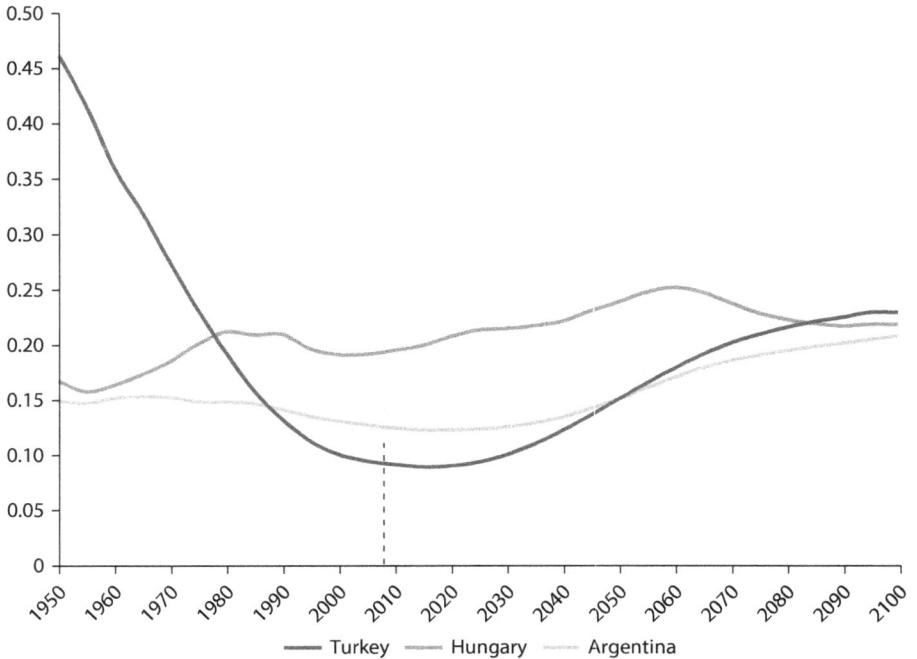

Source: Based on population projections from UN Population Division 2010.

favorable demographic chance, the health system in Argentina is set to experience increasing demographic pressures over the coming decades.

Striking differences are seen in health care expenditures by age between high-income and middle-income countries. Figure 4.9 shows health care expenditures per person of each age as a fraction of average labor earnings of primary workers (ages 30–49) based on data taken from NTA. For those below age 60, health spending in high-income and middle-income countries is surprisingly similar. This cross-sectional data imply that health care spending at these ages increases proportionally with income. Above age 60, the pattern is quite different. There we see that in high-income countries, health care expenditures per older adult are significantly greater in high-income countries; that is, as incomes rise, health care expenditures at these ages increase more rapidly than income. Health care after 60 acts as a luxury good. Note that Argentina presents a peculiar pattern that seems to lie between these two sets of countries. Its health spending profile is very similar to that of middle-income countries, although spending levels, especially at younger ages, are considerably higher.

It is very much an open question as to why societies show this striking difference in health spending profiles between developed and developing countries. Among the possibilities, experts point at a shift in medical protocol in which chronic diseases are more aggressively treated. Other possible causes may be

Figure 4.9 Spending on Health, by Age in Argentina and Middle- and High-Income Countries, 2010

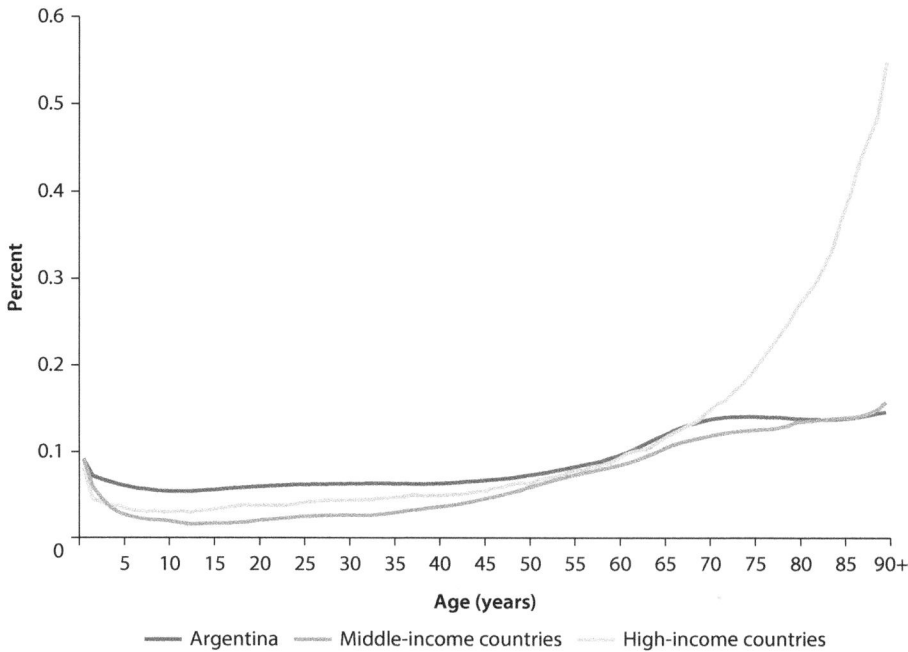

Source: Calculations based on NTA data.

related to the productive organization of a society or other issues less specific to the health sector. As an example, older and wealthier countries may provide some care for senior citizens in the market, whereas in poorer countries such goods are home produced. A primary example of this would be the shift from personal home care provided by family members toward institutional care provided in nursing home facilities.

Whatever the reasons for this pattern, the shift to higher expenditures at older ages magnifies the impact of population aging and is projected to lead to significant increases in health expenditures as a share of GDP.

We present two alternative scenarios for future public spending on health. For the education and pensions sector previously analyzed, we project aggregate public spending both for average benefit constant at 2010 levels and with convergence toward high-income countries' levels. However, based on the previous discussion, it is crucial to take into consideration that the distribution of health expenditure by single age will vary considerably as the country grows richer, with older ages having more weight on the total expenditure.

The eventual increase in health expenditure resulting from the demographic transition will be magnified by these behavioral and institutional changes.[9] If public health expenditure were expected to increase from 6.3 percent to 7.5 percent of GDP between 2010 and 2100 because of demographic factors only, the jump is estimated to be much more significant (up to 9.1 percent of

Figure 4.10 Public Spending on Health, Argentina, 2010–2100

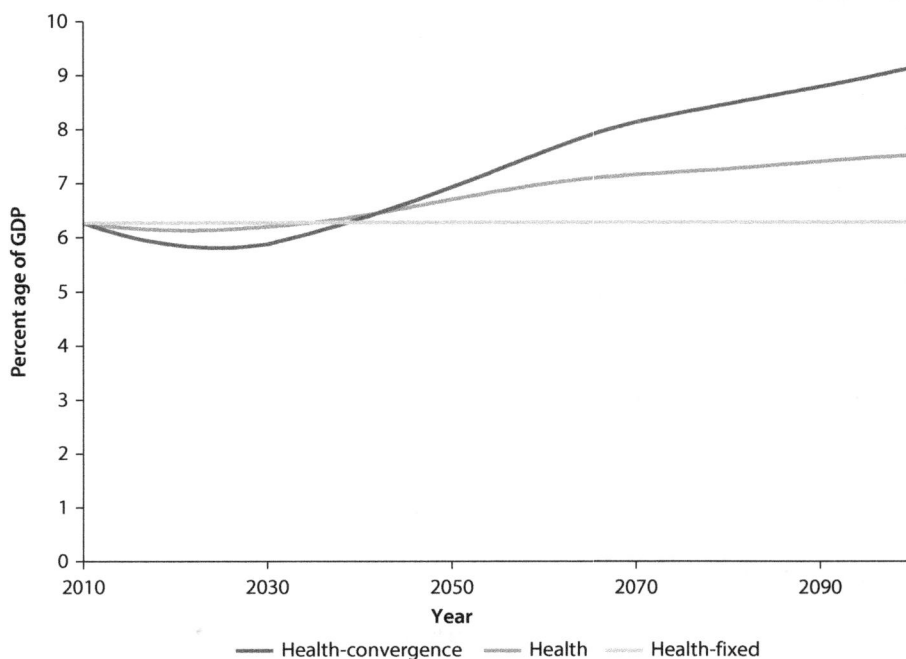

Source: Projection based on fiscal projection model.

GDP in 2100) when we take into account the shift of the country toward a different health consumption pattern. Figure 4.10 shows the magnitude of this divergence in public health consumption patterns as the weight given to older age grows larger. Note that, for both scenarios, these projections also foresee aggregate spending to stay constant or slightly decrease up to 2040, roughly. As a result of the first demographic dividend, this period will enjoy a relatively smaller proportion of people in ages where health expenditure is concentrated, namely, the very youngest and, especially in the convergence scenario, the very oldest.

Conclusions

The fiscal projections described in this chapter allow us to figure the possible implications of the demographic transition Argentina is currently experiencing, in terms of fiscal social expenditures and the welfare system. As discussed, the aim is not to estimate a number for Argentina social spending in 2100, but rather to prove the utility of taking into consideration a predictable factor as demographic transition when designing and projecting the impact of public policy.

We have recalled that the demographic and economic components are equally important in determining aggregate spending in each social sector. In fact, aggregate spending is the result of the relative generosity of social programs benefits, as well as the number of people in a determined age group that will be affected by that program. Put the other way around, we have shown that similar levels of aggregate spending in education, health care, and social security in different countries translate into very different benefits levels for citizens in those economies because of the different size of eligible populations in those countries.

What will the demographic changes mean for Argentina's social spending? Assuming no change in public policy, and hence in benefit generosity per person, the increase in the proportion of the elderly in the population will result in a disruptive increase in public expenditures in 2050, and even more in 2100. More important, in the short term (2030, roughly 15 years from now) we would observe a redistribution of resources from the young to the elderly, with public spending decreasing in the education sector and increasing in financing pensions.

As Argentina grows richer, however, it is likely to assume that its consumption patterns will tend to resemble those of high-income OECD countries. Assuming that public policies will change accordingly, we present a scenario in which benefit generosity in each social sector will converge to those of high-income countries in 2030. This involves higher spending per student in education, focusing on the human capital and productivity of future generations. At the same time, a decrease in the generosity of pensions will become necessary as the proportion of potential retirees increases to the levels of more developed countries. Finally, convergence toward the consumption patterns of rich economies will bring significant changes in health expenditure by age, as health services after age 60 are sure to increase proportionally as income per capita increases.

As discussed in the introduction of this chapter, Argentina has gone through a profound change in its welfare system in the last decade, and its current levels of social spending are more similar to those of wealthy economies than other middle-income countries. Because of this, convergence toward the spending profiles of high-income OECD countries would not imply such a difference in absolute levels in terms of public expenditures in social sectors, neither in the short nor long term, as illustrated in table 4.2. What convergence will imply, instead, is a different allocation of resources among sectors. With respect to the status quo scenario, relatively more resources will be devoted to education and health care, while less funds will go to finance pensions.

This chapter focused on the importance of taking into account the demographic factor when analyzing the potential impact of public policies in the future. The projections also highlighted the potential fiscal trade-offs between the education and health care sectors, and social security, that could arise over the long term as the age structure of the population changes. Nevertheless, many other factors are likely to play a role in the evolution of social policy, including trends and needs specific to each sector. Moreover, the impact of the demographic transition can be mitigated by adopting alternative policy options that would not necessarily be captured by our convergence scenario. The following chapters will offer an in-depth discussion of these issues.

As Time Goes By in Argentina • http://dx.doi.org/10.1596/978-1-4648-0530-1

Table 4.2 Projected Increases in Public Spending, 2010, 2030, 2050, and 2100

Sector	Scenario	Spending as percentage of GDP			
		2010	*2030*	*2050*	*2100*
Education, pensions, and health care	Age-specific education, pensions, and health public benefits fixed at current levels (status quo)	20.9	21.9	26.6	33.8
	Gradual increase in education investment; gradual decrease in pension benefits to wealthy OECD levels; increasing health expenditures at older ages	20.9	21.3	25.2	31.2
Education	Age-specific education spending fixed at current levels (status quo)	5.5	4.6	4.2	4.0
	Gradual increase in student investments toward wealthy OECD countries by 2030	5.6	5.6	5.1	4.9
Pensions	Average pension benefits fixed at current levels (status quo)	9.1	11.1	15.5	22.3
	Gradual decrease of pension benefits toward wealthy OECD levels by 2030	9.1	9.9	13.1	17.2
Health care	Age-specific health spending fixed at current levels (status quo)	6.3	6.2	6.9	7.5
	Increasing health expenditures at older ages to reflect OECD patterns, with benefits at wealthy countries' levels by 2030	6.3	5.9	6.9	9.1

Source: Based on fiscal projection model.
Note: OECD = Organisation for Economic Co-operation and Development.

Notes

1. The methodology in this section is the same as that used by Miller et al. (2009) in several papers. See Cotlear (2011) and Gragnolati et al. (2011).
2. Public spending on pension and health can be decomposed in an equivalent manner.
3. Most educational spending occurs in the school-age group, although increasingly expenditures are being directed at early education and lifelong learning.
4. NTA estimates are equal to zero when population of a certain age is not covered by that specific policy. See chapter 3 for more details on the NTA methodology.
5. High-income countries included as comparators are Austria, Finland, Germany, Japan, Spain, and Sweden. The choice of these countries was limited by availability of NTA estimates. Nevertheless, cross-checking with official spending data for the set of high-income OECD countries show very similar figures.
6. Assuming that total wage bill represents roughly two-thirds of GDP.
7. Note that we do not distinguish here between general health expenditure and specific spending on long-term care services, because of an insufficient level of data disaggregation for most of the countries considered.
8. As discussed earlier, NTA estimates may slightly differ from the ones available in international databases. These differences, however, do not affect conclusions in terms of the relative generosity in each social sector.

9. Note that as the country grows richer, the public sector share of total health expenditures is also expected to increase, creating a further impulse for rapid acceleration in public health care spending. These trends and their impact, specific to the sector, is discussed more in depth in chapter 6.

References

Carsten, J. 2007. "Fixed or Variable Needs? Public Support and Welfare State Refom." *Government and Opposition* 42 (2): 139–57.

Cotlear, D., ed. 2011. *Population Aging: Is Latin America Ready?* Washington, DC: World Bank.

Gragnolati, M., O. Hagen Jorgensen, R. Rocha, and A. Fruttero, eds. 2011. *Growing Old in an Older Brazil: Implications of Population Aging on Growth, Poverty, Public Finance, and Service Delivery*. Washington, DC: World Bank.

Lee, R., and A. Mason. 2010. "Fertility, Human Capital, and Economic Growth over the Demographic Transition." *European Journal of Population* 26 (2): 159–82.

Lee, R., and T. Miller. 2001. "An Approach to Forecasting Health Expenditures, with Application to the U.S. Medicare System." Document presented at Population Ageing and Health, Londres, January 27.

McGrail, K., B. Green, M. Barer, R. Evans, C. Hertzman, and C. Normand. 2000. "Age, Costs of Acute and Long-Term Care and Proximity to Death: Evidence for 1987–88 and 1994–95 in British Columbia." *Age and Aging* 29 (3): 249–53.

Miller, T., C. Mason, and M. Holz. 2009. "The Fiscal Impact of Demographic Change in Ten Latin American Countries: Projecting Public Expenditures in Education, Health, and Pensions." Paper presented at the Workshop on Demographic Change and Social Policy, World Bank, Washington, DC, July 14–15.

UNESCO (United Nations Educational, Scientific and Cultural Organization). 2012. UNESCO Institute for Statistics Data Centre. http://stat.uis.unesco.org.

Zweifel, P., S. Felder, and M. Meiers. 1999. "Ageing of Population and Health Care Expenditure: A Red Herring?" *Health Economics* 8 (6): 485–96.

CHAPTER 5

Argentine Social Protection in a Context of Demographic Transition

Rafael Rofman and Ignacio Apella

Introduction

Social security is usually defined as the set of programs and policies that have as their objective covering households' risk of income loss through schemes that utilize participants' contributions to fund themselves. In general terms, social security is established to provide certainty and insure individuals against the risk of income loss or spending *shocks* associated with retirement in old age, disability, sickness, accidents, and death.

In turn, social protection encompasses a field that is broader than social security, including not just traditional contributory social security, but also other noncontributory transfer schemes. Thus, social protection programs include contributory social security (old-age and disability pensions, death benefits, occupational hazards, unemployment benefits, family allowances) and noncontributory transfer programs, usually aimed at reducing the incidence of poverty.

The funding of noncontributory social protection thus comes from general revenues, specific taxes, and direct contributions from the state. Social security, on the other hand, tends to cover fewer people and is financed by three types of contributions (from the insured, employers, and the state) based on payroll.

Noncontributory programs in Latin America have traditionally been very limited in their reach, both in terms of budget as well as coverage. In recent years, we have begun to observe a change in the trend in social protection systems, as a result of which the importance of these programs has progressively increased. In Argentina, the implementation of the Unemployed Heads of Household Plan, the Moratoria Previsional (Pensions Moratorium or Pensions Inclusion Program), and the Universal Child Allowance (Asignación Universal por Hijo, AUH) are clear examples of the expansion of coverage to the population that has been excluded from the formal labor market and is living in poverty or vulnerability.

From a life-cycle perspective, monetary transfers for social protection reach the population in different ways for each age group. For example, family allowances are transfers to children, unemployed young adults are protected via contributory unemployment insurance and training and employment insurance, and older adults receive protection through pension programs.

As discussed in detail in chapter 2, Argentina is immersed in a demographic transition process toward an older population structure as a product of the decrease in fertility and mortality since the beginning of the previous century. On the basis of this process, growth is predicted for both the total dependency ratio and the elderly dependency ratio in the coming decades. The total dependency ratio reached 55 percent in 2010, and it is estimated that it will reach 72 percent by 2100. Furthermore, the proportion of the adult population older than 65 years of age relative to the working-age population was 10 percent in 2010 and is projected to reach 25 percent by 2100.

The increase in the number and proportion of the population older than 65 years of age in many countries around the world has generated interest in the impact this trend will have on social security systems. The apparent implication of this phenomenon is pressure on the sustainability of public and private expenditures on pensions. As social security spending increases, so too do controversies over the funding mechanisms for current and future benefits.

In this context, the process of demographic transition that is pushing Argentina toward an older population structure has direct effects on the quantity and adequacy of the transfers made through the social protection system. This is the result of two factors: (1) the demographic transition itself, which results in a change in the sizes of the contributor and beneficiary population groups as the population ages, and (2) the changes in public policy created as a response to these demographic trends. For this reason, this chapter presents an estimation exercise for coverage and the amounts transferred through social protection programs according to several alternative scenarios, with the goal of evaluating the potential costs of the system in different contexts.

The long-term projections are necessary to evaluate how the system will react in the face of the expected changes in economic, political, and demographic conditions. These are not predictions to "correctly guess the future," but rather to allow us to evaluate the system's prospects, given certain reasonable hypotheses about the long-term evolution of several determinant variables. In addition, the present exercise will allow us to evaluate the impact of alternative hypotheses and reforms of current regulations on the coverage and financing of social protection.

Social Protection in Argentina

In Latin America, Argentina forms part of the group of countries called "pioneers" in the development of their social protection systems, along with Chile, Cuba, and Uruguay. These countries introduced old-age and death pension schemes for some groups of organized workers at the beginning of the twentieth century. The development of social protection was undertaken gradually and was linked to formal employment, excluding unemployed and informal workers as a result. The formal sector's social security programs include pension transfers, family allowances, and contributory unemployment insurance. These schemes had their beginnings in negotiations between workers' unions and employers and were converted throughout the last century into national systems managed by the state.

The Pension System

Pension programs are considered to be important components of social security systems. The first formal scheme in Argentina was approved in 1904 with the creation of the Civil Fund for workers who held permanent positions in the government administration and whose salaries were part of the Annual Budget of Expenditures of the Nation (teachers and employees of the National Education Council, employees of official banks and of Argentine railroads, judicial magistrates, and elected officials). The system expanded slowly and beginning in 1944 started a process of expansion of social security benefits to the entire working population, including independent workers and employers. This expansion was carried out without any planning or coordination. According to Isuani and San Martino (1995), during the 1960s the system faced funding difficulties and was highly fragmented, with varying requirements for eligibility, contributions, funding, and benefit adequacy. For this reason, in 1969 the various existing systems were unified to create the National Social Security System. Law 18,037 established predetermined benefits for salaried workers, fixed as a percentage of the average of the three highest salary years during the final 10 years of employment according to retirement age, and Law 18,038 established an equivalent regime for independent workers. In addition, minimum and maximum benefits were established.

During the 1980s and the beginning of the 1990s, the financial sustainability problems worsened, in part because of the maturation of the system and the difficulty of adding new groups of workers to it, and also in part because of the process of population aging and the impossibility of maintaining such generous benefits in this context (such as a replacement rate of 82 percent). In this context, Law 24,241 was approved in 1993, introducing structural reform to the pension system. Thus, the Integrated Retirement and Pension System (Sistema Integrado de Jubilaciones y Pensiones, SIJP) was created, comprising two regimes: one public, organized as a pay-as-you-go scheme and managed by the National Social Security Administration (Administración Nacional de la Seguridad Social, ANSES), and a regime based on individual capitalization and administered by private firms, the Retirement and Pension Fund Administrators (AFJP). In addition, some parametric changes were introduced, including increasing the minimum retirement age from 55 to 60 years old for women and from 60 to 65 years old for men, along with a greater number or required years of contributions, which increased from 20 to 30 years, and an increase in workers' contribution rate, from 10 to 11 percent of salary.

These reforms signaled a clear strengthening of the contributory character of the social security system in terms of accessing entitlements. Not only was a clearer and more explicit rule introduced regarding the proportionality between contributions and benefits, but the number of years required to receive benefits also increased. Nonetheless, the introduction of the capitalization scheme implied a significant increase in the fiscal resources flowing into the system to finance the transition costs, resulting in a schism from the contributory principle in terms of funding (Rofman and Oliveri 2012).

From its implementation, the design and functioning of the SIJP were the subject of strong debates. On one hand, various observers pointed to the existence of market failures that made the capitalization regime less efficient than had been expected. At the same time, the fiscal pressure stemming from the transition process was considered by others as a key factor in the economic crisis unleashed in 2001–02 in Argentina. These considerations meant that from its approval in 1993, the system was the object of multiple modifications and adjustments. Among these, several stand out for their importance: in February 2007, Law 26,222 made it easier for members of the capitalization regime to switch to the pay-as-you-go regime, and Law 26,425 at the end of 2008 definitively ended the capitalization regime, directing all contributions to the public regime. This reform, however, did not modify the system's main parameters (such as contribution rates, minimum retirement age, or the number of contribution years required to receive benefits), which remained at the levels established in 1993.

The Family Allowances System

Family allowances consist of social income transfers, whereby all formal workers receive an amount based on the size of the family that they must support. Therefore, they are considered to be a complement to family income, aimed at increasing per capita resources in larger households (Rofman et al. 2001).

The system first appeared in Argentina in the mid-1930s as a maternity subsidy. In 1940 a per-child subsidy was incorporated, although this was only in the banking sector. Starting in 1957, the system was formalized with the creation of compensatory funds established by collective bargaining, subsequently expanding the subsidies for children younger than 15 years of age and disabled persons.

The funds' source of financing came from an employer contribution equivalent to between 4 and 5 percent of payroll, which later increased to 10 and 12 percent, and in mid-1985 was reduced to 9 percent. In 1991 the contribution designated for family allowances was reduced to 7.5 percent of payroll, and the remaining 1.5 percent was earmarked for the creation of the National Employment Fund. Also in 1991, the funds were dissolved and social security benefits were unified, including the family allowances system, under the jurisdiction of ANSES (Bertranou and Bonari 2005).

In 1996 a reform to the family allowances system was proposed with the goal of making it more redistributive and limiting its cost for employers. The reform established varying benefit amounts according to a worker's salary level. Four salary ranges that offered greater benefits to lower paid workers were established. Workers with salaries above a fixed limit were not directly eligible.

The benefits comprise birth, maternity, adoption, marriage, prenatal, children, disabled children, and school support. After the law was approved in 1996, the per-child benefits, school support, and maternity benefits were paid by employers, who recovered these expenses through a contribution compensation mechanism, whereas birth, adoption, and marriage benefits were requested from ANSES. This process was progressively changed during the first decade of this century, and by 2012 all of these benefits were paid directly by ANSES.

The 1996 law, approved during a period of economic stability, did not contemplate systemic adjustment mechanisms for benefit amounts, nor did it consider lower and upper limits for the salary bands that determined eligibility for the various benefits. Even though this restriction did not have important effects until 2002, the change in the economic regime implemented since then, with increases in salaries, resulted in a reduction of the system's coverage each time various groups of workers switched from one salary band to another or simply were no longer eligible. The adjustments to the amounts and salary eligibility bands came about gradually beginning in 2004 as we observe in figure 5.1. However, these modifications exhibit a frequency and irregularity in terms of amounts that denote the nonexistence of a parametric conditioning mechanism. The social security system faced similar difficulties until 2008, when a mobility

Figure 5.1 Salary Bands for Family Allowances and Average Salaries, 1996–2010
Current pesos

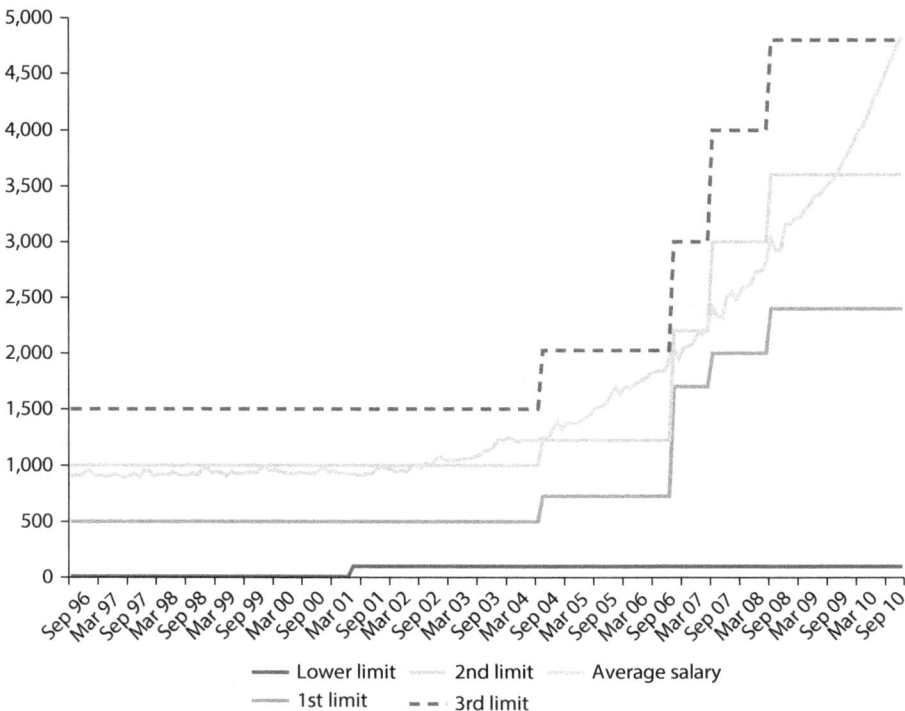

Source: Moreno 2012.

Table 5.1 Family Allowances per Child, by Household Salary Income Band, 2012

Household salary band	Benefit amount (AR$)
W < 3,200	340
3,200 < w < 4,400	250
4,400 < w < 6,000	160
6,000 < w < 14,000	90

Source: ANSES.
Note: w = salary in AR$.

index was approved, whose evolution is mostly explained by the changes in salaries and ANSES collections.

The structure of the salary bands was modified in 2012. Since then, instead of considering just the responsible adult's income, household income is used to determine eligibility, combining the formal salary income of both spouses, and establishing ranges according to table 5.1.

Households with total formal income greater than $14,000 are not eligible for benefits from this subsystem. This mechanism does not contemplate automatic adjustment mechanisms for benefit amounts or upper and lower salary band limits for determining eligibility for the various benefits the subsystem offers. Thus, salary increases will reduce the relative coverage of the system, unless the limits are adjusted at the discretion of the national government.

Unemployment Insurance

One of the instruments used to protect workers from the risk of a reduction in income associated with job loss is unemployment insurance. The traditional design of these programs is based on the principle of insurance. This, complemented by assistance programs, constitutes one of the most used protection mechanisms in industrialized countries. The main goal of unemployment insurance is to offer income security to avoid large fluctuations in household consumption when a member is unemployed, as well as to offer a base of stability that allows him or her to search for employment and rejoin the labor market in better conditions.

In Argentina, legislation on unemployment insurance appeared in 1991 with the imprimatur of Law 24,013 (National Employment Law). Workers protected from the risk of unemployment are those who maintain a labor contract governed by the Labor Contract Law (Law 20,744, which covers salaried workers in the private sector) and those included in the National Regime for the Construction Industry, who have a special regime.

To access the benefit, a worker cannot have left his or her job (i.e., quitting a job does not activate the benefit), must have contributed to the National Employment Fund for a minimum period of six months during the three years before losing the job, and cannot receive social security benefits or noncontributory benefits.

The benefit is equivalent to a percentage of the net amount of the highest paid month during the six months before being dismissed, with minimum and maximum limits. The percentage is 50 percent during the first four months of the benefit, subsequently decreasing as the unemployment period increases: From the fifth to the eighth month, the benefit is equal to 85 percent of the amount received during the first four months, and the benefit from the ninth to the twelfth month falls to 70 percent. As of June 2012, the benefit had a lower limit of $250 and an upper limit of $400; the average benefit was $357.51.

Even though the scheme is more than 20 years old, its coverage—measured as the ratio between beneficiaries and the total number of unemployed persons—is low. In this sense, labor informality is an obstacle to the program's operation because as a contributory scheme, only formal salaried workers can join.

Between Bismarck and Beveridge

Beginning in the mid-2000s several measures aimed at universalizing the social protection system were introduced. They targeted two dependent population groups in particular: the elderly and children. The two emblematic programs are the Moratoria, and the AUH.

In terms of the elderly, several studies highlight the decreasing trend in coverage since the beginning of the 1990s,[1] explained by the combined effects of the high level of labor informality and stricter eligibility requirements introduced in 1994. A study performed by the Secretariat of Social Security (2005) analyzing data from 1994 to 2003, shows that nearly 80 percent of the employed population was affiliated with the social security system. However, among this group only 20 percent (16 percent of the economically active population, EAP) made regular contributions at least 80 percent of the time, meaning they would be able to meet the requirements to retire upon reaching the minimum age. In contrast, around 50 percent had made less than one-third of the contributions. When this group is combined with those who have never made a contribution during their working life, it indicates that around 60 percent of the population would never be able to retire.

With the goal of reducing the coverage gap among the unemployed population, beginning in 2005 the Moratoria was implemented, establishing a regime of payment options for debtors to the social security system who were independent workers. This initiative created the possibility that any citizen who conformed to the minimum age requirements but not with the required number of contribution years could declare a debt corresponding to those years through the independent workers regime and set up a payment plan that would allow him or her to make payments while also receiving benefits.

In addition, these access options for social security benefits were extended to some family members of deceased workers, with the goal that these persons could obtain survivors benefits. The voluntary debt regularization regime created by these regulations is permanent, but it recognizes contribution years only before 1994, which means that the option to join the regime will gradually disappear.[2]

In operational terms, *Moratoria* means that workers assume a debt representing their unpaid contributions to the tax office and ANSES—the amount varies depending on the number of years that a person could have made contributions—and agree to a monthly payment plan for this debt. This recognition allows workers to receive retirement benefits or a pension, from which their monthly payment is discounted. ANSES became the main management institution of the program because it was responsible for registering and collecting the debt. The payment amount is limited to a maximum of $360 per month.

The impact of the Moratoria was massive: Between the end of 2005 and 2011, more than 2.7 million retirement benefits were awarded through this mechanism. As a result, by the end of 2011, the total number of benefits in the national system had reached 6.1 million,[3] and around 1.2 million people were receiving noncontributory pensions for disability or old age. This had a significant impact on coverage levels beginning in 2006, which marked a sharp break with the previous trend. In this sense, coverage of the elderly recovered quickly between 2005 and 2006, when it reached 84.3 percent, and continued growing gradually until reaching 90.8 percent of the population older than 65 years of age in 2011.

In terms of the population group younger than 18 years of age, in October 2009 family benefits were expanded to unemployed children and informal workers. This initiative, the AUH, established that any family whose members do not participate in the formal labor market will receive $340 per child (as of 2012).[4] Eighty percent of this amount is transferred monthly, and the remaining 20 percent is delivered annually when the family presents documentation to prove school attendance for children older than 5 years of age and a checkup and vaccination certificate for those aged four and younger. According to Rofman and Oliveri (2012), the AUH has not significantly increased its coverage since it was created, remaining at around 3.5 million children since 2009.

This change to the family allowances scheme signaled a profound change in the social protection system because it created a permanent income transfer system that was not linked to an economic emergency. Jointly with the Moratorium, these programs represented a paradigm shift in terms of the design and role of social protection in Argentina because they abandoned the (Bismarckian) principle of contributions as an access requirement, replacing it with a (Beveridgian) scheme based on citizenship as the only condition. The massive inclusion of beneficiaries should have a strong impact on the incidence of poverty and its age profile, inasmuch as social protection programs—both contributory and the new noncontributory initiatives—assist different age groups.

Figure 5.2 presents ANSES expenditures as a percentage of gross domestic product (GDP) for each budget category. Between 1998 and 2012, social security benefit expenditures grew by 50 percent as a percentage of GDP, increasing from 4.9 to 7.4 percent. This is the result of various factors, among them the increase in benefits, first discretionarily and subsequently through an automatic

Figure 5.2 National Social Security Administration Expenditures by Budget Category, 1998–2012

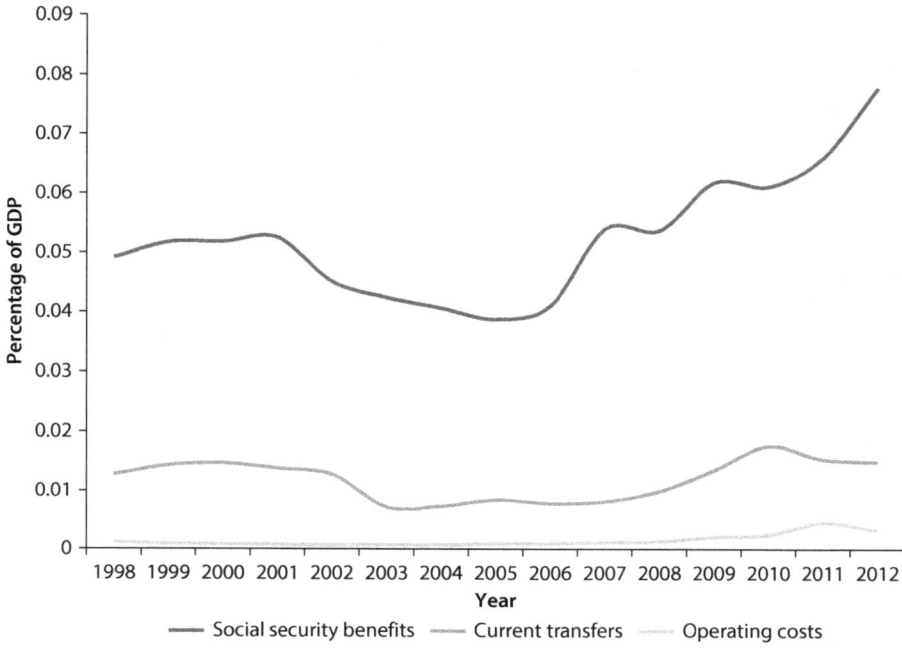

Source: Elaboration based on ANSES and the Treasury Ministry.

update mechanism; and the inclusion of 2.7 million beneficiaries through the Moratoria. The latter signified an average expenditure increase of 2.1 percent of GDP between 2008 and 2012.

In the same way, following a period of contraction, the transfers exhibit a significant increase beginning in 2009 (27 percent) associated with the implementation of the AUH, which, on average, was equivalent to an additional effort of 0.5 percent of GDP.

Social Protection and Poverty

The gap and the incidence of poverty before and after taxes and transfers can be explained, in part, by differences in the taxation systems, but the role of public spending is important. This expenditure allows households to use certain goods and services, such as health care, education, and other general government services, including social protection policies.

The level of poverty is affected by labor and social protection policies because salaries, independent workers' income, and social protection transfers constitute the principal sources of income among Argentine households. The main goal of social protection programs is to replace labor income, ensure a base level of income or consumption, and even promote the accumulation of human capital.

It is possible to identify the association between the social protection programs' specific goals and the age of beneficiaries. More specifically, whereas pension programs are targeted at the elderly population with the goal of replacing labor income during old age, family allowances are designed to increase the disposable income of households that care for children. In between, we find transfers for unemployment insurance (contributory and noncontributory) targeted at young adults with employment problems.

The aforementioned resource distribution pattern gains significance as we consider poverty's heterogeneous profile depending on the household life cycle. The evolution of the poverty profile by age follows the pattern of transfers and consumption throughout the life cycle, during which we can identify three periods. In the beginning, during childhood, individuals face a deficit inasmuch as their expenditures are higher than the resources that they generate. In effect, in this stage, people are not able to generate their own income and rely on the adults in charge to finance their consumption. Subsequently, during the second stage, as a result of their entry into the labor market, their income can surpass their level of consumption, enabling them to generate savings and accumulate assets. Finally, as they pass through the third stage, a period of disaccumulation of assets occurs that is frequently associated with the retirement of the heads of household from the labor market.

This division into three periods has significant consequences for the analysis of the incidence of poverty, insomuch as depending on where an individual is in the life cycle the determinants of poverty will vary, as will the potential policies for combating it. For example, although the incidence of poverty during the first period could be a consequence of null or low resources generated during childhood, an individual that is just above the poverty line during the second period, when he or she is economically active, could present a more worrying case because of the fewer years remaining to save and accumulate assets to fund the third period.

Various authors have estimated the potential impact of income transfer programs on the incidence of poverty and the income distribution in Argentina (Gasparini and Cruces 2010; Rofman and Oliveri 2012), generally considering each program individually. These works usually use the Continuous Household Survey as an information source, identifying beneficiaries of some programs (such as the social security system) when possible or estimating their numbers by applying the eligibility criteria to the survey population (in the case of the AUH). These analyses show that the transfers have positive effects, on both poverty and equity, although in some cases with very limited significance. In all cases, the estimates do not include the effects on the behavior of household members related to the transfers, which are assumed to be static regardless of the presence or absence of the transfers. As a result, the analysis is unavoidably biased, but it allows researchers to identify the existence of trends related to the studied effects.

Figure 5.3 Persons in Poor Households, by Age Group and Type of Transfer, 1998 and 2012

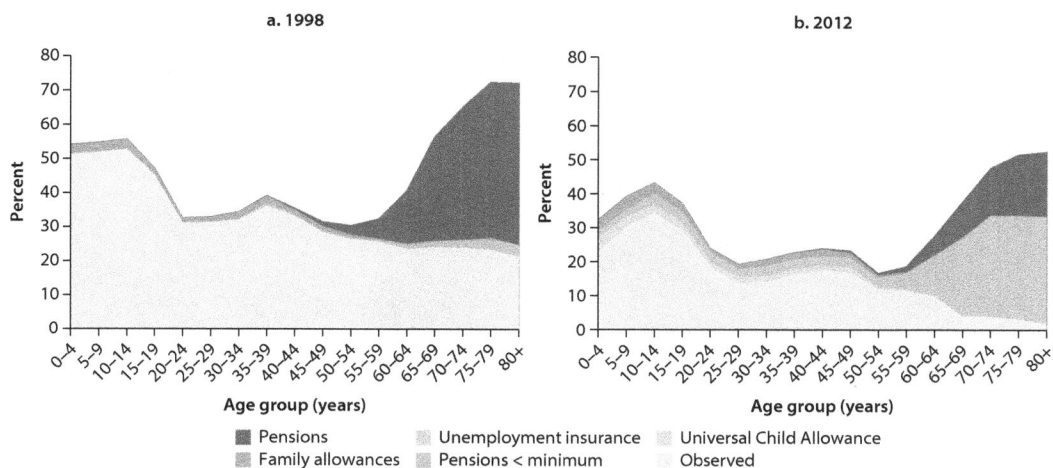

a. 1998

b. 2012

Age group (years)

Pensions   Unemployment insurance   Universal Child Allowance
Family allowances   Pensions < minimum   Observed

Source: Elaboration based on EPH-INDEC.
Note: AUH = Universal Child Allowance.

Adopting a similar methodology, here we evaluate the aggregate impact of social protection policies.[5] We subsequently present the potential impact that social protection as a whole had on the incidence of poverty by age among the population during 1998 and 2012.

Figure 5.3 presents, for 1998 and 2012, the percentage of people in poor households by age group, identifying the impact that eliminating each type of transfer program would have. Thus, it is evident that in 1998 poverty affected 36.7 percent of the population, but if transfer programs had not existed, this level would have reached 43.4 percent. The principal program that affects the poverty level is the pensions system, and as a result, the simulated impact was concentrated on the elderly population. In 2012 the incidence of poverty was significantly lower (18.8 percent) than the level recorded in 1998, a difference that was observed among all age groups. Here again, the importance of income transfers from the social protection system stands out, because without these programs the proportion of individuals belonging to poor households would have reached 29.7 percent. This impact is greater than that observed in 1998; the change is associated with the expansion of social protection coverage through noncontributory programs.

Nonetheless, in future discussions the results uncovered should be analyzed in the context of the household. In other words, given that poverty is a household concept, the analysis related to the life cycle and the incidence of poverty should contemplate not just the individual's life cycle, but also that of the household itself.

Figure 5.4 presents the poverty gap, that is, the average percentage of income needed to reach the value of the poverty line, by age group and type of transfer.

Figure 5.4 Poverty Gap, by Age and Type of Transfer, 1998 and 2012

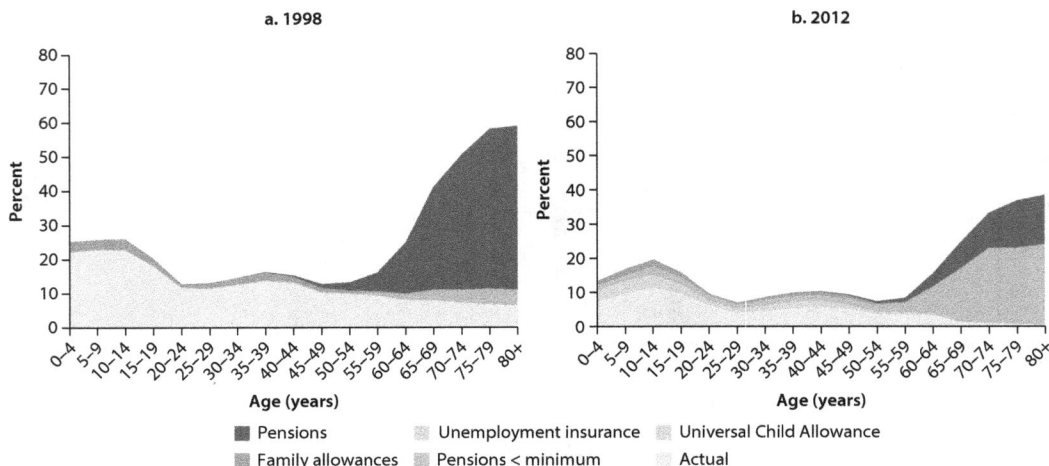

a. 1998

b. 2012

Age (years)

- Pensions
- Family allowances
- Unemployment insurance
- Pensions < minimum
- Universal Child Allowance
- Actual

Source: Elaboration based on EPH-INDEC.

In 1998 those individuals living in poverty needed, on average, 12 percent of the value of the poverty line to reach it. Moreover, poor children had a gap of 21 percent, and young adults and the elderly exhibited gaps of 11 and 7 percent, respectively. Figure 5.4 helps highlight the importance of social protection programs not just in reducing the incidence of poverty, but also in reducing the gap for persons whose income remains below the poverty line. This is particularly noticeable among the elderly, a group that without transfers from the social security system would have maintained an average gap of 51 percent in 1998 and 36 percent in 2012. In terms of family allowances the effect is important, but less significant. This type of transfer increases the income available in young households. For this reason, its impact on both poverty reduction as well as the gap is evident not only among children, but also among young adults.

The role that the two programs implemented during the last decade played in expanding social protection coverage is clear in figures 5.3 and 5.4. The AUH had the effect of reducing total poverty by approximately 1.7 percentage points, with an expected concentration among children and the young adult population, enabling a potential reduction of poverty of between 3 and 1.2 percentage points, respectively. Along with contributory family allowances, this program facilitated a joint reduction of 3.4 points, with the greatest effect felt among children (6.0 points). Even though the potential impact on the incidence was notable, it also enabled a reduction of the gap by 7 percent, targeting its effect on children and young adults—14 and 6 percent, respectively.

In terms of the elderly, the impact of the Moratoria (29 points) is added to the impact from the traditional contributory pension system (15 points). The expansion of social security coverage, through the Moratoria, signified the integration of a large number of the elderly that had been excluded from receiving a social protection transfer and enabled them to rise above the poverty line.

Social Protection Beneficiaries in 2010

In this section, we present an approximation of the beneficiary profile of the social protection programs, based on estimates made from information from the Continuous Household Survey and adjusting these values as a function of the data from ANSES' administrative records.[6] Figure 5.5 presents the beneficiary profile for social protection by age and type of transfer received in 2010.

Argentine social protection is characterized by its concentration of benefits on the two most vulnerable age groups in terms of income: children and the elderly. In 2010 a little more than 6.7 million children were beneficiaries of family allowances, with 48 percent receiving contributory benefits and 52 percent the AUH. For their part, pension benefits reached not only the elderly, but also other age

Figure 5.5 Beneficiaries, by Social Protection Program and Age, 2010
thousands

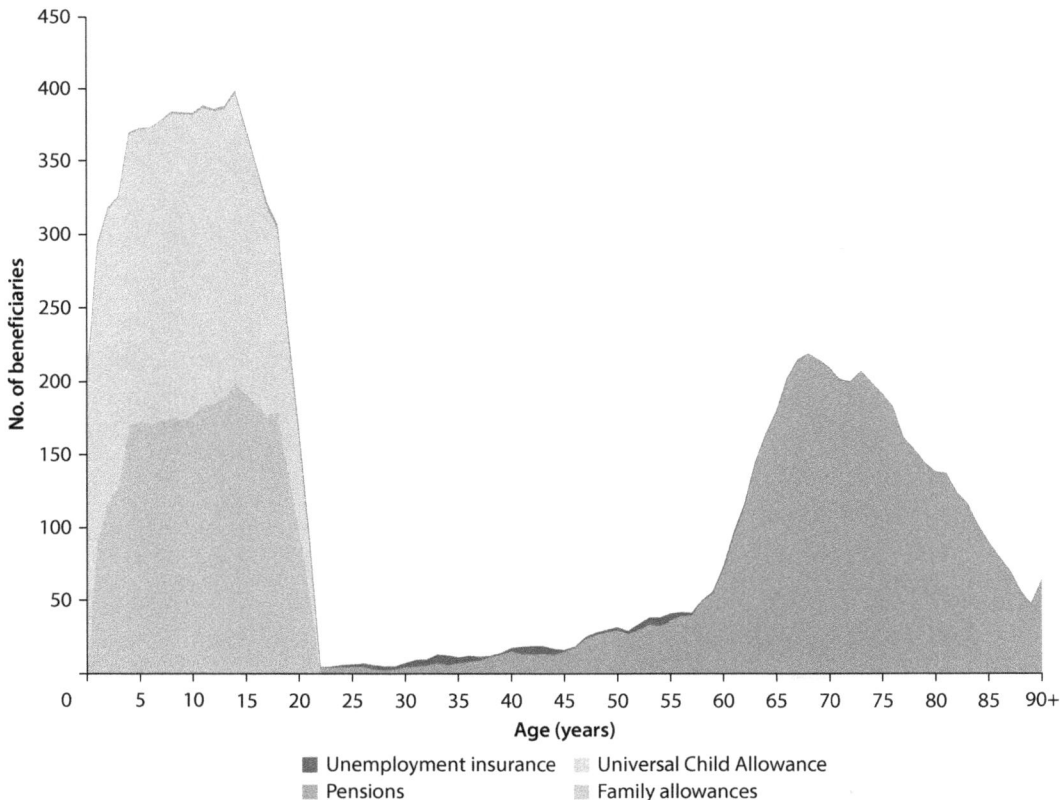

Legend: ■ Unemployment insurance ▨ Universal Child Allowance ■ Pensions ▨ Family allowances

Source: Elaboration based on information from INDEC and the MTEySS.

groups because the pension system offers entitlements not just for retirement, but also for disability pensions and survivors benefits. However, the largest concentration of beneficiaries was among adults older than 60 years of age.

In 2010 monetary transfers from social protection (consolidated national-provincial), excluding operating expenses, reached $156.4 million, equal to 10.8 percent of GDP. On the basis of the distribution of beneficiaries by age group, figure 5.6 presents the profile of total transfers from social protection by age group and type of program in 2010.

Seventy-two percent of social protection expenditure is concentrated within the population of adults older than 60 years of age, basically explained by transfers for pensions. In turn, children younger than 18 years of age receive 15 percent of social protection spending. This asymmetry in the distribution of social protection resources is associated with the difference in the average benefits paid by each program. In the month of December 2010, the average social security benefit was $1,359, and per-child family benefits and the AUH were set at $220.

Although total social protection expenditure by age exhibits a strong bias in favor of the elderly, the effect is even more notable if one considers per capita

Figure 5.6 Total Expenditure on Social Protection, by Age and Program, 2010

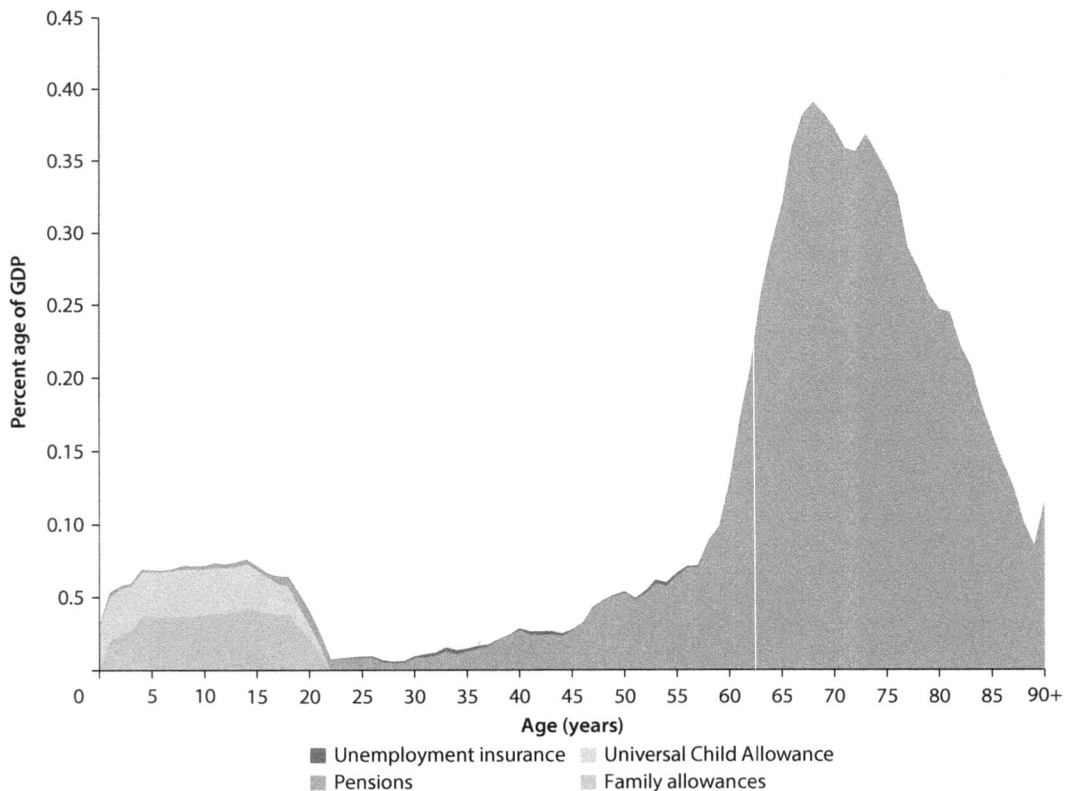

Source: Based on information from INDEC, Treasury Ministry, and MTEySS.

As Time Goes By in Argentina • http://dx.doi.org/10.1596/978-1-4648-0530-1

Figure 5.7 Annual Expenditure Per Capita on Social Protection, by Ages and Programs, 2010
Current AR$

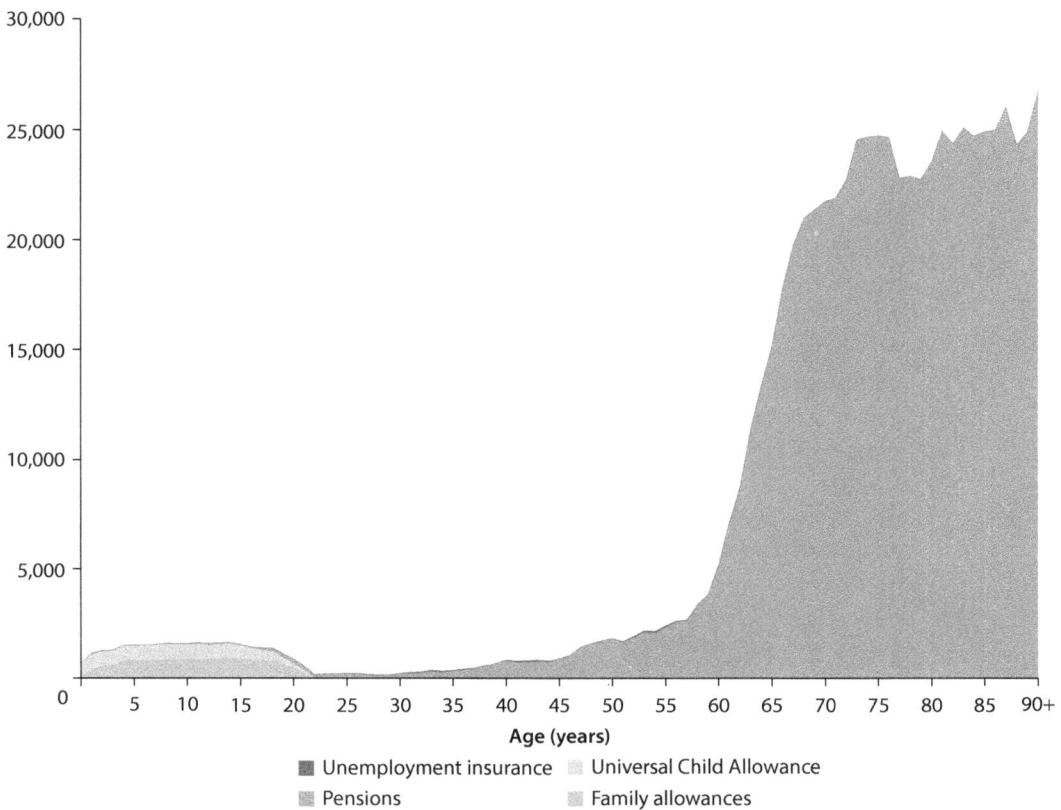

Source: Elaboration based on information from INDEC, Treasury Ministry, and MTEySS.

expenditure. Figure 5.7 shows a strong bias in expenditure for the elderly, who, on average, receive transfers worth some 10–15 times the value of those that children and youth receive. This difference is explained by the combination of the high value of retirement benefits relative to transfers to children, as well as greater coverage among the elderly.

The differences reflected in figure 5.7 give rise to a debate about the system's intergenerational equity. This debate has two dimensions. On the one hand, in terms of the period, it is clear that the elderly strongly benefit from these transfers, although it is possible that part of this difference is compensated for through intrafamily transfers (i.e., the elderly use part of these resources to fund the consumption of their children and grandchildren). Even if this were the case, it is worthwhile to question the reasonableness of a social protection policy with such a strong bias.

On the other hand, in a cohort analysis it would be possible to view this apparent inequity as not so significant. The principal arguments in favor of this point would be that (1) all groups pass through childhood and old age during their life cycle, thus eventually all will benefit from this model, and (2) the elderly who are currently receiving these benefits have made contributions both via contributory social security systems and through their work and general tax payments throughout their lives, so these transfers basically represent the fruits of their labor during decades past.

This last argument is associated with the idea that pension benefits consti- tute deferred salary income. Given the current configuration of the pension system, financed by both salary-based contributions and general tax revenue, both formal and informal workers have made contributions as a way of post- poning some of their income from their economically active period for their retirement period. In any case, it would appear that beyond the normative discussion of intergenerational equity that these data should spark, it seems that it is important to also consider the question of efficiency. Even if we assume that the cohort focus is more appropriate and, therefore, the intergen- erational transfers are less, it would be worthwhile to consider the effectiveness in terms of promoting human capital accumulation and economic and social development of waiting until the final stages of life for the bulk of transfers of public resources to households. A transfer earlier in the life cycle could facili- tate the accumulation of human capital through, for example, greater spending on education, which would redound in better living conditions throughout the life cycle, including during old age.

The Impact of Demographic Trends and Public Policy Assumptions

In the current section, we present simulations of predicted expenditures on mon- etary transfers for social protection for the period 2010–2100 based on some long-term behavioral assumptions for some variables.

The first proposed scenario supposes the continuity of the four programs considered (pensions, unemployment insurance, contributory family allowances, and the AUH) in their current condition and with current rules. Under this assumption, it is expected that there will not be any significant changes in the last three programs in terms of eligibility or the value of benefits (which are assumed to be constant relative to salaries). In contrast, however, the mere appli- cation of the current rules will have a significant effect on pension coverage.

As we pointed out earlier, trends in labor formality, combined with the reforms in access requirements for retirement benefits in recent decades, signi- fied a declining trend in pension coverage that would have continued if the Moratoria had not been implemented. In an analysis of medium- and long-term trends, Grushka (2011) predicted that if the current rules were maintained,[7] the percentage of the elderly receiving retirement benefits or a pension would fall uninterruptedly to near 50 percent in 2040. After that, and assuming a continu- ous increase in the rate of labor formality of approximately 0.3 percent per year,[8] a recovery would begin, reaching a coverage level of 69 percent in 2100.[9]

On the basis of the aforementioned assumptions, and considering the demo- graphic projection presented in chapter 2, the percentage of the elderly covered

Figure 5.8 Percentage of Adults Older Than 65 Years of Age with Income from Retirement Benefits and/or Pensions, 2010–2100

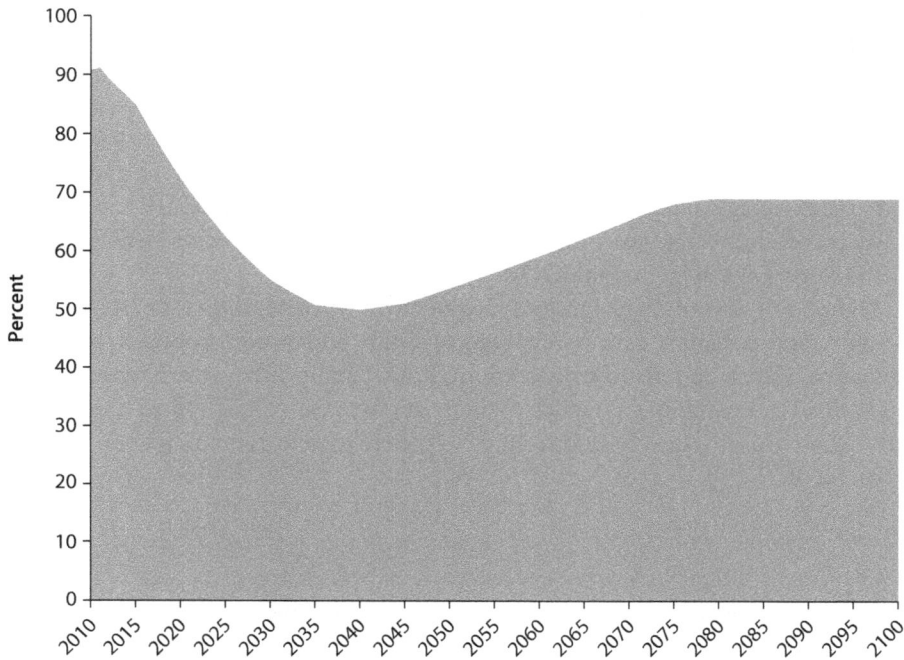

Source: Based on Grushka 2011.

by the pensions system would exhibit a reduction until around 2040 and after that point would recover at a constant rate (figure 5.8). The reasons behind this behavior are partly because the starting point of the analysis includes the significant impact of a program that is assumed to have closed after 2012 (the Moratoria), which will gradually fade in importance. Near the midpoint of the predicted period, we can expect that the predicted improvements in labor formality will foster increasing pensions coverage among the elderly.

Eligibility requirements and the difficulties in developing the formal labor market allow us to foresee a significant reduction in pension coverage in the coming decades, with a growing proportion of the elderly without access to retirement benefits or a pension. In this context, it appears reasonable to expect that political and social pressures in favor of the implementation of normative reforms that will ease access to benefits will increase during this period.

Consequently, an alternative scenario that is interesting to evaluate is the possibility of establishing additional benefits that recognize some level of compensation for individuals who contributed to the pensions system for a minimum period of time or who did not join the formal labor market. For example, it is possible to model an alternative scenario that includes allocating a basic benefit, set at 66 percent of the current average benefit, that is distributed in such a way as to maintain coverage of the elderly at 90.8 percent. To predict the cost of this additional benefit, it is necessary to determine the total number of persons entitled to such a benefit. This number of beneficiaries emerges as the difference between contributory coverage and the desired level of coverage.

On the basis of these projections for coverage, the financial effort required to pay these benefits is simulated below. Given that we prefer to prioritize a long-term vision and the structural analysis of the social protection system under relatively stable conditions, we chose to present a scenario in which GDP and salaries grow according to the assumptions described in chapter 4, while benefits grow at the same pace as per capita GDP.

Figure 5.9 presents the projected trajectory of expenditure on retirement benefits and pensions as a percentage of GDP under the proposed coverage scenarios. Given the assumptions adopted, the main difference between both scenarios is the system's coverage, which in one case would follow the trajectory shown in figure 5.8, but in the other would remain stable around 90 percent.

Figure 5.9 Projection of Total Expenditure on Retirement Benefits and Pensions, 2010–2100

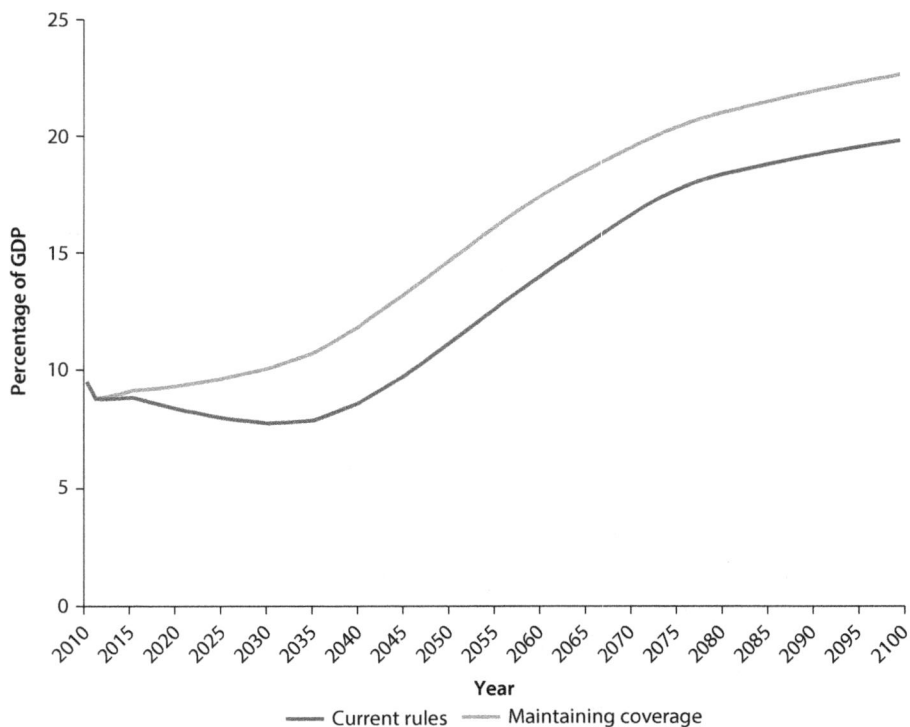

On the basis of our assumptions, if the current rules are not modified, the aging process will not affect social security expenditure until the middle of the century because the increasing elderly population will be offset by decreasing coverage. Beginning in 2040, when coverage will begin to recover because of projected increases in labor formality, expenditure will also increase and will reach approximately 18 percent of GDP by 2100. In contrast, if a policy were adopted that guaranteed a benefit of at least 66 percent of the average contributory system benefit for 90 percent of the population, the increase in spending would be apparent immediately and would reach 21 percent of GDP by 2100.

The projected evolution of expenditures in the other programs follows demographic trends; we do not assume any changes in coverage or benefit levels. Thus, figure 5.10 shows how the trends in family allowances, both contributory and noncontributory, will decline, given the reduction in the relative size of the population of children and adolescents. This will not occur in the case of unemployment insurance because the participation rate among the economically active population will remain stable. Of course, the relative importance of

Figure 5.10 Estimate of Expenditure on Family Allowances, Universal Child Allowance, and Unemployment Insurance, 2010–2100

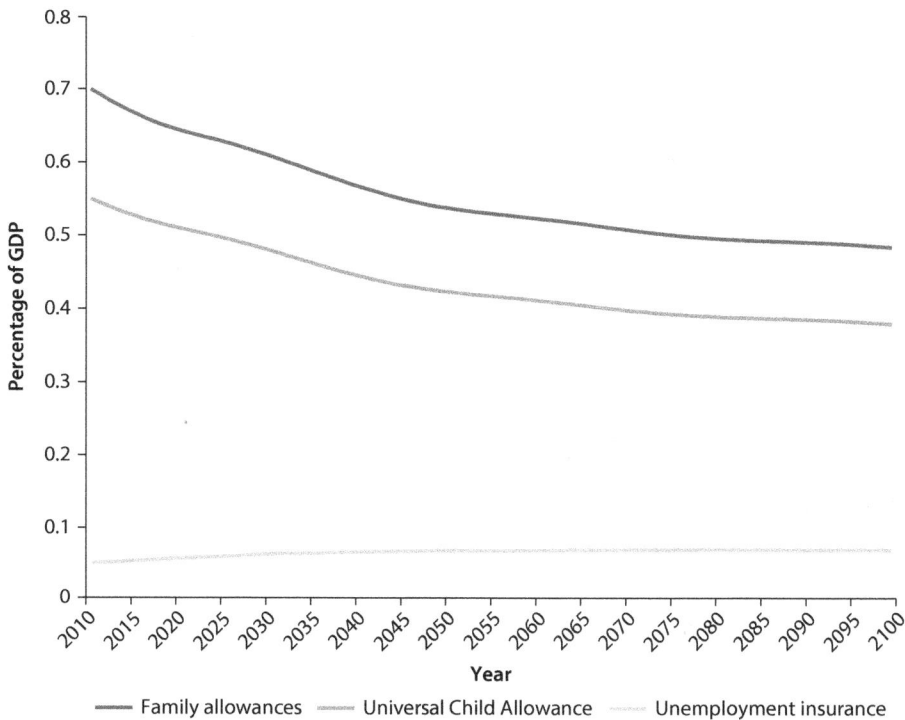

Figure 5.11 Projection of Total Social Protection Expenditure, 2010–2100

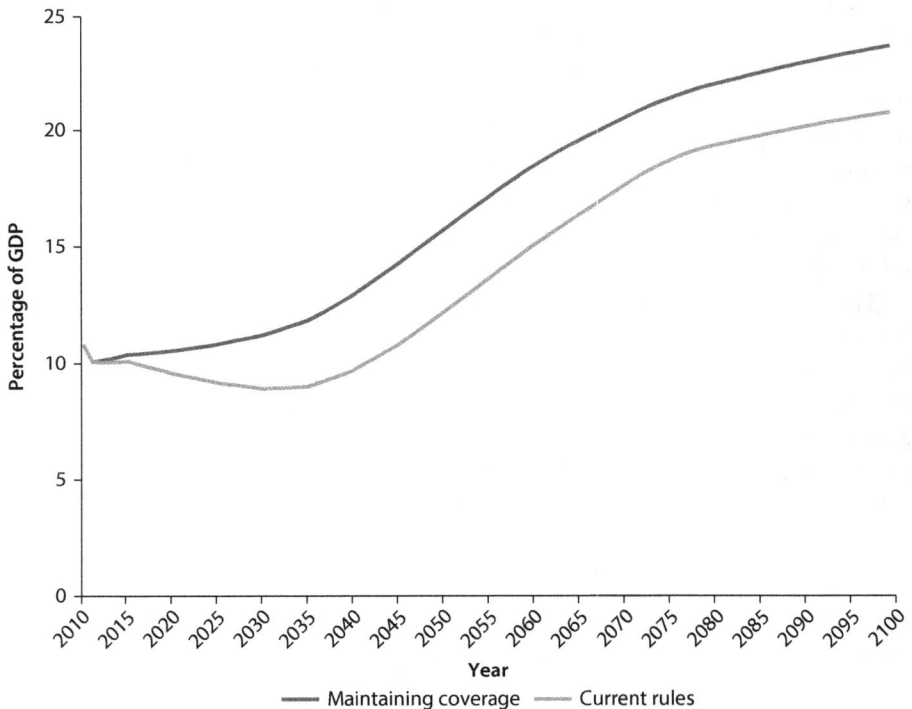

Year

—— Maintaining coverage ——— Current rules

expenditures for these three programs will continue to be minor (and will even decrease) relative to pensions spending.

Finally, figure 5.11 shows that total expenditure in the sector (i.e., including all four programs), which in 2010 reached 9 percent of GDP, will follow an increasing trend in any scenario in the coming decades. If the current rules are maintained, it will reach 19 percent of GDP; under an alternative scenario that sustains current coverage levels, it could reach 21 percent of GDP. In any case, it is clear that this spending will represent a significant demand for fiscal resources that the state must confront by combining various sources of alternative financing.

Final Reflections

Both the actuarial sustainability of the Argentine social protection system (i.e., its ability to maintain a flow of contribution funds sufficient to finance the flow of benefits) as well as the fiscal sustainability (the state's capacity to generate sufficient resources to fund promised benefits) will depend on different factors.

On the one hand, as we have seen in this chapter, the demographic transition process toward an older population creates pressure as a larger portion of the population is dependent on income from others. On the basis of our simulated results, it is evident that population aging has a direct impact on the level of monetary transfers made by the social protection system. In 2012 society spent around 10 percent of GDP on monetary transfers on the following group of social protection programs: family allowances, unemployment insurance, AUH, and the pension system.

Under various alternative pension coverage scenarios, the demographic transition process would lead to an increase in future social protection expenditures, reaching 15 percent of GDP during the 2050s and surpassing 21 percent in 2100.

Under any scenario, beginning in the mid-2030s, a period of growing demand for spending could begin. This situation is the result of the end of the demographic dividend and the resulting increase in the number of retired elderly persons relative to the economically active young adult population. In other words, the *baby boomers* from the 1970s and 1980s will be elderly by the 2040s–60s, increasing the financial requirements for sustaining their consumption.

However, some changes in personal behavior could smooth, and even offset, the effect of aging on the dependency of the elderly population. As analyzed in chapter 10, the dependency ratio is a static indicator, insomuch as it is defined by the age of the population. Nonetheless, age is not a determinant of a worker's decision to retire from the labor market. According to information from CELADE, a continuous increase in the economic participation of the elderly is predicted, especially among workers ages 65–79. This behavior represents a natural increase of the retirement age and thus removes financial pressure from the social protection system.

In any case, the medium- and long-term social protection policies (especially in terms of social security) cannot wait for a possible evolution of the dependency ratio. The situation demands an adequate forecast of outlays and sources of funding. Currently, the Argentine social security system is funded in part with contributory resources (contributions based on payroll), although it also requires alternative sources of financing, especially those coming from tax revenues. The practice of using funds other than those collected from the system to fund pension commitments has been in place for decades, and even though labor formality increased in the last ten years, there is still a high percentage of persons working informally.

The discussion presented in this chapter focused on the problems of coverage and fiscal sustainability of social protection programs in the medium term, showing that both dimensions face important challenges in the coming decades. The principal challenge will be finding mechanisms that, institutional definitions and the selection of responsible parties in management processes notwithstanding, facilitate the ability to maintain a social protection scheme that can replace income for those who lose it, whether as a result of old age, disability, or labor market dynamics, and to limit the risk of falling into poverty for these individuals and other social groups.

As Time Goes By in Argentina • http://dx.doi.org/10.1596/978-1-4648-0530-1

These mechanisms must be sustainable, not just from a fiscal point of view (i.e., the state must be able to fund the commitments it assumes in the short and medium term), but also from an economic one because expecting that the necessary transfers will take place outside public institutions will not solve the problem if the financing needs are substantial. In this context, it appears essential to ensure, on one hand, that there is sustained economic growth that guarantees that per capita GDP remains stable or increases even in the context of an increasing total dependency ratio, and moreover that institutional arrangements to deal with the demographic and social changes in the country are put in place.

Notes

1. See, for example, Rofman et al. (2008) or Secretariat of Social Security (2005).

2. As we were writing this chapter, the National Government changed the limit year to 2004.

3. The number of benefits includes retirements and pensions, from both the public regime and the capitalization regime, which was eliminated in 2008. It is important to note that this number does not represent the total number of beneficiaries because there is a significant number of beneficiaries that receive more than one benefit (for example, a person might receive a normal retirement benefit in addition to survivor benefits).

4. The amount was originally $180.

5. Starting with an estimate of the incidence of poverty according to the methodology applied in Argentina since 1988 (using the poverty line that has been adjusted since 2006 based on the Santa Fe consumer price index), we estimated the incidence of poverty both including reported or estimated payments from transfer programs in household income and not including them. In this way, we obtained an estimate of the impact of these programs on poverty.

6. The Continuous Household Survey does not specifically ask whether respondents receive family benefits. Thus, this population was identified indirectly based on the programs' eligibility criteria. Gasparini and Cruces (2010) and Rofman and Oliveri (2012) propose various scenarios in which either formal independent workers or students in private schools or with no schooling are excluded. Retirees, pensioners, and the beneficiaries of unemployment insurance are identified based on their direct declarations regarding receiving income from retirement benefits, pensions, and unemployment insurance, respectively.

7. Specifically, relating to the requirement to make contributions for 30 years to receive retirement benefits.

8. The assumption used here indicates that this increase takes place in the context of a strongly bimodal distribution in terms of the accumulation of contribution years during the economically active period.

9. The assumptions adopted by Grushka (2011) are similar to those used by Coppini (2000) and Thullen (1995) and, with some differences, to those adopted for Argentina by Rofman et al. (1997) and Grushka (2002).

References

Bertranou, F., and D. Bonari. 2005. *Protección social en Argentina. Financiamiento, cobertura y desempeño, 1990–2003*. Geneva: International Labour Organization.

Coppini, M. A. 2000. *Técnica de los seguros sociales*. Vols. 1 and 2. International Social Security Association, Ginebra.

Gasparini, L., and G. Cruces. 2010. "Las Asignaciones Universales por Hijo en Argentina. Impacto, discusión y alternativas." *Económica* 56: 105–46.

Grushka, C. 2002. "Proyecciones previsionales de largo plazo." Argentina, 2000–2050. Special Studies Series? Also, cf. under Rofman et al. 1997: Series Estudios Especiales. 14, Superintendence of AFJP, Buenos Aires.

———. 2011. "Evolución y perspectivas del SIPA." Draft, Universidad Nacional de General Sarmiento, Buenos Aires.

Isuani, E., and J. San Martino. 1995. "El nuevo sistema previsional argentino. ¿Punto final a una larga crisis?" Boletín Informativo Techint 281, Buenos Aires.

Moreno, J. M. 2012. "(Las partes del) sistema de protección social federal de Argentina." Draft.

Rofman, R., and L. Oliveri. 2011. "Las políticas de protección social y su impacto en la distribución del ingreso en Argentina." Serie de Documentos de Trabajo sobre Políticas Sociales 6, World Bank, Washington, DC.

———. 2012. "Un repaso sobre las políticas de protección social y la distribución del ingreso en Argentina." *Económica* 58: 92–123.

Rofman, R., C. Grushka, and V. Chevez. 2001. "El Sistema de Asignaciones Familiares como herramienta central en la política social Argentina." Paper presented at the VI International Congress of the Latin American Center for Development Administration, Buenos Aires, November 5–9.

Rofman, R., G. Stirparo, P. Lattes. 1997. "Proyecciones del Sistema Integrado de Jubilaciones y Pensiones 1995–2050." Serie Estudios Especiales 12, Superintendence of AFJP, Buenos Aires.

Rofman, R., L. Luchetti, and G. Ourens. 2008. "Pension Systems in Latin America: Concepts and Measurements of Coverage." Discussion Paper SP 161, World Bank, Washington, DC.

Secretariat of Social Security. 2005. "SIJP Actuarial Financial Valuation, 2005/2050." Ministry of Labor and Social Security, Secretariat of Social Security publications series, Year II, Buenos Aires.

Thullen, P. 1995. *Técnicas actuariales de la seguridad social. Regímenes de las pensiones de invalidez, de vejez y sobrevivientes*. Ministry of Labor and Social Security, Spain.

CHAPTER 6

Aging and Challenges for the Argentine Health Care System

Daniel Maceira

Introduction

The impact of aging on the health care system is a classic topic of discussion in the health sector that has regained some of its vigor in recent years. This debate includes three key elements that exert pressure on the health care model and are relevant to Argentine society. They are connected to both the country's relative success in caring for its population's health—with the resulting impact on the epidemiological profile—as well as external factors that require that additional resources be allocated to the sector.

The first of these key elements is a demographic environment in a country with improved living conditions. The population pyramid's slide, age group by age group, toward an older society is driven by a longer life expectancy at birth and a drop in the fertility rate, both characteristic of more developed nations.

The second element is associated with the epidemiological transition. Developing countries move beyond mortality profiles linked to infectious diseases to make room for cardiac problems and tumor-related ailments. On many occasions, unequal income distribution leads to the coexistence of both scenarios, a phenomenon known as epidemiological accumulation.

Finally, the third factor involves the need for greater resources to be invested in the health care sector: Constant technological change in diagnostics and treatments, preventative medicine, and the development of new drugs increase the quality of life and the ability to fight illnesses, with an impact on the financial mechanisms for health care coverage. The demand phenomenon encouraged by the health care system itself pushes the trend in the same direction, promoting increased spending.

Looking beyond the relative weight of each of these factors and the interactions between them, it is evident that the health care system, even as it implements efficient and equitable prioritization mechanisms and effective resource use, envisages a horizon of growing needs for funding and organization in the system.

These requirements will generate a public policy debate, not just throughout the life cycle, but also across generations.

Argentina spends approximately US$1,200 per person per year to fund health care, making it one of the highest-spending middle-income countries for this sector. Evaluating the achievements and the coming challenges from a population-aging point of view means that we must review some of the health care system's strengths and identify characteristics to keep in mind in any future action plan.

The analysis of such challenges is reflected not just in the tensions normally found in terms of the fragmentation of the insurance system, the existence of inequality in access to certain treatments, and differences among social groups and provinces. There is also a need to discuss the presence of new sectorial demands now and in the future to plan initiatives that facilitate a systematic approach to deal with them.

All of these arguments are challenges for social coverage policies in health care in that they identify and reveal new needs. These needs are not only pertinent in terms of entitlement to access to health care, promotion, prevention, and care, but also because they require that mechanisms to prioritize health care actions be coherent and rational. Integrating these new topics into the health care system will present a challenge to the system's financial capacity.

The second section of this work offers a brief description of the situation of the Argentine health care system. The third section completes this analysis with a comparison of health care indicators in the regional context. The fourth section defines, based on the earlier discussion, the themes of the analysis to move toward an estimation of the determinants of the health care system's financial requirements. These results start with the population and gross domestic product (GDP) growth projections estimated in chapter 2 and include elements linked to the epidemiological change and the impact of economic growth on prescription and health care spending patterns. Next, we discuss the policy instruments designed to satisfy Argentina's existing needs, an analysis of the tools currently in use, and the potential improvements to others that would enable economic growth and social protection in health care. In particular, the discussion concentrates on cancer prevention policies, public initiatives dealing with nutrition, and the development of normative instruments to promote appropriate responses from lenders and service providers in terms of health care policies from the life-cycle perspective. Finally, we offer a policy discussion that emphasizes the implications on equality and efficiency for the proposed approach. A discussion of long-term care, which overlaps with the general health care discussion, is presented in chapter 7.

Salient Features of the Argentine Health Care System

Organization of the Health Care System

The health insurance system in Argentina is based on two pillars. The first is a public health care subsystem associated with a supply subsidy structure that is designed to care for the lower-resource population. This structure exhibits broad geographical coverage, with hospitals and primary care clinics managed primarily at the provincial and municipal levels throughout the country.

The second component is the coverage of the formal social protection system, through the social security health insurance system (Obras Sociales), both provincial plans (OSP) and national plans (OSN). As a whole, this second block covers approximately 60 percent of the country's total population, a proportion that surpasses the Latin American average. In the rest of the region, the relative weight of formal employment is markedly less (Maceira 2010).

The social insurance subsystem also includes the National Institute of Social Services for Retirees and Pensioners (Instituto Nacional de Servicios Sociales Para Jubilados y Pensionados, INSSJyPI), which covers a population of between 7 and 9 percent of the entire country. The institute offers a Comprehensive Medical Assistance Program (Programa de Asistencia Médica Integral, PAMI) to the elderly, the only entity to do so in the region, and exercises special influence over the operations of the Argentine health care sector.

In terms of the resources available by subsector, 27 percent of health care expenditure in Argentina corresponds to public institutions, 38 percent to social security institutions, and 35 percent in private spending.[1]

Within the public subsystem, 68 percent of spending corresponds to direct outlays to the provinces and 14 percent to municipalities, demonstrating the high level of responsibility that subnational governments take in funding health care. Just 18 percent of public resources (approximately five of every 100 pesos of the total dedicated for health care) comes from the Ministry of Health.

Table 6.1 reflects this distribution of responsibilities in terms of funding, as well as the distribution of funds within social security. Within this subgroup,

Table 6.1 Health Care Expenditure, by Funding Entity, 2009

Entity	Millions AR$, 2009	%	% of total health expenditure	%, 2009 GDP	%, 2006 GDP
Public and social security health care expenditure	71,152	65	65	6.21	4.59
Public health care	29,420	27	27	2.56	1.91
National	5,378	18	5	0.47	0.31
Provincial	20,046	68	18	1.75	1.35
Municipal	3,996	14	4	0.35	0.25
Social security	41,732	38	38	3.64	2.68
National social security health insurance plans	21,418	51	20	1.87	1.40
Provincial social security health insurance plans	9,967	24	9	0.87	0.70
INSSJyP	10,347	25	10	0.90	0.58
Private household health care expenditure	37,667	35	35	3.29	2.56
Total health care expenditure	108,819	100	100	9.5	7.15

Source: Elaboration based on data from the Directorate of Expenditure and Social Programs Analysis, Ministry of the Economy and Public Finances; Ministry of Health; and the World Health Organization.
Note: INSSJyP = National Institute of Social Services for Retirees and Pensioners; PAMI = Programa de Asistencia Médica Integral.

the PAMI is responsible for 25 percent of the investment in the sector, which is equivalent to 10 percent of the total health care spending in the country.

Public Subsystem

The evolution of public resources over time and across jurisdictions also highlights significant differences. As figure 6.1 illustrates, national public expenditure (including federal agencies, social security institutions, and the PAMI) continued to grow until reaching AR$6 billion in constant pesos of 2001. This amount subsequently fell by about one-third and then beginning in 2002 grew continuously, surpassing AR$13.5 billion pesos in 2009.

Provincial expenditures followed the same trend (ministries and provincial social security health insurance plans), converging at AR$11 billion in the last period of the sample. The municipal level had not yet reached AR$2 billion in health care spending in 2009, although its expenditure had been growing.

On the whole, health care expenditure showed a marked increase, growing from approximately AR$8 billion in 2002 to AR$25.5 billion by the end of the decade.

Despite the primary role played by the provinces in funding public health care, the differences among jurisdictions are extremely important. During 2009, the gap between the province with the highest public per capita expenditure and the one with the lowest was 9.4–1. This gap is reduced to 5.1 to 1 when the analysis is focused on expenditure per provincial social security beneficiary. As figure 6.2 demonstrates, such differences do not necessarily favor those jurisdictions with the greatest relative needs, but rather those that have the greatest ability to spend the money.[2]

Figure 6.1 Public Health Care Expenditure, by Jurisdiction, 1980–2009

Millions of 2001 constant pesos

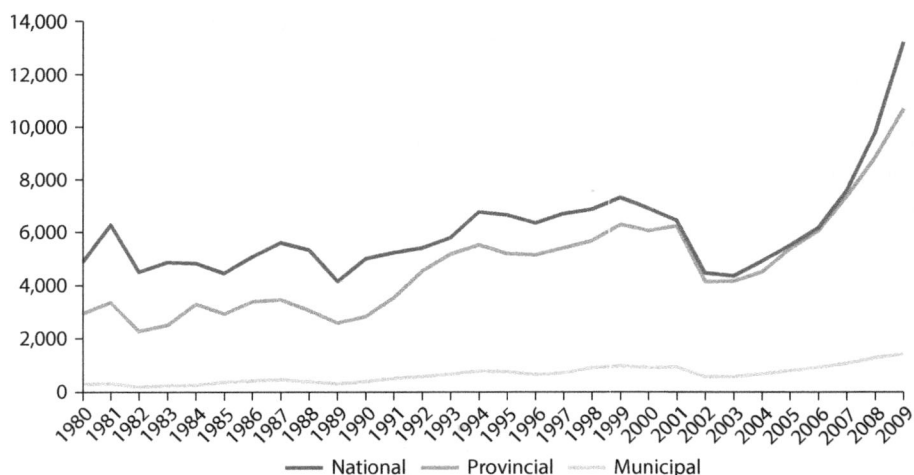

Source: Elaboration based on data from the Directorate of Expenditure and Social Programs Analysis, Ministry of Economy and Public Finances.
Note: National and provincial expenditure on health care includes public care and social security.

Figure 6.2 Provincial Public Sector Expenditure Per Capita and Provincial Employer-Based Health Plans, 2009

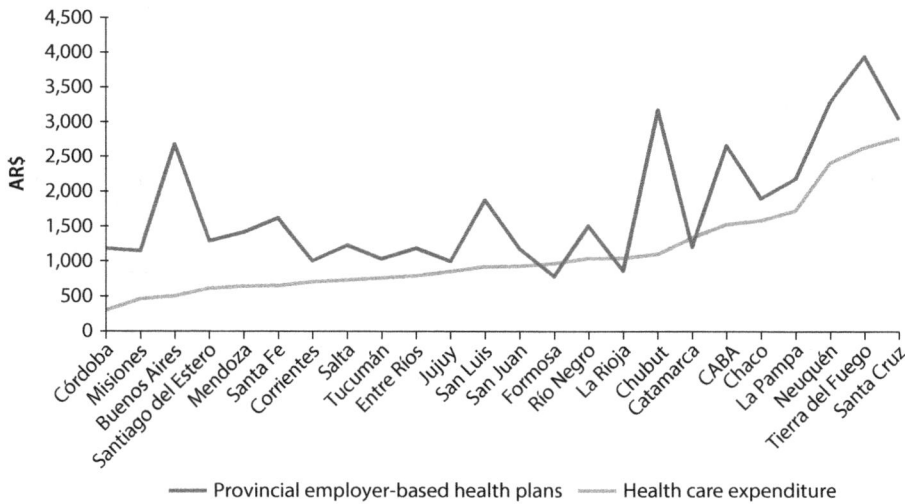

Provincial employer-based health plans ——— Health care expenditure

Source: Based on data from Directorate of Expenditure and Social Programs analysis, Ministry of the Economy and Public Finances.
Note: The estimated population enrolled in provincial employer-based health plans is from 2005.

The growth of public expenditure and the health care funding gap among provinces feed the debate over the determinants of public health care spending and the disparity of allocations within the social protection scheme. It is important to identify the effect of the demographic transition and epidemiology on health care spending, especially from a health and aging point of view, with the goal of contributing arguments to the policy debate.

Employer-Based Health Plan Subsystem

A structure organized with funding from taxes on formal employment facilitates the financial sustainability of the model while strictly linking the health care system to the fluctuations of the labor market. Thus, the labor market directly influences the funding mechanisms for health care entitlements for formal workers and their families.

Formal health care coverage exhibited a significant increase following the 2002 crisis, evidencing nearly double-digit growth rates. The available values (Maceira 2012a; Maceira and Cicconi 2008) show that from 1997 to 2011, the population covered by national employer-based health plans (for both union members and management) increased by more than 50 percent on average.

Comprehensive Medical Assistance Program (PAMI)

Typically, when individuals near retirement age, their family members should make savings plans to protect themselves from health care shocks given a context of weak institutions. In many cases, this situation is aggravated by women's longer life expectancy, with the result that they outlive their husbands and do not have retirement benefits or pensions of their own.

This is not necessarily the case in the Argentine system because it contemplates pension coverage for surviving spouses and has an institution like the PAMI that guarantees coverage for the elderly in cases where they are not covered by any other protection mechanism. This is an indicator of the success of the national social protection system.

The institution is a public entity created by Law 19,032 approximately 40 years ago, called the National Institute of Social Services for Retirees and Pensioners (INSSJyP), and commonly known as the Comprehensive Medical Assistance Program or PAMI. The program was subsequently renamed For an Argentina with Integrated Elders (Resolution No. 654/DE/2009). The law created an autonomous, self-governing, public, nonstate institution with financial and administrative independence.

The organization specializes in care for the elderly based on Argentine society's decision (expressed in the law) to establish a protection system for the elderly through asset contributions (principally) based on services from a specialized health plan that offers them social and health care services (PAMI 2012).

The institution currently has 4.5 million members, mostly retirees and pensioners from the contributory regime, their family members, and veterans from the Islas Malvinas. According to official data, the INSSJyP-PAMI offers coverage to 82 percent of persons older than 65 years of age and to more than 96 percent of persons older than 79 years of age in Argentina. In recent years, the PAMI extended membership to groups of people without a history of contributions to the social security system, increasing its coverage. This was the case for housewives and workers who were underemployed or informally employed during their economically active periods.

Figure 6.3 shows how the PAMI's formal coverage evolved between 2007 and 2012, along with the average budgeted expenditure for each period.

Figure 6.3 Evolution of the Number of Beneficiaries and Budgeted Expenditure Per Capita, 2007–2012

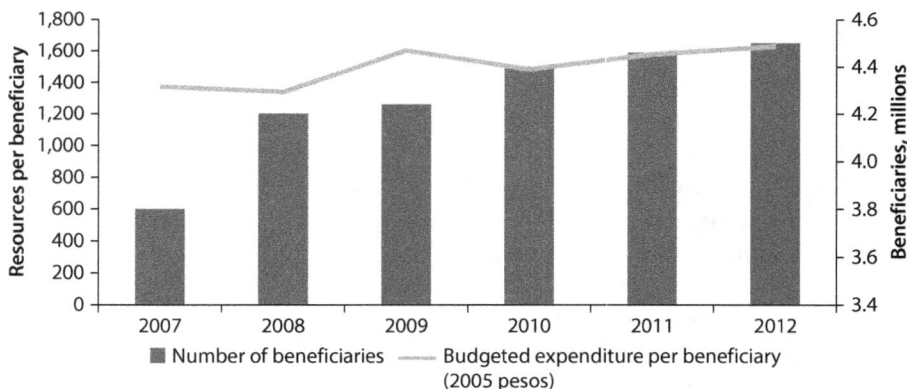

Source: National Institute of Social Services for Retirees and Pensioners Report 2012.

The institution's income comes mainly from the contributory system: 78 percent from contributions by active workers, 4 percent from investments, and 18 percent from contributions by retiree members of the INSSJyP-PAMI.

Regional Factors

An analysis of health care expenditure and GDP per capita in Latin America shows a positive and significant correlation between the creation of wealth and the priority given to the health care sector, as measured in international U.S. dollars per person per year (Maceira 2012b). This link also shows an intuitive association between the creation of greater wealth and better results on indicators such as infant mortality, life expectancy at birth, and the fertility rate, although this correlation has not been shown to be strict. This is the product of the importance of other factors with implications on the population's health, beyond the organization of the health care system, usually presented as social determinants of health, including education level, housing conditions, family situation, etc. A summary of these variables is presented in table 6.2.

Table 6.2 Latin America and the Caribbean, Basic Health Care Sector Indicators, 2009

Country	GDP per capita, USD PPP	Health care expenditure per capita, USD PPP	Total health care expenditure (% of GDP)	Public health care expenditure (% of THE)	Out-of-pocket health care expenditure	Population >65 years (%)	Fertility rate	Life expectancy
Trinidad and Tobago	23,107	1,743	6	48	43	7.1	1.6	70
Bahamas, The	22,644	1,633	7	45	23	7	1.9	75.5
Barbados	18,723	1,456	7	64	29	11.6	1.6	76.7
Argentina	13,202	1,235	10	66	20	10.7	2.2	75.8
Chile	13,033	1,172	8	47	35	9.5	1.8	79
Mexico	12,507	846	6	48	48	6.5	2.3	76.9
Uruguay	11,937	979	7	63	12	13.8	2	76.4
Panama	11,883	1,081	8	72	24	6.7	2.5	76.1
Venezuela, RB	11,190	737	6	40	54	5.8	2.5	54.3
Costa Rica	10,085	1,165	10	67	29	6.7	1.8	79.3
Brazil	9,438	943	9	46	31	7.2	1.8	73.4
Cuba	9,300	503	12	93	7	12.7	1.5	79.1
Colombia	8,250	569	6	84	8	5.8	2.1	73.6
Peru	7,843	400	5	59	31	6.2	2.5	74
Dominican Republic	7,658	495	6	41	39	6.4	2.5	73.4
Ecuador	7,507	503	6	48	45	6.4	2.4	75.6
Jamaica	7,127	383	5	56	31	7.9	2.3	73.1
Suriname	6,931	548	8	49	12	6.5	2.3	70.6
El Salvador	6,020	427	6	60	35	7.1	2.2	71.9
Belize	6,019	355	5	73	27	4	2.7	76.1

table continues next page

Table 6.2 Latin America and the Caribbean, Basic Health Care Sector Indicators, 2009 *(continued)*

Country	GDP per capita, USD PPP	Health care expenditure per capita, USD PPP	Total health care expenditure (% of GDP)	Public health care expenditure (% of THE)	Out-of-pocket health care expenditure	Population >65 years (%)	Fertility rate	Life expectancy
Guatemala	4,283	337	7	37	56	4.4	3.9	71.1
Bolivia	4,206	213	5	63	30	4.7	3.3	66.6
Paraguay	4,107	305	7	43	51	5.2	2.9	72.5
Honduras	3,488	230	6	57	36	4.4	3.1	73.1
Guyana	2,649	258	8	90	10	4.4	2.2	69.9
Nicaragua	2,411	254	10	57	40	4.6	2.6	74
Haiti	1,045	71	6	22	47	4.4	3.3	62.1
Latin America and the Caribbean	9,133	698	7	57	32	7.0	2.4	73.0

Source: World Bank, World Development Indicators, 2009, except Cuba, CIA World Factbook, 2009.
Notes: PPP = purchasing power parity; THE = total health expenditure.

The table also ranks the countries in terms of per capita income, allowing one to observe how the decrease in wealth is accompanied by a reduction in health care spending, lower indicators for life expectancy (around 75 years in the upper portion of the table, higher than the values near 70 in the lower portion), and fertility rate (with extremes of 1.6 in the Bahamas and 3.9 in Guatemala).

At the same time, the link between wealth, health care spending, and improved health results is correlated with lower out-of-pocket expenses for families and a greater proportion of health expenditure originating in the public sector as a percentage of the total. In other words, relatively wealthier countries not only invest more in health care, but they also possess a state with a greater relative participation in funding and regulating the health care system, lowering the proportion of total expenditure that families pay. This results in improved performance in the sector and more satisfactory health results, shifting the life expectancy thresholds and redefining morbidity levels.

This has generated, on the one hand, an increase in the prevalence of illnesses associated with the elderly and a greater relative proportion of these illnesses in terms of years of potential life lost corrected for morbidity. Figure 6.4 shows how the epidemiological transition in Latin America has evolved, revealing the greater relative weight of years of potential life lost associated with noncommunicable diseases (NCDs), although high variability exists in the region's interior.

In the particular case of Argentina, approximately 75 percent of the years of potential life lost is associated with NCDs (chronic illnesses, cancer, and cardio-vascular illnesses), while around 17 percent of the years of potential life lost are related to communicable diseases.

The country's evolution over time relative to countries with similar epidemiological patterns shows a certain relative lag in terms of life expectancy at birth, although there are greater advances related to the infant mortality rate (figure 6.5). In the first case, Argentina—at 76 years—shows an increase of nearly

Figure 6.4 Epidemiological Profiles in Latin America and the Caribbean

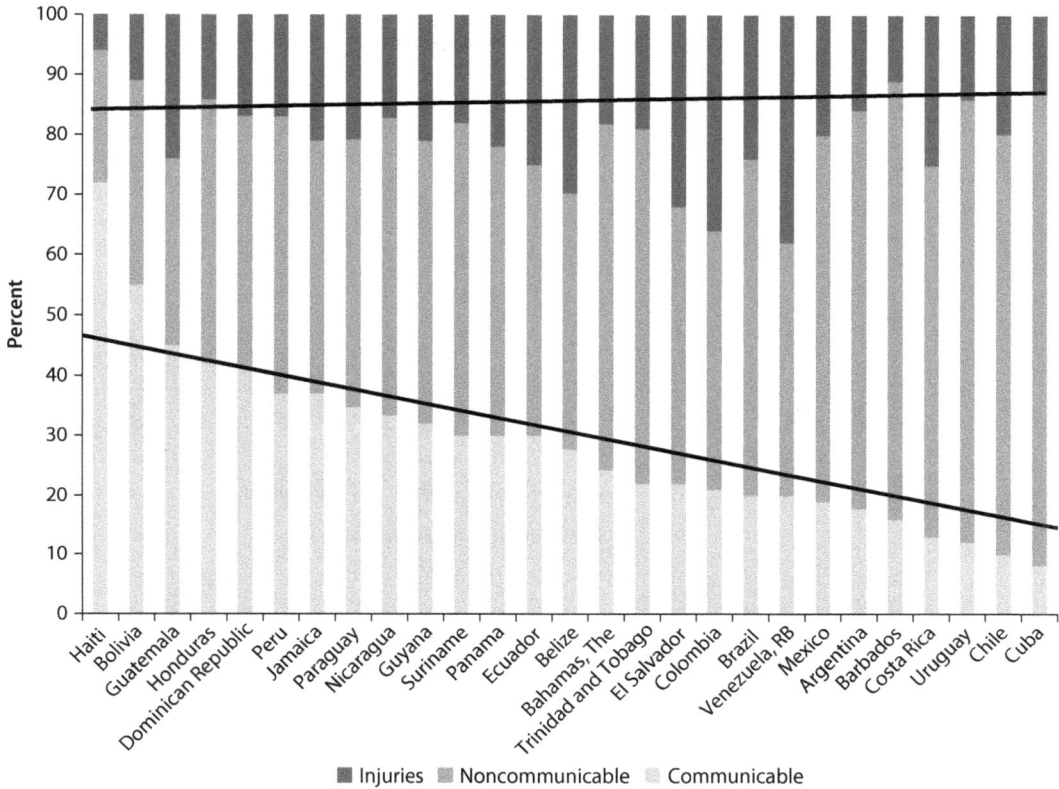

Source: WHO, Global Health Observatory, 2008.

5 percent between 1995 and 2012, slightly less than in Chile, where in the final year, values reached levels similar to those in Costa Rica at around 79 years. The infant mortality rate in the country decreased by 39 percent during the same period of analysis (1995–2012), more than in Costa Rica (−34 percent) and Chile (−32 percent). This dynamic suggests Argentina's values will converge with those of its regional peers during the next four or five years.

This case of epidemiological accumulation (having a systematically greater proportion of NCDs relative to overall illnesses, while still maintaining a significant volume of communicable diseases) creates a challenge for health care policy planning in that it forces a debate regarding resource allocation and defining priorities.

The regional outlook possesses an analogue within the country. Table 6.3 summarizes various economic, demographic, and health indicators for the 23 Argentine provinces and the Autonomous City of Buenos Aires. The gross geographic product per capita column is used to rank the provinces, with the relatively wealthier jurisdictions in the upper rows (primarily the federal capital and the Patagonian provinces), while those located in the northeast and northwest are located near the bottom.

Figure 6.5 Mortality Indicators in Argentina, Chile, and Costa Rica, 1995–2010
Per thousand live births

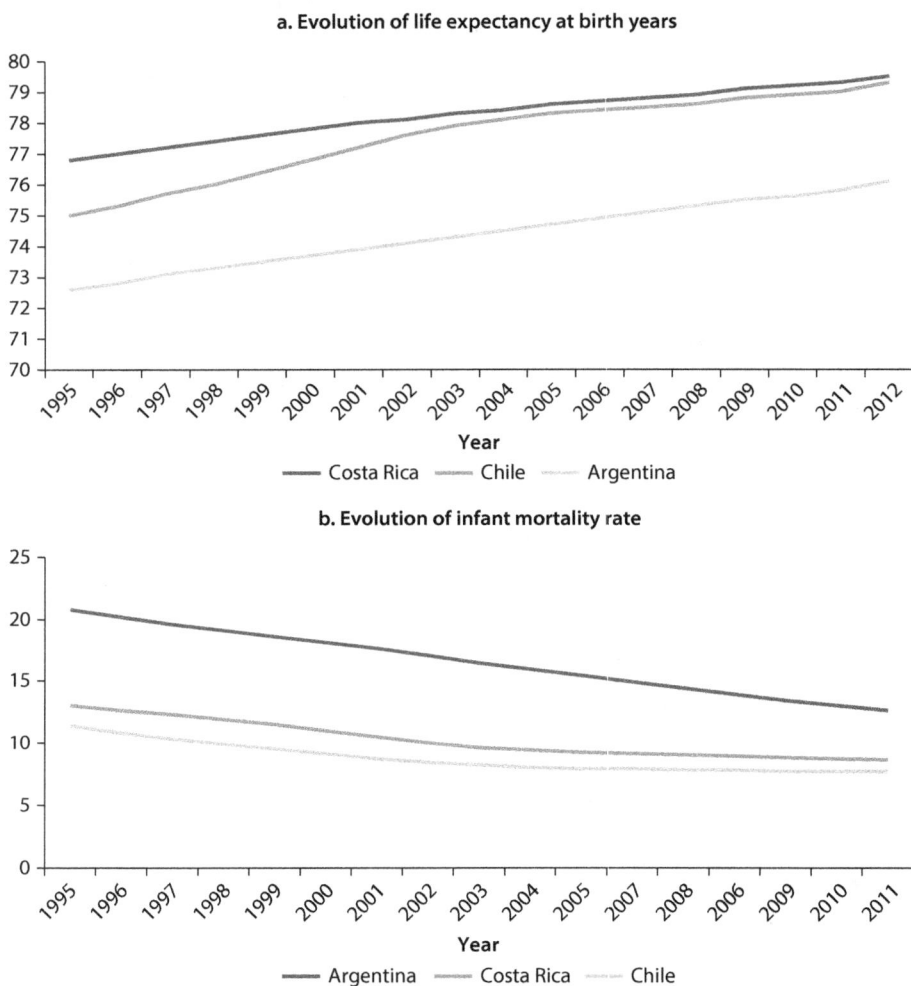

a. Evolution of life expectancy at birth years

— Costa Rica   —— Chile   —— Argentina

b. Evolution of infant mortality rate

— Argentina   —— Costa Rica   —— Chile

Source: Level & Trends in Child Mortality. Estimates made by the UN Inter-agency Group for Child Mortality Estimation (UNICEF, WHO, World Bank, UN DESA, UNDP).

The more rural jurisdictions and those with lower levels of formal coverage are concentrated near the bottom of the table, where the epidemiological profiles identify a greater presence of infectious diseases. At the opposite extreme, the weight of tumor-related diseases is markedly above average, as well as lower rates of infant mortality and a greater proportion of the elderly in the total population of the province.

From the comparative analysis of Latin American countries, one observes that the income difference between extremes (Argentina–Haiti) is 12.63 times, with a gap in the occurrence of infectious diseases of 7:1, and the life expectancy of the highest performing country is 15 years greater than in the lowest. In Argentina's interior the income gap is significantly high and resembles the regional profile (11.1:1).

Table 6.3 Argentina: Economic, Epidemiological, and Demographic Indicators, by Province

Provinces	GDP per capita	Population[a]	% rural population[b]	% employer-based health plan coverage	Infant mortality[f]	Life expectancy at birth[d]	Cardiac causes	Tumor causes	Infectious causes	% population <5 years (1)	% population >65 years (1)
							— Potential years of life lost every 10,000 inhabitants[e]			% population	% population
CABA	92,293	2,890,151	0.0	44	8.8	75.91	95.92	119.73	46.14	5.7	16.5
Tierra del Fuego	56,850	127,205	2.9	55	7.1	74.84	54.97	73.74	29.31	9.0	4.0
Santa Cruz	49,178	273,964	3.9	61	9.7	72.93	58.63	123.88	75.85	9.7	6.2
Neuquén	47,280	551,266	11.4	50	7.5	75.24	43.54	102.82	34.9	9.1	6.7
Chubut	40,019	509,108	10.5	56	10.2	72.16	60.51	123.1	46.95	8.9	7.7
Santa Fe	33,176	3,194,537	10.8	46	10.8	74.17	63.65	115.84	38.9	7.5	11.9
Catamarca	30,200	367,828	26.0	51	14	73.38	68.56	57.9	53.3	8.8	7.3
Buenos Aires	26,816	15,625,084	3.6	47	11.8	73.99	94.32	109.88	69.77	8.3	11.0
Córdoba	25,913	3,308,876	11.3	47	10.8	74.9	84.33	95.32	34.94	7.9	11.6
Mendoza	22,707	1,738,929	20.7	50	9.7	74.95	66.07	100.46	26.45	8.9	10.4
Entre Ríos	20,714	1,235,994	17.5	52	11	74.08	68.03	116.3	43.11	8.1	10.4
Misiones	19,291	1,101,593	29.6	43	13.7	72.69	96.87	86.85	66.53	10.3	6.2
San Luis	15,836	432,310	12.9	47	12.3	74.06	69.12	94.84	45.02	8.8	8.3
La Pampa	15,486	318,951	18.7	52	10.4	74.78	67.76	113.76	42.27	8.0	11.1
Río Negro	14,565	638,645	15.6	50	6.6	73.86	59.85	108.07	34.08	8.4	8.9

table continues next page

Table 6.3 Argentina: Economic, Epidemiological, and Demographic Indicators, by Province *(continued)*

Provinces	GDP per capita	Population[a]	% rural population[b]	% employer-based health plan coverage	Infant mortality[c]	Life expectancy at birth[d]	Potential years of life lost every 10,000 inhabitants[e]			% population <5 years (1)	% population >65 years (1)
							Cardiac causes	Tumor causes	Infectious causes		
San Juan	13,631	681,055	14.0	42	9.9	73.63	71.33	93.12	38.95	9.7	8.7
Corrientes	13,565	992,592	20.6	39	15.7	72.03	62.99	101.4	53.42	8.9	7.6
La Rioja	12,542	333,642	16.9	48	16.5	72.54	54.79	83.32	60.06	8.8	6.7
Tucumán	12,079	1,448,188	20.5	45	14.1	72.42	73.78	80.66	41.29	8.9	7.8
Chaco	12,041	1,055,259	20.3	33	11.4	69.97	64.87	112.67	101.86	9.1	6.7
Salta	10,806	1,214,441	16.6	40	14	71.88	59.59	83.09	117.26	10.0	6.5
Jujuy	9,979	673,307	15.0	41	12.9	72.5	46.1	76.08	62.13	9.0	7.1
Sgo del Estero	8,581	874,006	33.9	33	11.7	71.53	60.64	75.67	82.33	9.8	7.2
Formosa	8,305	530,162	22.3	35	21.2	70.8	80.95	85.34	116.88	9.4	6.2
Total		40,117,093	10.6	46	11.7	73.77	80.93	104.25	59.5	8.3	10.4

Sources:
a. INDEC, 2010 census.
b. INDEC, 2001 census.
c. Ministry of Health of the Nation, Dirección de Estadística e Información de Salud, Vital Statistics, 2011.
d. Ministry of Health of the Nation, Basic Indicators, 2000–2001.
e. Ministry of Health of the Nation, Basic Indicators, 2012.
Note: CABA = Autonomous City of Buenos Aires.

However, the health care gap is lower: four times in terms of infectious diseases between Tierra del Fuego and Salta (the provinces at the two extremes), and the difference in life expectancy is almost six years between the two extremes.

Advanced epidemiological profiles and the greater proportion of the elderly in the population pyramid are associated with the presence of new technologies and drugs that are able to treat the population afflicted by sicknesses associated with aging, the greater proportion of NCDs, as well as the presence of the so-called new diseases.

These new illnesses are mainly products of behavioral changes by individuals, including problems associated with nutrition and addictions (tobacco, alcoholism, drug addiction), as well as illnesses linked to pollution, poor treatment of the environment, etc.

The relative weight of these recent illnesses as a proportion of the total is increasing and represents a new challenge, not just for the health care system, but also for the criteria used to train health care workers.

Distribution of Coverage, Determinates of Expenditure, and Projections

Predicting health care expenditure requires that one account for the fact that individual and family behavior patterns are not homogeneous. These patterns are subject to income structures, not just in terms of spending capacity, but also depend on perceptions of needs for health care goods and services related to well-being, which differ according to coverage and available information.

On the whole, relatively richer countries allocate more resources to health care, because they have been able to increase their population's average life expectancy. Their epidemiological profiles also require different types of investments than they did when communicable diseases were more prevalent. Moreover, the utilization of technology occurs more frequently, and the perception of quality of coverage requires new procedures. Obviously, the supply of innovation in treatments, medicines, and diagnostic studies validates these demands.

The segmentation of coverage in the Argentine health system requires that the expansion of its different components be approached separately. The effects of each of the potential determinants of expenditure are not necessarily homogeneous among subsystems. Thus, we propose to capture these differences by estimating them separately, creating a weighted sum for the group during a second stage. In addition, this mechanism will facilitate the calculation of future expenditure, as a result of the identification of the potential impact of each factor individually (income, aging, epidemiological change).

To make this task possible, we relied on information about three different segments of health care expenditure: public provincial spending (which in the aggregate will give us the public total nationally), the corresponding spending for provincial employer-based health plans (which will resemble the rest of social security institutions), and families' out-of-pocket health care spending.

The information sources cover spending undertaken by the respective health care authorities and come from the Ministry of Economy and Public Finances of the Nation, Secretariat of Fiscal Relations with the Provinces for a period of 15 years up to 2009. The out-of-pocket spending figures are gathered from the 2005 National Household Expenditure and Consumption Survey performed by INDEC.

We assume that the resource utilization patterns in the public sector do not necessarily resemble those that we see in social security, given that the former produces many public goods for health care (regulation, prevention, communication) and focuses on providing services to lower income groups. In contrast, social security provides coverage mainly to individuals and families with formal jobs, who are able to contribute resources to funds that will cover their eventual needs for health care services, and not just receive care when a need must be attended to. In addition, we estimate the determinants of out-of-pocket spending separately. Recognizing the possible differences between subsectors should help us obtain a more plausible consolidated expansion pattern.

As a first step, each of them will be estimated using least squares multivariate econometric models. Second, the coefficients obtained separately will be used to expand the level of expenditure by subgroup for the period 2010–2100, for which we will use the population and GDP growth trajectories presented in chapters 2 and 4. Third, we will proceed to sum the results obtained for each year, weighing each of them according to the relative weight corresponding to the different health care subsystems.

In each of the three cases, we estimated the determinants of expenditure, based on four arguments: the growth of the population, population aging, epidemiological change, and income growth. The final argument attempts to explain the changes in spending associated with new technologies, greater incentive to spend, and increased need to consume health care goods and services as part of a revealed need, and including comfort. The provincial population, the percentage of the population older than 65 years of age, and the gross geographic product indicators were chosen as explanatory variables, using the 2001 National Population and Housing Census as the source for the first two, and the Ministry of Economy and Public Finances for the last one. To capture the epidemiological transition gap, a rate calculated in the following manner was added to these indicators: the years of potential life lost from heart- and tumor-related illness as the numerator, and the impact of infectious diseases on causes of death in the denominator. This rate used data produced at the provincial level from the Health Ministry and the Pan American Health Organization.

In the annex, a descriptive summary of the information used is presented (table 6A.1), along with the corresponding regressions for public expenditure and social security (table 6A.2), and the estimate of out-of-pocket spending (table 6A.3). The coefficients calculated in each case show the incidence of each of the arguments identified in the determination of spending.

The elasticities presented in table 6.4 were calculated based on the average of each variable and obtained based on the coefficients from the econometric estimates. They show the effects in percentages of a one percentage point increase in the explanatory variable on health care expenditure for each case (public expenditure, social security, and out-of-pocket). In all cases, the results of the estimates and the associated elasticities show the expected results: Greater expenditure is linked with larger population and an increase in the number of elderly persons (whether in absolute terms or as a proportion of the total). An epidemiological profile characterized by a higher prevalence of chronic and noncommunicable illnesses (in the numerator of the indicator) operates similarly to a spending trigger, inasmuch as an alternative variable from the health care profile, tested based on the infant mortality rate, is correlated with pushing spending in the same direction.

The application of these coefficients to the expenditure profile estimated in chapter 3 allows one to recalculate the elasticities for each year of the series, generating a cumulative effect for each one of the variables. In this way, the individual effects of epidemiological factors, aging, and income growth are added to the projections proposed in chapter 4 based on the growth of the population until 2100.

Table 6.4 also provides information on two relevant features: the impact of the formal coverage structures and an estimate of the implications of different age groups on health care expenditure.

In the first case, the response of expenditure to formal coverage by employer-based health plans (third and fourth columns) reflects a progressive link between financial health care protection through social insurance and the level

Table 6.4 Estimated Elasticities for Expenditure by Health Care Subsector

| | Elasticities (%) | | | | |
| | Public health care expenditure | | Employer-based health plan expenditure | | |
	Estimated model 1	Estimated model 2	Estimated model 1	Estimated model 2	Out-of-pocket expenditure
GDP per capita (2009 prices)	1.308	1.216	0.738	0.719	
Population	1.077	1.077			
Epidemiological profile[a]	1.423		0.367		
Infant mortality rate		0.825		0.312	
Beneficiary population of provincial employer-based health plans			0.281	0.265	
Proportion older than 65 years of age	3.324	2.533			
Population older than 65 years of age			4.962	5.039	0.169
Income					0.573
Coverage					−0.209
Younger than 14 years old					−0.053
Household members					0.014

Source: Based on results from the tables presented in the annex.
a. Incidence of noncommunicable diseases divided by communicable diseases in years of potential life lost, corrected for morbidity.

of spending. This relationship, discussed in the literature, is supported by two arguments. On the one hand, the structure for provision permits larger outlays associated with health care: Need is translated into care. However, this also implies a greater possibility of inducing demands and health care expenditure that are not necessarily effective. Together, they drive institutional expenditure in the same direction, which is verified by the results of the econometric exercise. In addition, the analysis of the last column shows the elasticities defined by the individual determinants of out-of-pocket health care spending. As a counterpart to the previous argument, formal coverage reduces individual spending (as a result of the increase in financial protection).

To the second feature, and of particular relevance for this study, we verify that in all the cases the effect of the population older than 65 years of age on the total is the most powerful determinant impacting the level of expenditure. This evidence supports the classic argument that observes growing health care expenditures associated with age. In the same direction, the presence of elderly in the household increases the risk of financially catastrophic shocks, as is presented in the following pages. In this way, the greater proportion of the population that is elderly increases the sector's needs for funding and is evidence of the need to invest in interventions which promote healthy aging. This argument will be discussed in greater detail in the section on policy predictions.

Concurrently, an additional variable was explored in the regression of household out-of-pocket spending associated with the age structure: Isolating the scale effect (number of household members) and the presence of formal coverage, the impact of the presence of minors younger than age 14 years on out-of-pocket spending is negative and not statistically significant. As such, the trajectory of health care spending throughout one's life tends to increase, nearing the parameters identified in the analyses of developed countries.

Finally, in the Latin American comparison, presented earlier, Argentina exhibits a proportion of elderly adults older than 65 years of age of 10.7 percent of the total population, higher than the regional average of 7.7 percent and the fourth highest in the region, behind Uruguay, Cuba, and Barbados (13.8, 12.7, and 11.6 percent, respectively).

Each family of elasticities by subsector is weighted by the relative weight of the corresponding expenditure as a portion of the total (table 6.1), in such a way as to be able to sum the group to calculate total expenditures for public health care and social security, separating it from private spending on health care.[3]

Figure 6.6 shows the estimated trajectory of public health care and social security spending based on the estimates presented in chapter 4, accompanied by the new calculations, which highlight the complementary effects discussed above. In this scenario, total social expenditure on health care exhibits an increase that is disproportionate over the years relative to the scenario of demographic change as the only trigger of cost, representing some $300 million in additional costs for the final projected period.

The argument that accompanies this projection is that an increase in the population increases average health care expenditure and that this occurs

Figure 6.6 Public and Social Security Health Care Expenditure: Original Projection and Corrected Projection Including the Effects of Epidemiological Change and Growth, 2010–2100

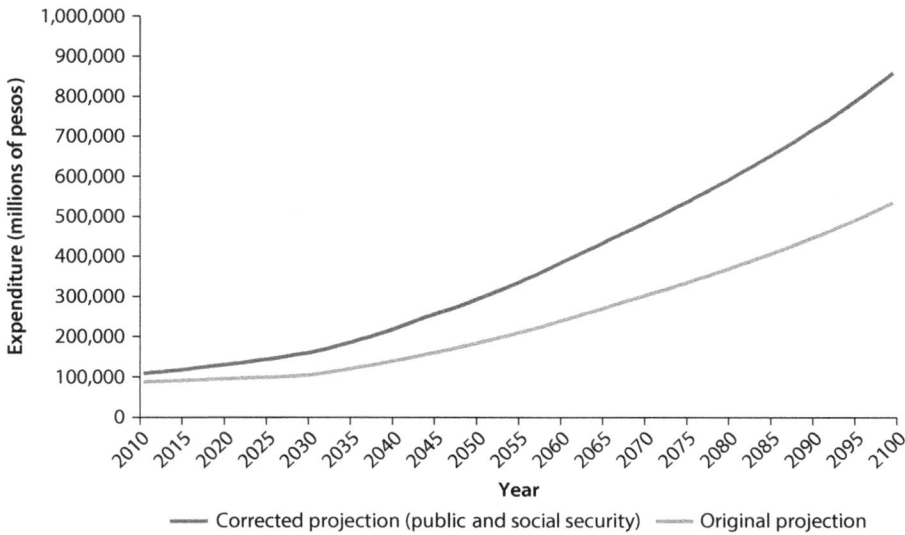

disproportionately when such demographic growth originates in a population possessing an epidemiological profile with a persistent bias toward NCD, and with a relatively greater portion of the population of adults older than 65 years of age. Similarly, as a society's average income increases, it demands more health care, the expected quality of services increases as new technologies are introduced, and their inclusion in the system facilitates the development of demand induction. On the whole, expenditure is expected to increase throughout the life cycle along with income, as has been evidenced in countries with greater relative economic development.

The particular nature of the Argentine case—and perhaps the Latin American pattern—with respect to the projections for European nations is the existence of severe inequalities in income distribution. In the medium term, income gaps will cause the epidemiological accumulation to develop mixed patterns of health care expenditures. Medium- and high-income groups who enjoy continuous income growth will follow the pattern observed in more economically advanced nations and will eventually reach their type of consumption. If poverty reduction policies are successful, this phenomenon will capture more and more of the total population. Alternatively, the dual model will persist over a longer period of time. These trends will be revisited in the following section, through predictions of the impact of specific policies on the sector.

The trends calculated here affect the proportion of public and social spending on health care in terms of total GDP, as figure 6.7 reflects. On the basis of the same projections, a disproportionate increase is also seen in terms of the health

Figure 6.7 Public and Social Security Health Care Expenditure: Original Projection and Corrected Projection Including the Effects of Epidemiological Change and Growth, 2010–2100

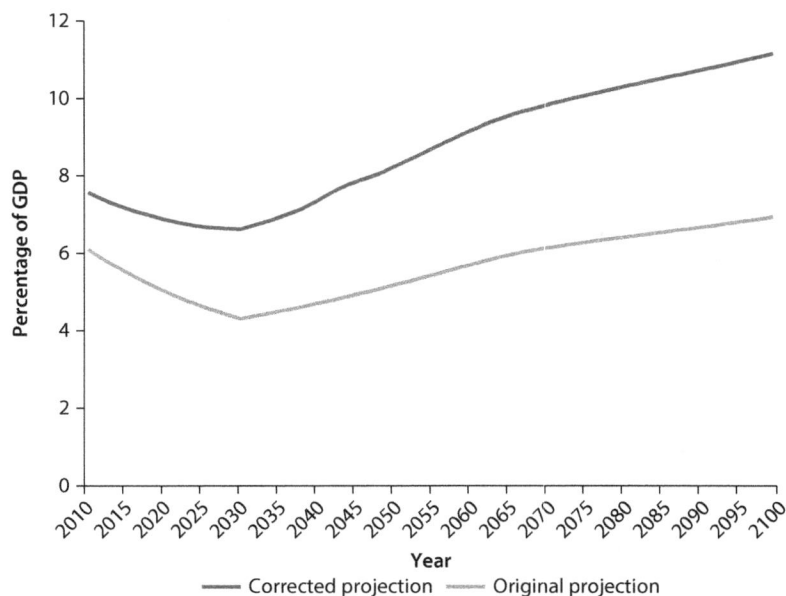

care expenditures by public or social sources only, reaching 11 percent in 2100, while total spending (including the private sector) has not currently exceeded 10 percent of GDP.

Policy Predictions

The definition of an inclusive strategy for health care in an aging population such as that observed in Argentina requires that one consider a spectrum of interventions that facilitate a rational regulatory policy that incorporates technology, initiatives that promote the systemic management of NCDs, while not neglecting the development of healthy habits among the population.

The following section proposes dealing with these varying aspects by examining the international literature and using it as a way to identify the arguments to be analyzed in the context of the national health care system.

Regulation of Service Packages

In line with what has been presented in this book, Mulligan et al. (2006) suggest that the coming decades will present dramatic changes in the needs of the population in developing countries. According to the authors, while developing countries are still under pressure combating communicable diseases (HIV, malaria, and tuberculosis in particular), an increase in mortality from NCDs is evident, including conditions such as depression, coronary diseases, and cancer.

These illnesses replace infectious diseases as the most prominent causes of sickness and premature death. Factors associated with rapid urbanization in cities and industrialization have been implicated in the increase of neuropsychiatric disorders such as depression, among others.

Even though estimates of the present and future patterns of illness have firmly placed NCDs on the agenda, they do not provide guidelines for dealing with them. If the decisions that officials and policymakers will consider refer to the use of limited resources, it is necessary to know which of the interventions available are the most efficient and equitable to apply them.

However, the use of these capacities in the definition of decision-making mechanisms, the establishment of priorities, and impact measurement is still not widely disseminated, even for relatively standardized topics such as performing cost-effectiveness studies. According to Hutubessy et al. (2003), occasionally there are political causes, social preferences, and systemic barriers that limit their implementation.

In the same vein, in 2000 the World Health Organization emphasized the role of cost-effectiveness analyses in identifying which interventions generate the best results given available resources. However, the greater the spectrum of interventions to be compared, as is the case for epidemiological accumulation, the lower the probability that the results that come from these analyses will be combined.

This strategy of analysis, measurement, and establishment of intervention guidelines should also be sensitive to the type of service provider or subsystem. However, it is important to maintain the ability to present recommendations that standardize clinical criteria among providers, recognizing the differences among them, not just in effectiveness, but also in available resources. Because technology is frequently seen as a determinant of the cost of services (Cohen and Hanft 2004), research applied to health care, especially the discipline of health technology assessments, has increased the importance of being able to adequately inform decision makers about the costs and benefits of including innovations.

In Argentina, the national state is home to a group of institutions with the capacity to establish regulatory structures with a broad reach that, beyond their function as funders, define insurance, provision, and organization strategies for services as well as far-reaching behavior guidelines.

In particular, the Superintendence of Health Care Services is responsible for, among other things, defining, analyzing costs, and complying with the Compulsory Medical Program (Programa Médico Obligatorio, PMO), a broad set of entitlements that must be complied with by all national social security institutions (National Social Security Health Insurance Plans) and prepaid medical firms, that is used as a standard of care, in content and price, for provincial social security institutions.

In this way, the PMO provides a far-reaching mechanism for allocating resources, establishing care and coverage strategies, and promoting a trend toward equality between the social and private insurance systems in the country. The required cost and design criteria imply the inclusion of factors linked to epidemiological aspects and the structure of the provider market. The inclusion of mechanisms that capture the differences among the provinces and regions leads to a more efficient allocation of resources, insomuch as it incorporates the epidemiological prevalence and health care coverage of each subnational jurisdiction.

Similarly, the PMO as a regulatory instrument offers the opportunity to regulate the vast majority of public and private providers in Argentina, making it one of the most important health care policy instruments in the country.

Strengthening the PMO and similar instruments requires that they be given greater flexibility to face the differing needs and health and demographic profiles, as well as a rigorous methodological framework and the ability to be updated systematically based on technological evaluation institutions.

From a systemic point of view, the PMO is a regulatory instrument with a highly expansive potential to incorporate efficiency and equality into the system, especially in the face of scenarios contemplating the epidemiological and demographic changes discussed in these pages, offering signals to funders, providers, and users regarding contracting, prescription, and health care behavior guidelines.

Noncommunicable Diseases

The epidemiological and demographic transition in recent decades has generated an increase in so-called NCDs, principally cardiovascular disease, diabetes, cancer, chronic respiratory disease, and injuries from external causes. In total, these NCDs account for more than 70 percent of the deaths in the country (Ministerio de Salud de la Nación 2011). The sustained growth of these diseases around the world threatens the future response capacity of health care systems. Argentina is not an exception to this reality. The addition of NCDs to infectious diseases is confronting the health care system with significant challenges in dealing with this "double burden" of illnesses.

In 2009 the Argentine Ministry of Health approved and began to implement the National Strategy for the Prevention and Control of Non-Communicable Chronic Illnesses (ECNT—Estrategia Nacional de Prevención y Control de Enfermedades Crónicas no Transmisibles). It is based on the regional strategy formulated by the Pan American Health Organization and includes public policies, advocacy, health promotion through population base actions, integrated management of the ECNT in health care services, and the strengthening of epidemiological monitoring among its lines of action.

Inadequate levels of coverage and accessibility to health care services suggest the need for policies designed to increase them, but they also highlight the role of health promotion policies, which are cost-effective actions with the ability to reduce the future demand for services.

In effect, evidence exists that the reduction in mortality from cardiovascular diseases observed in developed countries can be attributed specifically to changes in habits and behaviors. In Great Britain, the largest portion of the decrease in mortality from NCDs was due to the reduction in tobacco consumption and other risk factors at the population level. In Argentina, tobacco-free environment laws have reduced admittances for acute coronary syndrome (Ministerio de Salud de la Nación 2011).

In addition to representing the most frequent causes of mortality, NCDs significantly affect the health-related quality of life of the persons who suffer from them, requiring significant combinations of financial resources and family or institutional care (Suhrcke et al. 2006).

Similarly, there is evidence that strategies can be adopted to promote improved nutrition to reduce future cardiovascular risks. On the basis of these effects, initiatives were proposed through the National Noncommunicable Diseases Commission and the Argentine Nutrition Code was modified in 2010, establishing the elimination of trans fats over time so that the food industry could implement the changes.

Concurrently, physical inactivity is responsible for 3.2 million deaths annually worldwide (5.5 percent of the total), strongly impacting women and the elderly. This phenomenon, meanwhile, increases the risk of ischemic heart disease, cerebrovascular disease, breast cancer, colorectal cancer, and diabetes. A sedentary lifestyle is estimated to affect around 17 percent of people worldwide, but if one considers both insufficient physical activity and physical inactivity, this figure grows to 41 percent.

Among the cost-effective interventions that promote physical activity, we find changes to urbanization and transport, community organization, changes to school curricula, and local communication strategies (Norum 2005). At the national level, the most recent risk factors survey reported a physical activity prevalence of 54.9 percent, which was higher than the level (46.2 percent) recorded in the previous survey in 2005. Similarly, the 2009 National Risk Factors Survey (Encuesta Nacional de Factores de Riesgo, ENFR) recorded a greater occurrence of low physical activity in persons with lower levels of income and education. This differs from the data observed in the 2005 EFNR, which reported that the prevalence of low physical activity did not vary significantly depending on those variables.

Lifestyles, Nutrition, and Health

The sustained development of demographic and health care patterns drives the necessity to advance toward models of social protection designed to change behaviors, redirecting health care policy toward health promotion and prevention strategies that increase the value of essential public health functions.

A focus that encompasses the entire life cycle emphasizes the social perspective and the perspective through the years and allows us to examine a single cohort or various generations to find the keys to its state of health or sickness, determined by the social, economic, and cultural environment. In epidemiology, the life-cycle perspective is used to study physical and social risks present from pregnancy, childhood, and adolescence up until maturity. This perspective facilitates the analysis of the intertemporal risk of contracting diseases, especially chronic ones, and health outcomes in the later stages of life. The objective is to "identify the biological, behavioral, and psychosocial processes that intervene throughout life" (Kuh and Ben-Shlomo 1997).

There is growing proof that indicates the existence of critical periods for growth and development, not just during pregnancy and early infancy, but also during childhood and adolescence. During these periods, exposure to certain environmental factors can be more harmful to one's health and have a greater effect on long-term potential health than during other stages of life (WHO and International Longevity Center UK 2000).

The cumulative effects on health are not limited to the life of a single individual, but rather they are transmitted to successive generations (Lumey 1998). Numerous studies, such as Fogel (1996), have shown that traditional development indicators, such as weight, height, and cranial perimeter, are persistent across generations.

This focus informs one approach to development of policies with significant implications in terms of morbidity and mortality and that affect the costs associated with restoring and maintaining health. Thus, the links between nutritional, education, and social protection policies in health care are important, especially in the developing world.

From a public policy perspective, the approach to food security initiatives has passed through various stages; in Argentina, this process has occurred during the last 30 years of democratic life. The National Surveys of Nutrition and Health (ENNyS 2005) have allowed researchers to measure the incidence of phenomena associated with the nutritional deficit in the country, while recording the burden of chronic and acute malnutrition in Argentine provinces, as well as the growing prevalence of obesity. During the last two decades, nutrition programs have been implemented systematically both at the federal and local levels. They have evolved from distribution plans for boxes of dried foodstuffs for low-income families to the development of workshops promoting certain preparation and cooking techniques, community gardens, and school cafeterias, among other initiatives. School cafeterias, in particular, have enjoyed a long tradition in the country. The Food Security Program developed by the Ministry of Social Development at the national level, in cooperation with provincial initiatives, has been among the most important recent policy actions. The program is based on the distribution of purchasing cards for supermarkets and warehouses among target population groups, identifying a list of priority foodstuffs.[4]

Risk factors tend to be grouped in socially conditioned ways. Exposure to negative factors in early stages of life can increase the risk of illnesses for adults. A perspective that encompasses the entire life cycle helps to identify risk chains and points when interventions would be especially effective.

The advance of broad-based population pyramids and the emergence of increased incidences of chronic illnesses in epidemiological patterns, even though communicable diseases rooted in poverty have not been eradicated, offer a wide open environment for the development of these initiatives. Furthermore, technological advances, which have been so successful in delivering longer and better life spans, also put strong pressure on funding mechanisms designed to offer universal coverage.

Despite the advances made in this area, Argentina's work is not yet completed in terms of increasing coordination in the joint implementation and evaluation of these initiatives among the Ministries of Social Development (which is usually in charge of implementing these plans), Education, and Health.

The literature has begun to shift markedly toward highlighting the increased importance of healthy behaviors, from considering them as social protection tools themselves (Lustig 2001) to developing proposals for a change in "patterns of physical activity" (Kelley et al. 2009), including sleeping disorders and chronic stress as risk factors for cardiovascular diseases.

As part of this shift in direction, mental health topics have joined the main discussion of health care strategy, particularly as a result of the emergence and spread of new social pathologies, including eating disorders, drug addiction, and other types of addictive behaviors.

In 2002 psychiatric and neurological ailments had more than doubled, 22.2 percent, according to data obtained from the website of the World Morbidity Burden project from the World Health Organization. The growth of mental illnesses is, in part, a result of the fact that they appear at an earlier age than other chronic illnesses (Kohn et al. 2005).

Policy Impacts

On the basis of this debate, and keeping in mind the expenditure estimates for 2010–2100 presented in the previous section, this section will consider the impact of four selected policies on health care expenditure in the public and social security systems. The selected topics are relevant to the Argentine epidemiological profile: comprehensive tobacco control policy, reduction of salt consumption, promoting physical activity, and controlling hypertension.

For each case, a local and international literature review was performed that contributed arguments to the discussion of impact. A summary of the review is presented in table 6A.4.

Table 6.5 presents a summary of the policy impacts that emerged from the material reviewed. Each row identifies a policy, the indicator examined in the references mentioned, and its effect on different elements of health, measured in percentages. For example, according to the literature, the impact of a comprehensive tobacco control policy is a reduction of deaths from noncommunicable causes by 0.432 percent compared with existing patterns.

These percentages were applied to the estimators that emerged from the regression analysis, allowing us to predict the impact of policies on the original expansions. Their inclusion is performed by applying the impact percentage to the original database that was used to make the estimates (they are incidence of infectious diseases, total population, and population older than 65 years of age). Once the new variable corrected by the cumulative impact created by the policy (year to year) was obtained, it was incorporated into the formulas used to calculate the expenditure projections.

As Time Goes By in Argentina • http://dx.doi.org/10.1596/978-1-4648-0530-1

Table 6.5 Policy Impacts: Annual Variations

Policies	Indicator	Impact on			
		% noncommunicable deaths	% total deaths	% population >65 years	% infectious and others[a]
Comprehensive tobacco control policy	−1% per year in cardiovascular deaths	−0.432	−0.323	0.010	−0.025
Reduction of salt consumption	−0.16% in noncommunicable deaths	−0.160	−0.120	0.002	−0.009
Promotion of physical activity	−1.5% in noncommunicable deaths	−1.500	−1.121	0.015	−0.087
Hypertension control	−1.75% in cardiovascular deaths	−0.756	−0.565	0.018	−0.044
Total				0.044	−0.165

Source: Elaboration based on Health Bureau of Statistics and Information (Dirección de Estadísticas e Información de Salud, DEIS) and results from table 6A.4.
a. Proportion of infectious, maternal, perinatal, and nutritional illnesses.

In all cases, the policy impact prediction summarizes the joint impact of two partial effects. First, the impact on the epidemiological profile is seen, reducing the costs associated with the treatment of the illness, especially in the case of the impacts from preventative policy measures. Second, an indirect impact is observed on the age burden. Effective health policies increase life expectancy and quality of life, triggering an increase of health care expenditure in the long term.

Figure 6.8 shows the partial impact of each one of these dual effects, which exhibit opposite signs: savings linked to prevention and expenditure increases as life expectancy improves.

The coefficients that were originally determined by the regressions for the public sector and social security are reapplied after having been corrected for the effects identified in the literature in each case. The total net effect is located in the center of each figure and is positive in all cases (an increase in health care spending over time), although it is only marginally significant in the cases of tobacco and hypertension control policies. The corrected expenditures for physical activity promotion and reduction of salt consumption exhibit an envelope near zero: The decrease in social health care spending almost completely offsets the increase due to improved survival.

The joint impact of the selected policies on public and social health care expenditure reaches $950 million by 2100. The increase appears insignificant based on the length of the period of analysis, while control of hypertension and the implementation of a comprehensive tobacco control policy are the two actions with the greatest potential effect. The promotion of physical activity and the reduction in salt consumption will have lesser effects in terms of health care expenditure.

The evolution of expenditure by age group is not significant over time, nor is the time accumulated between 2010 and 2100. In any case, an increase in

Figure 6.8 Estimate of Impact on Expenditure of Four Preventative Health Policies, Argentina, 2010–2100

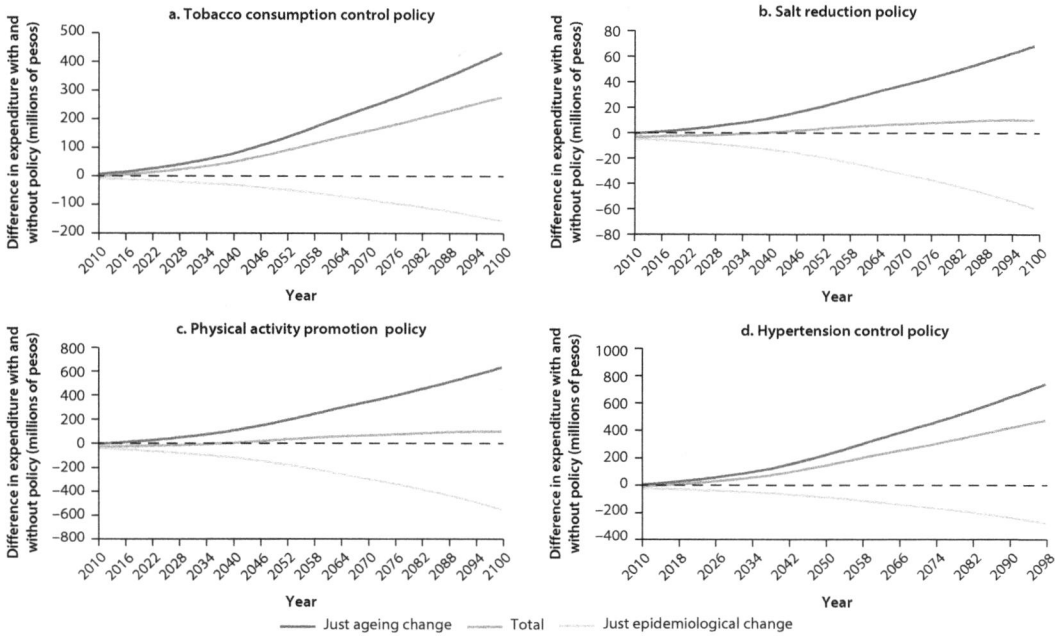

Source: Based on the results of table 6.5.

this type of policy initiative tends to smooth the effect of health care expenditure during the life cycle, insomuch as it triggers investment at younger stages of the life cycle with the goal of reducing pressure on expenditure at older ages.

Figure 6.9 summarizes the difference between the increase in expenditure for each period and the cumulative effect of implementing the four selected policies. The bold line represents the total spending resulting from the four initiatives, compared with the estimated expenditures accounting for both the demographic change as well as the increase in spending related to the change in consumption patterns and the epidemiological evolution.

In the aggregate, one observes that the investment in preventative policies that improve the quality of life, particularly among the elderly, precipitates an improvement in the quality and quantity of years of life and a reduction of the expenditures associated with the disease burden. Nonetheless, this investment does not result in resource savings, which is the product of increasing expenditures over time. However, the monetary cost of applying the four policies simultaneously does not represent a significant expense for the health care system. In terms of the public and social expenditures expanded and presented in the previous section (figure 6.6), they constitute 0.08 percent of total spending in 2020, increasing marginally to 0.10 percent in 2050 and eventually to 0.11 percent in 2100.

Figure 6.9 Health Care Spending Projection, with and without Impacts of Preventative Policies, 2010–2100
Millions of pesos

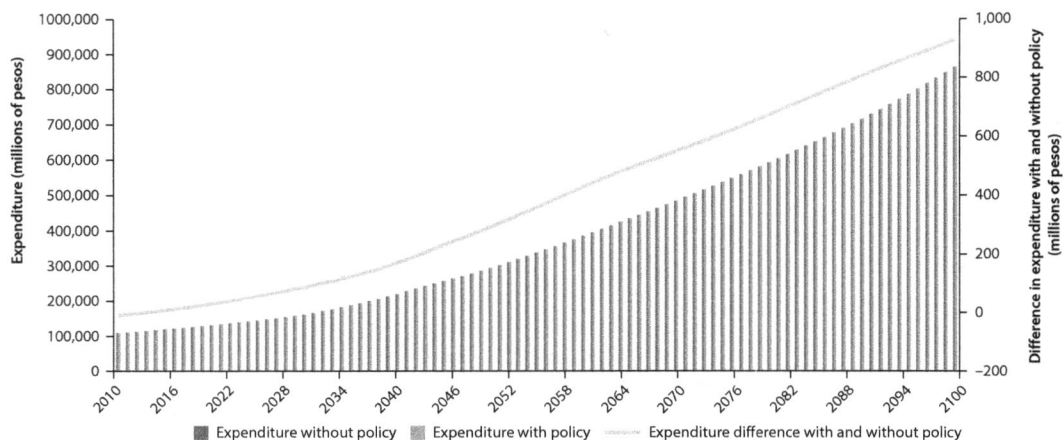

Source: Based on the results of table 6.5.

Equality and Access to Health Care

The literature on financially catastrophic expenses underlines the need for an institutional response to the probability that families' out-of-pocket spending will increase in general and as it relates specifically to the aging of the family unit. Recent literature on direct household expenditure (Knaul et al. 2012) has estimated the impact of health care on the family budget for various countries in the region. In Argentina, Maceira and Reynoso (2012) present a study based on the comparison of two household expenditure surveys for the years 1997 and 2005 analyzing how the families face catastrophic expenses. Using the Wagstaff and Van Doorslaer (2002) calculation methodology, the study calculates the incidence of catastrophic expenses in the country for both periods based on the national poverty line. As figure 6.10 shows, the probability of incurring catastrophic expenses increases with the level of poverty, mimicking the regressive structure of out-of-pocket health care spending.

Despite this situation, the comparison between periods allows one to identify a movement associated with increased financial protection for all families in general, and particularly for those most economically challenged, with an improvement of 33 percent in the poorest quintile and a reduction of 0.07–0.04 in the richest group. The same study also uncovers the impact of population aging on private health care expenditure.

For 1997, the work identifies a differential of approximately 21 percent in out-of-pocket health care spending as a proportion of total expenditure in households that include elderly members. However, the incidence of this additional expenditure drops by 12 percent in comparison with the 2005 survey, allowing one to infer the impact of the policies aimed at the elderly in the country.

Figure 6.10 Probability of Falling Below the Poverty Line as a Result of Health Care Expenditure, 1997 and 2005

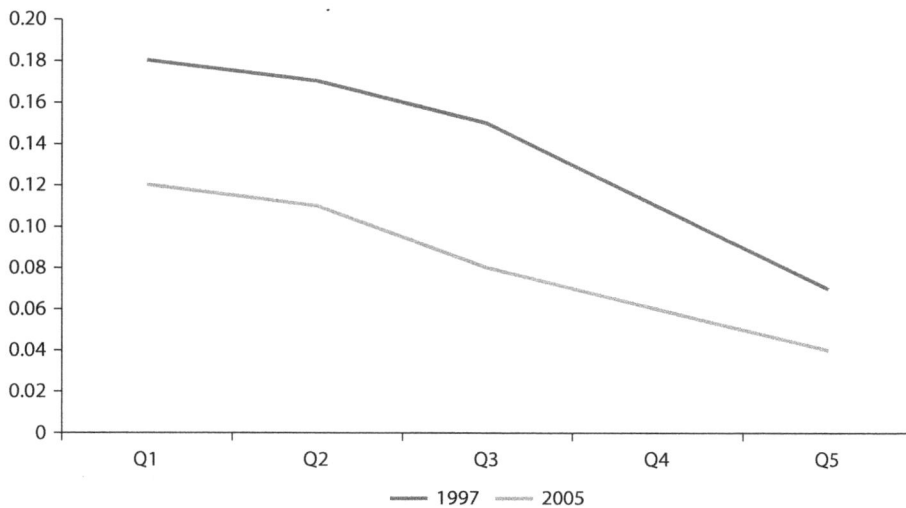

Source: Maceira and Reynoso 2012, based on ECH1997–ECH2005, INDEC.

Thus we find that the structure of the Argentine health care system exhibits some challenges that have been dealt with and successfully resolved in addition to a pending agenda related to the fragmented organization of insurance and resource management. This has not impeded the establishment of a satisfactory level of coverage for specific population groups or population needs. This is the case with the medicine policy, which started in 2003 and has been successful in reducing out-of-pocket expenses in this area for families. Within the public strategy, specific policies associated with certain types of illnesses exist, as well as general programs, such as the Law of Generic Prescriptions and the REMEDIAR program.

As a group, these initiatives guarantee coverage for the entire population of between 40 percent and 100 percent of medicines associated with primary care, 100 percent of medicines for chronic cancer conditions, as well as full coverage for persons living with HIV/AIDS.

Similarly, the existence of the PAMI as a coverage program for the elderly establishes a conceptual regional comparator as an initiative that has been consistently sustained over the years with the goal of covering those individuals who require more care and health care system expenditure via a unified national mechanism.

Public policy's effect on households' out-of-pocket expenditure reflects the regressiveness or progressiveness of sectorial decisions. In Argentina, as in many nations in Latin America, the proportion of income directed to health care among the lowest income quintiles is relatively higher. In 2003, for example, the poorest families spent 16 percent of their income in the health care system, compared with 9 percent among the wealthiest quintile.

These percentages improved two years later, primarily as a result of the medicine access policy, which in 2003 represented two-thirds of families' direct expenditures. In 2005, the first quintile utilized approximately 11 percent of their income to care for their health, compared with 6 percent among the wealthiest families.

Similarly, the presence of elderly individuals in a household increases the probability of out-of-pocket health care expenses and increases the prevalence of catastrophic expenses by between 14 and 21 percent, depending on how the indicator is defined (see box 6.1).

As has been mentioned in earlier sections of this chapter, relatively wealthier nations exhibit higher levels of public and social security participation in health

---

Box 6.1 Catastrophic Health Care Expenses

With the goal of measuring and comparing various institutional arrangements' ability to offer financial protection to households, indicators have been developed that facilitate comparisons across time and between dissimilar health care systems.

The household financial contribution, as it has been called by Xu et al. (2003), represents the financial burden met by families that corresponds to payments in the health care system. This concept translates into a rate that links contributions to the system through general taxes, social security contributions (in the Argentine case, the employer-based health plans), private insurance, and out-of-pocket payments to a family's payment capacity, defined as a family's consumption minus the subsistence cost of living (poverty line). The definition of this measurement gives rise to indicators of catastrophic and impoverishing expenses.

An out-of-pocket expense is considered catastrophic if the *percentage* of the payment capacity that it represents is greater than a specified threshold (x percent of available income). The *catastrophic expense* indicator is supposed to measure the severity with which out-of-pocket health care expenses impact a family's bottom line after accounting for subsistence expenditures. There is no consensus in the literature regarding the threshold that an expense must exceed for it to be considered catastrophic. Xu et al. (2003) use a threshold of 40 percent. An *impoverishing* health care expense is one which pushes a nonpoor household below the poverty line. The impoverishing expense indicators allow one to evaluate the impact of health care expenditure on the household's finances in the short term.

Figure B6.1.1 shows the probability that an out-of-pocket health care expense will exceed 30 percent of household income, once food costs are accounted for. This probability varies considerably: Chile and Costa Rica occupy the extremes in terms of financial protection, whereas Argentina is in the middle, where the probability that a household will suffer a catastrophic health care expense is 8.4. However, these values do not identify subutilization— the lack of attention to a need not translated into demand (and expense)—or the probability of demand induction (and expense) associated with formal coverage systems that lead to the existence of moral hazard. Thus Costa Rica and Mexico share the lowest extreme, and

box continues next page

Box 6.1 Catastrophic Health Care Expenses *(continued)*

Argentina and Nicaragua are in the second group of countries. This argument is particularly important when analyzing coverage for the elderly and their exposure to catastrophic expenses in the face of growing spending requirements. In the Argentine case, one observes how out-of-pocket expenditure among the elderly is reduced by the existence of specific social protection mechanisms (PAMI; see table 6.5).

Figure B6.1.1 Probability of a Financially Catastrophic Health Care Expense Selected Latin American Countries
Percent

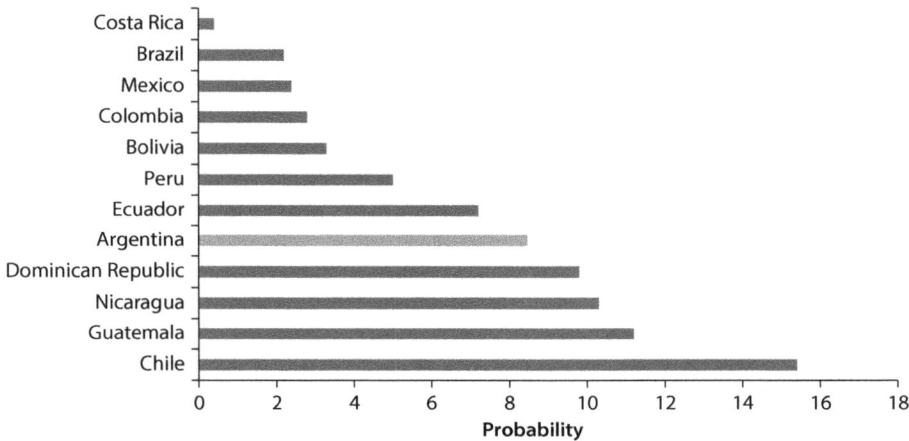

Source: Muiser and Vargas 2009.

care spending than their developing peers. This can be explained as a movement toward improved resource allocation in countries with greater financial capacity, but also with more stable and solid institutions that are capable of establishing a long-term strategy to identify priorities and implement consistent policy actions.

Relatively less developed countries have less capacity for social protection of health care entitlements, leaving the primary responsibility for care with their inhabitants, who pay for it through direct out-of-pocket payments.

Using the same expansion methodology as in the previous section, and relying on the estimation of the determinants of out-of-pocket spending based on the 2005 Survey of Consumption, we improved the 2010–2100 projection of private health care spending and its analogue in terms of public and social expenditure.

As figure 6.11 shows, the predicted level of private expenditure grows, but at a significantly slower pace than the public and social security subsystems, consistent

Figure 6.11 Social Expenditure and Private Expenditure in Health Care

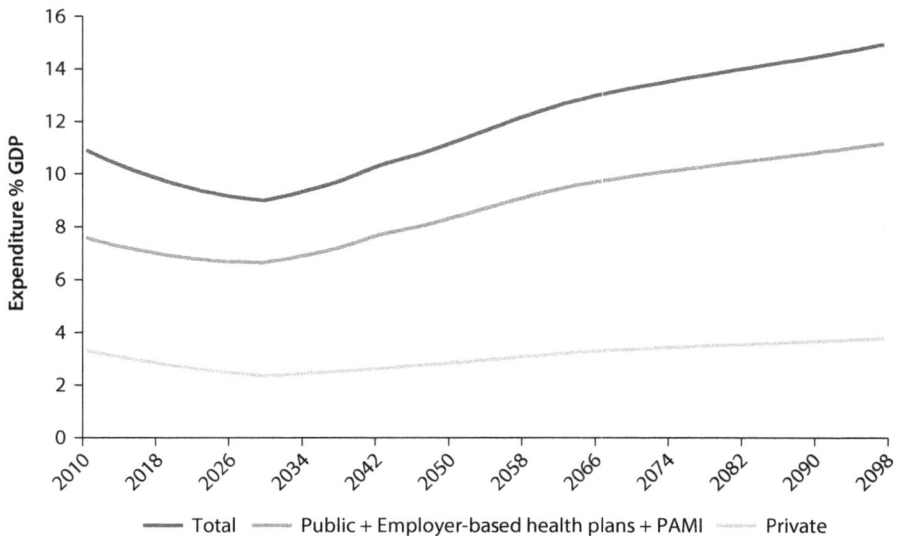

Source: Based on the results from table 6.4.

with the pattern seen in countries that are relatively more developed than Argentina's current state. However, as we have pointed out, it is necessary to analyze the expenditure according to its components, its effectiveness in terms of use, and its allocation equality in order to understand how productive such an investment will be from a redistributive perspective. The figure presents two important points. First, the vertical sum of the components of total expenditure reaches 15 percent of GDP by 2100. Second, private participation in spending exhibits a lower growth rate than its peers in the public and social security sectors. The final estimate projects a direct contribution from families of 27 percent of total health care expenditure, compared to 35 percent currently.

Final Reflections

Lee et al. (2010) asked a crucial question for developing nations: Will the countries grow old before they grow wealthy? The argument is that nations with greater proportions of their population at older ages have less capacity to generate wealth and, on the other hand, require greater resources to care for an age group that typically demands higher levels of health care services. The preceding argument is connected not just to the subject of monetary income, but also with the construction of institutions that show they can sustainably guarantee social protection for their population.[5] Moreover, from an insurance and health care system management perspective, Argentina must advance toward an adequate health care risk management structure, planning income transfers between populations with fewer needs relative to others with greater requirements for care.

As Time Goes By in Argentina • http://dx.doi.org/10.1596/978-1-4648-0530-1

The increase in health care expenditure associated with population aging comprises two different components. The first is linked to the presence of a greater proportion of the elderly population, as a result of the reduction in birth rates. In this way, the total funds collected by the health care system decrease, while the demand for services increases. The second component originates in the possibility of increasing life expectancy, associated with healthier behaviors and environments, as well as the development of technologies and medicines that require larger budgets and better management of funds at the sectorial level.

Beyond the economic factor, as the population ages, the prevalence of chronic and disabling diseases increases. In general, the illnesses diagnosed among the elderly are not curable and tend to provoke complications and consequences that limit personal independence and autonomy if they are not treated adequately and opportunely. Despite the fact that the majority of older people with NCDs maintain their functional ability, the degree of disability increases with age. In general, depression, osteoarthritis, ischemic heart disease, and hip fractures account for the greatest number of cases of physical disability among the elderly who are not institutionalized (see Menéndez et al. 2005 for a study of Latin American cities). The elevated prevalence of these illnesses among the elderly constitutes an important challenge for health insurers because they raise health care costs and increase disability, negatively affecting perceived quality of life.

The PAMI for the elderly in Argentina plays an important role in this framework of financial protection. As the largest social security institution in the country, its ability to organize a coverage plan of interventions at all levels of complexity is particularly expansive, and it can hire both public and private providers. Excluding the topics of resource management and user satisfaction, which are outside the scope of this project, three elements stand out in terms of its operations.

First, as we have shown in this work, the PAMI reduces household financial risk, although it does not mitigate it completely, which means there is still room to develop an institutional financial protection and resource use strategy. Second, as a complement to its role as a system funder, the PAMI—on its own or in coordination with the Superintendence of Health Care Services—could be used as a tool to regulate private supply. Given its broad network of providers and its ability to set quality standards and incentivize the unification of networks, it could increase the resource utilization effectiveness among the age group with the greatest funding requirements. Finally, the PAMI must be analyzed from a systemic point of view using a life-cycle health care model. Faced with a fragmented social protection system—not just among subsectors, but also by age groups—there is a negative incentive to underestimate preventative actions if the cost of treatment is covered by another funder.

This systemic point of view encompasses a debate that reaches beyond any particular institution to all sectors. The lack of interconnections favors the existence of equality of access gaps for all age groups and creates areas where existing resources are utilized inefficiently. From this perspective, the guiding role of the state is particularly important, given that it possesses two tools that are especially suitable for creating a life-cycle strategy: the PAMI and the task of evaluating new technologies. Both are potential tools to promote the rational utilization of resources and will allow the state to push practices in the provider system that will foment biases in favor of preventative medicine, evidence-based medicine, and coordination among institutions.

The Ministry of Health, along with authorities from the education and social development sectors, have the basic responsibility to create spaces for debate, technical assistance, training, promoting healthy nutrition, and care. The application of policies that promote and strengthen the essential public health functions in a federal funding and resource management environment presents a special challenge, in which not just executive authorities must participate, but also provincial legislatures and the judicial branch, to generate a consistent and consensus-based design over time.

Beyond the relative weight of each of these factors and the interaction among them, it is evident that the health care system, even when efficient and equitable prioritization and efficient resource utilization mechanisms are implemented, envisages a horizon of growing financial requirements. These requirements lead to a public policy debate, not just throughout the life cycle, but also across generations.

Annex 6A

Table 6A.1 Descriptive Statistics

Variable	Average	Standard deviation	Minimum	Maximum
Total health care expenditure	413.98	715.22	37.60	7,841.40
Public health care expenditure	272.70	467.29	23.30	4,498.40
Employer-based health plan expenditure	141.27	274.00	14.40	3,343.00
GDP per capita	2,512.79	1,771.84	762.25	10,327.40
Population	1,545,598.00	2,774,554.00	76,068.00	15,200,000.00
Beneficiary population of employer-based health plans	233,740.40	226,421.30	8,383.00	1,338,174.00
Population older than 65 years of age	155,416.50	307,628.90	2,282.04	1,670,387.00
Proportion older than 65 years of age	7.94	2.76	3.00	17.30
Prop. of deaths from infectious diseases, others[a]	9.90	4.63	3.28	25.05
Infant mortality rate	17.33	5.67	4.10	34.40
Out-of-pocket expenditure	81.46	203.43	—	5,020.00
Income	1,389.24	1,598.88	6.67	46,733.33
Coverage	1.37	0.66	1.00	9.00
Younger than 14 years of age	1.05	1.40	—	12.00
Household members	3.62	2.05	1.00	19.00
Older than 65 years of age	0.32	0.60	—	4.00

Source: Elaboration based on the 2005 National Household Expenditure and Consumption Survey.
a. Proportion of total deaths from infectious, maternal, perinatal, and nutritional diseases.

Table 6A.2 Estimates: Determinants of Public Expenditure and Provincial Social Security Expenditure

	Public health care expenditure		Employer-based health plan expenditure		Total health care expenditure	
	Specification 1	Specification 2	Specification 1	Specification 2	Specification 1	Specification 2
GDP per capita	0.142***	0.132***	0.0415***	0.0404***	0.157***	0.139***
	(0.00880)	(0.0134)	(0.00919)	(0.00930)	(0.0107)	(0.0148)
Population	0.000190***	0.000190***			0.000334***	0.000334***
	(8.30e–06)	(8.91e–06)			(1.69e–05)	(1.73e–05)
Proportion older than 65 years of age	114.1***	86.97***			106.4***	79.77***
	(6.291)	(7.631)			(8.146)	(9.086)
Prop. of deaths from infectious diseases, others[a]	39.22***		5.245**		35.37***	
	(3.099)		(2.160)		(3.475)	
Infant mortality rate		12.99***		2.540*		6.270*
		(2.892)		(1.316)		(3.471)
Beneficiary population of employer-based health plans			0.00017	0.00016		
			(0.000155)	(0.000156)		
Population older than 65 years of age			0.00451***	0.00458***		
			(0.000202)	(0.000212)		
Constant	−1,428***	−1,027***	−642.6***	−641.8***	−1,308***	−809.1***
	(85.38)	(118.4)	(53.28)	(59.04)	(96.03)	(131.6)
Observations	374	374	374	374	374	374
R^2	0.937	0.910	0.676	0.674	0.945	0.934
Number of provinces			24	24		

Source: World Bank elaboration.
a. Proportion of total deaths from infectious, maternal, perinatal, and nutritional diseases.
*$p < 0.1$, **$p < 0.05$, ***$p < 0.01$.

Table 6A.3 Determinants of Household Out-of-Pocket Expenditure

Variable	Out-of-pocket health care expenditure
Total Income	0.0336***
	(0.000760)
Coverage	−12.38***
	(1.764)
Older than 65 years of age	43.15***
	(1.962)
Younger than 14 years of age	−4.111***
	(1.361)
Members	0.305
	(0.922)
Constant	118.8***
	(4.984)
Observations	28402
R^2	0.135

Source: World Bank elaboration.
Note: Standard deviations appear in parentheses.
*$p < 0.1$, **$p < 0.05$, ***$p < 0.01$.

Table 6A.4 Summary of Empirical Evidence on Health Policy

Study	Study year	Country	Period of analysis	Intervention	Result
Tobacco control					
Konfino et al.	2012	Argentina	2012–2020	Tobacco Control Law and 100% price increase	Reduction in the quantity of deaths from cardiovascular illnesses (3%), heart attacks (3%), and strokes (1%), approximately 0.4% per year Reduction in the quantity of deaths from cardiovascular illnesses (8%), heart attacks (7%), and strokes (8%), approximately 1% per year
Meyers et al.	2009	Canada, Italy, Scotland, and the United States	2004–2009	Workplace smoking ban	Reduction of the risk of heart attacks by 17%
Ferrante et al.	2007	Argentina	2001–2034	Comprehensive tobacco control policy	Reduction in the quantity of deaths associated with tobacco use by 16,000 per year (22%) compared with the situation without the policy, by 2034, approximately 0.7% per year
Promotion of physical activity and diet					
Pang Wen et al.	2011	Taiwan, China	1996–2008	Promotion of physical activity, 92 minutes per week (experimental method)	Reduction of death by any cause by 14%, approximately 1.1% per year Increase in life expectancy of 3 years
Byberg et al.	2009	Uppsala, Sweden	35 years	Physical activity	Middle-aged men who practice intense physical activity increase their life expectancy by 2.3 years compared with inactive men
Myers et al.	2005	United States?	1987–2000	Physical activity	Spending 1,000 calories/week (30 minutes of moderate physical activity per week) produces a reduction of 20% in total deaths, approximately 1.5% per year
Reduction of salt consumption					
Basu et al.	2012	India	2013–2043	Reduction of salt consumption by 3 grams per day over 30 years	Annual reduction of deaths from heart attacks and strokes of 4.9%, approximately 0.16% per year
Bibbins-Domingo et al.	2010	United States	2010–2019	Reduction of salt consumption by 3 grams per day	Reduction in the mortality rate from any cause by 5% (per 10,000 people)

table continues next page

Table 6A.4 Summary of Empirical Evidence on Health Policy *(continued)*

Study	Study year	Country	Period of analysis	Intervention	Result
Asaria et al.	2007	23 countries	2006–2015	Reduce salt consumption by 15% and a comprehensive tobacco control policy	Reduction in the quantity of deaths by 13.8 million 10 years after implementing the policies. Represents 7.1% of total noncommunicable deaths per year, approximately 0.71 percent per year
Selmer et al.	2000	Norway	1995–2020	Reduction of salt consumption by 6 grams per day	Increase in life expectancy of 1.8 months for men and 1.4 for women Reduction in the annual mortality rate of 4% and 3.8% for stroke and heart attack, respectively
Control of alcohol consumption					
Wagenaar et al.	2008	Alaska	1976–2004	Increase of taxes on alcoholic beverages in 1983 (36%) and 2002 (200%)	Reduction in the quantity of alcohol-related deaths by 29% after 1983 and 11 percent after 2002
Treatments for hypertension					
van Vark et al.	2012	United States?	4 years	Hypertension treatment with ACE inhibitors	Reduction of 7 percent in cardiovascular-related deaths and 5% of total deaths, in patients with hypertension
Rubeinstein et al.	2009	Argentina		Analysis of 6 interventions	Years of life adjusted for disabilities avoided: * 713 by reducing the amount of salt in bread * 1,426 in communications campaigns * 8,033, 13,913, and 17,409 from combined pharmaceutical therapy provided to patients with a 20%, 10%, or 5% global risk of cardiovascular diseases, respectively * 5,919 by arterial hypertension reduction therapy * 449 by quitting use of tobacco with bupropion * 712 by treatment to reduce high cholesterol with statins

171

Notes

1. Private expenditure is primarily made up of direct out-of-pocket spending by families, generally paying for medicines, coinsurance, and payments, in addition to direct out-of-pocket payments for private insurance (prepayments). Prepaid private insurance covers about 10 percent of the population.

2. The group of relatively lower per capita expenditure provinces includes Buenos Aires, Córdoba, and Santa Fe. Municipal governments in these provinces have greater budget authority because of specific decentralization policies. The lack of available disaggregated information limited the ability to identify the relative contribution from local governments within the provincial total.

3. The corresponding estimates for provincial employer-based health plans serve to expand both the spending of these institutions as well as that of the provincial employer-based health plans, and, separately, that of PAMI. In terms of PAMI, we decided to apply each independent variable multiplied by the weight of the coefficient that accompanies the population over age 65 years variable. In this way, we estimated the direct impact of the elderly population and added in the indirect effects of the epidemiological, population, and income changes, weighted by the phenomenon of more than proportional increase in health care expenditure during old age.

4. For a comparative study of nutrition policies in Argentina, see Maceira and Stechina (2008).

5. See the John Lennon-Paul McCartney song "When I'm Sixty-Four" from their album *Sgt. Pepper's Lonely Hearts Club Band* (1967).

References

Asaria, P., D. Chisholm, C. Mathers, M. Ezzati, and R. Beaglehole. 2007. "Chronic Disease Prevention: Health Effects and Financial Costs of Strategies to Reduce Salt Intake and Control Tobacco Use." *Lancet* 370: 2044–53.

Basu, S., D. Stuckler, S. Vellakkal, and S. Ebrahim. 2012. "Dietary Salt Reduction and Cardiovascular Disease Rates in India: A Mathematical Model." *PLoS One* 7 (9): e44037. doi:10.1371/journal.pone.0044037.

Bibbins-Domingo, K., G. M. Chertow, P. G. Coxson, A. Moran, J. Lightwood, M. J. Pletcher, and L. Goldman. 2010. "Projected Effect of Dietary Salt Reductions on Future Cardiovascular Disease." *New England Journal of Medicine* 2010 (362): 590–99.

Byberg, L., H. Melhus, R. Gedeborg, J. Sundström, A. Ahlbom, B. Zethelius, L. G. Berglund, A. Wolk, and K. Michaëlsson. 2009. "Total Mortality after Changes in Leisure Time Physical Activity in 50 Year Old Men: 35 Year Follow-Up of Population Based Cohort" *British Medical Journal* 338: b688.

Cohen, A., and R. Hanft. 2004. *Technology in American Health Care: Policy Directions for Effective Evaluation and Management.* Ann Arbor: University of Michigan Press.

ENNyS (Encuesta Nacional de Nutrición y Salud). 2005. "Documento de resultados 2007." Ministerio de Salud de la Nación, Buenos Aires.

Ferrante, D., D. Levy, A. Peruga, C. Compton, and E. Romano. 2007. "The Role of Public Policies in Reducing Smoking Prevalence and Deaths: The Argentina Tobacco Policy Simulation Model." *Revista Panamericana de Salud Pública* 21 (1): 37–49.

Fogel, R. 1996. "A Life of Learning: The Charles Homer Haskins Lecture for 1996." American Council for Learned Societies (ACLS) Occasional Paper 34, American Council of Learned Societies, New York.

Hutubessy, R., D. Chisholm, and T. Tan-Torres Edejer. 2003. "Generalized Cost-Effectiveness Analysis for National-Level Priority-Setting in the Health Sector." *Cost Effectiveness and Resource Allocation* 1: 8.

Kelley, K., G. Petteey, and B. Ainsworth. 2009. "Building Healthy Lifestyles Conference: Modifying Lifestyles to Enhance Physical Activity and Diet and Reduce Cardiovascular Disease." *American Journal of Lifestyle Medicine* 3: 6S.

Knaul, F., X. Wong, and A. Ornelas. 2012. *Financing Health in Latin America*. Vol. 1 of *Household Spending and Impoverishing*. Cambridge, MA: Harvard University Press and International Development Research Centre.

Kohn, R., I. Levav, and J. Caldas de Almeida. 2005. "Los trastornos mentales en América Latina y el Caribe. Asunto prioritario para la salud pública." *Revista Panamericana de Salud Pública* 18 (4/5): 229–40.

Konfino, Jonatan, Daniel Ferrante, Raul Mejia, Pamela Coxson, Andrew Moran, Lee Goldman, and Eliseo J. Pérez-Stable. 2012. "Impact on Cardiovascular Disease Events of the Implementation of Argentina's National Tobacco Control Law." *Tobacco Control* 1–8.

Kuh, D., and Y. Ben-Shlomo. 1997. *A Life Course Approach to Chronic Disease Epidemiology*. 2nd ed. Oxford: Oxford University Press.

Lee, R., A. Mason, and D. Cotlear. 2010. "Some Economic Consequences of Global Aging." Health, Nutrition, and Population (HNP) Discussion Paper, World Bank, Washington, DC.

Lumey, L. H. 1998. "Reproductive Outcomes in Women Prenatally Exposed to Undernutrition: A Review of Findings from the Dutch Famine Birth Cohort." *Proceedings of the Nutrition Society* 57 (1): 129–35.

Lustig, N. 2001. *Shielding the Poor: Social Protection in the Developing World*. Washington, DC: Brookings Institution Press.

Maceira, D. 2010. "Evolución de la inversión pública social en salud en Argentina." *Revista de Salud Pública*.

———. 2012a. "La seguridad social en salud en la Argentina." Documento de Trabajo CEDES, CEDES, Buenos Aires.

———. 2012b. "Cuadrantes de análisis de los sistemas de salud de América Latina." Draft manuscript, UNICEF, Buenos Aires.

Maceira, D., and A. Reynoso. 2012. "Catastrophic and Impoverishing Health Expenditures in Argentina, 1997–2005." In *Financing Health in Latin America*. Vol. 1, *Household Spending and Impoverishing*, edited by F. M. Knaul, X. Wong, and A. Ornelas. Cambridge, MA: Harvard University Press and International Development Research Centre.

Maceira, D., and M. Stechina. 2008. "Salud y nutrición. Problemática alimentaria e intervenciones de política en 25 años de democracia." Documento de Trabajo CIPPEC. February. Centro de Implementación de Políticas Públicas para la Equidad y el Crecimiento, Buenos Aires.

Maceira, D., and V. Ciccioni. 2008. "Obras sociales nacionales. Financiamiento y equidad." Documento de Trabajo 40/2008, CEDES, Buenos Aires.

Menéndez, J., A. Guevara, N. Arcia, E. León Díaz, C. Marín, and J. Alfonso. 2005. "Enfermedades crónicas y limitación funcional en adultos mayores. Estudio comparativo en siete ciudades de América Latina y el Caribe." *Revista Panamericana de Salud de Pública* 17 (5/6): 353–61.

Meyers, D. G., J. S. Neuberger, and J. He. 2009. "Cardiovascular Effect of Bans on Smoking in Public Places: A Systematic Review and Meta-Analysis." *Journal of the American College of Cardiology* 54 (14).

Myers, J., A. Kaykha, S. Georgie, J. Abella, N. Zaheer, S. Lear, T. Yamazaki, and V. Froelicher. 2005. "Fitness Versus Physical Activity Patterns in Producing Mortality in Men." *American Journal of Medicine* 117: 912–8.

Ministerio de Salud de la Nación. 2011. "Segunda encuesta nacional de factores de riesgo." Government of Argentina, Buenos Aires.

Muiser, J., and J. F. Vargas. 2009. "Health Care Financing and Social Protection in Latin America: The Design of the Costa Rican Health Financing System in View of Financial Risk Protection." In *Financing Health in Latin America.* Vol. 1, *Household Spending and Impoverishing,* edited by F. M. Knaul, X. Wong, and A. Ornelas. Cambridge, MA: Harvard University Press and IDRC.

Mulligan, J., D. Walker, and J. Fox-Rushby. 2006. "Economic Evaluations of Noncommunicable Disease Interventions in Developing Countries: A Critical Review of the Evidence Base." *Cost Effectiveness and Resource Allocation* 4: 7.

Norum, R. 2005. "World Health Organization's Global Strategy on Diet, Physical Activity and Health: The Process behind the Scenes." *Scandinavian Journal of Nutrition* 49 (2): 83–88.

PAMI. 2012. "Informe Instituto Nacional de Servicios Sociales para Jubilados y Pensionados." Tercera Conferencia Regional Intergubernamental sobre Envejecimiento en América Latina y el Caribe. Plan de Acción Internacional sobre el Envejecimiento. Seguimiento de la Declaración de Brasilia. Draft, May, San José de Costa Rica, May 8–11.

Pang Wen, C., J. Pui Man Wai, M. Kuang Tsai, Y. Chen Yang, T. Cheng, M. Lee, H. Ting Chan, C. Keng Tsao, S. Pou Tsai, and X. Wu. 2011. "Minimum Amount of Physical Activity for Reduced Mortality and Extended Life Expectancy: A Prospective Cohort Study". *Lancet,* August 16.

Rubinstein, Adolfo, Sebastián García Martí, Alberto Souto, Daniel Ferrante, and Federico Augustovski. 2009. "Generalized Cost-Effectiveness Analysis of a Package of Interventions to Reduce Cardiovascular Disease in Buenos Aires, Argentina." *Cost Effectiveness and Resource Allocation* 7:10.

Selmer, R., I. Kristiansenb, A. Haglerødc, S. Graff-Iversena, H. K. Larsend, H. E. Meyera, K. H. Bønaae, and D. S. Thellef. 2000. "Cost and Health Consequences of Reducing the Population Intake of Salt." *Journal of Epidemiol Community Health* 54: 697–702.

Suhrcke, M., R. Nugent, D. Stuckler, and L. Rocco. 2006. *Chronic Disease: An Economic Perspective.* London: Oxford Health Alliance.

van Vark, L. C., M. Bertrand, and E. Boersma. 2012. "Los IECA reducen la mortalidad en pacientes con hypertension." IntraMed. http://www.intramed.net/contenidover .asp?contenidoID=78528.

Wagenaar, A. C., M. Maldonado-Molina, and B. Wagenaar. 2008. "Effects of Alcohol Tax Increases on Alcohol-Related Disease Mortality in Alaska: Time-Series Analyses from 1976 to 2004." *American Journal of Public Health* 99 (8): 1464–70.

Wagstaff, A., and E. Van Doorslaer. 2002. *Catastrophe and Impoverishment in Paying for Health Care: With Applications to Vietnam, 1993–98.* Washington, DC: World Bank.

WHO (World Health Organization), International Longevity Center UK, Ministerio de Salud del Gobierno de Chile, and Facultad Latinoamericana de Ciencias Sociales Sede Chile. 2005. "Construyendo la nueva Agenda Social desde la mirada de los Determinantes Sociales de la Salud." Documento Síntesis del Ciclo de Diálogos Democráticos, Santiago de Chile.

Xu, K., D. Evans, K. Kawabata, R. Zeramdini, J. Klavusy, and C. Murray. 2003. "Household Catastrophic Health Expenditure: A Multicountry Analysis." *Lancet* 362: 111–17.

CHAPTER 7

Long-Term Care in Argentina

María Eugenia Barbieri

Introduction

Long-term care represents a growing sector of the economy, although it is still relatively small. It is broadly defined as services required by people who have lost the ability to live independently (OECD 2011). Alternatively, long-term care includes all of the actions designed to guarantee social and organic survival for persons who lack personal autonomy and need the assistance of others for essential acts of daily living (Huenchuan 2009).

Adults older than 65 years of age, especially those older than 80 years of age and women, are the most likely group to require this type of care. Globally, estimates show that more than 46 percent of adults older than 60 years of age live with some type of disability (UNFPA 2012). However, long-term care is not just limited to the elderly; advances in modern medicine have allowed many people to survive major health problems despite the existence of physical, psychological, and cognitive disabilities. As a result, more and more children, adolescents, and adults with severe health conditions require this type of care (Wunderlich and Kohler 2001).

This sector is labor intensive, and the services tend to be fragmented as a result of the variety of target groups and forms of governance, provision, funding, and types of care offered. The ways in which societies approach this topic depends on social, moral, and ethical norms, government policies, and the specific situations that each country faces. For some, this type of care is the responsibility of individual families, whereas for others it is a collective responsibility or rests with the government. For example, in the majority of countries in Latin America, people believe that each family is responsible for ensuring good living conditions for the family elders, with some minor assistance from the state, while individuals have the least amount of responsibility (Huenchuan 2009). These differences have implications for how long-term care systems develop. Moreover, the formal system is a small part of the entire system because the majority of care is provided informally by friends and family members (OECD 2011).

Older adults' need for care is not new. In all societies, there have always been elderly persons who need the help of others (ECLAC 2009). However, the way in which societies respond to this need is changing, and the pressure on formal long-term care systems is increasing for at least four reasons (OECD 2011; WHO 2003): (1) the demographic transition will increase demand for these services; (2) changes in social roles (for example, fewer births and women's increased participation in the labor market) will result in a decrease in informal care offered, transferring this demand to the formal system; (3) as the population increases its use of these services, increased demands for quality and more responses from the social and health care systems are expected; and (4) technological changes will allow for more long-term care to be delivered in the home but could require that the system be organized in new ways.

Worries about long-term care in Latin America are relatively recent, and this responsibility primarily falls to the family. Even though the region currently faces demand for care mainly directed to ward children, in the future the elderly will make up the principal group (ECLAC 2012).

This topic is especially sensitive because the demographic and epidemiological transition process has been more accelerated in developed countries, and socio-economic conditions have not been conducive to establishing adequate public measures to meet the elderly's need for care, instead favoring other areas of action (ECLAC 2009; United Nations 2007). At the same time, the elderly in the region are expected to be less healthy than their peers in developed countries because the increases in life expectancy have been more a product of the reduction in infectious diseases and better treatments than of improvements in terms of living conditions. The growing number of cases of chronic illnesses and the prevalence of risk factors (obesity, hypertension, tobacco, alcohol), as well as the particularities of a system of care that prioritizes acute episodes of sickness, lead one to predict that the risks of elderly dependence in the region will be significant (Huenchuan 2009).

Argentina has one of the highest levels of population aging in Latin America. According to information from the National Institute of Statistics and Censuses (Instituto Nacional de Estadística y Censos, INDEC), the population older than 65 years of age has been increasing: In 1970, it represented 7 percent of the total and in 2010 it represented 10.2 percent. In terms of the population older than 80 years of age, in 1970 it was 1 percent of the total number of inhabitants, increasing to 2.5 percent in 2010 (INDEC 2004).

The increase in the average age of the population is directly associated with the incidence of pathologies that create dependence and, therefore, with the increased need for care. According to information provided by the 2004 National Disability Survey (Encuesta Nacional de Incapacidad, ENDI), the prevalence of disability among the elderly (older than 65 years of age) is 28.3 percent, compared with 5.5 percent for persons between the ages of 15 and 64 years and 3.0 percent for those younger than age 15 years. This percentage increases to 37.8 percent if we consider the age group of adults older than 75 years.

The ENDI also allows one to observe that 9.0 percent of persons older than 75 years require assistance to feed themselves, 15.6 percent to perform domestic chores, 27.1 percent to wash themselves and care for their physical appearance,

13.6 percent to go shopping, 38.8 percent to leave the house, and 19.6 percent to travel on public transportation. Nonetheless, many tell us that they cannot perform these activities; for example, 49.5 percent say they cannot travel on public transportation, and 46.3 percent cannot leave home to go shopping.

Argentina has taken action in the health care, promotion, and social assistance fields to deal with the elderly population's need for care. The organization of service providers is fragmented, not just as a result of the unique features of this type of care (OECD 2011), but also because of the country's federal structure and the fragmentation of the health care system (Maceira 2002; Tobar et al. 2012). Within the health care sphere, the National Institute of Social Services for Retirees and Pensioners (INSSJyP), known as the Comprehensive Medical Assistance Program (PAMI), exists as an organization created with the specific task of providing health care and social services to elderly adults and currently offers coverage to 82 percent of elderly adults older than 65 years of age. In addition to this program, other services are offered by social security institutions (national and provincial social security health insurance plans) and government plans, such as the Federal Plan to Include Health. The National Directorate of Policies for the Elderly is under the Ministry of Social Development, where it implements specific social promotion, protection, and integration programs for the elderly.

This chapter's objective is to present the long-term care service provision strategies implemented in Argentina. To accomplish this, we define long-term care and describe which two types of services it involves, followed by the different ways countries have found to organize systems that provide this type of care. Another section describes the principal actions implemented in Argentina toward this end. Finally some conclusions are offered.

Definition of Long-Term Care

The term *long-term care* refers to the organization and provision of a range of services and care to persons whose ability to live independently has been limited for an extended period of time. This care can include attention to personal, domestic, and health care needs. These services can be provided in a variety of environments, including geriatric centers, residences for the elderly, and the home. They can be provided by trained personnel or informal caregivers (family members, friends, neighbors) (OECD 2007; Sprah et al. 2011). This definition has two main components: (1) care should be provided over a long period of time, uncertain in terms both of duration and of the intensity of care needed, and (2) the type of care provided includes a variety of services.

Evaluating a person's need to receive this type of care has been based, in general, on two measures of dependency: difficulty performing activities of daily living (ADLs), and the degree of difficulty faced in carrying out instrumental activities of daily living (IADLs). The degree of difficulty that individuals experience performing one activity or another demonstrates their level of dependence. ADLs consist of a set of personal or self-care activities that include bathing and grooming oneself, getting dressed, feeding oneself, getting in and out of bed, using the bathroom, and controlling one's bowels. Limitations on these activities indicate that an individual has serious difficulties in carrying out basic personal care activities. IADLs are related to activities that maintain an individual's environment, such as going shopping, washing clothes, cleaning the house, cooking, and dealing with personal issues. Restrictions in terms of these activities can be understood as limitations on community participation or on daily problem solving. In general, assistance with ADLs is considered to imply a greater level of dependence than assistance with IADLs, and therefore it is associated with a higher level and more complex type of care (Casado and López 2001; OECD 2007).

Long-term care encompasses services from the *health care* and *promotion and social assistance sectors*,[1] because it has components from both fields, as figure 7.1 demonstrates. The challenge is comprehensively and practically defining the limits between these fields. To this point, we have proposed at least three approaches (OECD 2007):

1. *Functional approach:* This is based on whether the type of service provided is to assist in the development of ADLs or IADLs. For this approach, we assume that the first set deals with health care, and the instrumental activities correspond to the promotion and social assistance sector.
2. *Approach based on the provider's or funder's characteristics:* This approach can be divided into three types:
   - *Personnel characteristics:* If the service is provided by medical, paramedic, or nursing personnel, then it is health care.
   - *Type of institution:* If the services are provided by health care institutions, they should be categorized under that heading.
   - *Source of funding:* If the services are paid for from health care or health insurance budgets, then they should be categorized with this group.

Figure 7.1 Components of Long-Term Care

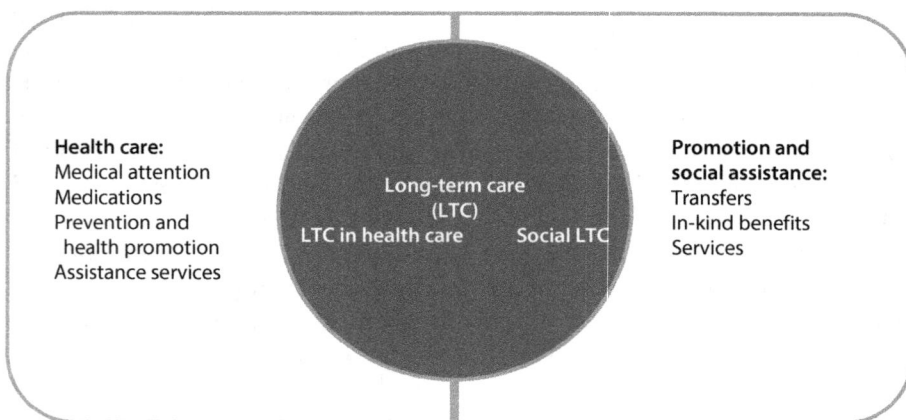

Source: Adapted from OECD 2007.

3. *Approach based on the individual's health:* If the individual needs care to carry out ADLs, then this care should be categorized as health care, whereas care to assist with instrumental activities is considered to be a component of the promotion and social assistance sector.

The functional approach has been recommended for making comparisons between countries because it is able to discern the recipient of the service and thus can avoid the complexities that various existing institutional arrangements bring with them. However, it is also important to delve into and improve current definitions, especially on the subject of personal care. On the other hand, the approach based on the provider's or funder's characteristics is useful if one wants to analyze the services provided or spending at the institutional or governmental agency level without the need to focus on a single population group in particular. Nonetheless, this approximation is not exempt from debate because, for example, it could be the case that health care professionals are providing a service under the auspices of an organization considered to belong to the social sector. On the basis of a survey of OECD countries, the majority agreed to use a functional approach, although some suggested complementing this approach with other information sources that would assist with the service classification process. Similarly, it is important to maintain a flexible framework that can adjust to the changes that are expected to develop in the sector.

The next section presents the services that should be included in the concept of long-term care, by order of decreasing intensity in terms of the health care component (OECD 2006, 2007):

1. *Palliative care* (end-of-life care): This category includes hospice care (nursing homes and similar institutions) and care provided by doctors, paramedics, and nurses for terminal patients.
2. *Long-term nursing care:* This category covers intensive services, is highly complex, and assists with ADL. It includes daily care provided by qualified nurses, as defined by national standards that regulate the profession. The type of care that they provide includes administering medication, medical diagnostics, and performing minor surgeries and dressing wounds. Sometimes this category refers to services provided by less qualified personnel who provide complex care under the supervision of a health care professional. These services are provided in specialized institutions, such as nursing homes, mental hospitals, and homes for persons with disabilities. However, the term is also increasingly used to include in-home care from professional nurses for individuals with chronic illnesses or disabilities.
3. *Personal assistance with ADL:* These services refer to intermediate care, mostly help with one or more ADLs via psychological support or supervision of an individual with a disability or who cannot take care of him or herself. They are provided by caregivers who do not have medical training but who are generally trained for these tasks.

4. *Services and funding in support of informal care:* This includes social services that support care offered by families and can include support ranging from social protection for informal caregivers, training, counseling, and even subsidies.

5. *Home-based help and care and other types of assistance with the performance of instrumental activities of daily life:* Home-based help refers to care at any level of need and intensity. In general, this type of care is less complex than care received in an institution.

6. *Other residential services:* These services meet the needs of elderly or disabled persons, providing a variety of services that range from lodging to help with ADL and personal assistance, but that comprise a less complex level of care than that provided in an institution such as those contemplated below. These establishments combine the idea of living independently, for example in a personal apartment with a high degree of personal decision making, but with the provision of different types of social support activities: cafeteria service and house cleaning, recreational activities, and so forth.

7. *Other social services provided in the context of long-term care:* These services include day care, case management and coordination, special transportation, and other social activities for people with functional limitations.[2]

Formal Long-Term Care Systems

Elder care can be offered by three sources: the family, the state, and the market. None of these sources is exclusively responsible for providing care, and, as a result, a clear division is not always possible among the types of care that each one provides (ECLAC 2009). Even though most care currently falls to the family, the creation of formal coverage mechanisms for long-term care to supplement them is highly justified. First, costs can be very high and represent a significant burden for users, especially for those that have low income or high levels of dependence. In addition, a high level of uncertainty exists regarding the type of needs to cover, the duration, and their severity. For this reason, prepayment and risk pooling mechanisms, subsidies, and targeted assistance offer an answer for the high level of uncertainty and high costs.

Countries have tried to meet this demand for care in very different ways. The following section describes the solutions provided, first by OECD countries, which have a longer history of worrying about how to improve living conditions throughout the life cycle, and then countries from Latin America and the Caribbean, which have taken up this agenda more recently.

Formal Long-Term Care Systems in OECD Countries

The OECD has proposed a taxonomy to describe how formal long-term care systems are organized based on two characteristics: (1) the systems' reach, either universal or targeted (by income level), and (2) coverage based on a single system or from multiple benefits, services, and programs. On the basis of this classification system, one can discern three categories of systems: universal coverage via a single program, mixed systems, and targeted systems based on an evaluation of economic means. These three broad categories can be subsequently divided based on the source of funding (taxes, for example), if the system is part of the health care system, and the combination of services it provides. Next, the various coverage schemes based on this taxonomy are presented, along with their main features (OECD 2011).

Universal Coverage via a Single Program

Long-term care in this system is provided by a single program that may or may not form part of a health care system. In general, these systems provide coverage for nursing and personal care for eligible persons based on their level of dependence. Despite the fact that they are universal systems, they require either copayments or other out-of-pocket expenses and are subject to income level, with possible exceptions for some payments, or social assistance mechanisms for the most vulnerable individuals. Three different models are identifiable in this scheme:

1. *Models based on tax collection:* The Scandinavian countries are a typical example of these systems, which are based on universal coverage, funding from taxes, and including this service as an integral part of health care services. One distinguishing feature of Denmark, Finland, Norway, and Sweden is that local governments enjoy a high level of autonomy to organize, provide, and fund long-term care. In general, service coverage is very broad, including providing personal care in homes and institutions, household adaptations, accessories, and transportation. These systems' expenditure level is high, and eligible persons see few out-of-pocket expenses.
2. *Insurance-based models for long-term care:* This category includes countries that have based their health care systems on insurance systems, such as Germany, Japan, the Republic of Korea, the Netherlands, and Luxembourg. These schemes offer broad coverage, not just in terms of the population reached, but also in the types of services that are provided. Users must also contribute to cover some of the costs. These schemes have three common properties: (1) health care and long-term care have different sources of funding, although they are organized similarly; (2) participation in these insurance schemes is compulsory for the entire population or a certain segment; (3) the scheme is funded primarily from payroll taxes, although there is also a contribution from the government's general revenues.
3. *Services provided by the health care system:* In this case, long-term care is provided as an integral part of the health care system. The vision underlying this scheme is that long-term care is a health risk and the institutional agreements to provide these services are based on an assistance-based medical model, in which professional nurses are the principal providers. Belgium is an example of this type of arrangement.

Single-program universal coverage schemes have the advantage that they ensure broad coverage, not just in terms of population, but also for the types of services provided. Similarly, they do not limit access based on individual income levels, although they can consider that criterion to define out-of-pocket spending limits. In general, they are regulated to ensure service provision with minimum quality standards, and their separate sources of funding from the health care system (except in the case of Belgium) guarantee that they do not use resources for very costly health care services. Nonetheless, these systems are generally very expensive, and the division between these services and health care can create continuum-of-care problems and incentives to shift costs among different providers, requiring greater coordination.

Mixed Systems

Mixed systems provide long-term care through a combination of various universal programs or a combination of various universal and targeted programs. Countries with these schemes do not have a single, comprehensive system, but rather a variety of benefits and programs depending on the groups, costs, service coverage, and jurisdiction. Some provide monetary benefits, whereas others offer in-kind services. It is difficult to categorize the various institutional arrangements in this scheme, but an approximate classification is as follows:

1. *Parallel universal schemes.* These systems are based on the coexistence of different universal programs that provide services with varying features. In general, nursing care is offered through the health care system, while personal care is a separate program. For example, in Eastern European countries universal access to nursing homes or qualified nursing care, through the health care system, is combined with subsidies to cover other types of costs, such as home-based care and assistance.
2. *Universal income-adjusted benefits or subsidies.* Countries that opt for this system, such as Australia, Austria, France, and Ireland, offer benefits to all individuals classified as eligible based on a care needs evaluation. Nonetheless, the benefit amount is adjusted based on income level.
3. *Mix of universal and targeted benefits.* This group of countries provides universal coverage for some services, whereas for others assistance is subject to a prior evaluation of an individual's economic conditions. Canada is one example, in which several of its provinces apply the universal concept of health care provision and in-home personal care, although income-level evaluations are used to determine admissions for elder care residences.

These systems, like their universal counterparts, do not cover all costs associated with care. In fact, they consider individuals' income levels and assets to determine the subsidy level. Nonetheless, mixed systems cover at least a portion of the costs that individuals face, providing a stable source of resources.

Costs are variable in each of the countries, although out-of-pocket expenses tend to be higher in countries with universal coverage via a single program. On the other hand, the variety of programs creates fragmentation and incentives to transfer costs among providers and benefit systems. Thus, it is necessary for these systems to have good coordination.

Targeted Systems

Countries that opt for this system evaluate individuals' income level and assets to establish eligibility limits for receiving public funding. Those who are below a fixed level receive aid, and priority is given to those with the greatest need. Under this approach, only individuals who are unable to pay for services with their own means are protected. Eligibility criteria vary widely from one scheme to another.

Targeted schemes can control costs, but the burden on users can be very high, creating inequalities and incentives to overuse health care services for long-term care purposes. At the same time, implementing targeting schemes can be a costly process, and inclusion and exclusion errors can occur. These errors will grow in importance given the increase in demand that is expected over the coming years because a significant group of people could be excluded.

All of the schemes for provision, funding, and governance of long-term care systems presented here are targeting common lines of action. The increase in public coverage is one common goal, although one also finds attempts to increase targeting even in the most comprehensive systems. Similarly, a desire for greater consumer choice has been reflected in the most recent reforms that these systems have experienced. On the other hand, targeted schemes have been questioned in terms of equality and growing needs. However, the coverage level of the most comprehensive schemes has also been the subject of observation, as they face challenges related to offering greater choice and flexibility to the consumer, while controlling costs and providing quality services (OECD 2005).

Long-Term Care in Latin America and the Caribbean

The institutions dedicated to the elderly in the region are heterogeneous, and in general countries provide public health services. The first countries in the region to begin to discuss these topics were the English-speaking Caribbean countries. As a result, these nations exhibit a greater degree of development in the provision of elder care services than in Latin America (ECLAC 2012).

Housing for the elderly represents one of the areas of long-term care in which Latin American countries have advanced. Again, Caribbean countries and territories (Anguilla, Antigua and Barbuda, Aruba, and the Bahamas, among others) have a longer tradition in this sector. For example, in the Bahamas, the government provides support for individuals to rent housing that facilitates their ability to live independently—there are eight buildings with 40 units in each one—and government representatives regularly visit the individuals who live there. Similarly, the government provides 24-hour in-home services for dependent elderly persons, and private residential centers and day care centers are found throughout the country. In addition, the Department of Social Affairs, part of the Ministry of Labor and Social Services, provides assistance to the elderly in the acquisition of wheelchairs, walkers, hearing aids, and home help, as well as providing counseling and information for family members of the elderly (Bethell-Bennett 2012).

Many countries in the region—Argentina, Chile, Costa Rica, Mexico, and Uruguay, for example—have focused on regulating long-term stay residences.

In the majority of cases, the regulations are weak and mainly deal with administrative measures. An analysis of experiences shows that the majority of the regulations fail to guarantee fundamental rights for the elderly, resulting in continual complaints regarding violations of the rights of those who use these services (ECLAC 2012). Another report demonstrated that this situation is common in the rest of the world and that the lack of international guidelines and national regimes for regulating and monitoring these practices makes the situation even more difficult (Casado and López 2001).

The ways in which long-term care is provided and funded in the region vary widely. Using the OECD's classification system as a basis, one can say that in general Latin American countries use a model of mixed provision that combines multiple programs (universal and targeted) from the Ministries of Health and Social Development and social security institutions.

In Costa Rica, for example, the elderly enjoy total coverage to access health care services based on the policies defined by the Costa Rican Social Insurance Fund (the public institution in charge of social security), as well as access to basic extended-use medicines. In effect, a large portion of the adult population uses this service.

Similarly, elder care is supplemented with other programs. The Friendly Care Program for the Elderly has led to the implementation of initiatives that improve the accessibility of services, household adaptations, and support for aging in the household with family and with caregiving tasks. At the same time, the Network of Progressive Attention for Integral Elder care represents a social organization composed of individuals, families, organized community groups, nongovernmental organizations, and government institutions that are connected by actions, interests, and programs that seek to guarantee adequate care and the ability to meet the needs of the country's elderly population in order to promote old age with good quality of life. A training program for family and community caregivers has been organized by the Costa Rican Social Insurance Fund in coordination with other institutions (Rivera Meza 2012).

In the case of Mexico, a single fund does not exist, and coverage is fragmented. The health insurance system is divided in three components. Social security institutions, such as the Mexican Institute of Social Insurance (IMSS) and the Institute of Social Security and Services for State Workers, among others, cover formal workers and their dependents and reach almost half of the population. The second component is the Health Care Social Protection System, directed by the Ministry of Health, which provides coverage to the population not covered by the social security funds. Finally, private sector funds reach less than 3 percent of the population (Gómez Dantés et al. 2011).

Long-term care services in Mexico are rare and dispersed (OECD 2011). In general, social security covers this type of care and in some cases there are individual initiatives. For example, the IMSS carries out the In-Home Care for the Chronically Ill Program with the goal of caring for and dealing with the complications for patients with chronic and degenerative diseases, including temporary or permanent disability. Some private institutions also exist (both for profit and nonprofit) that offer day care or residential services, but little is known about the costs of the services, coverage, and how they are provided.

The aforementioned actions are complemented by government initiatives, such as the National Institute for Adult Persons, which provides access to day care centers, shelters, and daytime residences (with support from family members); the National System for the Comprehensive Development of the Family, which provides assistance to individuals in residential centers and nursing homes and manages four of its own homes and offers daytime care; and the National Council for Persons with Disabilities, which promotes the social inclusion of disabled persons.

Chile is characterized by providing health care coverage through the public and private sectors. In the former, the National Health Care Fund, through the National System of Health Care Services and its network of regional health care services, and the municipal primary care system cover around 80 percent of the national population. The private sector is made up of social security health care institutions, which cover the other 20 percent and provide services through both private and public institutions (Becerril-Montekio et al. 2011). As in the previous examples, the Chilean state also complements these actions with various initiatives that range from construction programs and funding for extended stay centers and day care centers, to providing complementary social services and rest services for family caregivers (Government of Chile 2012).

In 2002, Law 19,828 created the National Service for the Elderly (SENAMA), focused on designing and implementing policies, plans, and programs in the aging and elderly sector. The service has developed projects that aid the vulnerable elderly (those who belong to the first three income quintiles or live in violent environments) and those dependent on housing based on management improvements or increases in the available spaces at institutions managed by the National Council for the Protection of the Elderly. The service has also constructed and begun operations of government extended stay institutions and assisted living condominiums to provide a comprehensive solution for individuals who need housing and care services.

The Ministry of Health promotes the In-Home Care Program for individuals with severe dependence. This program consists of periodic visits by health care teams to elderly persons confined to their homes to deliver health care. In addition, this program delivers anti-bedsore mattresses and wheelchairs. Working with SENAMA, the ministry has also established regulations that specify the rights of elderly persons living in extended care facilities. Finally, the Ministry of Health through the Explicit Health Care Guarantees Plan, seeks to ensure guarantees of access, opportunity, financial protection, and quality to confront a set of health problems specific to the elderly, in both the public and private sectors.

The countries of the region have gradually formulated responses to the elderly population's need for care. They have invested resources in both improving and expanding benefits, as well as in the supervision of long-term care. Currently, however, a large part of the burden still rests with families, although the decrease in fertility, the incorporation of women into the labor market, and the increase in

life expectancy will make protection in the face of the need for care a challenge
for the region's public policies in the coming years (United Nations 2007).

Long-Term Care in Argentina

Argentina has one of the oldest population profiles in the region. By the 1970s,
the country had already created the primary institution for public health care for
the elderly, the INSSJyP-PAMI. In addition to this institute, one must add the
actions undertaken by the Federal Health Care Program (PROFE), currently
Include Health, and the provincial and national social security health insurance
plans. According to information from the census, in 2010, 86 percent of the
population older than 65 years of age had health coverage through a social security health insurance plan, including the PAMI (INDEC 2010). The Ministry of
Social Development, through the National Directorate of Policies for the Elderly,
has also created various public policies aimed at dealing with population aging.
One of the most highlighted programs in terms of long-term care is the National
Program of In-Home Care.

The following section describes the care offered by each of these initiatives, as
well as the debates about the future regarding public policies in this sector. One
will note that the fragmentation existing in the health care system is also an issue
in the long-term care sector, where various initiatives coexist, but they do not
necessarily offer the same type of service or quality.

Health Care Sector Institutions

National Institute of Social Services for Retirees and Pensioners

The INSSJyP, also known as the PAMI, is a public entity created in 1971 by Law
19,032. It is a health plan designed to protect the elderly with the goal of offering
comprehensive, integrated, and equitable social and health care benefits aimed at
health promotion, prevention, protection, recovery, and rehabilitation. It is organized as a solidary benefit model that responds to the particularities and idiosyncrasies of each of the 24 provinces.

The PAMI currently serves 4.5 million members, mostly retirees and pensioners from the contributory regime, and provides coverage to 82 percent of the
population older than 64 years of age and more than 96 percent of the population older than 79 years of age in the Argentine republic, making it the primary
provider of care for the elderly in the country. The services that it provides are
mostly delivered by third parties (almost 20,000 public and private providers)
with whom it normally establishes contracts based on volume. The PAMI has
only two health care effectors and five extended-term residences of its own.
The institution's income mainly comes from the contributory system: 78 percent
of income derives from contributions from active workers, 4 percent is generated
from investments, and 18 percent comes from contributions from retirees and
pensioners affiliated with the INSSJyP-PAMI (PAMI 2012).

The PAMI's current budget has increased because of improved labor registration and contributions to social security, which have allowed it to increase

Figure 7.2 Evolution of the Budgeted Income for INSSJyP-PAMI, 2007–13

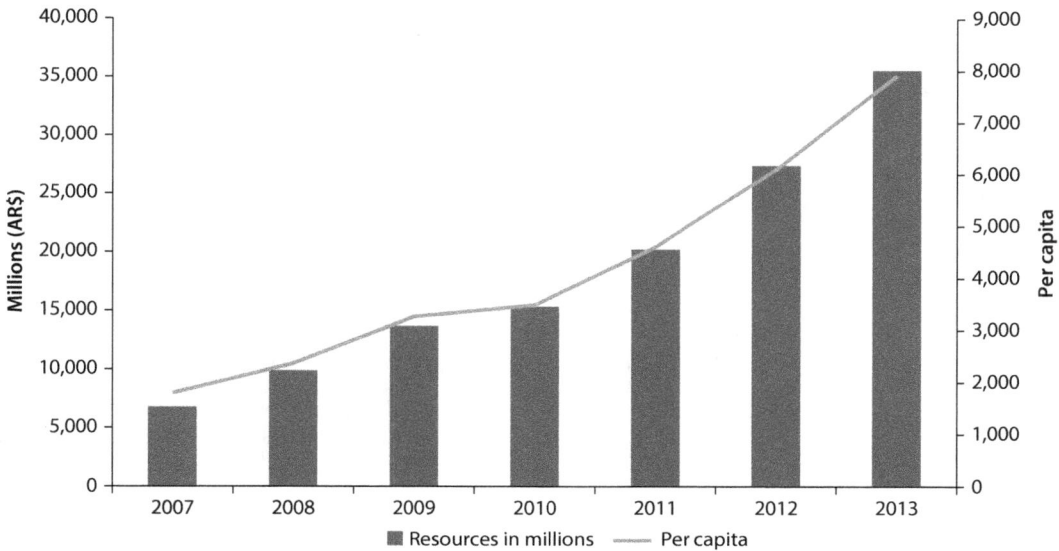

Source: Based on the Budget Reference Messages, 2007–13.

protection through benefits and health care and social programs. Figure 7.2 shows the evolution of the level of funding in aggregate and per capita terms. One can also observe that in 2013, income of AR$35.6 billion is estimated, or AR$7,914 for each beneficiary of the institute, an increase of 30 percent compared to the level estimated in 2012 (Oficina Nacional de Presupuesto 2013).

The increase in the PAMI's resources has also been accompanied by an increase in the beneficiary population. As was discussed in chapter 5, beginning in 2005, through the Social Security Inclusion Program (Moratorium) citizens outside the contributory regime were added to social security, making them beneficiaries not just of the social security benefit, but also of health insurance offered by the PAMI. As a result, it is estimated that between 2005 and 2013 the rolls increased by 45 percent, from 3.1 million beneficiaries to almost 4.5 million.

The institute's budgeted expenditure recorded increases of around 35 percent between 2007 and 2013, as figure 7.3 shows. In addition, annual expenditure never exceeded income during the period of analysis. In per capita terms, in 2013 the PAMI budgeted expenditures of AR$7,902 per beneficiary, which represents an increase of 43 percent compared to 2012.

PAMI Programs
The PAMI directly provides a variety of health care and social services, without shortage periods, and does not charge coinsurance payments. Provision of primary, secondary, and tertiary health care, coverage of medications (which in some

Figure 7.3 Evolution of INSSJyP-PAMI Budgeted Expenditures, 2007–13

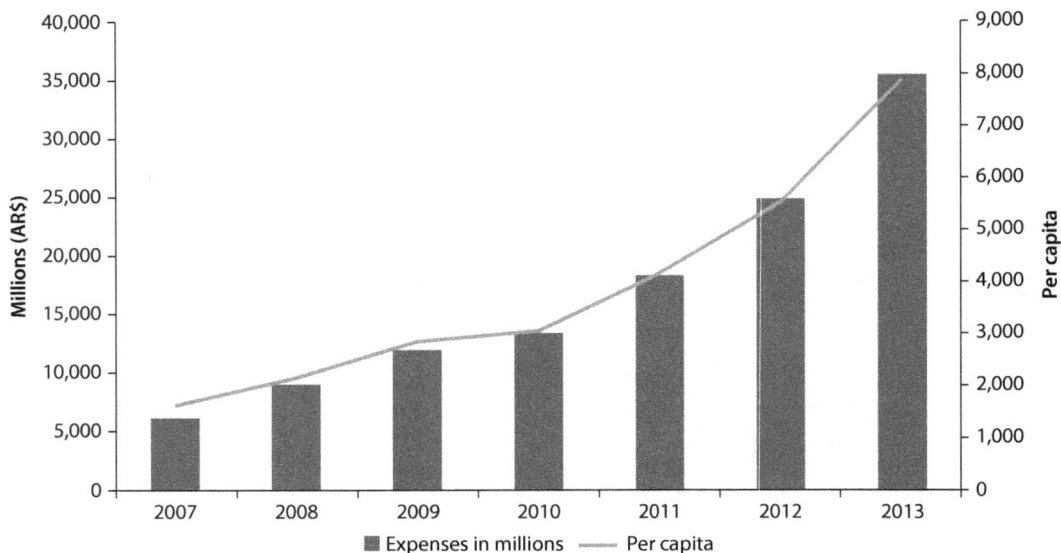

Source: Based on the Budget Reference Messages, 2007–13.

Table 7.1 Programs Implemented by the PAMI to Care for the Elderly

Health care programs	Social programs
• Care for the elderly with disabilities • Equitable access to health care services: health care (mental health, dentistry, ophthalmology, physical therapy and rehabilitation, kidney dialysis, special services, organ transplants), medication delivery, vaccination • HADOB Program (care for arterial hypertension, diabetes, and obesity) • Specialized residential centers • Supervision of extended-term institutions • Palliative care services • Health care access for persons with HIV	• National program to detect and assist vulnerable groups • Program to provide care in high-risk public health situations • Care program for rural populations • Day centers • Social tourism • Cultural pathways program • National in-home care program • Pro-well-being program (food security policy for the elderly)

Source: Based on Rivera Meza (2012). HADOB = Hipertensión Arterial, Diabetes, y Obesidad.

cases reaches 100 percent), subsidy allocations for high-risk situations, and actions related to food security stand out among the activities that have the greatest effect on protection of beneficiaries.

Table 7.1 presents the various programs that the organization is currently implementing, based on their categorization as health care or social services. One can also appreciate the variety of activities implemented, which range from recreational activities (tourism and cultural programs) and highly complex medical care to extended term centers.

The aforementioned programs, even though they offer care and support for the elderly, are not necessarily all included in what we consider to be the long-term care category, defined as care for persons who cannot live independently. This is the case for tourism and cultural activities, care for chronic illnesses in their early stages, preventative care and health promotion, and even a portion of the subsidies offered. Next, we differentiate between the PAMI's specific components aimed at providing long-term care by whether they are health care or social programs.

Health Care Programs

Care for elderly persons with disabilities: The PAMI, through the Office of Disabilities, offers educational, therapeutic, and assistance services to adults with disabilities. This program is based on current international agreements on the subject, on Law 24,901 for the system of basic enabling and comprehensive rehabilitation services in favor of persons with disabilities, and on the services required by the Basic Framework for the Organization and Functioning of Services and Establishments for Attention to Persons with Disabilities (Resolution 1,328/06 of the Ministry of Health). On the basis of this normative framework, the office instituted a basic system of comprehensive care for persons with disabilities, which includes prevention, care, promotion, and protection activities. In 2011 it reached 15,122 beneficiaries.

Specialized residential centers: PAMI Resolution 559/01 instituted the extended-term residences regime, keeping in mind that the comprehensive vision of the human being requires not just dealing with his or her symptoms, whether they are persistent, transitory, or progressive, but also tapping into aspects that formed part of his or her identity that can still reemerge through limited expressions. The regime seeks to provide comprehensive treatment through a multi- and interdisciplinary team, prioritizing the stimulation of abilities and the resocialization of the elderly.

Supervision of extended stay institutions: The extended-term residences contracted by the PAMI are subject to Resolution 682/08 from the institute, which establishes the mechanisms for evaluations of services and physical installations at geriatric or specialized residential centers. The areas reviewed in the evaluations are administration (enabling documentation), medicine, nursing, nutrition, social prevention, and physical installations. During 2011 the institute carried out 2,142 control activities that involved complete audits and follow-ups on identified shortcomings.

Creation of palliative care services: Resolution 379 of 2008 established the palliative care unit for cases in which there is no longer a possibility of rehabilitation. The program is aimed at chronically afflicted patients or those who have potentially lethal pathologies that do not respond to available treatments. The services include care from clinical doctors, physical therapists, nurses, occupational therapists, audiologists, as well as all of the disposable materials needed.

Social Programs

Assistance program for high-risk public health situations: This program was created in 2008 with the goal of increasing the economic capacity of vulnerable members to face public health crisis situations through the delivery of an economic subsidy as part of a plan for comprehensive social treatment. This subsidy is intended to cover nutritional or housing needs, hire an elder care assistant for the home, social reinsertion, guidance for complex pathologies, transfers, and household modifications. In 2011, 150,477 members received this benefit.

Day center: The day center is a therapeutic tool for providing social support and specific daytime stimulation where preventative activities, professional care, and rehabilitation take place aimed at improving personal autonomy and independence. Its goal is to provide daytime care and stimulation for elderly persons whose overall strength is diminishing by implementing comprehensive, specialized, and personal treatment tending toward strengthening functional autonomy and continuity in the family environment.

National in-home care program: The PAMI provides economic subsidies for in-home care. The activities included in this category include domestic tasks, health support activities, personal activities, and sociocultural activities. In-home care is essentially preventative and for rehabilitation; it tries to minimize situations that would increase the risk of loss of independence by creating healthy hygiene and nutritional habits, avoiding falls and accidents in the home, in addition to strengthening family ties. The program attempts to recover lost functional abilities by stimulating individuals' independence, training them in ADL, such as dressing, grooming, and performing household chores, and reinforcing elderly individuals' communication abilities and social, leisure, and recreational activities.

Include Health Federal Plan

The Include Health Federal Plan provides medical care coverage to beneficiaries of noncontributory pensions and their family members. This group is made up of pensioners receiving disability or old-age benefits, mothers of seven or more children, ex gratia pensions awarded by Congress, and beneficiaries of special laws. In 2011, the plan has 997,498 members, of which 61.8 percent receive disability pensions and 3.5 percent receive old age pensions (Oficina Nacional de Presupuesto 2011). In recent years, the government has implemented various policies that have expanded the beneficiary rolls. In particular, beneficiaries with disabilities stand out, having increased by 58 percent between 2009 and 2011.

Care for beneficiaries is decentralized in each province, responding to coverage, accessibility, utilization, and service quality regulations. The plan hires, through quotas, mostly public practitioners, although some private practitioners are included. Beneficiaries can also receive care through the PAMI if he or she so chooses.

The program's resources are earmarked almost exclusively for transfers to the provinces. Transfers are made based on quotas and other criteria, such as

Figure 7.4 Budget Expenditure for the "Include Health" Program, 2007–12

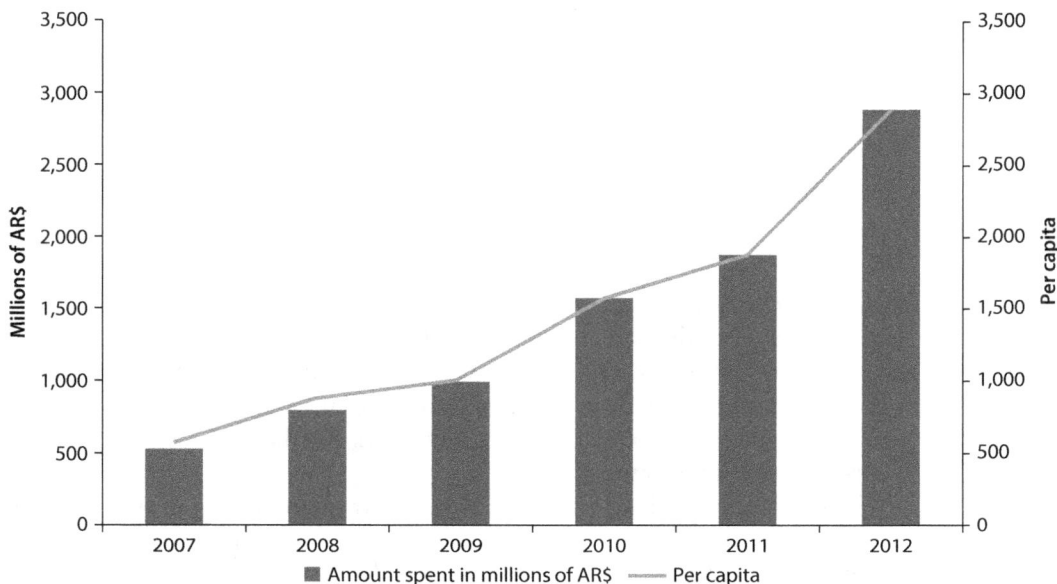

disabilities, dialysis, and high-cost services and low-incidence ailments (PACBI).[3] The program's budget expenditure has increased in recent years, with variations of 41 percent on average between 2007 and 2012, as seen in figure 7.4. In per capita terms, in 2012 the program spent $2,938 per beneficiary, which represents an increase of 46 percent compared to 2011.

Currently the most disaggregated information available for the Include Health expenditure is information from the Savings-Investment-Financing Account from the Secretariat of the Treasury of the Ministry of Economy for 2011. This information specifies that the spending components be distributed as follows: 39.5 percent to services for disabilities, 26.6 percent to quotas, 21.0 percent to dialysis, 7.8 percent for nonquota services, and 5.1 percent to PACBI.

Incluir Salud Services

Even though not solely aimed at elderly adults, the services provided by Incluir Salud contemplate several practices included in the long-term care category, as table 7.2 shows. At present, more details are not available regarding each of these practices, although long-term care items in the health care category broadly include health attention, geriatric internment, and the provision of medicines, prostheses, and orthopedic braces. In terms of social long-term care items, care at day centers and in the home as well as transportation stand out.

Table 7.2 Incluir Salud Services

Health care	Social
• Health care attention	• Day centers
• Dialysis	• In-home care
• PACBI	• Transportation
• Prostheses and orthopedics	
• Medications	
• Geriatric internment	

Source: Based on the 2011 Savings-Investment-Financing Account.

Social Security Health Insurance Plans

Social security health insurance plans are divided in two large groups: the OSN and OSP. The former comprise approximately 300 institutions that include all formal workers by mandate. Provincial social security health insurance plans provide coverage to public employees who work for the 24 provincial governments as well as their retirees.

The OSNs provide long-term care, although they are unique in that they are paid for (via reimbursements) by a fund, called the Solidary Redistribution Fund, which is financed based on a percentage of the contributions that the plans' members make. These resources were administered until July 2012 by the Administration of Special Programs, which was charged with providing financial support to the institutions to ensure that their beneficiaries had timely access to the services required for low-incidence, high-cost illnesses, as well as long-term treatment. Per Decree 1198/12-PEN, the Administration of Special Programs was absorbed by the Superintendence of Health Care Services, and with Resolution 1200/2012 the Single Reimbursement System was created, which is the new entity in charge of implementing and administering the funds earmarked to support the financing of these practices.

Resolution 1200/2012 includes in its regulations the list of pathologies, practices, and medicines for which the OSNs can request reimbursements, as well as their maximum amounts. The regulations contemplate several practices related to long-term care. Table 7.3 lists these practices. However, the division between health care services and social services is rather complex because in some cases the same item can involve distinct levels of complexity of care.[4] In addition, practices are included that do not apply to the elderly, even though they are associated with long-term care (educational centers, for example). For other practices, the description specifies that coverage does not apply to the elderly population.

The OSPs are heterogeneous institutions that, unlike the OSNs, do not have a global set of regulations about what types of services to provide for low-incidence, high-cost pathologies and long-term treatment. Regarding long-term care, seven of the 24 OSPs specify that these services are covered,[5] generally in terms of disabilities. Broadly speaking, the services included are rehabilitation, day centers, homes, residences, and transportation and in some cases in-home care. Special education services are also included for minors younger than 18 years of age.

Table 7.3 Services Included in the Single Reimbursement System, National Employer-Based Health Plans, Associated with Long-Term Care

Health care	Social
• Day centers (single shift and full-time totally dependent persons) • Day hospital (single and double shift) • Simple or intensive ambulatory care (rehabilitation) • In-home ambulatory care (includes support teachers in the case of children) • Homes (Monday to Friday and permanent care for totally dependent persons)	• Day centers (single shift and full time) • Therapeutic educational centers (single shift and full time)[a] • Early stimulation center (single shift)[a] • Homes (Monday to Friday and permanent in-home care, nutrition, and specialized care for disabled individuals) • Homes with educational centers (general/basic/job training)[a] • Residences (for individuals with an adequate level of self-sufficiency and independence)[b] • Transportation

Source: Based on Resolution 1200/2012 from the Superintendence of Health Care Services.
a. Practices for minors younger than 18 years of age.
b. Disabled persons between 15 and 65 years old.

Social Promotion and Assistance Institutions
Ministry of Social Development: National Directorate of Policies for the Elderly

The National Directorate of Policies for the Elderly, which is overseen by the Secretariat of Childhood, Adolescence, and Family in the Ministry of Social Development, participates in activities aimed at protecting the elderly. Its responsibilities include strategies for prevention and promotion of quality of life for the elderly and in-home and institutional care, while also dealing with direct care via residential and day centers and setting service quality criteria.

One of the initiatives that the directorate promotes is the National In-Home Care Program. The program seeks to ensure that the elderly continue to live in their own homes for as long as is possible and advisable, and it also trains suitable human resources and implements in-home care services for the elderly, persons with disabilities, and chronically ill patients in socially and economically vulnerable situations in need of care. The program is implemented in a decentralized manner, via agreements with provinces, municipalities, universities, nongovernmental organizations, and work cooperatives (ECLAC 2009). Total program investment is estimated to have reached $27.7 million between 2007 and 2011 (Dirección Nacional de Políticas para Adultos Mayores 2012).

Another program that the directorate implements is related to institutional strengthening (technical, management, equipment) of organizations that care for the elderly, including centers for retirees and elderly organizations and clubs. The directorate has also provided technical assistance related to replacement parts and furnishing residential and day centers with the necessary equipment in order to contribute to improving living conditions and create a family environment. Investment between 2007 and 2011 is estimated to have reached $14.8 million. Along the same lines, the directorate has also provided training to directors and professionals within these institutions regarding management techniques specific to elder care issues. In addition, the directorate oversees nine extended-term residences that care for 391 older adults via an interdisciplinary team.

Future Debates Regarding Long-Term Care

Long-term care policies face numerous challenges given the overlap that exists between health care and social services and the informal care that family members and friends provide. Moreover, the coordination problems among acute care, rehabilitation, and long-term care services can create unsatisfactory results for patients and also lead to inefficient resource utilization.

Policies to improve coordination can be implemented starting with the establishment of a national strategic framework that defines the major objectives and priorities along a continuum of care. This type of coordination is especially relevant in the Argentine context, where one must not only confront the overlap of health care and social services, but also the fragmentation that the current structure of the health care system exhibits.

In addition, the quality of long-term care services varies widely, and, consequently, many users and their families are unhappy with the situation. A number of examples of inadequate service provision exist: poor living conditions in residential centers, a lack of social interaction and privacy, and inadequate treatment for pain and depression. Some countries have tried to deal with these problems by increasing public spending or improving the regulation of these services, establishing quality measures and monitoring for results (OECD 2005).

The PAMI has improved somewhat in this area because Resolution 682/08 established evaluation mechanisms for services and physical installations at geriatric and specialized residential centers. In addition, the National Directorate of Policies for the Elderly is also charged with promoting quality of life for the elderly and strengthening (technical, management, and equipment) institutions that care for this population group. However, national rules and monitoring schemes need to be established, while also focusing on developing programs that incentivize service quality improvement.

Human resources represent another central concept to which public policy needs to devote attention, in terms of both the quantity and the quality of the care provided. Many countries have approached this topic through salary increases, improvements to working conditions, and designing and supporting professional training initiatives. Even though training programs exist in Argentina, such as the program for in-home caregivers carried out by the Ministry of Social Development, their reach must be broadened, while also defining the traits and qualities that these professionals should possess.

Both public and private resources devoted to long-term care will continue to increase as the growth trend among the elderly population deepens. Public expenditures could be limited by requiring greater private participation (from those who can afford these costs), targeting benefits to low-income individuals or based on the level of disability, as well as through the implementation of health care policies that prevent or delay disability in old age.

Regarding the role of the private sector, long-term care insurance schemes have emerged in some countries (OECD 2011). In general, these insurance policies have one of two goals: complementing the services provided by the public sector or providing services that are not included in public coverage. The most common insurance models are reimbursement and compensation. The former awards an amount to cover necessary expenses up to a certain limit. The latter provides a fixed monthly amount for the life of an insured person who presents a level of dependence according to established criteria.

Even though a strong rationale exists in support of implementing this type of insurance (for example, uncertainty and the intensity and duration of benefits), the market is still very small in countries where these policies are offered. Some of the reasons are related to information failure as a result of the information asymmetry present in this type of market; the uncertainty regarding costs, evolution of supply, and future arrangements for these services; premium volatility; and individual shortsightedness in terms of the risks associated with long-term care, combined with the various obligations and priorities that individuals and their families face.

Some interventions that have been undertaken to encourage the development of this market deal with establishing rules, for example, through the development of standard contracts and the establishment of minimum requirements and tax write-offs that lower the cost of premiums and stimulate demand. Regulations have also been developed with the goal of protecting individuals, increasing the quality of services, and ensuring the plans' financial sustainability. Other options that have been implemented are related to building public-private partnerships or sales of an insurance mix. However, the public's lack of recognition of the financial risks associated with long-term care and the role that these insurance policies can play in mitigating this effect have kept the market small.

Final Reflections

The need for long-term care, defined as services required by individuals who have lost their ability to live independently, is not new. Older adults who require the assistance of others have always existed. However, the demographic transformation, marked by the increase of the elderly population and the decreasing proportion of youth, as well as new social roles, such as women's increased participation in the labor market, among other factors, have provoked changes in the way society responds to this need.

The institutional and programmatic arrangements that countries have developed to deal with these problems are very heterogeneous because they depend on the norms, policies, and particular situations in each nation. In addition, a large part of the responsibility for this type of care is currently met by informal care provided by family members and friends. Since the 1970s, the OECD countries have placed this concern on the agenda, and they have shaped a diverse group of systems (for example, universal, targeted, with numerous programs, with a single program) that seek to expand coverage. Meanwhile, in Latin American and

Caribbean nations, the construction of a formal long-term care framework is much more recent and has focused on regulating extended-term care institutions.

Argentina exhibits one of the most marked population aging profiles in Latin America. Eleven percent of the total population is older than age 65, and it is estimated that 28.3 percent of this group presents some degree of disability. The answers to their needs have materialized as actions from both the health care field as well as from other social services. The way in which they are organized is a replica of the fragmented health care system, combined with the federal structure of the country. The creation as early as the 1970s of an organization intended to provide medical and care services exclusively to the population of adults older than 65 years of age, the INSSJyP-PAMI, stands out. In addition, national programs under the Ministry of Social Development, the PROFE, and the provincial and national social security health insurance plans carry out related activities.

Annex 7A

Table 7A.1 Taxonomy of Long-Term Care Systems, OECD Countries

Structure		Main features	Positive aspects	Negative aspects	Examples
Universal with a single program	Tax collections	Provides services through a single program (that may or may not belong to the health care system) to all eligible individuals depending on their level of dependence	(1) Broad coverage (population and services) (2) Regulated (3) Separates the funding sources, guaranteeing that health care resources will not be overused	(1) Very costly (2) Separation of sources: problems with continuum of care and coordination	Scandinavian countries
	Insurance	Schemes based on insurance systems with three features: (1) different sources of funding for health care and long-term care; (2) compulsory participation for the entire population or a certain segment; (3) primarily funded via payroll taxes	(4) Out-of-pocket expenses, but the burden is less than in other systems		Germany, Japan, Korea, Rep., Netherlands
	Services from the health care system	Long-term care services an additional component of the health care system			Belgium
Mixed	Parallel universal schemes	Various universal programs that provide distinct services coexist	(1) Provide a stable source of resources	(1) Larger out-of-pocket expenses compared to universal systems with a single program	Eastern Europe

table continues next page

Table 7A.1 Taxonomy of Long-Term Care Systems, OECD Countries *(continued)*

Structure		Main features	Positive aspects	Negative aspects	Examples
	Income-adjusted universal benefits	Provides care to all individuals according to their degree of dependence, but the benefit amount varies as a function of income			Australia, Austria, France
	Mix of universal and targeted benefits	Combination of universal coverage for some services, whereas for others, assistance is subject to a prior evaluation of the individual's economic situation		(2) Fragmentation and cost transfers among systems	Canada
Targeted		Evaluate individuals' income and assets to establish eligibility limits for receiving public funding	(1) Control costs	(1) Inequalities and incentives to overuse health care services (2) Targeting a potentially very costly process and can leave many families without coverage	United States, United Kingdom

Source: Based on OECD 2011.

Table 7A.2 List of Long-Term Care Services by Program/Institution in Argentina

Institution/program	Health care	Social
INSSJyP-PAMI	• Care for elderly individuals with disabilities • Specialized residential centers • Supervision of extended-term centers • Palliative care	• Assistance program for high-risk public health situations • Day centers • In-home care
PROFE	• Health care: medications, prostheses, and orthopedic equipment • Geriatric internment	• Day centers • In-home care • Transportation
Single Reimbursement system, national social security health insurance plans	• Day centers (single shift and full-time totally dependent individuals • Day hospital (single and double shift) • Ambulatory care (rehabilitation) simple and intensive • In-home ambulatory care (includes support teachers in cases with children) • Internment care • Homes (Monday to Friday and permanent care for individuals with total dependence)	• Day centers (single shift and full-time) • Therapeutic education centers (single shift and full-time) • Early stimulation centers (single shift) • Homes (Monday to Friday and permanent in-home care, nutrition, and specialized care for disabled persons) • Homes with educational centers (general/basic/job training) • Residential centers (for persons with adequate levels of self-sufficiency and independence) • Transportation
Ministry of Social Development National Directorate of Policies for the Elderly	• Extended-term residences (institutional) • Strengthening of extended-term residences	• National In-Home Care Program • Strengthening of day centers

Notes

1. According to the Manual of Budget Classifications for the National Public Sector, promotion and social assistance includes actions inherent to protection and direct assistance to persons in need, offering them both financial and material support as well as support aimed at reeducation and resocialization of the individual.

2. Even though not included in this definition because it is focused on elder care, special schools for children with disabilities could be included in the other social services in the context of the long-term care category.

3. Includes care for cystic fibrosis, multiple sclerosis, Gaucher's disease, HIV/AIDS, hemophilia, and posttransplant immunosuppressant treatment by enzyme replacement, with growth hormone, among others.

4. For example, day centers and therapeutic educational centers include care for dependent patients and patients with total dependence.

5. The OSPs that detail some long-term care practices include the provinces of Buenos Aires, Mendoza, Santa Fe, Tucumán, City of Buenos Aires, Chaco, and La Pampa.

References

Becerril-Montekio, V., J. Reyes, and A. Manuel. 2011. "El sistema de salud de Chile." *Salud Pública de México* 53 (2): 132–43.

Bethell-Bennett, B. 2012. *Report on the Major Improvements in the Quality of Life of Older Persons in the Bahamas, 2007–2011.* Latin American and Caribbean Demographic Centre (CELADE), Tercera Conferencia regional intergubernamental sobre envejecimiento en América Latina y el Caribe, San José de Costa Rica, May 8–11.

Casado, D., and G. López. 2001. "Vejez, dependencia y cuidados de larga duración. Simulación actual y perspectiva de futuro." Fundación La Caiza Colección Estudios Sociales no. 6.

Dirección Nacional de Políticas para Adultos Mayores. 2012. *Avances Nacionales en la implementación de la Declaración de Brasilia, 2007–2012.* Latin American and Caribbean Demographic Centre (CELADE), Tercera Conferencia regional intergubernamental sobre envejecimiento en América Latina y el Caribe, San José de Costa Rica.

ECLAC (Economic Commission for Latin America and the Caribbean). 2009. "Envejecimiento y sistemas de cuidado ¿Oportunidad o crisis?" Colección Documentos de Proyecto, Santiago de Chile.

———. 2012. "Informe sobre la aplicación de la Estrategia Regional de Implementación para América Latina y El Caribe del Plan de Acción Internacional de Madrid sobre Envejecimiento y la Declaración de Brasilia en América Latina y El Caribe." Latin American and Caribbean Demographic Centre (CELADE), Tercera Conferencia regional intergubernamental sobre envejecimiento en América Latina y el Caribe, San José de Costa Rica, May 8–11.

Gómez Dantés, O., S. Sesma, V. Becerril, K. Knaul, H. Arreola, and J. Frenk. 2011. "El sistema de salud en México." *Salud Pública de México* 53 (suppl. 2): S220–32.

Government of Chile. 2012. "Examen y evaluación de la Declaración de Brasilia en América Latina y El Caribe. Informe de Gobierno Chile." Latin American and Caribbean Demographic Centre (CELADE), Tercera Conferencia regional intergubernamental sobre envejecimiento en América Latina y el Caribe, San José de Costa Rica.

Huenchuan, S., ed. 2009. "Envejecimiento, derechos humanos y políticas públicas." Latin American and Caribbean Demographic Centre, Population Division of ECLAC. Santiago, Chile.

INDEC (Instituto Nacional de Estadística y Censos). 2004. "Encuesta Nacional de Personas con Discapacidad 2002/2003." INDEC, Buenos Aires.

———. 2010. "Censo Nacional de Población y Vivienda 2010." INDEC, Buenos Aires.

Maceira, D. 2002. "Financiamiento y equidad en el sistema de salud Argentino." Serie de Seminarios Salud y Política Pública, Documento de Trabajo no. 7, CEDES, Buenos Aires.

OECD (Organisation for Economic Co-operation and Development). 2005. *Ensuring Quality Long-Term Care for Older People*. OECD Health Project, OECD. http://www.oecd.org/els/health-systems/Ensuring-quality-long-term-care-for-older-people.pdf.

———. 2006. *Guidelines for Estimating Long-Term Care Expenditure in the Joint 2006 SHA Data Questionnaire*. OECD.

———. 2007. *Conceptual Framework and Methods for Analysis of Data Sources for Long-Term Care Expenditure*. OECD.

———. 2011. *Help Wanted? Providing and Paying for Long-Term Care*. OECD Health Policy Studies, OECD.

Oficina Nacional de Presupuesto. 2011. "Cuenta Ahorro-Inversión-Financiamiento 2011." Secretaría de Hacienda, Ministerio de Economía de la Nación Argentina, Buenos Aires.

———. 2013. "Mensaje de Remisión de Presupuesto 2013." Secretaría de Hacienda, Ministerio de Economía de la Nación Argentina, Buenos Aires.

PAMI (Programa de Asistencia Médica Integral). 2012. "Informe del Instituto Nacional de Servicios Sociales para Jubilados y Pensionados en la Tercera Conferencia regional intergubernamental sobre envejecimiento en América Latina y El Caribe." Latin American and Caribbean Demographic Centre (CELADE), Tercera Conferencia regional intergubernamental sobre envejecimiento en América Latina y el Caribe, San José de Costa Rica.

Rivera Meza, E. 2012. "Informe Nacional Costa Rica." Latin American and Caribbean Demographic Centre (CELADE), Tercera Conferencia regional intergubernamental sobre envejecimiento en América Latina y el Caribe, San José de Costa Rica.

Sprah, L., C. Romero, M. Ruiz, G. Tibaldi, and S. Johnson, eds. 2011. *Evaluation and Classification of Services for Long-Term Care in Europe*. Spain: Psicost and Catalunya Caixa DESDE-LTC Group. http://www.edesdeproject.eu/images/documents/eDESDE-LTC_Book.pdf

Tobar, F., S. Olaviaga, and R. Solano. 2012. "Complejidad y fragmentación. Las mayores enfermedades del sistema sanitario argentino." Documento de Políticas Públicas/Análisis 108, Centro de Implementación de Políticas Públicas para la Equidad y el Crecimiento, Buenos Aires.

UNFPA (United Nations Population Fund). 2012. "Envejecimiento en el siglo XXI. Una celebración y un desafío." UNFPA.

United Nations. 2007. "El desarrollo en un mundo que envejece. Estudio Económico y Social Mundial 2007." Departamento de Asuntos Sociales y Económicos, United Nations, New York.

WHO (World Health Organization). 2003. *Key Policy Issues in Long-Term Care.* World Health Organization Collection on Long-Term Care. http://www.who.int/ncd/long _term_care/index.htm.

Wunderlich, G., and P. Kohler, eds. 2001. *Improving the Quality of Long-Term Care.* Washington, DC: Committee on Improving Quality in Long-Term Care, Division of Health Care Services, Institute of Medicine–National Academy of Science.

CHAPTER 8

Funding Basic Education throughout the Demographic Transition in Argentina

Mariana Marchionni and Javier Alejo

Introduction

As has been discussed in previous chapters, the significant decrease in fertility and, to a lesser extent, mortality have led Argentina to a period known as the demographic window of opportunity or demographic dividend, characterized by a low ratio between the population in inactive age groups (children and the elderly) and the population at active or middle ages. The low dependency ratio during the dividend period presents a set of demographic circumstances that offers opportunities at the same time that it poses challenges for economic growth.

In the educational system, the demographic opportunity materializes as a reduction in the education dependency ratio: the public expenditure effort required to fund education diminishes when the ratio between the number of school-age children and the active population drops, as long as factors like educational service coverage and investment per student remain constant. The savings that are potentially generated as a product of the demographic structure can be reinvested to achieve gains in the education system itself, for example, expanding access, reducing dropouts, and increasing graduation rates. Thus, the question becomes whether the dividend will be sufficient to reach these goals.

This chapter's objective is to estimate the impact of the demographic change on educational funding needs according to various policy scenarios, working under the assumption that spending in the sector is efficient. The methodology is based on simulation exercises that allow us to project the evolution of public expenditure on education as a percentage of gross domestic product (GDP) (ECLAC 2008; Miller et al. 2011) and that incorporate the expected changes to the demographic structure estimated in chapter 2, along with various education policy objectives.

The analysis centers on basic education, which in Argentina comprises the early childhood, primary, and secondary levels and encompasses children from age 3 to 17 years old. First, we simulate goals that aim for universal access and an increase in the efficiency of educational trajectories at the basic level. The increase in coverage, grade completion, and graduation are explicit objectives of the current legal framework, and despite undeniable improvements during recent decades, there are still challenges that are expressed as goals in the simulations.

In addition, we simulated increases in expenditure per student as a percentage of GDP per worker, aiming for the goal of the average level for this indicator in Organisation for Economic Co-operation and Development (OECD) countries in 2010. Argentina's level of education expenditure is elevated, comparable with that in countries with higher levels of development. However, educational expenditure per student in terms of GDP per worker works out to be less as a result of the relatively high education dependency ratio.

The following section presents a set of education system indicators that describe the system's recent evolution, the current situation, and pending challenges in terms of enrollment, coverage, and public funding of Argentine basic education. Next, Argentina's education system in 2010 is placed in an international context, comparing the public expenditure effort intended for basic education funding with the levels of other countries and regions, and evaluating the how demographic factors and policy have contributed to the level of resources per student. Then, we present simulation exercises in which the evolution of the level of expenditure necessary to achieve various education policy objectives is projected as the demographic transformation intensifies. Finally, we discuss the principal conclusions.

Enrollment, Coverage, and Funding Trends for Basic Education in Argentina

Basic education in Argentina is organized into three levels: early childhood, primary, and secondary. In early childhood education, kindergartens serve children between three and five years old.[1] Age six marks entry into the primary level of the education system, which can last for six or seven years depending on the jurisdiction: some opt for six years of primary school and six years of secondary school (6–6 option), whereas others choose seven years of primary school and five years of secondary school (7–5 option).[2]

The number of students enrolled in basic education has been expanding continuously over time, as figure 8.1 shows. During the four decades between 1970 and 2010, enrollment more than doubled, growing from 4.6 million to 9.8 million students (1.5 million at the early childhood level, 4.6 million in primary, and 3.7 million in secondary).[3] Enrollment grew the most in the 1980s, increasing by 2.6 million students, a 45 percent increase in a single decade. The subsequent expansion was much slower: 1.1 million students in the 1990s and just 0.5 million during the 2000s.

Figure 8.1 Total Number of Students Enrolled in Basic Education by Educational Level, 1970–2010

Millions

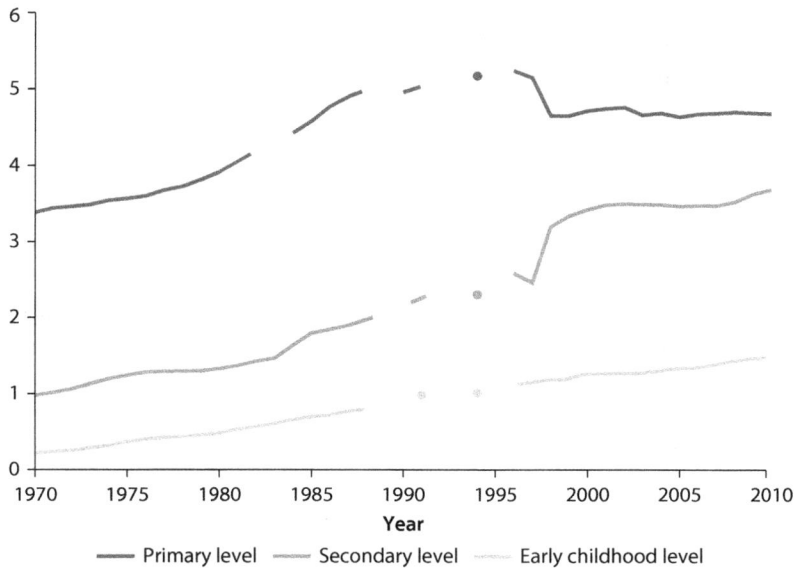

Source: Based on data from the UNESCO Institute for Statistics.
Note: The jump in the series for primary and secondary levels is due to a UNESCO classification change for the seventh year of the primary level, which after the reform introduced by the National Education Law (Law 24,195) was deemed part of the secondary level.

This pattern over time can be linked to the demographic and policy changes that took place during this period. On the one hand, the increase in fertility rates during the prior decade helps explain the strong enrollment growth during the 1980s. On the other hand, the slowing of enrollment growth starting in the 1990s occurred during a period of falling fertility rates and an extension of the number of years of compulsory education.

The legal mandate for compulsory education seeks to promote universal basic education. During the last two decades significant changes have been made to the legislation governing basic education in Argentina. In 1993, National Education Law 24,195 increased compulsory education from 7 to 10 years, which subsequently included, in addition to the primary level that was already compulsory, the final year of early childhood education and the first stage of what is currently the secondary level.[4] Subsequently, with the approval of the National Education Law 26,206 (Ley Nacional de Educación, LEN) in 2006, which is currently in effect, compulsory education was extended by another three years. Currently, compulsory education encompasses the five-year-old level of early childhood education through the end of secondary school, which in theory covers a total of 13 years (Art. 16, LEN). In addition to increasing the compulsory levels, the applicable legislation also aims for universal coverage of education for four-year-olds and the expansion of coverage for three-year-olds in the early childhood level, recognizing the fundamental role that education at young ages plays for pedagogical and social benefits that affect children's future opportunities.[5]

A significant increase in basic education coverage was linked to the expansions of compulsory education. Figure 8.2 shows the evolution of net enrollment rates, which measure the population enrolled in school as a proportion of the total population at the appropriate age for each level, that is, the coverage of educational services among the target population. The enrollment rate for the primary level has historically been high as a consequence of the legal mandate for compulsory education and of education policies that have guaranteed universal access through no-cost, free access to public education.[6] Currently, coverage at the primary level is nearly complete, with a net enrollment rate of 99 percent in 2010, comparable to and even higher than that in the most developed countries.[7]

Although coverage at the primary level has remained fairly stable, greater than 97 percent since the end of the 1980s, the successive expansions of compulsory education contributed to a substantial expansion in the other levels of education (DiNIECE 2011). Since the mid-1990s, there has been strong growth in net enrollment rates at the secondary level, which grew from 61 percent in 1997 to 81 percent in 2006 and continued growing after the approval of the LEN, until they exceeded 84 percent in 2010 (SEDLAC).

At the early childhood level meanwhile, coverage more than doubled in the last 20 years, from around 30 percent at the beginning of the

Figure 8.2 Net Enrollment Rates by Education Level, 1980–2010
Percent

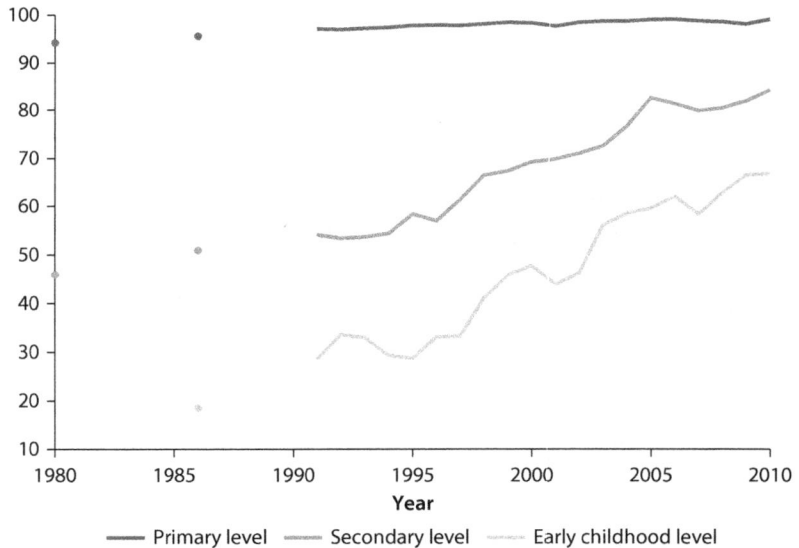

Source: Based on Socio-Economic Database for Latin America and the Caribbean (Centro de Estudios Distributivos Laborales y Sociales–World Bank).
Note: Only urban areas: 1980–92 includes only Greater Buenos Aires and the City of Buenos Aires; 1992–97 includes the 15 principal cities; 1998 and later includes the 28 principal cities. The early childhood level series corresponds to the school attendance rate for children between ages three and five years old.

1990s to 67 percent in 2010. Marked differences among the levels of early child-hood education exist as a consequence of the various legal mandates related to the compulsory nature of education and the commitment to universal access: Coverage exceeds 95 percent for five-year-olds, the only compulsory level, but falls to three of every four children at the four-year-old level and to just one in three at the three-year-old level (DiNIECE 2010).

However, the objective of universal access to basic education requires not only guaranteeing access, but also grade completion and graduation. Figure 8.3 presents the proportion of youth who completed the primary and secondary levels for the 15- to 24-year-old and 20- to 24-year-old age groups, respectively. At the primary level, nearly perfect coverage is combined with a high percentage of students who complete the level: 96 percent of youth between ages 15 and 24 had completed at least primary education in 2010. Despite improvements in the indicators in recent decades, guaranteeing grade completion for students in secondary school still presents important challenges: in 2010, just 63 percent of youth between ages 20 and 24 had completed this level.

Basic education constitutes the first attempt to reduce inequalities of opportunity among various population groups (UNESCO 1996). Argentine legislation explicitly establishes inclusion and completion within education system as priority objectives for children and youth from the most deprived social sectors and regions. For example, Education Funding Law 24,075 (Ley de Financiamiento Educativo, LFE), approved in 2005, states that the government should "include in the early childhood level 100 percent of the population aged five years old and

Figure 8.3 Percentage of Youth That Have Completed Primary and Secondary Levels of Education, 1980–2010

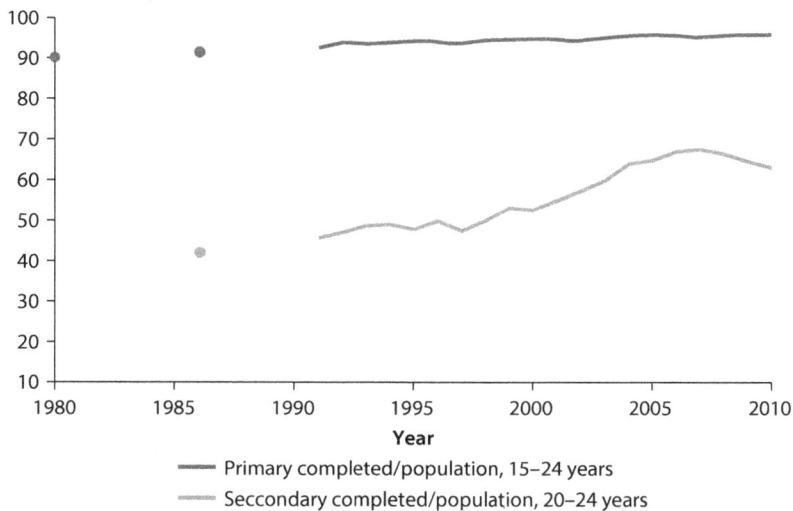

Source: Based on SEDLAC (CEDLAS–World Bank).
Note: Primary level uses data from the population between ages 15 and 24 and secondary level from 20 to 24 years old. Only urban areas: 1980–92 only includes Greater Buenos Aires and the City of Buenos Aires; 1992–97 includes the 15 principal cities; 1998 and later includes the 28 principal cities.

ensure increasing incorporation of children aged three and four years old, prioritizing the most underprivileged social sectors" (LFE, Art. 2, sec. a) and "promote strategies and mechanisms to allocate resources intended to guarantee the inclusion of and grade-level completion for children and youth that live in households that are below the poverty line through compensation systems that favor equality of opportunities in the national education system" (LFE, Art. 2, sec. c). However, the gaps are still very marked, as figure 8.4 shows. At the secondary level, for example, coverage among youth from the highest income quintile is 95 percent, but is just 77 percent among those from the first quintile (figure 8.4a). The difference widens if one considers the probability of completing the level for each group: In 2010, almost 90 percent of youth from the highest quintile had completed at least the secondary level of education, compared with less than half of youth from the first quintile (figure 8.4b).

Both the magnitude of the gaps and their persistence over time are reasons for worry. During the last two decades, the probability of completing the secondary level remained relatively stable around an average of 83 percent for youth from the richest quintile, but just 40 percent for those from the poorest quintile. The persistence of these gaps may in part reflect the growing problems associated with universalization of access to secondary education (ECLAC-OIE 2009). The increase of coverage, especially among the most disadvantaged social sectors, was accompanied by an increase in the repetition and desertion rates, which highlights the importance of focusing efforts not just on access, but also on promotion and completion of the education cycle, especially for the poorest population. This means that policies promoting universal basic education must continue improving in terms of inclusion and promotion, so that greater access also translates into an improvement of the educational trajectory efficiency and graduation indicators.

Figure 8.4 Coverage and Education Level Completion by Family Income Quintile, 1990–2010

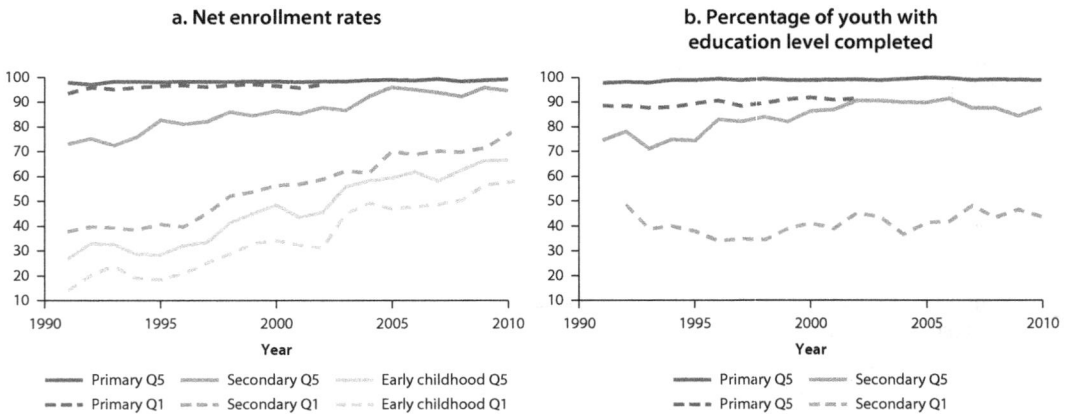

a. Net enrollment rates

b. Percentage of youth with education level completed

Legend panel a: Primary Q5, Secondary Q5, Early childhood Q5, Primary Q1, Secondary Q1, Early childhood Q1

Legend panel b: Primary Q5, Secondary Q5, Primary Q5, Secondary Q1

Source: Based on SEDLAC (CEDLAS–World Bank).
Note: Only urban areas: 1980–92 only includes Greater Buenos Aires and the City of Buenos Aires; 1992–97 includes the 15 principal cities; 1998 and later includes the 28 principal cities. Family income equivalent quintiles. In panel (a) the early childhood series corresponds to the school attendance rate for children between the ages of three and five years old. In panel (b) for the primary level the population between ages 15 and 24 was used, and the population between 20 and 24 years old was used for the secondary level.

Figure 8.5 Consolidated Public Expenditure on Education, 1980–2010

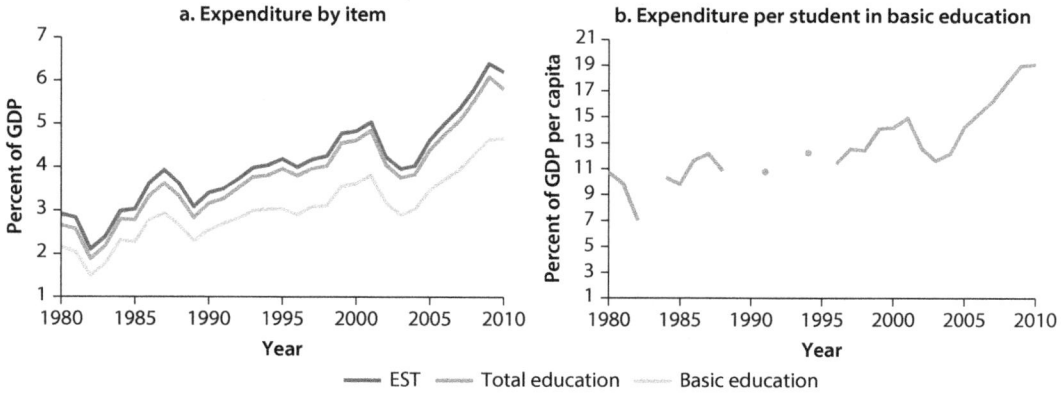

Sources: For 1980–2008, Consolidated Public Expenditure Series, Directorate of Macroeconomic Policy, Secretariat of Economic Policy and Development Planning, Ministry of Economy and Finance. For 2009 and 2010, estimates based on expenditures published by the Coordinación General de Estudio de Costos del Sistema Educativo, Ministry of Education. For panel (b) population data from the UN Population Division, *World Population Prospects: 2012 Revision* and total enrollment data from the UNESCO Institute for Statistics.
Note: EST = education, science, and technology.

As part of universal access policies, and in the face of new needs that the growth in enrollment was creating, public resources intended to fund education increased continuously during recent decades. As figure 8.5a shows, consolidated public expenditure on education, science, and technology (EST) increased its proportion of GDP from an average of 3 percent in the 1980s, to 4 percent in the 1990s, and reached 5 percent in 2001. After weakening as a result of the 2001–2002 crisis, spending recovered until reaching historic levels of more than 6 percent of GDP in 2009 and 2010, surpassing the goal set by the LFE to achieve a gradual and progressive increase of EST expenditure during the 2006–2010 period until reaching 6 percent of GDP (LFE, Art. 1).[8]

Spending on basic education, which accounted for an average of 75 percent of EST expenditure and 80 percent total education spending, also exhibited an upward trend: from a little more than 2 percent of GDP in the 1980s, to almost 3 percent in the 1990s, and 4.6 percent of GDP in 2010.[9] This increase in spending was proportionally greater than the expansion of enrollment in the basic levels, provoking an increase in expenditure per student that can be observed in figure 8.5b. After fluctuating between 10 and 12 percent of GDP per capita in the 1980s and 1990s, expenditure per student increased significantly during the last decade, especially after the LFE was approved in 2005, until reaching 19 percent of GDP per capita in 2010.

Public Expenditure Effort to Fund Basic Education: Argentina in the International Context

A considerable increase in public efforts to fund Argentine education has been observed, especially after the approval of the LFE at the end of 2005. But, how do the levels of expenditure effort in Argentina compare with other countries and regions? How much do the most developed countries spend per student? This section places the Argentine situation in 2010 in the international context, based on information provided by the UNESCO Institute for Statistics, which allows for comparability among countries.[10]

Figure 8.6 compares education expenditure's proportion of GDP in Argentina with other Latin American countries and OECD member countries for 2010. Argentina ranks the third highest in Latin America (LA) in terms of basic education expenditure as a proportion of GDP, after Bolivia and Brazil. Expenditure on basic education in Argentina is 4.6 percent of GDP, one percentage point higher than the Latin American average, slightly above (0.3 percentage points) the OECD average, and very similar to some of the most developed countries, such as Finland, Ireland, Norway, and the United Kingdom.

In addition, Argentina is among the countries in the region with the highest public spending per student. Figure 8.7 shows the variability of total education spending and expenditure per student among countries, normalized as a percentage of GDP and as a percentage of GDP per adult in the active age range (15–64 years old), respectively. All of the countries in LA, except for Brazil and Bolivia, spend less in the aggregate and less per student than Argentina earmarks for funding basic education. On the other hand, independent of the level of aggregate expenditure, all of the OECD countries spend more per student than Argentina.[11] Even if we compare countries that spend a similar proportion in the aggregate on education, the differences in terms of investment per student are considerable. For example, Finland and Argentina spend a similar proportion of their respective GDPs to fund basic education, but Finland's expenditure per student is, on average, 5.4 percentage points higher in terms of GDP per potential worker. The gap relative to the OECD average is four percentage points of GDP per potential worker (12 percent in Argentina versus almost 16 percent for the OECD), which indicates that expenditure per student must increase by around 30 percent to reach the levels of investment per student attained by the OECD countries.

Even though on average the countries that spend more on education in the aggregate are the same ones that achieve higher per-student spending levels, the relationship is not perfect: A little more than half of the variability of per-student expenditure in terms of GDP per potential worker is associated with other factors, in particular the coverage of the education system and the population's age structure, as will be analyzed next.[12]

International Comparisons Based on Expenditure Breakdown

Depending on the population's age composition and the education system's coverage, the same percentage of GDP earmarked for education can result in high or low levels of spending per student. It is possible to utilize the expenditure breakdown formula introduced in chapter 4 to organize this discussion:

$$\frac{B_t}{Y_t} = \frac{B_t/E_t}{Y_t/P_{15-64,t}} \times \frac{E_t}{P_{e,t}} \times \frac{P_{e,t}}{P_{15-64,t}} \qquad (1)$$

Figure 8.6 Public Expenditure on Basic Education in Latin America and the OECD, 2010

Percentage of GDP

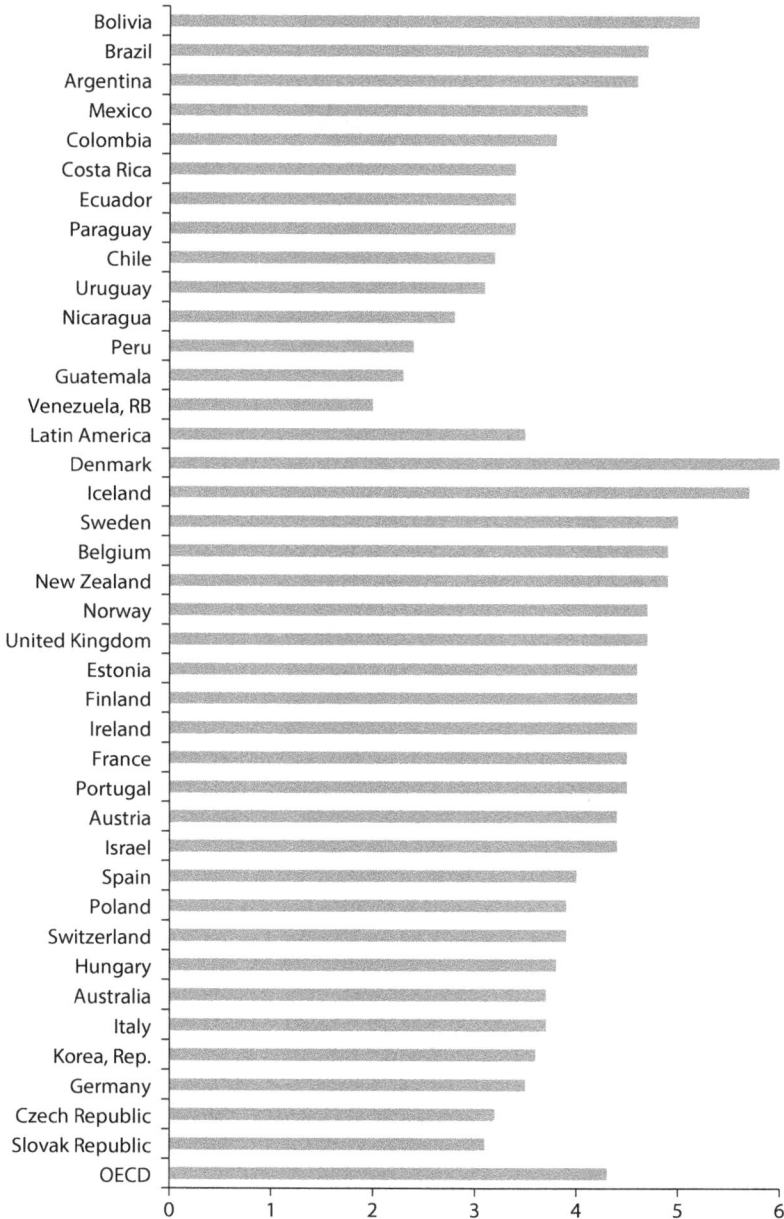

Source: Based on information from the UNESCO Institute for Statistics.
Note: OECD is the average of all member countries that provide information on expenditures for the three basic levels, excluding Chile and Mexico, which are considered to be part of Latin America (LA). LA is the average of Latin American countries that provide information on expenditures for the three basic levels. Expenditure data are from 2010, except for Australia, Brazil, Colombia, Costa Rica, Finland, and Republic of Korea (data from 2009), Uruguay (from 2008), and República Bolivariana de Venezuela (from 2007).

Figure 8.7 Public Expenditure on Basic Education and Spending per Student in Latin America and the OECD, 2010

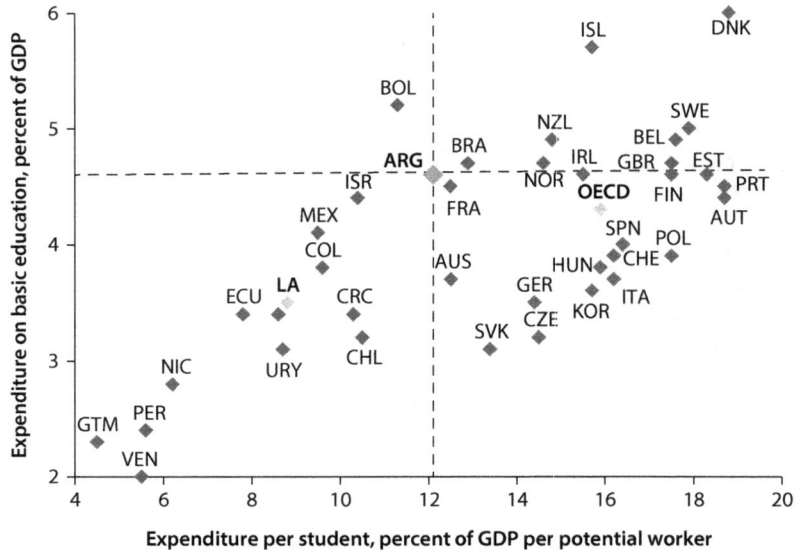

Source: Based on information from the UNESCO Institute for Statistics and population estimates from the UN Population Division, *World Population Prospects: 2012 Revision.*

Note: OECD is the average of all member countries that provide information on expenditures for the three basic levels, excluding Chile and Mexico, which are considered to be part of Latin America (LA). LA is the average of Latin American countries that provide information on expenditures for the three basic levels. Expenditure data are from 2010, except for Australia, Brazil, Colombia, Costa Rica, Finland, and Republic of Korea (data from 2009), Uruguay (from 2008), and República Bolivariana de Venezuela (from 2007). The potentially active population is considered to comprise individuals in the 15- to 64-years-old age range. ARG = Argentina; AUS = Australia; AUT = Austria; BEL = Belgium; BOL = Bolivia; BRA = Brazil; CHE = Switzerland; CHL = Chile; COL = Colombia; CRC = Costa Rica; CZE = Czech Republic; DNK = Denmark; ECU = Ecuador; EST = Estonia; FIN = Finland; FRA = France; GBR = United Kingdom; GER = Germany; GTM = Guatemala; HUN = Hungary; IRL = Ireland; ISL = Iceland; ISR = Israel; ITA = Italy; KOR = Republic of Korea; LA = Latin America; MEX = Mexico; NIC = Nicaragua; NOR = Norway; NZL = New Zealand; PER = Peru; POL = Poland; PRT = Portugal; SPN = Spain; SVK = Slovak Republic; SWE = Sweden; URY = Uruguay; VEN = República Bolivariana de Venezuela.

The expression can be interpreted as follows: for time t, B is public expenditure on basic education, Y is the GDP, E is the total number of students enrolled in basic education, P_{15-64} is the population in the active age range (between 15 and 64 years old), and P_e is the legal school-age population for the basic levels (from age 3 to 17 years old). Equation 1 breaks down expenditure on basic education as a percentage of GDP in three factors. The first is per-student expenditure as a percentage of the average GDP per potential worker. The second factor is the gross enrollment rate, defined as the number of students as a percentage of the population at the legal school age, and the third and final factor is the education dependency ratio that measures the ratio between the size of the basic-school-age population and the population in the active age range.[13]

The breakdown of equation 1 allows one to quantify to what level education policy and the evolution of economic and demographic indicators determine the magnitude of per-student expenditure that can be achieved based on a given

Table 8.1 Breakdown of Basic Education Expenditure, International Comparisons, 2010

Country	Expenditure on education (% of GDP) (1)	Expenditure per student (% GDP/potential worker) (2)	Gross enrollment rate (3)	Education dependency ratio (4)
Argentina	4.6	12.1	98.3	38.5
Bolivia	5.2	11.3	84.0	55.3
Brazil	4.7	12.9	100.4	36.5
Chile	3.2	10.5	97.0	31.4
Colombia	3.8	9.6	94.5	41.2
Costa Rica	3.4	10.3	99.9	33.3
Ecuador	3.4	7.8	106.6	41.1
Guatemala	2.3	4.5	89.5	56.5
Mexico	4.1	9.5	101.1	42.8
Nicaragua	2.8	6.2	86.9	52.5
Paraguay	3.4	8.6	73.2	53.8
Peru	2.4	5.6	95.9	43.6
Uruguay	3.1	8.7	98.7	36.0
Venezuela, RB	2.0	5.5	89.2	41.6
Latin America	3.5	8.8	93.9	43.1
OECD	4.3	15.9	102.2	26.9

Sources: (1) and (3) UNESCO Institute for Statistics; (4) UN Population Division, *World Population Prospects: 2012 Revision*, and UNESCO Institute for Statistics; (2) computed as the residual based on the rest of the variables and equation 1.

Note: OECD is the average of all member countries that provide information on expenditures for the three basic levels, excluding Chile and Mexico, which are considered to be part of Latin America. Expenditure data are from 2010, except for Australia, Brazil, Colombia, Costa Rica, Finland, and Republic of Korea (data from 2009), Uruguay (from 2008), and República Bolivariana de Venezuela (from 2007).

expenditure effort on education. Table 8.1 presents the results of applying the basic education expenditure breakdown formula to various countries in Latin America and the average of OECD countries.

Argentina earmarks one percentage point more for funding basic education than the Latin American average and attains a per-student benefit that is almost 40 percent higher (12 percent compared with less than 9 percent of GDP per potential worker). Even if Argentina reduced education expenditure as a proportion of GDP to the regional average, the per-student benefit would continue to be higher, mainly as a consequence of the differences in the dependency ratios. Argentina is one of most advanced countries in terms of the demographic transition in Latin America, which makes its education dependency ratio one of the lowest in the region (39 school-age children for every 100 adults in the active age range, compared to 43 for the regional average). This situation, combined with higher expenditure, more than offsets the also high Argentine enrollment rates, with the result that per-student expenditure is among the highest in the region.

Staying with the Latin American context, Argentina's situation is very similar to that of Brazil, not just in terms of education expenditure's proportion of GDP, but also in the breakdown of the various factors. Chile and Bolivia, meanwhile, also attain relatively high levels of per-student benefits within the region, but with very different education spending efforts and demographic circumstances. Chile, for example, earmarks almost 1.5 percentage points less of its GDP than Argentina to fund basic education, but its population is older, with 31 school-age children and youth for every 100 adults in the active age range, eight less than in Argentina. The opposite occurs in Bolivia, which even though it spends a greater proportion of its GDP on education than Argentina and has one of the lowest enrollment rates in the region, at the same time it also has one of the highest dependency ratios (55 percent) in the region.

If one uses the average of the OECD countries as a point of comparison, with public expenditure earmarked for basic education that is slightly less than in Argentina, they attain a per-student benefit that is four percentage points higher in terms of GDP per potential worker. In other words, per-student expenditure as a percentage of GDP per potential worker in Argentina must increase by 31 percent to close the gap with the OECD in 2010. This is basically a consequence of the large difference in the education dependency ratios, which are 43 percent higher in Argentina (43 school-age children and youth for every 100 adults in the active age range, compared with 27 for the OECD average). Intuitively speaking, whereas in the OECD the burden of funding each school-age child can be shared among four workers, in Argentina that burden weighs on just 2.5 workers. If Argentina seeks to increase per-student expenditure to OECD levels while maintaining current enrollment rates and the population's age structure, basic education expenditure's proportion of GDP must increase from 4.6 to 6 percent, a figure near the amount spent on EST in 2010 (see figure 8.5). In other words, to achieve per-student expenditure levels comparable to the OECD average, Argentina must spend 1.7 percentage points more of its GDP on education than the 2010 OECD average.[14]

The following section presents a series of simulation-based exercises with the goal of estimating the magnitude of expenditure necessary to attain different education policy objectives as the population's age structure changes.

Expenditure Effort in Basic Education throughout the Argentine Demographic Transformation

During the course of a demographic transition, the age structure of the population changes based on the speed at which fertility and mortality descend. As discussed in the previous chapters, it is useful to summarize these changes using the total dependency ratio (TDR), which measures the ratio between the population in the inactive age groups and the population in the active age range. Following the analysis proposed in chapter 2, if the active population is defined as the group between ages 15 and 64 years old and the inactive population as those younger than 15 years old and older than 65 years old, the TDR fell from a maximum of 66 percent at the beginning of the 1990s to 55 percent in 2010. As figure 8.8a shows, the TDR will remain near this value for several more decades until the trend reverses. The period during which lower levels of dependency are recorded is known as the demographic dividend or the demographic window of opportunity, because it exhibits a population age composition that favors economic growth. If one sets an arbitrary limit of 60 percent for the TDR (a maximum of six individuals in the inactive age groups for every 10 in the active age range), the demographic dividend period for Argentina began around 2000 and will extend until nearly 2050.

Demographic changes directly impact the education system via changes in the school-age population, and the ratio between the school-age population and the population in the active age range directly impacts the amount required to fund education.[15] The education dependency ratio, defined as the ratio between the basic-school-age population (age three to 17 years old) and the population in the active age range (15–64 years old), allows one to summarize the magnitude of the demographic opportunity that is presented for the education system during the dividend period.

Unlike the TDR, the education dependency ratio will decrease throughout the entire period of analysis, continuing the trend that began 20 years ago, and the most significant contraction will occur during the demographic dividend period. Between 2010 and 2050, the number of school-age children and youth will fall from 39 to 31 for every 100 potential workers, which will allow the government to save an amount on the order of 25 percent per potential student, all else constant. Figure 8.8b shows the projected education dependency ratios for the legal age groups corresponding to each of the three education levels. In the primary and secondary levels, one observes similar education dependency ratios, which will contract from a little more than 15 to 12 percent between 2010 and 2050. The initial level of dependency will fall from around 8 to 6 percent during the same period. These changes again suggest a possible savings on the order of 25 percent for each education level.

This potential savings in the education system as a result of demographic changes could be reinvested in attaining educational improvements that have not yet been achieved, such as coverage expansion, especially at the early childhood and secondary levels, and greater efficiency of education trajectories through reductions of underachievement and dropouts. These savings could also be reinvested to attain per-student expenditure levels comparable to the most developed countries over the long term, without losing sight of the fact that increases in per-student expenditure alone are neither necessary nor sufficient conditions to increase education quality (see boxes 8.1 and 8.2).

With the goal of including these concerns in the analysis, we again turn to the expenditure breakdown from equation 1, which shows that for a given level of aggregate spending on education, the per-student benefit depends on the demographic circumstances (education dependency ratio), but also on the education policies reflected in the gross enrollment rate. The gross enrollment rate, in turn, can be expressed as the product of the net enrollment rate (percentage of the school-age population that attends school, $E_{e,t}/P_{e,t}$) and the overage ratio (ratio between the total number of students and the number whose age corresponds to the theoretical age for the level that they are studying, $E_t/E_{e,t}$), which allows us

Figure 8.8 Dependency Ratios, Projections, 2010–2100

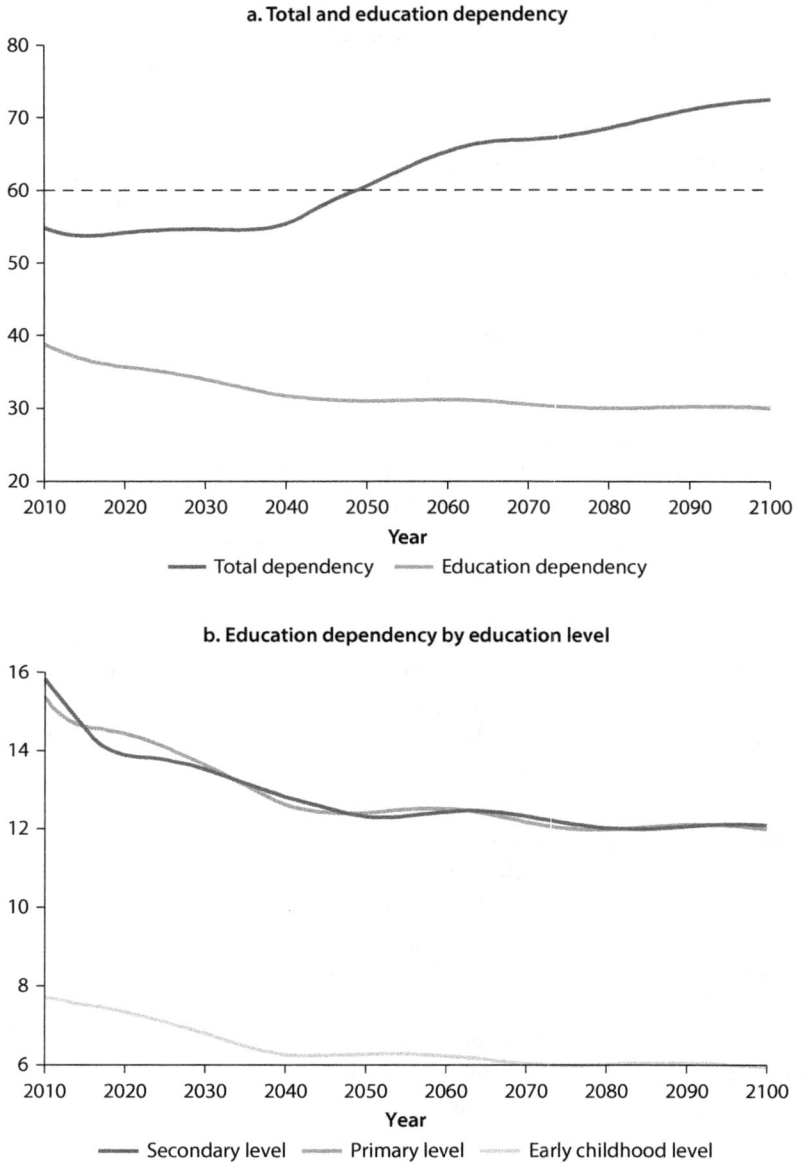

a. Total and education dependency

b. Education dependency by education level

Source: Based on projections made in chapter 2.
Note: For all of the ratios, the denominator is the active-age population (between 15 and 64 years old). The numerators are the following: the population younger than 15 years old or older than age 64 for the total dependency ratio; the population between ages three and five years old for the early childhood dependency ratio; the population between ages six and 11 years old for the primary level dependency ratio; and the population between ages 12 and 17 years old for the secondary level dependency ratio.

Box 8.1 Expenditure per Student and Education Quality

Consensus exists among specialists that some of the dimensions that describe education quality can be estimated using the results of standardized tests like the Programme for International Student Assessment (PISA). PISA seeks to measure the abilities of 15-year-olds to deal with the challenges of adult life, particularly working life. Argentine students' results on the PISA tests are relatively low and have fallen in the last decade. Of a total of 60 countries that participated in the 2009 edition of the PISA, Argentina ranked 50th in mathematics, 52nd in sciences, and 55th in reading. The results from the 2012 edition of the PISA portray a panorama that continues to be discouraging: According to the test, Argentine students rank between 58th and 61st out of a total of 65 participating countries. Within Latin America, Argentina is the only country that unfortunately forms part of the low-performing, worsening group (Auguste 2012; Marchionni et al. 2013).[a]

Even though a positive relationship exists between PISA test results and per-student expenditure across countries, it is well known that this relationship is not causal in terms of expenditure driving educational quality, but rather is owed to institutional, political, and cultural factors that determine the efficiency of spending and the education results for a given spending level (Hanushek 2003; PISA 2012). If increasing spending does not change how schools are organized, or the incentives that teachers, directors, parents, and students face, it will be difficult for it to affect the quality of education (Glewwe et al. 2011; Hanushek and Woesmann 2011). In this sense, for a broad group of countries, evidence exists that expenditure increases do not translate into substantial improvements in education results (Gundlach et al. 2001; Gundlach and Woessmann 2001), and the Argentine experience in recent years appears to follow this trend (Auguste 2012). Argentina has been increasing per-student expenditure, but the country lacks improvements in terms of the efficiency of this investment, in particular the pedagogical and organizational transformations that will facilitate improving education quality and teacher training (LFE, Art. 2, sections f, e, i). The 2009–11 and 2012–16 National Plans for Compulsory Education point in this direction, but it remains to be seen what concrete impact they will have on the quality of education services.

a. Other international and national evaluations exist. For example, at the national level, since 1993 the Ministry of Education has carried out the National Evaluation Operation (Oficina Nacional de Evaluación, ONE). According to results from the ONE, between 1995 and 2003 no significant changes were seen in the performance of students in the final year of secondary school in language and mathematics. The changes between 2005 and 2010 are encouraging on the one hand and discouraging on the other: There has been a significant reduction in the percentage of low-performing secondary students, although the proportion of high-performing students has fallen across all levels evaluated. For more information on the ONE tests, see DiNIECE (2003, 2005) and Delich et al. (2009), among others.

to consider policies that affect the coverage of the system and the efficiency of education trajectories independently. Equation 2 is obtained by incorporating these changes to equation 1:

$$\frac{B_t}{Y_t} = \frac{B_t/E_t}{Y_t/P_{15-64,t}} \times \frac{E_{e,t}}{P_{e,t}} \times \frac{E_t}{E_{e,t}} \times \frac{P_{e,t}}{P_{15-64,t}}.$$

(2)

Box 8.2 The Experiences of the Republic of Korea and Japan during the Demographic Dividend Period

Japan and the Republic of Korea are two examples of how economic development can be led by strong investment in human capital during the demographic dividend period. Japan's demographic window of opportunity began early, near the end of the 1950s and is currently in its final stage. For Korea, the demographic dividend period started at the beginning of the 1980s and will continue until the beginning of the 2030s.

Historically, both countries have demonstrated great interest in investing in human capital. At the beginning of the 1970s, both already exhibited nearly universal coverage of primary education, which meant that the subsequent expansion was principally aimed at the secondary and higher education levels. Since then, Japan was able to increase secondary coverage from 70 percent to nearly universal coverage in a little more than three decades, while Korea managed to achieve a comparable feat in half the time, taking advantage of the demographic dividend that began in the 1980s (Tilak 2002). Currently, both countries exhibit universal primary coverage and net enrollment rates above 95 percent in secondary education (UNESCO).

The expansion of coverage during the dividend period was accompanied by a significant increase in investment in education. Public expenditure on education in Japan grew from 4 percent of GDP in the mid-1960s to more than 6 percent in the 1990s. During the same period, Korea, which entered the dividend period 20 years later, increased education expenditure from 2 to 4 percent of GDP. But these countries did not just increase education expenditure effort; they also increased per-student investment. Between 1980 and 1995, when the demographic opportunity stage had recently begun, Korea increased per-student expenditure (in terms of GDP per capita) by five points at the primary level and two points at the secondary level. In Japan, the increases were four points and two points, respectively, during the same period (Tilak 2002). Today, basic education quality in both Korea and Japan is highly recognized. In the 2012 edition of the PISA, for example, Korea ranked 5th out of 65 countries in the reading and math tests, and Japan ranked 7th and 4th, respectively.

Next, we present a series of simulation exercises based on the breakdown offered by equation 2, with the goal of estimating the magnitude of public expenditure effort that will be necessary to achieve various education policy objectives over the course of the demographic transition.

Before discussing the results, it is necessary to provide an explanation regarding the interpretation of these exercises. The demographic transformation is a very long-term process, which means that evaluating its impacts requires one to analyze a period of such length that it exceeds what would appear reasonable to obtain a minimally reliable economic projection. Even though these predictions encompass the 2010–2100 period to capture the demographic changes, the current analysis focuses on the dividend period that will end just before 2050, but even more specifically in the first two decades, from 2010 to 2030, when demographic opportunities appear and when the challenges that are simulated for education policy are valid.

Education Expenditure, Per-Student Benefits, and the Demographic Opportunity: Projections Based on Simulation Exercises

The question that drives these exercises is if the opportunity that the demographic dividend offers is sufficient or if a greater effort will be necessary to achieve the goals of increasing coverage and the efficiency of educational trajectories in basic education while simultaneously increasing per-student expenditure as a percentage of GDP per worker. Using the breakdown of Argentina's basic education expenditure in 2010 (status quo) as a starting point, we simulate the trajectories of total expenditure and per-student expenditure (normalized by GDP and GDP per potential worker, respectively) that would result from alternative education policy scenarios while the age structure of the population changes in accordance with the estimates discussed in chapter 2.

In line with the application of the National Transfer Accounts methodology used in the other chapters of this book, the analysis in this section focuses only on current expenditures, which in any case represent nearly all of public spending on basic education.[16] Consolidated public expenditure on basic education was 4.6 percent of GDP in 2010, of which 4.5 percent of GDP was current expenditure, mostly salaries.[17] In the simulations, we consider this 4.5 percent of GDP level of effort to fund basic education as the status quo.[18]

The status quo and the objectives related to net enrollment rates, the overage ratio, and the per-student benefit that were set for the simulations are summarized in table 8.2. In general, one can interpret these goals as designed to close the gap observed in 2010 between Argentina and the average of the OECD countries.[19] In terms of coverage, the proposed objectives differ by education level: increasing early childhood coverage from 67 to 85 percent, the secondary level from 84 to 95 percent, and the primary level from 99 percent to complete universalization. Together, these goals imply 95 percent coverage for basic education as a whole, that is, the population between ages 3 and 17 years old. In terms of per-student expenditure, the goal is an increase of 31 percent, from 12 percent to nearly 16 percent of GDP per potential worker, similar to the OECD average.

Although increasing net enrollment rates in the basic levels appears to be an indisputable policy objective, the interpretation of the rules to reduce overage enrollment is less obvious: On the one hand, overage enrollment can be understood as an indicator of failure, that students' educational pathways are not efficient (education lag, repetition), but it also can reflect the efforts of reinsertion and completion policies in the system. Keeping this double reading of the indicator in mind, we set an intermediate goal of reducing the proportion of overage students by half from the value observed in 2010.[20]

In terms of the amount of time necessary from the status quo until the completion of the goals, two alternative scenarios are presented: a rapid

Table 8.2 Status Quo and Policy Objectives Set for the Simulations

		Argentina 2010 status quo	Policy objectives 2020/2030
Current public expenditure on basic education/GDP (1)		4.5%	Endogenous
Expenditure per student/GDP per potential worker (2)		12.0%	Increase 31%
Education dependency ratio (3)			
	Total basic education	39%	Estimated
	Early childhood level	8%	Estimated
	Primary level	15%	Estimated
	Secondary level	16%	Estimated
Net enrollment rate (4)			
	Total basic education	87%	95%
	Early childhood level	67%	85%
	Primary level	99%	100%
	Secondary level	84%	95%
Overage ratio (5)			
	Total basic education	1.12	1.06
	Early childhood level	1.00	1.00
	Primary level	1.10	1.05
	Secondary level	1.18	1.08

Sources: Figures for the status quo are estimates based on (1) CGECSE, Ministry of Education; (3) chapter 2; (4) SEDLAC (CEDLAS-World Bank); and (5) 2009 Annual Survey and 2010 Statistical Yearbook (DiNIECE), except for the early childhood level, where it was assumed that overage enrollment did not exist. (2) Obtained as the residual value based on the previous variables and using the breakdown from equation 2. The education dependency ratio for 2020/2030 (estimated) is calculated based on the population projections presented in chapter 2.

convergence scenario during the 2010–20 decade and another more moderate convergence scenario that extends for 10 more years and encompasses the period from 2010 to 2030. If one considers that the difficulty of expanding coverage increases as coverage nears universality, then the moderate convergence scenario seems more realistic.[21] This would be the case particularly for primary education and the final grade of the early childhood level, where coverage is nearly perfect and any progress means improving the inclusion and completion of children in very vulnerable situations. It is important to note that with either of the two trajectories, the adjustment is completed during the demographic dividend period and that, even in the more moderate scenario, the education coverage goals are achieved in time to impact the final, largest group of students.[22]

Figure 8.9 shows the estimates for the number of students under the different scenarios. The "natural" evolution of enrollment, that is, that which is just a product of the demographic change, is represented in the figure. The effect of incorporating these education policy objectives on the number of students is a result of the net effect of two opposing forces: the expansion of coverage and the reduction of overage enrollment. In other words, all else constant, the expansion of coverage increases the number of students, while the reduction of overage enrollment reduces it. For example, the extra expansion of the number of

Figure 8.9 Projections of the Number of Students: Total Basic Education and by Level

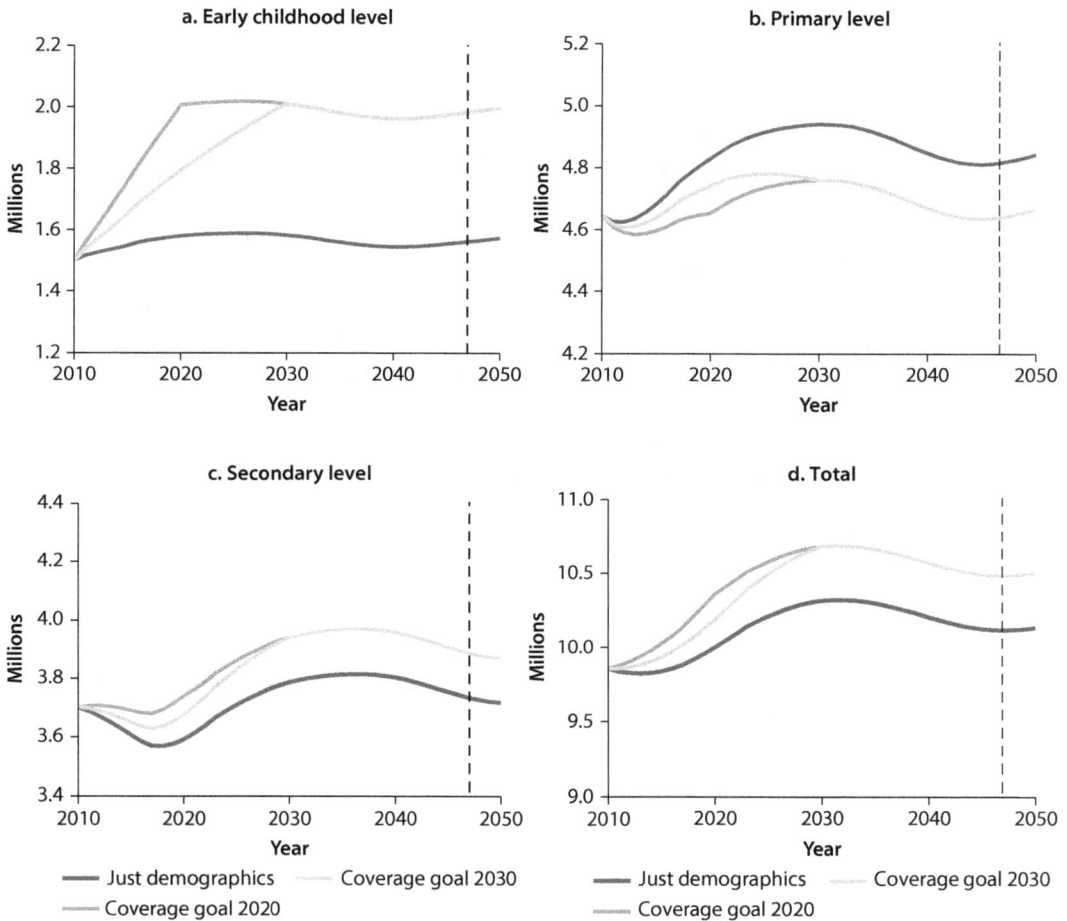

Source: Based on the estimates presented in chapter 2 and on the assumptions for each scenario. The scenarios "Coverage Goal 2020 (2030)" assume constant growth of the net enrollment rates and decreases of overage enrollment for the year 2020 (2030). See target values in table 8.2.

students in the early childhood level relative to the estimate that includes only demographic changes (figure 8.9a) is only a result of the change in the net enrollment rate. In contrast, at the primary level, where the net enrollment rate is nearly perfect (99 percent), the effect of the decrease in overage enrollment overshadows the coverage factor, and as a result the number of students estimated with these policy changes would be less than in their absence (figure 8.9b). The opposite occurs at the secondary level (figure 8.9c), where the decrease in overage students is more than offset by the expansion of the net enrollment rate (from 84 to 95 percent).

Finally, the effect that predominates in the aggregate of the three basic levels (figure 8.9d) is related to the expansion of coverage in the secondary level and in the first years of the early childhood level. Despite the simulated reduction of overage enrollment in the system, the expansion of coverage combined with a school-age population that continues growing (which will be the case until shortly after 2030) will increase the total enrollment in basic education by a little more than 800,000 students, an increase on the order of 8 percent relative to the 9.8 million students enrolled in 2010.

As discussed in chapter 4 regarding basic fiscal projections, the demographic changes that are expected in the coming decades, with the resulting reduction in the dependency ratios, will allow the government to increase the per-student benefit without needing to increase the expenditure effort for education. As figure 8.10 shows, this result remains the same, if one considers just basic education, and even if coverage and education trajectory efficiency increase. Naturally, the extra expansion of the number of students resulting from the increase in coverage would have a cost in terms of per-student benefit, represented as the gap of nearly half a percentage point of GDP per potential worker relative to the estimate that only accounts for demographic changes. The dashed horizontal line in figure 8.10 represents the goal of an increase of 31 percent in per-student expenditure as a percentage of the GDP per potential worker. The gap relative to that goal in the scenarios with coverage expansion is almost 2.5 percentage points of GDP per potential worker in 2030 and 1.2 percentage points toward the end of the demographic dividend period. As a result, if the challenge is to

Figure 8.10 Estimates of Per Student Expenditure: Simulations with Constant Expenditure Effort, Total Basic Education

Percent of GDP per potential worker

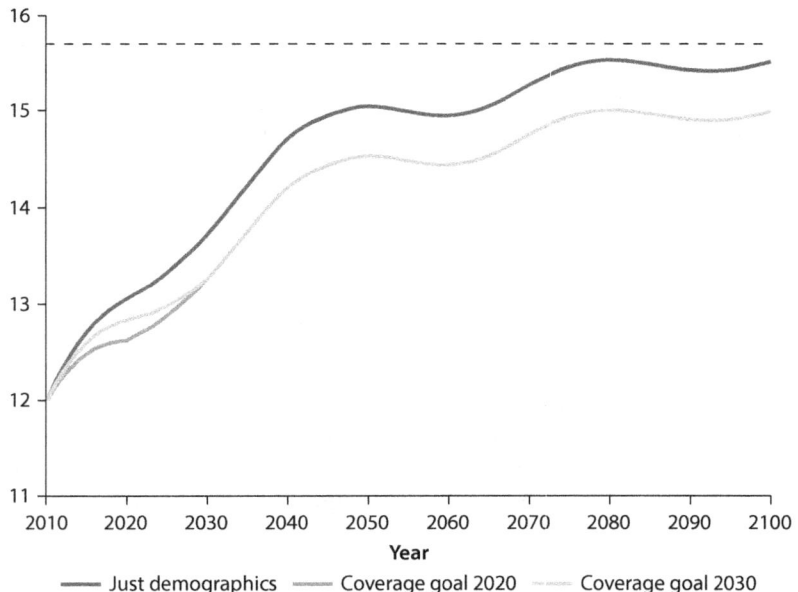

Source: Based on the estimates presented in chapter 2 and on the assumptions for each scenario.
Note: The scenarios "Coverage Goal 2020 (2030)" assume constant growth of the net enrollment rates and decreases of overage enrollment for the year 2020 (2030). See target values in table 8.2.

As Time Goes By in Argentina • http://dx.doi.org/10.1596/978-1-4648-0530-1

simultaneously achieve the goals of coverage, overage enrollment, and per-student expenditure, then the system will require a greater spending effort on education than Argentina made in 2010. Figure 8.11 illustrates this point.

If the per-student benefit were to remain fixed at the 2010 level (12 percent of GDP per potential worker), the reduction in the education dependency ratios would more than offset the increases in coverage and education trajectory efficiency (the series of solid lines in figure 8.11), resulting in a reduction in the effort required to fund basic education from 4.5 percent of GDP to 3.7 percent of GDP toward the end of the dividend period. More ambitious goals that contemplate a real increase in resources per student would require a higher level of spending on education. This funding requirement would increase progressively until it attained the per-student expenditure goal, which would occur in 2020 or 2030, depending on the scenario under consideration. The maximum effort required under the rapid convergence scenario would be a little more than 5.6 percent of GDP in 2020, and almost 5.4 percent of GDP in 2030, in the case of the more moderate convergence. Sustaining these levels of spending per student as a percentage of GDP per potential worker over the long term does not appear to leave any room for generating aggregate savings from the education system. As Figure 8.11 shows, once the demographic dividend period

Figure 8.11 Projections of Basic Education Expenditure

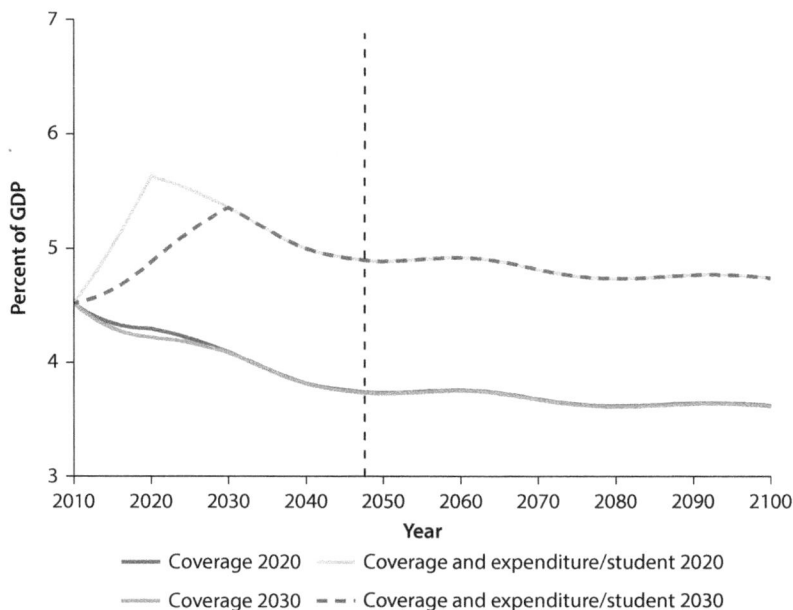

Source: Based on the estimates presented in chapter 2 and on the assumptions for each scenario.
Note: The scenarios "Coverage 2020 (2030)" refer to achieving the coverage and overage enrollment goals for 2020 (2030). In addition, "Coverage and Expenditure/student 2020 (2030)" assume constant growth of per-student expenditure until reaching the 31 percent increase in 2020 (2030). See target values in table 8.2.

concludes, the effort required to fund basic education will stabilize around 4.8 percent of GDP, greater than the 4.5 percent that Argentina spent in the 2010 status quo as well as the 4 percent that OECD countries currently earmark for education.

Simulations Disaggregated by Education Level

In this subsection, the previous simulation exercises are repeated, but instead of using basic education expenditure in the aggregate, the distribution of this expenditure among the three levels is considered. In this way, the goals related to per-student expenditure no longer focus on the average student enrolled in basic education but are redefined in terms of the average student enrolled in each level separately.

To this point, some limitations exist associated with the availability of information disaggregated by education level. The most complete data set known is from the General Coordinating Office for the Study of Education System Costs in the Ministry of Education, which publishes the education expenditures allocated to each level for the provinces and the City of Buenos Aires. On the basis of these data, it is estimated that for 2010 the percentage allocation of current expenditure on basic education by levels was 11 percent for early childhood education, 44 percent for primary, and 45 percent for secondary.[23]

Earlier, we noted that the gap between Argentina and the OECD in terms of spending translated to average student benefit in basic education was around 31 percent in 2010. Disaggregating this expenditure by levels, one observes that this gap varies between one education level and another (see table 8.3). The benefit per secondary student must increase by 26 percent to close the gap with the OECD countries, an increase of 31 percent as we assumed in the earlier simulations would not be sufficient for the primary level, but at the early childhood level it would be almost double what is necessary. In the following discussion, the simulation exercises are repeated, this time considering each education level independently.

Figure 8.12 presents the estimates of per-student expenditure that emerge from the simulations when expenditure effort remains constant for each education level. Naturally, all else constant, the demographic effect favors the sustained increase of per-student expenditure in terms of GDP per potential worker for all the levels, which would even allow the system to surpass the goals in terms of spending per student at the early childhood and secondary levels.

Once again, the results vary significantly when the coverage expansion and overage enrollment reduction objectives are included. The extra increase in the number of students in the early childhood and secondary levels increases the distance to the per-student expenditure goal. Moreover, at the early childhood level, per-student expenditure falls relative to the status quo because the significant enrollment expansion more than offsets the savings (in terms of GDP per potential worker) resulting from the demographic change. At the primary level, in contrast, the increase of educational trajectory efficiency overshadows the (marginal) expansion of coverage, reinforcing the demographic effect.

Box 8.3 Spending on Higher Education

This chapter focuses on basic education, deliberately setting higher education aside. One reason for this is that the methodological approach utilized, which focuses on universalization policies that tie the evolution of enrollment to demographic changes, does not appear to be appropriate for this level. The optional nature of higher education as well as vocational considerations and the vast heterogeneity of educational offerings place additional limitations on the methodological approach used for basic education.

With the goal of evaluating the impact of the policies simulated for the basic level on the funding of the education system as a whole, expenditure effort estimates for higher education are added in this box. This exercise leaves per-student expenditure as a percentage of GDP per potential worker fixed for this education level, but does allow the changes predicted for the dependency ratio and coverage increases. The higher education dependency ratio is calculated considering potential beneficiaries as the estimated population between ages 18 and 23 years old. For the second factor, it is assumed that the enrollment rates for higher education will increase, accompanying the coverage expansion simulated at the secondary level, after a lag (five years later). The percentage of youth that attend higher education institutions will thus increase from 31.4 percent (Continuous Household Survey, second half of 2010) until reaching 36.8 percent as the change comes to an end in 2025 or 2035.

Panel (a) of figure B8.3.1 shows the projection resulting from current expenditure on higher education in terms of GDP. The demographic opportunity is reflected in the trend: If all else remains constant, the reduction in higher education dependency will allow spending efforts to decrease without sacrificing expenditure per student. In addition, if higher education coverage is expanded, then the demographic dividend will initially be more than offset by the

Figure B8.3.1 Projections of Education Expenditure

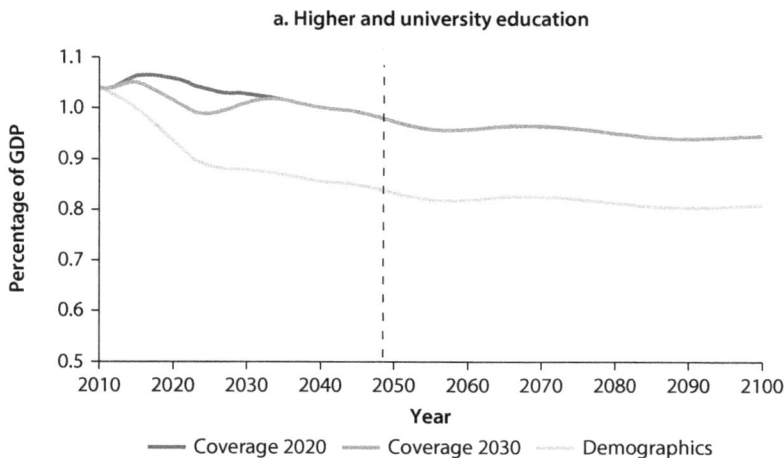

a. Higher and university education

Coverage 2020 —— Coverage 2030 ······ Demographics

box continues next page

Box 8.3 Spending on Higher Education *(continued)*

Figure B8.3.1 Projections of Education Expenditure *(continued)*

b. Basic+higher education

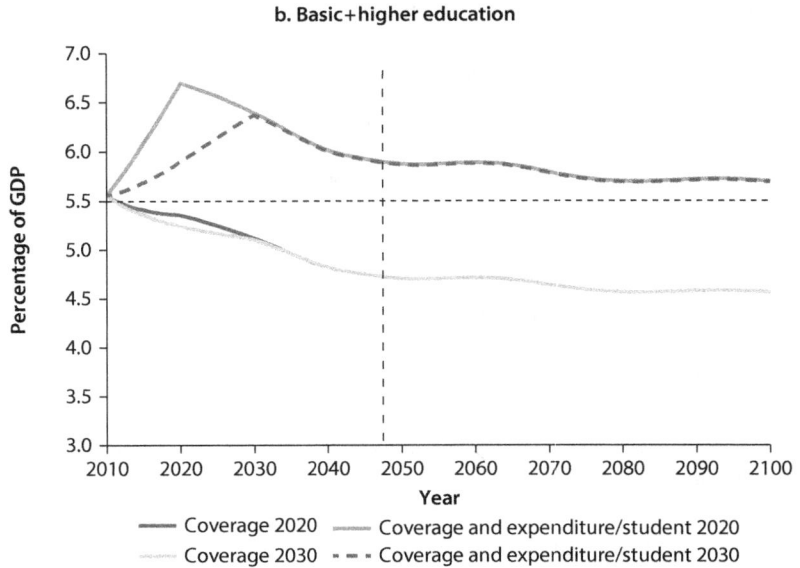

Source: Based on the estimates presented in chapter 2 and on the assumptions for each scenario.
Note: "Coverage 2020 (2030)" and "Coverage and Expenditure/student 2020 (2030)" refer to the scenarios
simulated for basic education according to the assumptions described in the text.

greater number of students. In the long term, funding requirements for higher education relative to the status quo will not decrease if an increase in enrollment rates is expected.

In panel (b) of the figure, the expenditure projections for higher education are added to
those that were obtained for basic education in figure 8.11. Again, one observes how after the
demographic dividend period, the effort required (current expenditure as percentage of
GDP) to fund the education system will stabilize around a level higher than the 5.6 percent in
the status quo scenario and also above the 5.5 percent that OECD countries currently earmark
for education.

In summary, in the proposed scenarios, none of the basic education levels could
achieve the goal of per-student expenditure given the effects of coverage expansion and reduction of overage enrollment if expenditure effort and the allocation
among levels remained fixed at the status quo levels.

Even though the aggregated simulations produced qualitatively similar results,
these simulations exhibit indications that the gap that must be closed to reach
the goals differs among levels. This suggests that if the expansion of expenditure
effort in basic education required to increase per-student expenditure were
accompanied by a reallocation of spending among levels, the effort required to
fund basic education could be less than was estimated in the aggregated

Table 8.3 Status Quo and Target Expenditure per Student in the Simulations Disaggregated by Education Level

	Early childhood level	Primary level	Secondary level
Status quo Argentina, 2010			
Public expenditure on education as a percentage of GDP (1)	0.5	2.0	2.0
Education dependency ratio (%) (2)	8	16	15
Net enrollment rate (%) (3)	67	99	84
Overage ratio (4)	1.00	1.10	1.18
Expenditure per student as a percentage of GDP per potential worker (5)	9.6	11.2	13.8
Goal of expenditure per student as a percentage of GDP per potential worker (6)			
Percentage increase by 2020/2030	17	34	26
Level to reach in 2020/2030	11.3	15.0	17.4

Sources: Based on (1) CGECSE, Ministry of Education; (2) chapter 2; (3) SEDLAC (CEDLAS–World Bank); (4) 2009 Annual Survey and 2010 Statistical Yearbook (DiNIECE), except for the early childhood level, where it is assumed that there is no overage enrollment; (5) the residual value of the breakdown of equation 2 and the earlier variables; (6) applying the gap between per-student benefit (normalized by GDP per potential worker) that existed between Argentina and the OECD average in 2010, estimated based on information from the UNESCO Institute for Statistics.

simulations. Figure 8.13 compares this alternative with the option of pursuing a uniform increase of 31 percent of per-student expenditure in all the basic levels (the colored series in this figure, the same one that was called "Coverage and expenditure/student 2030" in figure 8.11). The reallocation of resources among education levels as the goals are achieved would allow the system to free up some real resources; however, those resources would represent just one-tenth of a percentage point of GDP per year, which supports our earlier conclusion: In the long term, policy makers should not expect to find savings in the education system.

Final Reflections

This chapter measured the impact of demographic changes on the expenditure effort required to fund basic education in Argentina using simulation exercises. On the one hand, these exercises include the evolution of demographic variables, while on the other they incorporate policy objectives aimed at coverage expansion, increasing the efficiency of educational trajectories, and increasing per-student expenditure as a percentage of GDP per potential worker.

The first manifestation of the demographic and policy channels' effects on basic education is evident through the number of students. On the one hand, the population is evolving: The size of the basic-school-age population (age 3 to 17 years old) is forecast to continue growing until the beginning of the 2030s. On the other hand, the coverage expansion and reduction in the overage ratio objectives have contradictory effects on the number of students enrolled. As a result, at the primary level, where enrollment rates are nearly perfect, the

Figure 8.12 Projections of Expenditure per Student: Simulations with Constant Effort at Each Education Level

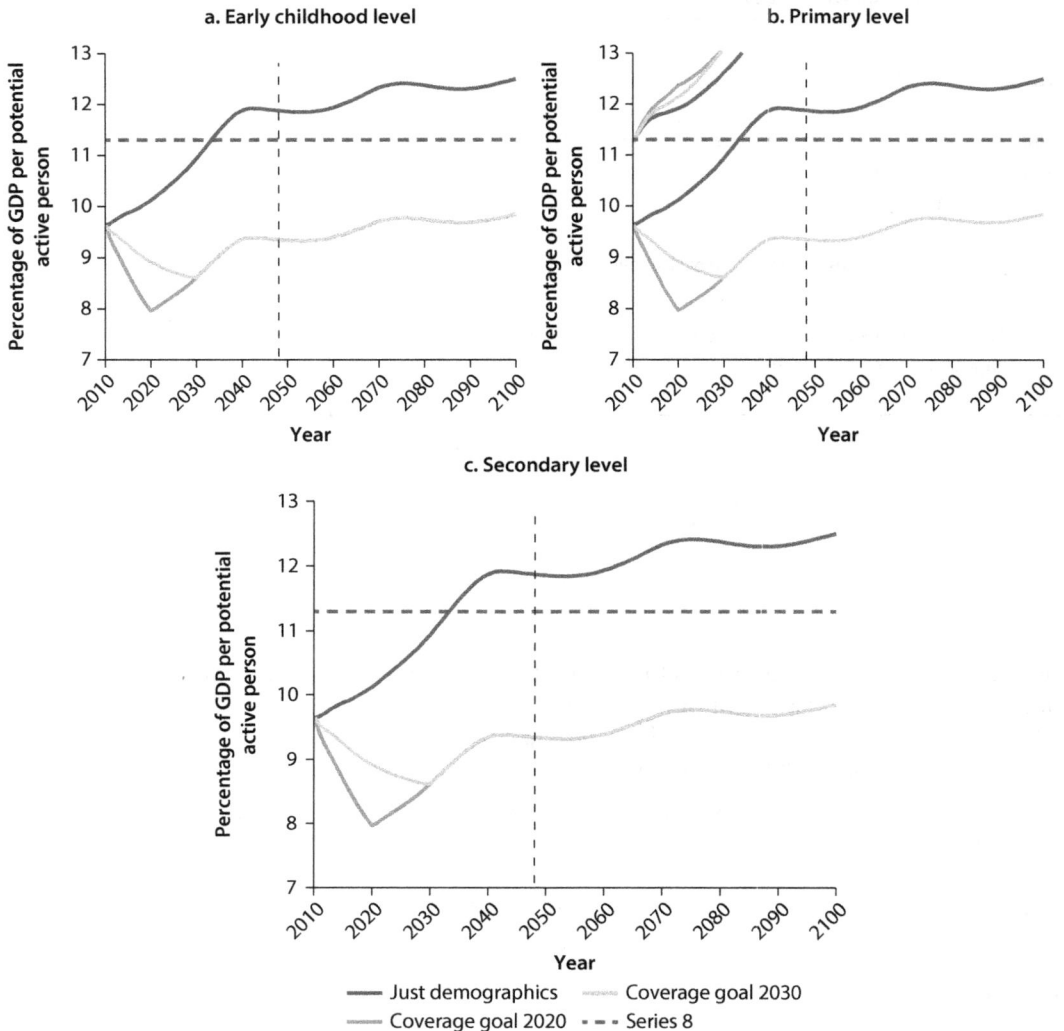

a. Early childhood level

b. Primary level

c. Secondary level

— Just demographics ⋯⋯ Coverage goal 2030
— Coverage goal 2020 - - - Series 8

Source: Based on the estimates presented in chapter 2 and on the assumptions for each scenario.
Note: The Coverage goal 2020 and coverage goal 2030 scenarios assume constant growth in the net enrollment rates and reductions related to overage enrollment for 2020 (2030). See the target values in table 8.3.

reduction of overage enrollment overshadows the effect of the expansion of coverage. In the other levels, the opposite occurs, and the effect that predominates in terms of total basic education enrollment is the expansion of coverage at the secondary level and in the first years of the early childhood level.

The demographic opportunity, which materializes through the contraction of the education dependency ratio, is evident in the simulations: If the expenditure effort earmarked to fund basic education maintains its 2010 levels (status quo), then per-student expenditure (as a percentage of GDP per potential worker) will

Figure 8.13 Projections of Expenditure on Basic Education

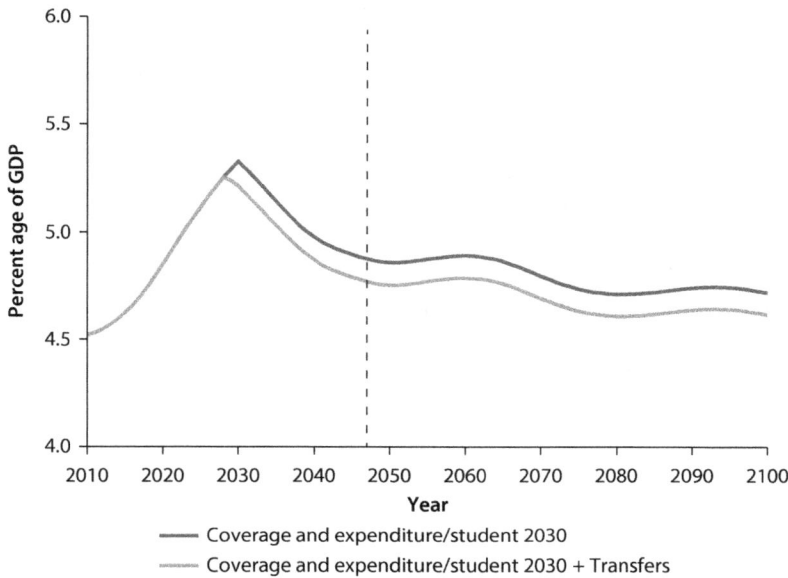

- Coverage and expenditure/student 2030
- Coverage and expenditure/student 2030 + Transfers

Source: Based on the estimates presented in chapter 2 and on the assumptions for each scenario.
Note: The Coverage and expenditure/student 2030 scenario assumes constant growth in the net enrollment rates and reductions to the overage ratio for 2030. The Coverage and expenditure/student 2030 + Transfers scenario includes transfers of savings among education levels (from early childhood and secondary to primary) once the goals are achieved. See the target values in table 8.3.

increase even as enrollment grows. According to the assumptions used here, the magnitude of the effect is an increase in per-student expenditure of 2.5 percentage points of GDP per potential worker by the end of the dividend period, which represents an increase of around 20 percent compared with the status quo. Nonetheless, this increase will not be sufficient if the goal is to achieve per-student expenditure levels (normalized in terms of GDP per potential worker) similar to those of the OECD countries in 2010. In other words, if policy makers seek to close the gap in per-student expenditure that separates Argentina from the most developed countries as well as expand coverage and reduce the overage ratio, then the expenditure effort to fund basic education must increase. According to our assumptions, the maximum effort required would be 5.6 percent of GDP (1.1 percentage points more than the status quo in 2010) and would be applied once the coverage goals are achieved (in 2020 in the more optimistic simulation, when the dividend is still in force and the school-age population is still growing). Nonetheless, in the long term, policy makers should not expect any resource savings from the basic education system if the achievements in terms of coverage, educational trajectory efficiency, and per-student expenditure are to be sustained. Following the most demanding years during which the adjustment is made, the (current) expenditure effort required to fund basic education will stabilize around 4.8 percent of GDP, higher than in

2010 (status quo), and more than the OECD countries currently earmark for education, which is around 4 percent of GDP.

In this chapter, the opportunity to make progress on some specific education goals provided by the transformation of the population's age structure was analyzed: increasing coverage, reducing overage enrollment, and increasing per-student expenditure. These are important goals linked to the objectives of universal access to basic education, which are also easily quantifiable and whose relationship with demographic processes can be established directly. However, these quantitative objectives should be understood as initial goals that must be accompanied by qualitative improvements in terms of quality and equality in the education system. The increase in investment per student is not sufficient to achieve improvements in education quality, as the Argentine experience in recent years and international evidence have shown. It is necessary that the increased effort to fund education be accompanied by improvements in the efficiency of spending to achieve the pedagogical and organizational transformations that will facilitate translating this increased investment into better educational quality that increases human capital and individual productivity, both of which are necessary to face the higher costs associated with and aging population once the demographic dividend has been exhausted.

Notes

1. Nursery schools, which also form part of the early childhood level, covering children from 45 days of age until age three, are excluded from this analysis.

2. Currently, Argentina's 24 jurisdictions (23 provinces plus the Autonomous City of Buenos Aires) are divided evenly between the two options. The 6–6 option has been adopted by the provinces of Buenos Aires, Córdoba, Corrientes, Chubut, Entre Ríos, Formosa, La Pampa, San Juan, San Luis, Santa Cruz, Tucumán, and Tierra del Fuego. Meanwhile, the jurisdictions that have chosen the 7–5 option are the Autonomous City of Buenos Aires, Catamarca, Chaco, Jujuy, La Rioja, Mendoza, Misiones, Neuquén, Río Negro, Salta, Santa Fe, and Santiago del Estero. See Ministry of Education portal, http://portal.educacion.gov.ar, and DiNIECE (2012).

3. These figures include students at public and private institutions in the common education modality, which represents 92 percent of the total number of students. Special education and the youth and adult education modalities represent 1 and 7 percent of the total student population, respectively, in the three levels of education. (DiNIECE 2010).

4. National Education Law 24,195 replaced the previous structure of seven years of primary education and five years of secondary with the General Basic Education (Educación General Básica, EGB) and the Multimodal level. The former was structured in three cycles of three years each, and the latter in a single three-year cycle. Along with this reform, compulsory education expanded from seven years of the previous primary level, to the three cycles of EGB plus the final year of early childhood education.

5. Examples of these regulations include the LEN, the Educational Funding Law, the 2009–2011 and 2012–2016 National Plans for Compulsory Education, and

commitment to the 2021 Educational Goals from the Organization of Ibero-American States.

6. Accompanying this expansion of enrollment and coverage at the basic levels, the private sector's participation grew significantly. In the last decade, for example, its proportion of total enrollment grew from 24 to 27 percent (DiNIECE 2012).

7. According to data from UNESCO, the net enrollment rate at the primary level as an average of the OECD countries was 97.3 percent in 2010.

8. For more on meeting the LFE's goals, see Bezem et al. (2012). In 2010 the LEN regulations took effect, which set a minimum of 6 percent of GDP for expenditure intended exclusively for education.

9. Transfers to subsidized private institutions are included in spending on basic education. Education funding is mostly the responsibility of the provincial jurisdictions and the Autonomous City of Buenos Aires, which in 2010 contributed 75 percent of total funding to the education system. Provincial expenditure is mostly earmarked for the payment of salaries at the basic levels and nonuniversity higher education, while investment in capital goods and university education is mainly funded by the national government. Current expenditures represent the greatest portion of public expenditure on education. In 2010 consolidated public spending on education was 5.8 percent of GDP, of which 5.6 percent of GDP corresponded to current expenditures. At the basic levels, total expenditure was 4.6 percent of GDP, of which 4.5 percent of GDP was current expenditure (estimates based on information from the CGECSE in the Ministry of Education).

10. The data on education expenditure in 2010 published by UNESCO coincide with our estimates based on official sources in Argentina, which are the sources we used in the rest of the sections of this chapter (see, for example, figure 8.5 and its sources).

11. The only exception in our sample is Israel.

12. The $R2$ of the linear regression between expenditure on basic education and expenditure per student (expressed as a percentage of GDP and of GDP per potential worker, respectively) is 49 percent.

13. The product of the first two factors is known in the intergenerational transfer literature as the benefit generosity ratio, because it measures the generosity or effort of the transfers that active generations make to fund the education of children and youth. For greater detail, see chapter 4.

14. Per-student funding needs in Argentina could possibly be less than those in the OECD for the same year. The cost per student may increase along with the level of development as the relative prices between tradable and nontradable goods change, which is known in the literature as the Balassa-Samuelson effect. Education expenditure mostly consists of teacher salaries (nontradable), which are expected to increase relative to the price of tradable goods as the country grows wealthier.

15. The school-age population (age 3 to 17 years old) will remain relatively stable around an average of 10.4 million children and youth during the 2010–2100 period. The largest variation will occur during the first two decades, when a moderate expansion (5 percent) is predicted from a minimum of 10.1 million to a maximum of 10.6 million. During the same period, the population in the active age range will increase more quickly, thus explaining the estimated drop in the education dependency ratio.

16. For more information on the National Transfer Accounts methodology, see chapter 3. An analysis of the expenditure of the university level of education is described in box 8.3.

17. The estimates are based on information from the General Coordinating Office for the Study of Education System Costs in the Ministry of Education, the Directorate of Macroeconomic Policy in the Ministry of Economy and Finance, and estimates from Bezem et al. (2012). The figures for consolidated expenditure coincide with those published by UNESCO. For more information, see the third section of this chapter.

18. This total includes current expenditure earmarked to fund public educational institutions from the three basic levels (4 percent of GDP) and transfers to the private sector earmarked for the same levels (0.5 percent of GDP). The transfers to the privately managed sector are also intended to fund nonuniversity higher education at subsidized private institutions, but information is not available regarding the proportional distribution of these transfers by education level. To allocate the portion of the transfers that corresponds to the basic levels, we assume the same distribution by level that is observed for provincial expenditure on public education from the total of all jurisdictions, using the data published by the CGECSE for 2010 as the source. Thus, of the 0.6 percent of GDP that corresponds to transfers to private institutions, we assume that 94.2 percent (i.e., 0.5 percent of GDP) is earmarked to fund the basic levels.

19. These convergence scenarios are common assumptions in other works that utilize similar methodologies to the one applied here, for example, Gragnolati and colleagues (2011), Miller and colleagues (2011), and ECLAC (2008), among others. In chapter 4, the authors present various fiscal projections assuming convergence scenarios that serve as the basis for our exercises.

20. Note that the overage ratio is defined as the ratio between the total number of students and the total number of students in the legal age range (see equation 2). If one starts with an overage ratio of 1.10, reducing the proportion of students that exceed the legal age would result in an overage ratio of 1.05.

21. The periods for rapid and moderate convergence (2020 and 2030, respectively) are similar to those that would result from extrapolating the coverage trend observed during the 2000–10 decade. Using a linear extrapolation of this trend, the goals would be met in 2017 or a little before 2030 if one assumed a decreasing rate of growth.

22. Keep in mind that the basic-school-age population will continue to grow until approximately 2031.

23. Even though provincial expenditure represents the largest portion of current public expenditure on education, there are two additional limitations to this information source: 27 percent of provincial education expenditure is not disaggregated by level, and 10 provinces of a total of 24 jurisdictions do not provide expenditure information disaggregated between early childhood and primary education. Given these restrictions, we opted to assume that (1) the percentage allocation by levels of expenditures that are disaggregated can be applied to total current expenditure on basic education, and (2) the allocation between early childhood and primary education from the provinces with disaggregated information can be extrapolated for use in all the jurisdictions.

    This distribution is similar to that published by the UNESCO Institute for Statistics, according to which 9 percent of current public expenditure on education corresponds to the early childhood level, 41 percent to the primary level, and 50 percent to the secondary.

References

Auguste, S. 2012. "La calidad educativa en la Argentina." Documento de Trabajo 116, Fundación de Investigaciones Económicas Latinoamericanas, Buenos Aires.

Bezem, P., F. Mezzadra, and A. Rivas. 2012. "Monitoreo de la Ley de Financiamiento Educativo. Informe final." Informe de Monitoreo y Evaluación, Centro de Implementación de Políticas Públicas para la Equidad y el Crecimiento, Buenos Aires.

Delich, A., G. Iaies, N. Savransky, and M. Galliano. 2009. "Análisis del informe de resultados del ONE 2007. Hacia un nuevo debate de los resultados de las evaluaciones de calidad educativa en la Argentina." Centro de Estudios en Políticas Públicas, Buenos Aires.

DiNIECE (Dirección Nacional de Información y Evaluación de la Calidad Educativa). 2003. "Informe de resultados. Operativo Nacional de Evaluación (ONE) 2003." Ministerio de Educación, Ciencia y Tecnología de la Nación, Buenos Aires.

———. 2005. "Aspectos conceptuales y resultados nacionales. Operativo Nacional de Evaluación (ONE) 2005." Ministerio de Educación, Ciencia y Tecnología de la Nación, Buenos Aires.

———. 2010. "Las cifras de la educación inicial y sus modelos de organización." Temas de Educación. Boletín DiNIECE, year 5, no. 8, Dirección Nacional de Información y Evaluación de la Calidad Educativa, Ministerio de Educación, Buenos Aires.

———. 2011. "La Transformación del nivel secundario (2006–2009)." Temas de Educación. Boletín DiNIECE year 6, no. 9, Dirección Nacional de Información y Evaluación de la Calidad Educativa, Ministerio de Educación, Buenos Aires.

———. 2012. "El nivel primario. Un análisis cuantitativo." Serie Informes de investigación no. 7, Dirección Nacional de Información y Evaluación de la Calidad Educativa, Ministerio de Educación, Buenos Aires.

ECLAC (Economic Commission for Latin America and the Caribbean), ed. 2008. "Capítulo III. El bono demográfico: una oportunidad para avanzar en materia de cobertura y progresión en educación secundaria." In *Panorama Social de América Latina* 2008: 143–69.

ECLAC-OIE (Economic Commission for Latin America and the Caribbean and Organization of Ibero-American States for Education, Science, and Culture). 2009. *Metas educativas, 2021: estudio de costos*. ECLAC and OIE. Santiago de Chile: United Nations.

Glewwe, P., E. Hanushek, S. Humpage, and R. Ravina. 2011. "School Resources and Educational Outcomes in Developing Countries: A Review of the Literature from 1990 to 2010." NBER Working Paper 17554, National Bureau of Economic Research, Cambridge, MA.

Gragnolati, M., O. Hagen Jorgensen, R. Rocha, and A. Fruttero, eds. 2011. *Growing Old in an Older Brazil: Implications of Population Aging on Growth, Poverty, Public Finance, and Service Delivery*. Washington, DC: World Bank.

Gundlach, E., and L. Woessmann. 2001. "The Fading Productivity of Schooling in East Asia." *Journal of Asian Economics* 12 (3): 401–17.

Gundlach, E., L. Woessmann, and J. Gmelin. 2001. "The Decline of Schooling Productivity in OECD Countries." *Economic Journal* 111 (471): C135–47.

Hanushek, E. 2003. "The Failure of Input-Based Schooling Policies." *Economic Journal* 113 (485): F64–98.

Hanushek, E., and L. Woessmann. 2011. "The Economics of International Differences in Educational Achievement." In *Handbook of the Economics of Education*, vol. 3, edited by E. Hanushek, S. Machin, and L. Woessmann, 89–200. Amsterdam: North-Holland.

Marchionni, M., F. Pinto, and E. Vazquez. 2013. "Determinantes de la desigualdad en el desempeño educativo en la Argentina." Anales de la Asociación Argentina de Economía Política, XLVIII Reunión Anual, Buenos Aires, November 13–15.

Miller, T., C. Mason, and M. Holz. 2011. "The Fiscal Impact of Demographic Change in Ten Latin American Countries: Projecting Public Expenditures in Education, Health, and Pensions." In *Population Aging: Is Latin America Ready?* edited by D. Cotlear, 233–72. Washington, DC: World Bank.

PISA. 2012. "Does Money Buy Strong Performance in PISA?" PISA in Focus 13. OECD.

Rivas, A. 2003. "Mirada comparada de los efectos de la reforma educativa en las Provincias." Serie de Estudios sobre el Estado, el Poder y la Educación en la Argentina, Documento 2, CIPPEC, Buenos Aires.

Tilak, J. 2000. *World Education Report, 2000: The Right to Education.* Washington, DC: UNESCO.

———. 2002. *Building Human Capital in East Asia: What Others Can Learn.* Washington, DC: World Bank.

———. 2007. "Operational Definition of Basic Education. Thematic Framework." http://www.unesco.org/education/framework.pdf.

———. 2008a. *Medium Term Strategy (2008–2013).* Paris: UNESCO.

———. 2008b. "Educación para todos en 2015 ¿Alcanzaremos la meta?" Informe de seguimiento de la EPT en el Mundo, UNESCO, Paris, France.

UNESCO. 1996. *Learning: The Treasure Within.* Report to UNESCO of the International Commission of Education for the Twenty-first Century. Paris.

CHAPTER 9

The Limits and Virtues of Reviewing Long-Term Fiscal Policy in Light of Demographic Change in Argentina

Oscar Cetrángolo

Introduction

Fiscal policy is designed and implemented in such a way that it affects each age group in a society differently. As a consequence, demographic changes will necessarily provoke changes in the levels and structure of public expenditure and its funding. The various chapters that make up this volume approach the impacts, policy options, and trade-offs of population aging from diverse perspectives. The current chapter should be viewed as a complement to the rest, in which a set of considerations is presented that, based on a reading of the previous chapters, should be taken with special consideration for the medium- and long-term planning of fiscal policy. Specifically this chapter examines the fiscal impacts that come from the adaptation of the various sectorial policies studied in terms of demographic changes and also attempts to approximate the aggregate impact on the public accounts.

The Argentine case exhibits features that make this type of examination a central element of economic policy. One must remember that two of the factors that have had significant impact on the public accounts during the last 30 years have been closely linked to intergenerational financial transfers: debt and the social security crisis. As such, now is a good time to analyze how the temporary existence of a demographic window of opportunity and its subsequent disappearance as a result of population aging could affect the public accounts and force policy makers to reflect on their reformulation. If the belief is that a good policy is one that manages to anticipate problems, this type of analysis is of enormous importance.

One obvious but essential clarification: What is presented here is not a prediction of what is expected to occur during the next 100 years; it is not even an approximation. In contrast, it is an exercise intended to detect points of conflict, the need for definitions that anticipate problems, and a sensitivity analysis of the accounts in terms of certain decisions or the lack thereof. What predictive capacity would this exercise have had 100 years ago, when a specific Ministry of Education did not exist,[1] the social security system had not been constructed—only a few isolated and autonomous retirement funds existed, and no one was thinking about the need for moratoriums—and penicillin would not be discovered for another 15 years? Nonetheless, it is of special interest to exhaust the available knowledge today to define the conflicts and decisions that must be dealt with in the future as a result of the demographic change, knowing that there will be other significant changes during this period. Among these, technological and climate change attract the most attention, but they will certainly not be the only changes to have a significant impact.

The speculation presented here does not attempt to hide the uncertainty about the future, but rather to make it more explicit to allow for a more correct evaluation of the changes that can certainly be expected as a result of population aging. In an attempt to point out the limitations and rescue the virtues of this exercise, this chapter begins by discussing the strengths and weaknesses at the beginning of the projections, presenting the persistent tensions in the public accounts to be able to evaluate the results of the sectorial studies and their impact on long-term fiscal evolution.

A Characterization of the Fiscal Situation at the Starting Point Chosen as the Base Year for the Estimates

This study uses 2010 as the base year (see chapter 3). Regardless of the factors that were considered to make this decision, any long-term projection is very much dependent on the situation at the beginning of the projection period. In the present section, this choice is not discussed. Rather, it is essential to evaluate the virtues and difficulties of choosing this year as a starting point for long-term estimates from a fiscal point of view. Three basic questions appear unavoidable: Did the public sector exhibit significant imbalances in 2010? Did unresolved tensions in terms of fiscal issues exist at that time, regardless of the eventual imbalance? What was the role of each age group in these potential tensions?

To begin thinking about the answers to these questions, we first present the fiscal situation during that period to subsequently, in the sections that follow, provide some historical perspective for the situation that year and point out the principal points of tension that the public accounts exhibited at that time.

Fiscal Indicators in 2010

As table 9.1 shows,[2] in 2010 the consolidated public sector (national and provincial) had a balanced budget and, as a result, a positive primary result equivalent to the payment of interest on the national debt (2 percent of gross domestic product [GDP]). This situation favors the utilization of this year as the base case for the estimates. However, we will attempt to evaluate this period more precisely.

Table 9.1 Nonfinancial Public Sector (Consolidated National and Provincial), Estimate of 2010 Results: Savings-Investment-Financing Account
Percentage of GDP

Current income	37.1
Tax income	26.3
Contributions to social security	6.1
Nontax	4.7
Current expenditures	32.5
Consumption and operating expenditures	14.8
Rents for property	2.0
Social security benefits	7.3
Current transfers	8.3
Capital revenues	0.3
Capital expenditure	5.0
Total income	37.4
Total expenditure	37.5
Financial result	−0.1
Primary surplus	1.9

Source: Elaboration based on information from the Secretariat of the Treasury.

The projections in the current study refer to just one portion of the public budgets. Essentially, this analysis has worked with public consumption expenditures in education, health care, pension payments, and other social protection transfers. In addition, spending by certain nonstate institutions has been included in what is called public consumption, such as national employer-based health plans and provincial social security institutions, whose activities are not included in public sector accounting performed by the Secretariat of the Treasury, although they provide valuable goods funded by compulsory contributions from workers. With the goal of clarifying the significance of the differences between the different measurements, table 9.2 outlines the composition of each of the methodologies considered.

The evaluation of the public sector's financial situation in 2010 should take into consideration the existence of public indebtedness. In that sense, it should be pointed out that following the jump in debt indicators during the crisis years at the beginning of the century, the ratio of public debt to GDP has decreased and stabilized around levels that can be considered solvent, near 40 percent of GDP, as shown in figure 9.1.

The calculations of the impact of demographic change included in the different sectorial studies related to social protection, education, and health care include only public consumption of the sectors involved and a group of transfers when they refer to public expenditures. Consequently, there is a segment of public expenditure nearly as significant as the portion analyzed that has remained outside the considerations included in these studies. Comments on the fiscal impact of this expenditure should be taken with care, especially when the

Table 9.2 Comparison of Fiscal Expenditures and NTA Estimates
Percent of GDP

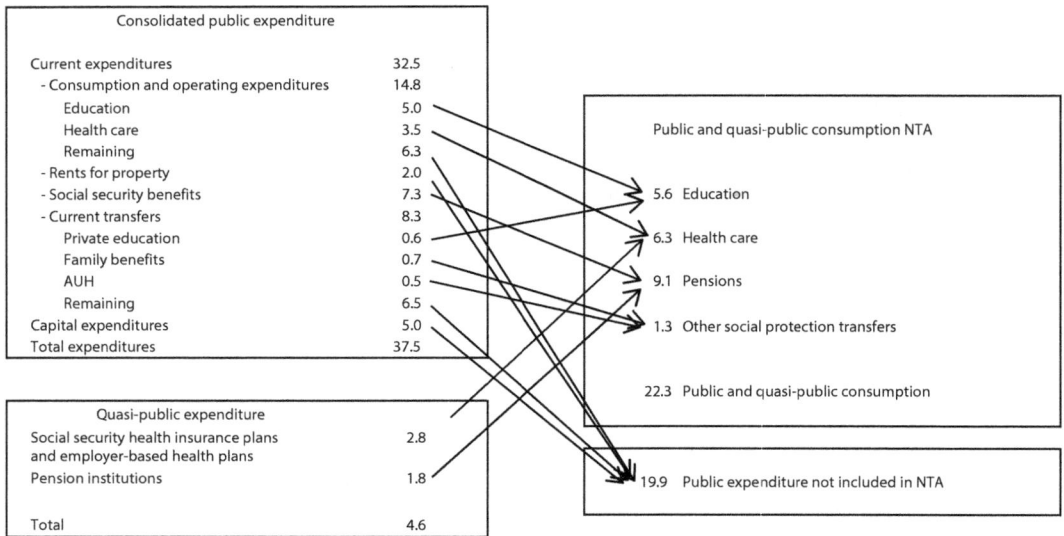

Consolidated public expenditure	
Current expenditures	32.5
- Consumption and operating expenditures	14.8
Education	5.0
Health care	3.5
Remaining	6.3
- Rents for property	2.0
- Social security benefits	7.3
- Current transfers	8.3
Private education	0.6
Family benefits	0.7
AUH	0.5
Remaining	6.5
Capital expenditures	5.0
Total expenditures	37.5

Public and quasi-public consumption NTA	
5.6	Education
6.3	Health care
9.1	Pensions
1.3	Other social protection transfers
22.3	Public and quasi-public consumption

Quasi-public expenditure	
Social security health insurance plans and employer-based health plans	2.8
Pension institutions	1.8
Total	4.6

19.9	Public expenditure not included in NTA

Source: Elaboration based on information from the Secretariat of the Treasury and chapter 3.
Note: AUH = Asignación Universal por Hijo; NTA = National Transfer Accounts.

Figure 9.1 Public Debt (Including Holdouts), 1994–2012

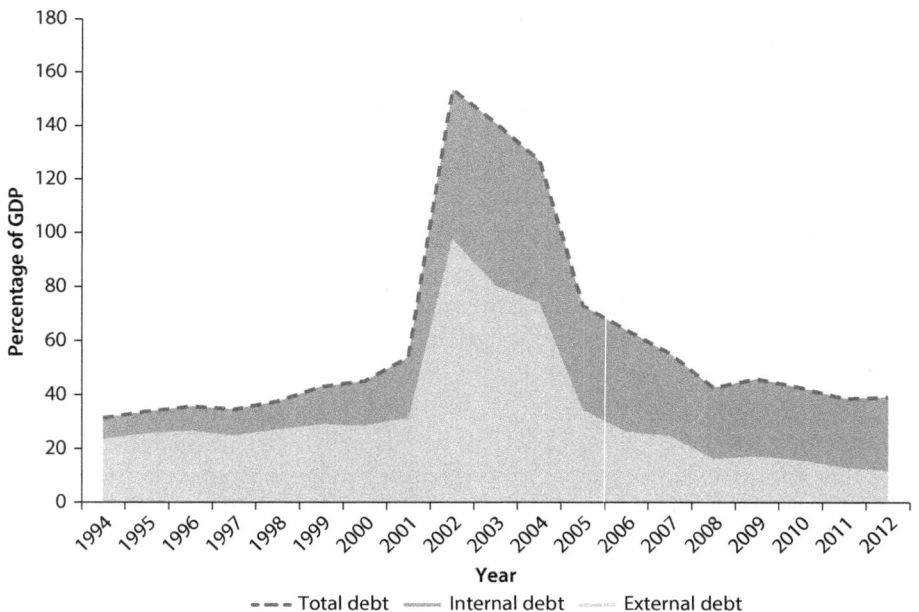

Source: Elaboration based on information from the Ministry of Economy and Public Finances.

remaining components of the savings-investment scheme shown in table 9.1 are assumed to remain constant (or are not considered).

It is especially important to keep in mind that this exercise does not account for capital expenditures. Because these are predictions about growth and aging in the long term, this is a significant limitation, especially considering the current consensus surrounding the weaknesses of energy and other types of infrastructure that characterize the Argentine economy at the beginning of these projections.

In contrast, from the revenue perspective, the breakdown by age groups that is presented in chapter 3 has accounted for the entirety of tax income (including social security contributions), and as a result the coverage is much higher.

In terms of the significance of the categories considered, it should be pointed out that the largest proportion of health care and public education expenditures are included in provincial government consumption spending. Meanwhile, social protection transfers are, for the most part, carried out by the national government. In contrast, the remaining transfers, interest on the debt, and capital expenditures are not covered by the present analysis.

The Base Year from a Historical Perspective

To evaluate the fiscal result of the base year it is essential to provide some historical perspective. During the three decades leading up to that year, the governments of the new Argentine democracy that emerged beginning in 1983 faced adverse economic situations that, generally, were characterized by significant fiscal restrictions.

In a first look at the Argentine public accounts over the long term,[3] a long period of the economic history of Argentina stands out. During this time, the consolidated public sector has exhibited a persistent imbalance in both financial and primary (not including interest expenditures) terms. Nonetheless, the trend toward recovery since the 1980s is notable. Without a doubt, the tensions that the democratic governments have faced following the debt crisis at the beginning of the 1980s and subsequent fiscal restrictions and macroeconomic volatility have had a significant impact on the structure and dynamics of the public accounts.

In summary, the fiscal solvency achieved after the 2001–02 crisis, even though it is extraordinary, should be understood as the culmination of a long and enduring process of improvement in the overall results of the national and provincial accounts. Consolidating this situation will depend on the ability of fiscal policy to confront the tensions implicit in the public budget.

Before naming the factors that have defined the evolution of the fiscal results, it is advisable to make an additional comment regarding public sector funding. How have such significant and tenacious imbalances been financed over such a long period? It is difficult to explain these imbalances without considering the existence of monetary financing of the fiscal deficit (normally called the inflationary tax). Until the beginning of the 1990s, issuing money was a very important way of funding the public sector. In figure 9.2, one can observe the long-term

Figure 9.2 Evolution of Consolidated Results, National and Provincial, 1961–2012
Percent of GDP

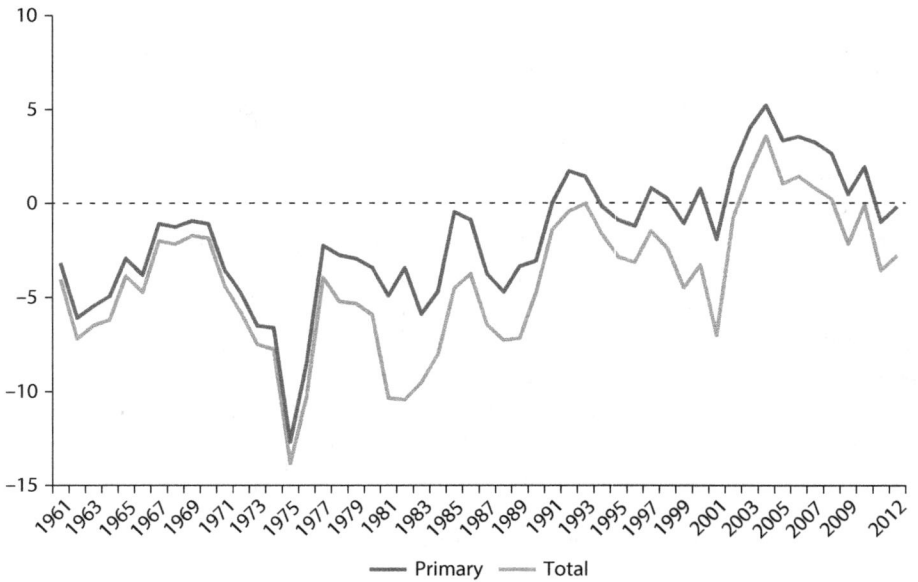

─── Primary   ─── Total

Source: Based on information from the Secretariat of the Treasury, INDEC, and BCRA.

Figure 9.3 Monetary Financing and the Fiscal Bottom Line, 1961–2011

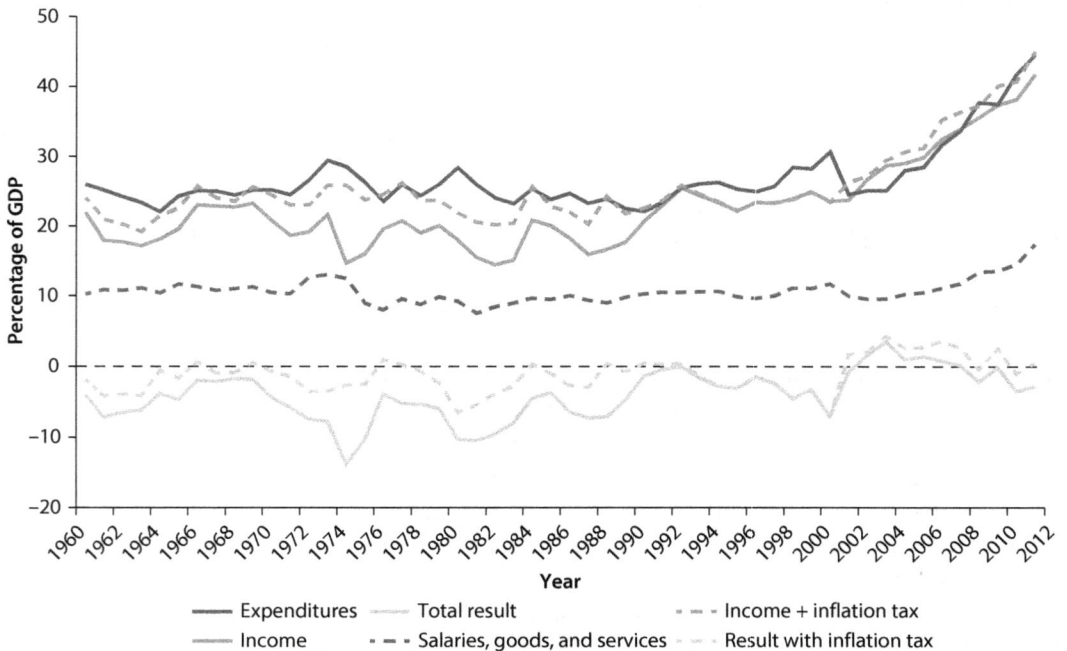

─── Expenditures   ─── Total result   ‒ ‒ ‒ Income + inflation tax
─── Income   ‒ ‒ ‒ Salaries, goods, and services   ‒ ‒ ‒ Result with inflation tax

Source: Based on information from the Secretariat of the Treasury, INDEC, BCRA, and Albrieu and Cetrángolo 2011.

Figure 9.4 Total Expenditure and Principal Components, 1961–2012
Percent of GDP

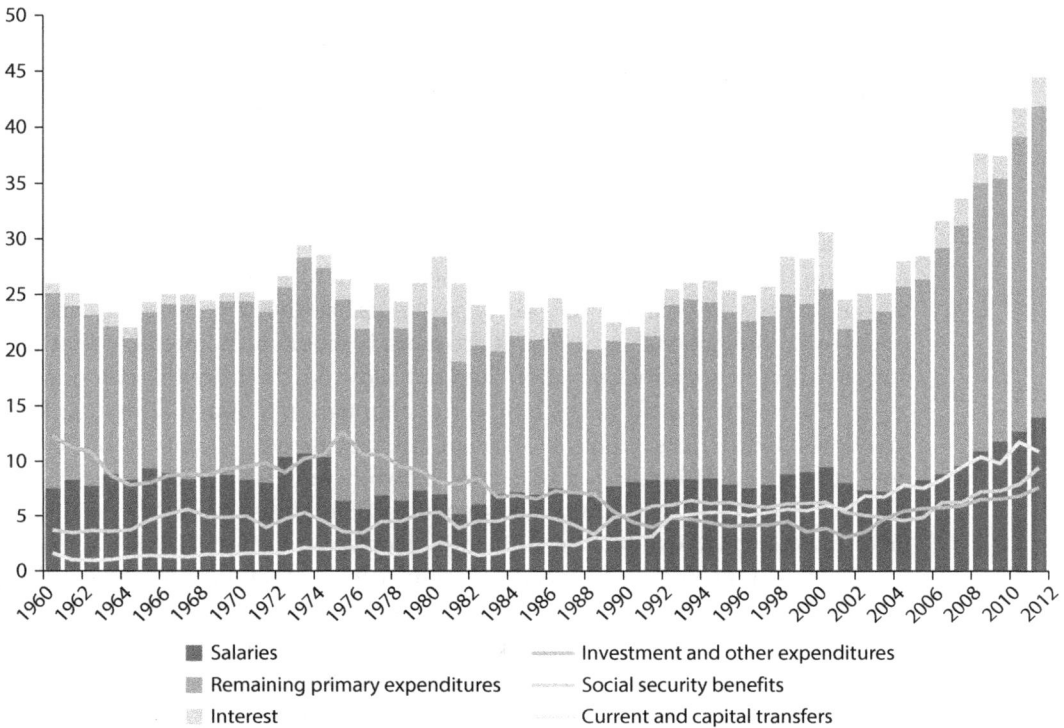

Source: Based on information from the Secretariat of the Treasury.

evolution of the consolidated public accounts with the inclusion of the inflationary tax. This aspect, which is illustrated in figure 9.3, must be evaluated as one examines the base period for the projections.

A blue, dashed line that shows the evolution of consumption expenditure for payment of salaries and purchases of goods and services is also included in figure 9.3, with the goal of assisting in the evaluation of the projections presented in this book in terms of the fiscal evolution. A comment of great significance emerges from this analysis: The evolution of public consumption turns out to be much less volatile than the rest of the fiscal indicators (expenditures, revenues, and results). We address this topic again in figure 9.4, which shows the evolution of the various components of the structure of public expenditures since the 1960s.

Some Factors That Explain the Evolution of Public Expenditure

Regarding recent years, it is advisable to point out, first, that the reduction of interest on the debt between the years before and after the crisis at the beginning of the century has been an important factor in explaining the greater fiscal room that the national public sector has had at its disposal. As one observes in figure 9.1, the amount of debt today is similar to the amount in 1999, but with a larger share of internal debt today. Nonetheless, as long as the method of renegotiation with the "holdouts" is not defined, it is difficult to describe 2010 as an ideal base year for long-term projections without first considering the various scenarios regarding this situation. However, the topics that are mentioned in the following discussion may be more relevant in this regard.

In effect, the second factor considered presents additional uncertainties. Salary payments represent significant amounts in the provincial accounts but are less significant in the national accounts. This is the result of the phenomenon that, following the decentralization of social services (education, health care, water, housing) during the last 30 years, salary payments have been increasingly concentrated in the subnational government accounts. It should be pointed out that the current salary negotiations situation does not allow one to judge this component to be relatively balanced in the long term, although it is also true that, as was mentioned before, it is important to point out the relative certainty of this component of spending in the past trajectory shown here.

Third, the transfers (current and capital expenditures) to families and the private sector have exhibited a substantial increase from insignificant levels to now represent a volume of expenditure similar to the total paid in salaries. This is explained by policies for transfers to households (Universal Child Allowance) as part of the new social protection policies and subsidies for firms with the goal of mitigating adjustments in prices and tariffs of privatized utilities. The reasons behind the introduction of these transfers and their continued existence today are precisely the proof that they are components of public expenditure that should not be considered permanent or even at a stable level in the long term.

Fourth, capital expenditures, which have fallen significantly since the mid-1970s as a result of the privatization processes and financial restrictions, have partially recovered in recent years, and it is difficult to predict their future evolution.

Finally, we have left to the end mentioning two factors that are among those that have most influenced the fiscal situation in the past and the present and are a source of uncertainty for the future. The first is related to the situation surrounding the social security system, which is one of most important causes of fiscal volatility. The second is associated with the joint participation in taxes and other financial transfer schemes among the levels of government. These internal transfers are not reflected in figures describing the consolidated public sector because they represent revenue transfers inside the consolidated fiscal sector illustrated in the series and figures presented up to this point. Both aspects will be the subject of specific comments below.

Comments Regarding What Has Occurred since 2010

Keeping in mind that this chapter was written in 2013 it would not be reasonable to evaluate the base year for the projections (2010) without considering what has happened since then. Even though definitive information regarding recent budget and investment account expenditures does not exist, with the goal of analyzing what has occurred in recent years more carefully, it is possible to utilize information from the Savings-Investment-Financing schemes from the national public sector called the cash approach. This approach allows one to follow the evolution in the short term and obtain more recent data than that offered so far.

Figure 9.5 offers a series of fiscal indicators from the national public sector as four-quarter moving averages, with the goal of minimizing the impact of seasonal factors. This allows us to obtain an approximation of what has occurred in the public accounts since the base year and, consequently, improve our evaluation.

In the upper portion of the figure, we can observe the rapid and significant recovery of the fiscal bottom line following the crisis at the beginning of the century and the slow but continuous erosion of the primary surplus throughout the decade, with a minor impact on the financial result, because of the lower weight of interest on the debt.

Figure 9.5 Evolution of the National Public Sector, Cash Approach, 1993–2013, Four-Quarter Moving Averages

figure continues next page

As Time Goes By in Argentina • http://dx.doi.org/10.1596/978-1-4648-0530-1

Figure 9.5 Evolution of the National Public Sector, Cash Approach, 1993–2013, Four-Quarter Moving Averages *(continued)*

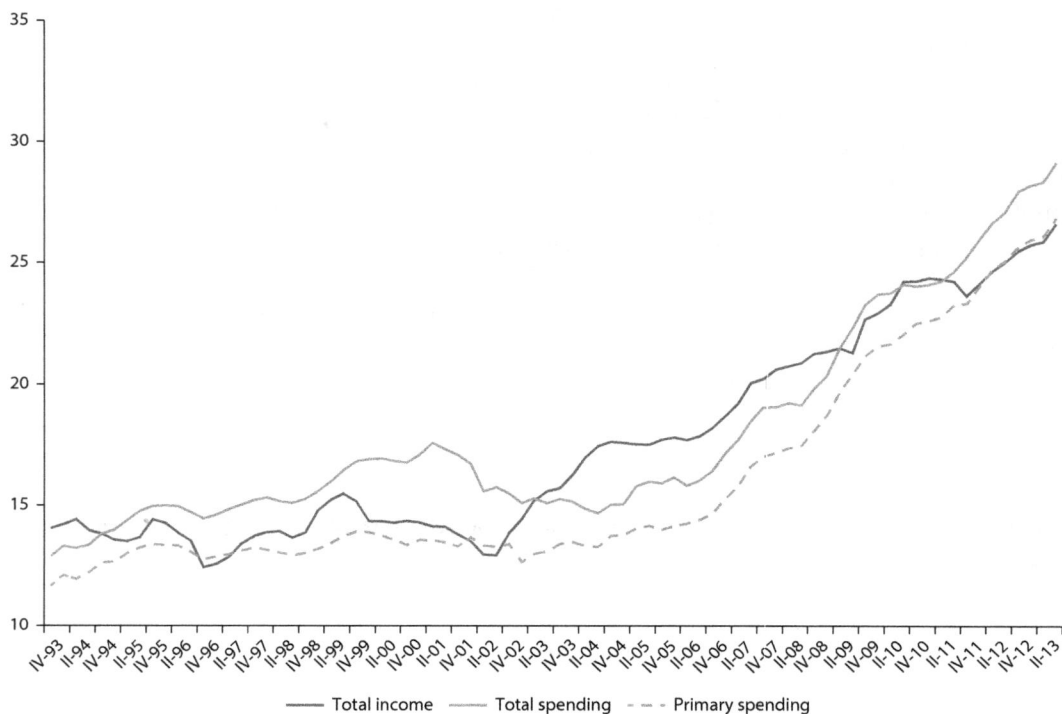

Legend: —— Total income   —— Total spending   - - - Primary spending

Source: Based on information from the Secretariat of the Treasury and Cetrángolo and Gómez Sabaíni 2012.

In turn, with the goal of breaking down the volatility in the fiscal space created in the first years following the crisis, the lower portion of the same figure presents the evolution of revenues and expenditures. This series demonstrates that in the creation of the fiscal space the increase in revenues was as important as the consistency of expenditures. Later, expenditure increases that outpaced revenue growth prompted the loss of the financial surplus.

In the second half of the decade, the increase of social security benefits and subsequent reform of the system, the increase in transfers (to provinces, households, and firms) and capital spending, as well as the increase in salaries brought about a spending trajectory that was rising faster than income, eroding the previous surplus. In the case of salaries, it should be kept in mind that this expenditure is not adequately reflected in that figure because they are mostly the responsibility of the provinces. In this case, the pressure created by the Education Funding Law drove increases to payroll spending that were higher than the GDP growth rate, both in the education sector as well as, indirectly, in the rest of the public sector in the provinces.

In addition, even though official information does not exist for the entire period, the provincial accounts should have suffered deterioration during the last three years. The pressures to increase expenditure in various sectors and the limited proportion of tax revenue that reached the subnational governments are part of the explanation. Consequently, during the period from 2010 until the writing of this chapter, the financial balance became a deficit of more than three percentage points of GDP and has completely wiped out the primary surplus.

Persistent Tensions

Without a doubt, many factors explain the evolution of the public accounts, and the space constraints of this chapter give us barely enough space to introduce them. It must be understood that there is a select group marked by particular importance relative to fiscal sustainability in the medium term and its impact on macroeconomic volatility: the situation surrounding the social security system, tax pressure, and the financial relationships between the national level and the provinces. These are just the three most important factors in a complex series of elements that should be kept in mind.

The Social Security System

The social security system's problems should be especially heeded to understand the reach of the Argentine fiscal crisis in the long term.[4] Even though its imbalances worsened during the 1980s and 1990s, they had been significant since the mid-1970s. The exhaustion of the initial surplus that results when any system matures and utilizes its accumulated funds to finance other public expenditure objectives resulted in an early imbalance to which demographic and macroeconomic factors, in addition to the sectorial policy's own answers, also contributed substantially.

Following a profound crisis, the Argentine social security system adopted and abandoned an individually funded scheme in less than two decades. In the middle of these structural reforms, starting in 2004 policy makers decided to increase coverage through an exceptional measure that allowed individuals that did not meet the requirements established by legislation to join the system, transforming it into one of the systems with the most coverage in the region.

Nonetheless, fundamental features of the system must be defined in the long term, making it difficult to make an adequate prediction of the system's trajectory in the medium term. The most important features yet to be defined are related to the effective replacement rate that has been promised and the coverage that will be given to those workers who do not manage to meet the requirements necessary to access the system's benefits under the current legislation.[5]

Sustainability of the Tax Burden

The total tax burden (including contributions for social security) showed a substantial increase of near 90 percent during the period from 1991 to 2012,[6] increasing from 18.4 percent of GDP in 1991 to a record level of 37.4 percent of GDP reached in 2012. This makes Argentina, along with Brazil, one of the highest-taxing countries in Latin America, comfortably surpassing the average of Latin American countries (18.9 percent in 2010), and placing it on the same level relative to the average recorded by the developed countries that form part of the Organisation for Economic Co-operation and Development (OECD) (34.3 percent in 2010) (Gómez Sabaíni and Morán 2012).

One observes that the increase in the tax burden was supported in large part by one-time impacts or effects on permanent taxes (value added tax and corporate earnings), and even by applying temporary levies (export tariffs and banking debits and credits), which evidences the high level of volatility in the tax system in the face of changes in macroeconomic circumstances (see figure 9.6).

The tax system has reached a level of burden that, on the one hand, depends on several factors that may lead to its long-term unsustainability. On the other hand, elements exist that indicate that it could be possible to increase this burden. Regarding the former, the following points should be made:

- The burden on payrolls could be judged exceptional, keeping in mind the existence of a significant social security moratorium. These revenues have become the most dynamic component in recent years and the second most

Figure 9.6 Gross Tax Collections, 1991–2012

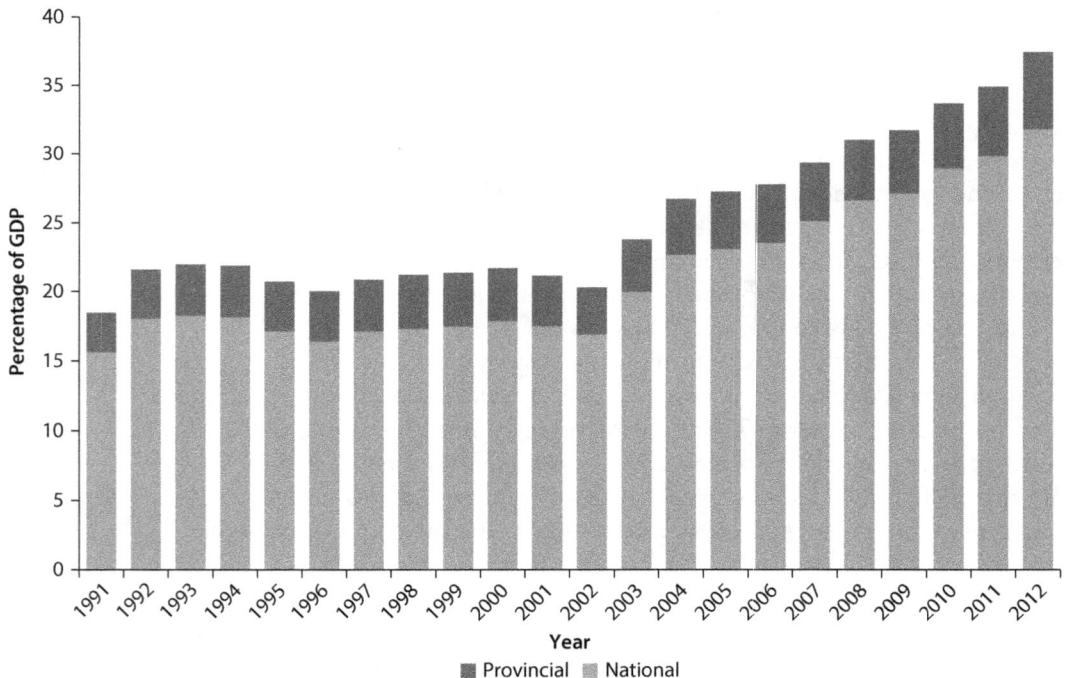

Source: Based on information from the National Directorate of Fiscal Research and Analysis, Ministry of Economy and Public Finances.
Note: Includes income from contributions to social security but does not include deductions from tax reimbursements.

important in the tax structure, representing almost 25 percent of tax income in 2011 (7.4 percent of GDP).

- Maintaining the level reached after the crisis related to export tariffs will depend on external conditions (international commodity prices) and the macroeconomic environment (real exchange rate). Having reached a maximum of 3.5 percent of GDP in 2008, these revenues represented almost 10 percent of total income at the national level.

- The growth of the tax burden following the end of the Convertibility Plan coincided with a change in the composition of the tax system, when the system began to consist of an elevated proportion of taxes that could be considered unorthodox, extraordinary, or emergency and that, because they are related to income and asset taxes, also tend to be called direct taxes (under subnational jurisdiction, at least in theory). However, these changes have various limitations in terms of their sustainability over time and create substantial effects on the efficiency and final distributive impact of the Argentine tax system. Currently, the unorthodox taxes that have these characteristics are, in addition to export tariffs, the tax on credits and debits in checking accounts, and the tax on minimum assumed earnings. Together, the three collect almost five percentage points of GDP, representing approximately between 15 and 20 percent of total national revenues during the last five years.

In turn, other factors could indicate the possibility of potential revenue increases:

- An elevated level of tax expenditure exists that comes from granting various promotional measures in terms of taxes. According to official estimates,[7] the level of tax expenditure has remained around a value of 2 percent of GDP between 2004 and 2009 (most recent data available).
- Tax evasion is a recurring problem for tax policy and administration in the country, for which we must recognize the achievement of significant improvements during the last two decades, although there are still significant inadequacies and much more that needs to be improved. To adequately evaluate tax administration in terms of the level of taxpayer compliance, it is essential to carry out official estimates periodically. The Directorate of Studies of the Administración Federal de Ingresos Públicos (AFIP 2008) last carried out such an exercise in 2007, examining the value added tax. At that time, researchers verified that the evasion rate for this tax had fallen from 34.8 percent in 2002 to 19.8 percent in 2007, accompanied by an increase in the taxable base for the levy that resulted in the plentiful amount of tax revenues that this charge has contributed during recent years. Using information from the National Accounts, Cetrángolo and Gómez Sabaíni (2009) carried out one of the few recent quantitative studies, estimating that the evasion rate for the earnings tax reached 49.7 percent of potential, or theoretical, collections in 2005.

Intergovernmental Financial Relationships

As a result of the substantial concentration of tax collection in the hands of the national government and the decentralization of expenditure processes to the provincial and municipal governments, the central government administers almost 80 percent of total revenues and spends just 50 percent of consolidated public expenditure (figure 9.7). Financing the subnational governments is accomplished through a complex and not always clear revenue transfer scheme from the national government to the provinces and from the provinces to the municipalities. In the case of the provinces, their collections are equivalent to about 40 percent of their expenditures, and they finance the rest through transfers from the central government and debt. This average hides large differences between some provinces that fund themselves almost exclusively with their own revenues (the Autonomous City of Buenos Aires, for example) and others in which revenue transfers from the national level represent more than 90 percent of their income (Santiago del Estero, La Rioja, and Formosa, for example). This financial imbalance among jurisdictions is one feature that has added conflict to the relationships between the national government and the provinces.

As a result of the aforementioned aspects, various provinces' financing is highly dependent on the revenue transfer system from the national level. Beginning with the approval of Law 23,548, the regime has become increasingly complex due to pressure caused by funding requirements at the national level—especially those of the social security system—resulting in numerous modifications to the distribution mechanisms and thus multiplying the channels through which revenues are routed to their final destinations in the provinces.

During some periods, the greater negotiation power of the national government versus the provinces or the gravity of the macroeconomic situation allowed it to

Figure 9.7 Percentage Breakdown of Revenues (Tax and Nontax) and Expenditures, by Level of Government, 1961–2009

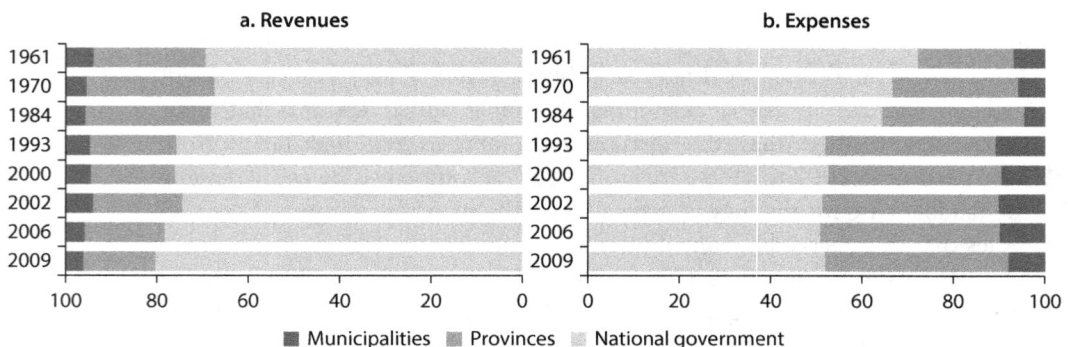

Source: Based on information from the Ministry of Economy and Public Finances.

negotiate reductions in the automatic revenue transfers established by the joint participation laws, through the preallocation of funds to areas managed by the national government (particularly the social security system). To illustrate the struggle surrounding the tax revenues collected by the national government over time, figure 9.8 reproduces the evolution of revenues differentiating between their destinations: the national level, the provinces, or the social security system. The figure demonstrates the long-term growth in financing for the provincial governments and social security. Beyond these experiences, it is important to point out the need to redefine these schemes in light of the new functions entrusted to each level of government.

This topic is of special interest for this study. Keep in mind that we have paid special attention to the impacts of aging on the national government's most significant expenditures (social security and other transfers for social protection) and those of the provinces (health care and education). The evolution of these expenditures and other functions of public spending (current and future) will define the type and magnitude of the future conflict surrounding Argentina's federal structure.

Figure 9.8 Distribution of National Tax Collections, 1935–2011

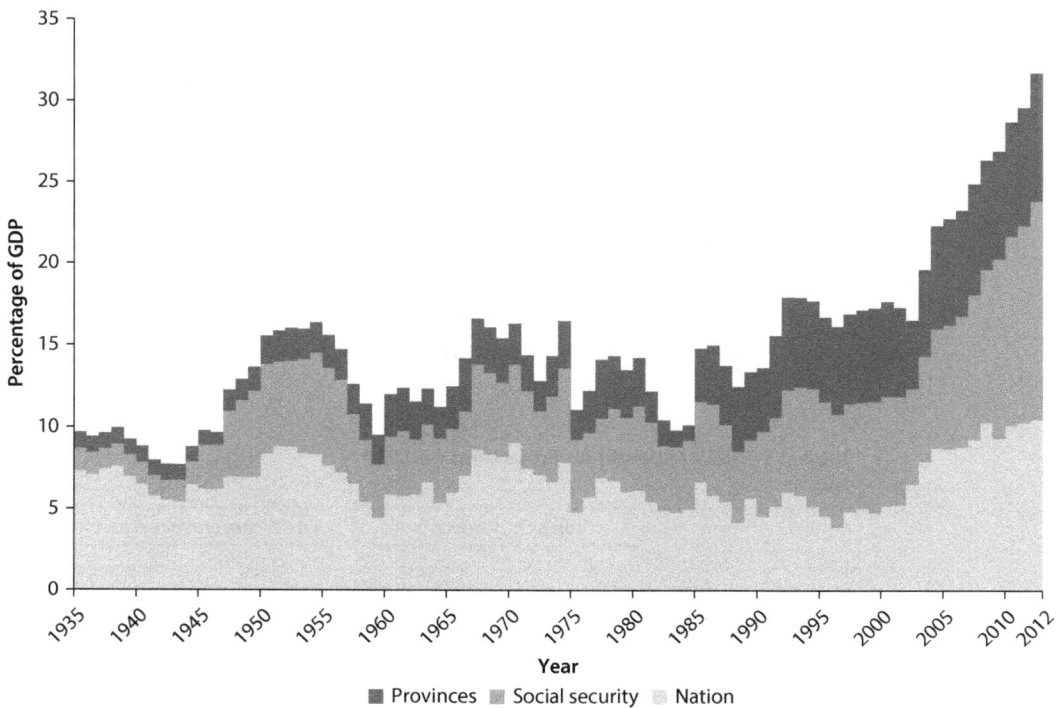

Source: Based on information from the Secretariat of the Treasury.

As Time Goes By in Argentina • http://dx.doi.org/10.1596/978-1-4648-0530-1

Fiscal Projections and Challenges

As part of this book, a series of sectorial studies has been performed with the goal of evaluating the impact of population aging on expenditure in certain specific areas of public intervention. Given that in the current section we attempt to evaluate the impact of demographic change on the public accounts, the comments that follow are necessarily very dependent on the aforementioned studies.

The Aggregate Information

As a first approximation of the fiscal impact, table 9.3 reproduces the results of the various studies regarding the measurement of the increase in public expenditure in the three sectors analyzed according to two scenarios.

First, the table presents a scenario in which expenditure levels by age group remain constant in reference to the base year. This scenario is called the Status Quo because the three policies analyzed are unaltered. Under these conditions, pressure would exist to increase spending in these three sectors by about one-third, the equivalent of about 13 percent of GDP.

Second, we evaluate, for each of the sectors, the effects of introducing policies that increase expenditure per age group to near the prevailing levels in developed (OECD) countries. In a long-term projection, without a doubt, this appears to be the more relevant scenario. Nonetheless, even within these sectors this is an attempt to chase a "moving target," because it is difficult to predict what public expenditure in developed countries will be in a century. Beyond this clarification, it should be noted that there is greater pressure in terms of health care and education expenditure and less in pensions. As we will see, this could affect the financial relationships among the levels of government.

As we have insisted throughout the current chapter, these are not predictions strictly speaking, but rather simulation exercises for certain components of public expenditure by age group to warn about the changes in intervention requirements that could result from demographic changes, in particular the aging of the population. Obviously, a more complete analysis must include the remaining services funded by public expenditure.

Table 9.3 Public Expenditure Projections for 2010

Percent

	Status Quo scenario		OECD convergence scenario	
	2100	Increase	2100	Increase
Education	4.0	−1.5	4.9	−0.6
Pensions	22.3	13.2	17.2	8.1
Health care	7.5	1.2	9.1	2.9
Total	33.8	12.9	31.2	10.3

Challenges for the Sectorial Policies under Analysis

Reviewing the specific conclusions of each sectorial analysis, it is advisable to begin with the sector that undoubtedly will demand the most revenues as a result of population aging. As chapter 5 pointed out, the demand for social protection policies for elderly adults will be significant and growing starting in the third decade of the present century, once the demographic dividend has ended. Even though some factors that could smooth this demand have been mentioned, it will still represent around 10 percentage points of GDP.

This could be the area of public policy that requires the most substantial and urgent redesigns. Keep in mind that if the current rules remain in place in the social security system, which require 30 years of contributions in order to access benefits, the percentage of elderly adults with retirement or pension benefits would fall to 50 percent by 2040. According to certain assumptions regarding increases in labor formality, it is estimated that coverage would reach 69 percent in 2100. This could mean a reduced demand for revenues for the contributory social security system, while there are significant fiscal and political pressures on the social protection policy.

In addition, chapter 5 estimates that if the current rules are not modified, social security expenditure would reach 18 percent of GDP by 2100. In contrast, if policy makers decided to guarantee 66 percent of the average contributory benefit for 90 percent of the population, the sector's expenditure would grow to 21 percent of GDP. As was pointed out in chapter 5, it is evident that Argentina will have to reassess its social security policy. If the three additional social protection programs considered (unemployment insurance, family benefits, and Universal Child Allowance) are included in the calculation, the expenditure level could be even greater; the same could happen if one also keeps in mind the need for public policies to reverse the economy's drop in productivity, including training programs for elderly adults (chapter 11).

Even though the system has various types of assets (including government bonds) that were incorporated when the individually funded scheme was abandoned and Argentina returned to a pay-as-you-go system in 2008, from a fiscal point of view, this should be taken into account as a reduction in net debt. This does not affect the functioning of the social security system because it is organized based on a pay-as-you-go scheme, as long as benefits are not promised that depend on the capitalization of these assets. The system requires financing from the rest of the public sector, which contributes a significant portion of tax revenues (Bertranou et al. 2011).

In summary, it would appear to be necessary that a debate begin on necessary and sustainable reforms in the social protection system for elderly adults before effects on the population's social situation, the public accounts, and the macroeconomic environment become irreversible.

Requirements for increases to public expenditure on health care are next in importance, on a horizon dominated by the growth of the elderly population (chapter 6). Here the predicament, even though it has some similarities to that faced by the pension system, can be read very differently in terms of the demand for fiscal revenues. Even though both sectors have in common that they are the fields that require the most urgent reforms, in the case of health care the equality and efficiency problems require institutional modifications and changes to financing methods without necessarily involving revenue increases. Moreover, certain evidence exists showing that health care expenses are not necessarily proportional to the number of years that an individual lives, but rather they are somewhat concentrated in the final years of each individual's life (Miller 2000).

Although the subject has not been studied specifically, the sector offers an excess of evidence of possible improvements to spending efficiency. The segmented structure of the sector, the overlapping coverage of a significant population group, the absence of instances of policy coordination, the existence of weakly regulated institutions, and the development of a disordered decentralization process are some of the factors that allow one to assume that the impact of policies can be improved without increasing spending.

The need to review the functioning of the social security health insurance plans and public provision should be evaluated jointly with the issue of reducing private spending. Of course, one specific point to be evaluated in these analyses is the advisability of maintaining an institution exclusively dedicated to caring for the elderly population: the PAMI—Programa de Asistencia Médica Integral (Comprehensive Medical Assistance Program).

Chapter 8, on the education sector, is of special interest for the evaluation of fiscal policy in Argentina. This will be the only sector for which the effects of aging could mean less pressure on public expenditure. Nonetheless, chapter 8 presents the case that it is not advisable to reduce spending given the quality problems that education in Argentina has shown, along with the advances toward universal access to basic education. In this sense, the demographic change may be a unique opportunity to improve results without requiring more revenues. In short, this analysis is a clear example of the deficiencies in the scope of public policies studied at the starting point of the estimates.

In summary, the considerations presented in the various chapters illustrate the potential pressure from increased demand for spending mainly coming from protection programs for the adult population (in the sectors that have been the subject of special attention in this book). In addition, it should not be forgotten that, in the long term, requirements may appear (it will surely occur) from sectors that are not analyzed here and new areas of public intervention will require increased resources. The following section offers some clarifications in this regard.

Additional Challenges

As we have seen, the studies performed have put the spotlight on a substantial portion of public expenditures, which have been commented on above. Table 9.2, meanwhile, has facilitated an approximation of the public expenditure items not included in the study. These include capital expenditures because, as was explained, the type of exercise undertaken using the present methodology puts the emphasis on consumption expenditures.

Without a doubt, it is important to point out that to appropriately evaluate the future evolution of the fiscal situation, it will be necessary to consider the pressure on the public accounts that comes from public investment requirements. The situation at the starting point signals the existence of serious deficiencies in terms of infrastructure. This manifests itself, undoubtedly, in the social sectors studied here (schools and hospitals) but is more evident in energy, transportation, and other sectors of the economy.

Since the beginning of the 1980s, as a result of the significant fiscal restriction that emerged from the debt crisis, public investment fell from levels near 5 percent of GDP to a minimum of 0.5 percent of GDP in 2002. The subsequent recovery never reached previous levels, and, in addition, during the period of privatizations, private investment did not manage to offset the reduction in public investment (Lucioni 2011). The need to strengthen the growth of the economy during the period when the population has not yet aged (chapter 12) will require more public funds for capital expenditures.

In relation to the discussion above, it should be pointed out that, given that all of the projections are presented as a percentage of GDP, more or less demand for funds thus measured will change if the economy grows more or less than the assumptions in these exercises.

It is pertinent to make a comment about the magnitude of the resources involved. Even for such long periods, increases of more than 10 percentage points of GDP seem very high. Nonetheless, this amount is less than the increase in tax revenues experienced in Argentina during the last 13 years. That does not mean that it will be easy to increase revenues by this magnitude again, but rather that it is necessary to reexamine the destination of the increased revenues.

Finally, a reflection is offered on another topic not explicitly studied in the book, although implicit in several of the chapters. In Argentina's public accounts, the intergenerational conflict manifests itself significantly and specifically in the federal conflict. The federal structure is characterized by strong conflicts in the financial relationships among the levels of government. In addition, the policies that care for the elderly population are principally in the hands of the central government (pensions and the PAMI), while the public policies aimed at building human capital (education and health care for the rest of the population) are in the hands of the subnational governments. Figure 9.9 illustrates this particular federal structure of social expenditure, with the exceptions that the education component includes the national universities (in addition to adding expenditure on culture, science, and technology to the figure), and in health care, a good portion of social security expenditure is in the hands of the national government. In summary, it should be stated that the demographic change process will certainly define modifications of financing for the levels of government and will affect the federal conflict. It should be especially kept in mind that collecting taxes is mostly the responsibility of the national tax administration, and significant changes are not expected in this area.

Figure 9.9 Jurisdictional Structure of Public Expenditure and Social Security in Various Social Sectors, 1980–2009

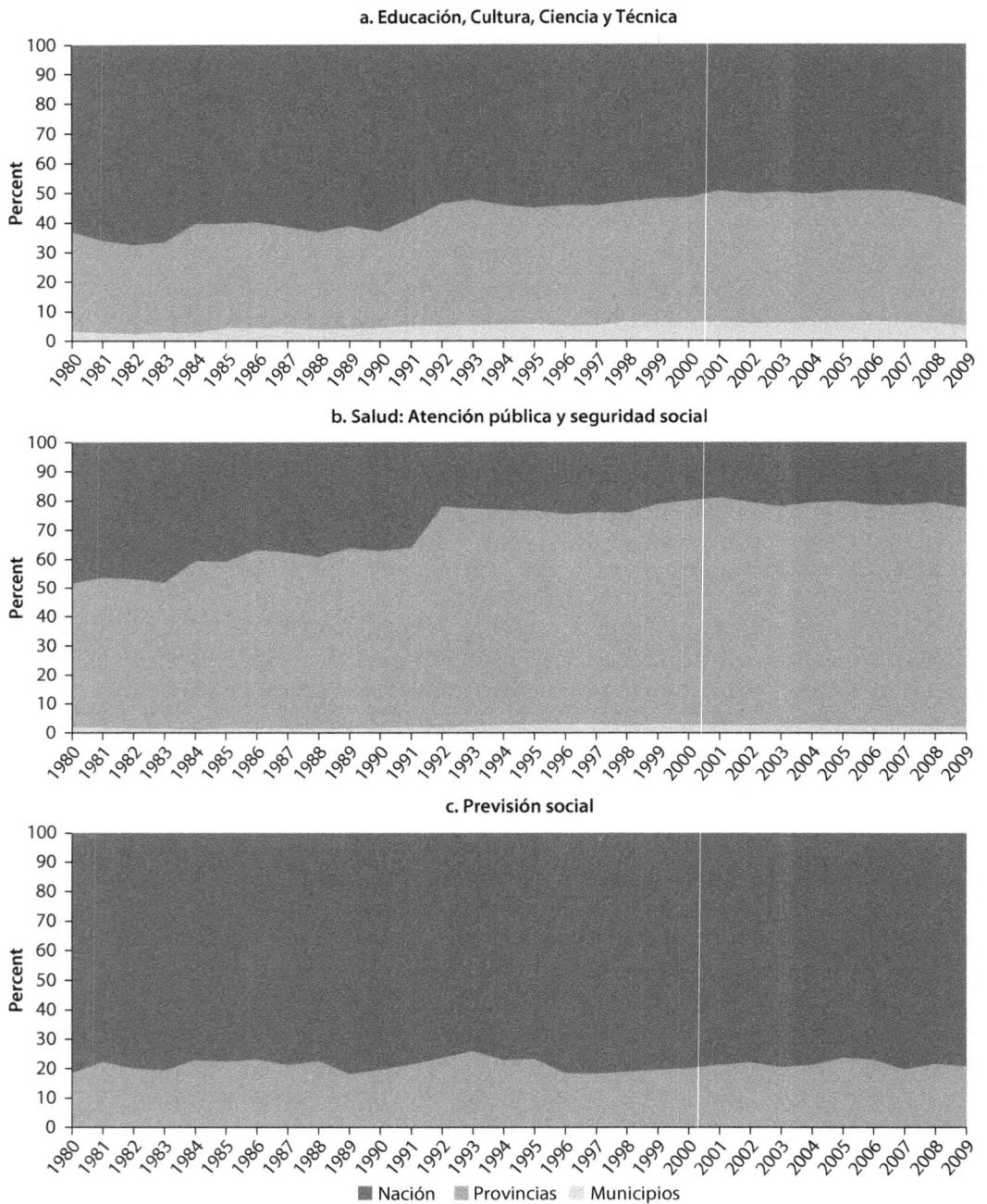

a. Educación, Cultura, Ciencia y Técnica

b. Salud: Atención pública y seguridad social

c. Previsión social

■ Nación   ■ Provincias   Municipios

Source: Based on information from the Ministry of Economy and Public Finances.

Final Reflections

Like any structural change, the population-aging phenomenon that will occur during the coming decades will require changes to the scope and design of public policies. On the basis of the results achieved in the different sectorial chapters of this book, this chapter has attempted to evaluate these changes' aggregate impact on fiscal policy.

In contrast with similar studies undertaken in developed countries, the Argentine case offers the special complexity of evaluating the impact of demographic change on a base scenario characterized by an elevated level of instability. Consequently, the well-known challenge of "growing rich before growing old" is incomplete and is added to the challenges represented by the multiple demands that, in a society like that of Argentina, weigh on the state, especially those related to the distribution of income and social cohesion. On top of the macroeconomic challenges that are studied in chapter 12, demands for reforms in many sectorial policies are added, some of which were evaluated in this book.

Moving beyond the many demands for reform that have been the subject of important studies and debates in recent years (though they did not include the impact of the demographic change), this new long-term outlook is of invaluable assistance to emphasize the need for reforms and warn about the direction of many of them.

We have seen that the demographic change involves several factors: first, the nation faces requirements for more funding for several policies studied here, especially the protection of the elderly population; second, even in the sectors in which a priori one would expect a reduction of these requirements, the demand for reforms will prevent this reduction from being recommendable, as is the case with education; third, Argentina must confront the need to increase the efficiency of expenditure (health care is one example); and fourth, one should expect increased demand for resources from those sectors that have not been the subject of specific analysis, such as infrastructure.

On the basis of the results presented in the previous chapters, one concludes that substantial pressure will be placed on the tax collector as a result of the need to finance the growth of social protection programs to attend to a greater proportion of the elderly population once the demographic dividend has passed. Gragnolati and colleagues (2011) pointed out various alternatives in the case of Brazil, and the same can be done for Argentina. Setting aside the possibility of financing the increased demands for assistance with debt, because that would mean transferring the burden to future generations, two extreme situations exist: maintaining levels of expenditure that can be funded with the available resources, thereby reducing average transfers per elderly individual, or maintaining benefits per adult by increasing the tax burden or reducing other expenditures. The path chosen will surely chart some intermediate course between these alternative extremes.

The present chapter has been able to prove the need for reforms to public policies and the existence of significant conflicts of interest inside the public sector, despite the spectacular increase in tax collections experienced during the last 15 years. Specifically, regarding the possibilities of expanding the sources of financing for public expenditure, it is worth highlighting that the situation of relative fiscal solvency at the starting point of the estimates coincides with the achievement of a record level of tax collections in the country. This level has been achieved with a tax structure that will be difficult to sustain without additional reforms. The existence of some taxes whose bases depend on special macroeconomic conditions or that affect economic efficiency call attention to the need for their review and, at the same time, the limitations of the assumptions of transferring the burden and incidence by age groups.

Nonetheless, the considerations presented concerning the long-term situation are of great help in evaluating the problems that Argentina's fiscal policy will have to confront in the coming years. We have attempted to explain that, keeping in mind the long-term demographic projections and the structural problems exhibited by the Argentine public sector, it is essential that the nation take advantage of the window of opportunities that will open in future decades to redefine the state's presence in the various sectors, improving the efficiency of expenditure and the distribution of income, while at the same time ensuring the consolidation of a macroeconomic scenario that will facilitate the strengthening of a path of economic growth and social development.

Notes

1. At that time, during the presidency of Luis Sáenz Peña, there were Ministries of the Interior, Foreign Affairs and Worship, Treasury, Justice and Public Instruction, Agriculture, Public Works, War, and Navy.

2. This table is an estimate based on officially available information, which may not coincide with the information presented in chapter 3 in some categories. Nonetheless, the discrepancies do not change the core of the arguments expressed here.

3. This discussion refers to the Savings-Investment-Financing Scheme series of the Consolidated National and Provincial Public Sector. Unfortunately, even when information exists for some years, there is not a long-term series available that includes the municipal governments. In any case, these governments make up a minimal part of the consolidated results.

4. Because this topic is dealt with specifically in chapter 5, here we will provide just a brief introductory reflection.

5. This topic is discussed exhaustively in chapter 5 and in Bertranou et al. (2011).

6. If one considers GDP growth during this period, the real increase is much higher than this figure.

7. National Directorate of Fiscal Research and Analysis, Ministry of Economy and Public Finances.

References

AFIP (Administración Federal de Ingresos Públicos). 2008. "Estimación del incumplimiento en el IVA–Año 2007." AFIP, Buenos Aires.

Albrieu, R., and O. Cetrángolo. 2011. "Volatilidad macroeconómica y política fiscal en Argentina." In *Volatilidad macroeconómica y respuestas de política*, edited by J. Fanelli, J. Jiménez, and O. Kacef. Santiago de Chile: ECLAC, AECID, and European Union.

Bertranou, F., O. Cetrángolo, C. Grushka, and L. Casanova. 2011. *Encrucijadas en la Seguridad Social Argentina. Reformas, cobertura y desafíos para el sistema de pensiones.* Buenos Aires: ECLAC-OIT.

Cetrángolo, O., and J. C. Gómez Sabaíni. 2009. "La imposición en Argentina. Un análisis de la imposición a la renta, a los patrimonios y otros tributos considerados directos." Serie Macroeconomía del Desarrollo 84, ECLAC, Santiago de Chile.

———. 2012. "Evolución reciente, raíces pasadas y principales problemas de las cuentas públicas argentinas." Boletin Informativo Techint 338, Techint, Buenos Aires.

Gómez Sabaíni, J. C., and D. Morán. 2012. "Informalidad y tributación en América Latina. Explorando los nexos para mejorar la equidad." ECLAC, Serie Economía del Desarrollo 124, Santiago de Chile.

Gragnolati, M., O. H. Jorgensen, R. Rocha, and A. Fruttero. 2011. *Growing Old in an Older Brazil: Implications of Population Ageing on Growth, Poverty, Public Finance, and Service Delivery.* Washington, DC: World Bank.

Lucioni, L. 2011. "América Latina. Tendencias en la provisión de infraestructura." In *La política fiscal para el afianzamiento de las democracias en América Latina. Reflexiones a partir de una serie de estudios de caso*, edited by A. Bárcena and O. Kacef. Santiago de Chile: ECLAC and UNDP.

Miller, T. 2000. "Increasing Longevity and Medicare Expenditures." Draft manuscript. University of California at Berkeley.

CHAPTER 10

The Argentine Labor Market in a Context of Demographic Transition

Ignacio Apella and Sara Troiano

Introduction

The demographic transition toward an older population poses questions related to the potential impacts on the labor market and, through them, about the level of national product and the social well-being of the population. This process has repercussions on the number of persons who are dependent on income from third parties and consequently on intergenerational income transfer systems.

The demographic transition consists of a process in which age groups change not only in size, but also in terms of their proportion of the total population. In particular, as a consequence of the fall in the mortality and fertility rates, along with increased longevity, the proportion of the elderly population grows, while the percentage of children and youth diminishes. However, certain periods can be delineated by examining the age composition of the population throughout this process.

The *demographic dividend*, defined as the period during which the proportion of dependent individuals is at a minimum, suggests the existence of a window of opportunities for generating savings and investment that give rise to what is known as the first dividend. The first dividend enables the accumulation of physical and human capital, which would lead to increased productivity, giving rise to a second dividend. Argentina, following the *baby boom* that occurred at the end of the 1970s and the beginning of the 1980s, is in the middle of the demographic dividend, which is projected to end around the beginning of the 2040s.

Once the window of opportunity passes, if society has not accumulated the capital necessary to enable labor force productivity to increase, then the only viable path to maintaining economic growth is to sustain the size of the labor force. Consequently, elderly adults could postpone their retirement and remain active as a reaction to increased potential demand for labor aimed at replacing the reduced availability of younger colleagues. In the same way, the growth of women's participation in the labor market could offset the adverse effects of aging on the labor force.

Moreover, an older population puts more pressure on the social protection system to maintain the level of consumption/income for a growing elderly population. However, given that pension systems are maturing, and in the absence of changes to eligibility criteria, such as the legal retirement age for example, the ability to fund these systems could face limits, and, consequently, many workers would be incentivized to remain active as a result of this situation. In other words, all else constant, the lower the level of income received from a pension, the higher the probability that one will remain in the labor market. For example, as a result of the natural maturation of the Argentine pension system, approximately 40 percent of the resources earmarked to fund pension payments come from general revenues.

However, the effects on the economy may be difficult to estimate, because the demographic transition creates processes of endogenous changes in the structure of the labor force, in terms of both participation as well as productivity.

For this reason, an analysis of the labor market dynamics in the context of aging should be accompanied by the consideration of two important features: on the one hand, individuals' decision to participate actively, and on the other hand, the choice they make regarding how to implement that decision. The first choice has two possible alternatives, to participate or not, whereas the second is associated with the characteristics of employment, such as salary, intensity, and field.

In particular, the participation decisions—jointly with demand—are the ones that define the potential for economic growth. Labor force dynamics vary by age and determine the number of individuals who are dependent on income from third parties. For this reason, depending on the magnitude of the changes in participation and their causes, the demographic dividend might not be strictly stable, but rather could vary according to the decisions workers make as a whole.

In this context, the objective of the present chapter is to study workers' behavior patterns in the labor market, particularly among youth and elderly adults, to understand how they make decisions to retire or to continue working. On the basis of this information, we define and study the economic dependency ratio with the goal of offering a hypothesis regarding its future behavior and its impact on the demographic dividend.

This chapter is organized as follows. The second and third sections discuss the theoretical framework of this analysis. The fourth section presents the evolution of the dependency ratio and its composition. The fifth and sixth sections examine the decisions made by youth and the elderly, respectively, related to their participation in the labor market. In the conclusion, we offer some final reflections.

Demographic Transition, Dividends, and the Labor Market

The Argentine population's age distribution is at the height of the transformation process. It is estimated that by 2050 the percentage of individuals older than 60 years of age will reach 43 percent, and those younger than 15 years old will represent 37 percent. This phenomenon occurs when a country's average age increases as a result of the reduction of the fertility and mortality rates as part of its development process and directly impacts the population dependency ratio.

Even though there is not a consensus on its definition, the demographic dependency ratio can be interpreted as the proportion of the population younger than 15 years old and those older than 65 years old in the total population. The idea behind this definition is to understand the relative importance of those population groups whose consumption is greater than the income they generate given their stage in the life cycle, requiring that they depend on income from third parties to finance their consumption. The United Nations utilizes this concept to make international demographic comparisons.

Changes in the age structures have an effect on a country's economic performance, insomuch as individuals' behaviors change with age. According to the life-cycle hypothesis, a person's life can be divided in three stages: pre-working life, working life, and post-working life. As discussed in chapters 1 and 3, during the first and last stages, individuals consume more than they produce, whereas in the second stage they produce more than they consume.

Consequently, during the first and last stages, individuals exhibit a life-cycle deficit given that their consumption is greater than their labor income. During both stages, this deficit must be financed through intergenerational transfers from working-age adults and young people to children and the elderly.

Keeping the previous discussions in mind, the demographic change process is not a sudden event, but rather occurs gradually, creating various periods depending on the process's advancement. In this sense, during the first stage and as a result of the reduction of the fertility rate, the percentage of children begins to fall while the proportion of working-age adults tends to increase. This entails a decrease in the dependency ratio and as a result a positive surplus from the life cycle.

In general, this situation is viewed as favorable for development because the aggregate life-cycle surplus facilitates increasing savings and thereby investment. The reduction of the dependency ratio frees up resources for public and private investment in physical and human capital, enabling per capita income to grow rapidly. This is commonly called the first demographic dividend.

A larger working-age population generates more revenues and therefore increased savings capacity. The challenge is to channel this savings toward internal investment, enabling the accumulation of physical and human capital. If this can be achieved, each worker will have more capital at his disposal in the future and production will increase as a result.

When the demographic transition reaches an advanced state, the elderly population will make up a relatively larger proportion of the population, that is, a higher number of individuals in the deficit phase of the life cycle. Simultaneously, the group of individuals usually known as the working-age population will be diminished. This stage, that is, the end of the demographic dividend, creates some concerns related to the pressure on public finances and economic growth.

As Time Goes By in Argentina • http://dx.doi.org/10.1596/978-1-4648-0530-1

Conventional wisdom is that this aging process diminishes aggregate savings capacity, insomuch as it diminishes the proportion of working individuals with savings capacity (*prime savers*) and increases the proportion of individuals who dissave, as one can infer from the life-cycle hypothesis. This effect redounds in the deceleration of economic growth (ILO 2013).

Nonetheless, the appearance of a second demographic dividend is possible. Given that the demographic transition also entails an increase in longevity—the increase of life expectancy at birth—under appropriate conditions this creates incentives for a higher savings rate with the goal of financing a longer post-working-life period. Thus, this results in an increased capacity to invest.

According to the ILO (2013), this second dividend will emerge to the extent that institutional frameworks and policies induce individuals, firms, and governments to accumulate capital. In contrast to the first dividend, the second dividend is not transitory in nature—because the aging phenomenon entails a permanent increase of capital per worker, and therefore per capita income—and, in theory, it is viable for it to continue growing in proportion to the increase in life expectancy.

However, in a context of low interest rates, undeveloped financial markets, and few investment alternatives, it is not very likely that the surpluses will sustain the investments required to maintain the accumulation of capital and the accompanying productivity gains and economic growth.

This argument posits that by not taking advantage of the first dividend, when the prime savers make up a larger proportion of the dependent population, especially the elderly, society lets a window of opportunities slip by that would not only maintain the rate of economic growth, but also accumulate capital that enables society to mitigate the negative pressure on growth (through increased labor productivity) that results from a reduction in the labor force. The current argument is based on the assumption that the group of prime savers is defined exogenously and is limited to the 15–65 age group, in accordance with the normal definition of the demographic dependency ratio.

Even though the life-cycle hypothesis offers three clearly defined stages, and these periods are to a greater or lesser extent associated with a pattern of consumption and income, this does not necessarily mean that they cannot be adapted to new scenarios. In other words, the duration of each stage (pre-working life, working life, and post-working life) could vary among individuals and depend on various factors, not just age.

In this sense, there is not an unambiguous definition that specifies which groups are dependent on third-party income. The ability to generate income is not just a function of age, although age does play a role indirectly through other factors.

First, individuals do not systematically abandon economic activity at a certain age. In general, advances in medicine (especially preventative) enable one to arrive at old age in better health than in the past, which creates favorable conditions for continuing to work for a longer period of time. In this way, the period of old-age dependence is delayed.

As the formal education cycle becomes more universally available and expands, a growing number of young people spend more time in the education system and delay their entry into the labor market, which extends the period of dependence during one's youth well beyond adolescence.[1]

In this context, the magnitude of the labor force is what enables us to define the population group that is dependent on others and the prime savers group. In turn, economic participation depends on various factors that range from individuals' health, the level of human capital, age, to the sector for which workers have the appropriate abilities, etc.

If we assume a gradual improvement in overall health and an increase in individual longevity, it is possible to expect that some will want to remain in the labor market longer, motivated on the one hand by the desire to be active and on the other to finance their longer lifespan. If at the same time, the education process is extended, it can be expected that on average young people will delay their entry into the labor market. Both phenomena together mean that the "ages" that define the demographic dividend will change along with this process.

For this reason, the challenge consists of recognizing that the demographic dividend possesses certain features that make it dynamic and this requires that society create conditions that enable its constant exploitation, recognizing that the demographic transition exerts pressure that at some point will cause the aforementioned dynamism to tend to diminish.

According to the ILO (2013), the problem is the global deficit of productive job opportunities. In the world, there are countries that lack the capacity to take advantage of the demographic dividend because a substantial proportion of their labor force is either looking for a job or is made up of unqualified workers with low-productivity and low-quality jobs in the informal economy who receive very low wages.

Labor Market Entry and Exit Patterns

On the basis of the previous discussion, next we briefly review the factors that determine when and why youth and the elderly enter and exit the labor market. This will enable us to understand the causes and use them to understand the evolution of the behaviors laid out in the previous section.

In general, *youth* is defined as the group of individuals between the ages of 15 and 24 years old. Our interest in this group is a result of the fact that it is the age range during which the transition from the formal education system to the labor market is made.

If we examine the population of youth between the ages of 15 and 24 years old, we see that their participation in the labor market has been diminishing. According to the Organisation for Economic Co-operation and Development (OECD 1999), this is the result of a variety of factors, not all of which are economic.

The principal argument to justify young adults' reduced participation in the labor market is the extension of the formal education period. France is one example worth mentioning because the average age of entry into the labor force was 22 at the end of the 1990s (OECD 1999), and, as a result, the least-educated youth make up more and more of the economically active population (EAP) of young people.

Young people are enrolling in the higher education system in massive numbers. This phenomenon is particularly clear in Western Europe, where enrollment in the postsecondary education system has increased noticeably, which contrasts with the United States, where this indicator has remained stable.

Moreover, the duration of the educational period is not the only explanatory factor. In the OECD countries, a change has been identified in the patterns of family formation, paternity/maternity, and couples' cohabitation. For example, in the United States, between 1971 and 1994, the proportion of young men between the ages of 16 and 24 years old who were heads of household fell from 22 to 11 percent, whereas in Canada it fell from 16 to 8 percent.

The aforementioned enables us to link the increase in the attendance rate and the average number of years of education in the advanced economies with the dynamics of the labor market. This, combined with new family customs and the postponement of the age at which children leave their parents' households, has changed the profile of youth in the main OECD economies and in the more developed economies in Latin America.

At the other extreme of the age distribution, we find the elderly age group. This group is made up of all adults older than 60 years of age.[2] The importance of this group of individuals resides in the fact that they are near the age at which they will retire from the labor market, based on current regulations in Argentina.

According to Bertranou and Mastrángelo (2003), the traditional approach proposes two sets of factors that determine the labor participation of the elderly, one from the supply side and the other from the demand side.

Within the first group, one finds the same incentives created by the social security system, the existence of an income effect, the presence of disability related or unrelated to work, the personal earnings from staying economically active, and the like. The way in which pension systems are organized can influence workers' retirement decisions. According to Stock and Wise (1990) and Gruber and Wise (2002), the elderly population's participation in the labor market is a function of the financial gains obtained by remaining economically active for some time in addition to the established minimum. These gains consist of two components: the present value of the salary obtained from the activity along with a higher future social security benefit associated with a "bonus" for the number of additional contribution periods acquired and the lower quantity of years during which they will enjoy the expected benefit (*incentive measure*).

The results uncovered for OECD countries support the hypotheses of early retirement motivated by the benefits from pension programs, related to the generous elderly benefits offered early in old age (Sigg 2005). In Latin America, meanwhile, studies on the participation of the elderly in the labor market are limited. According to Bertranou (2005), in 12 countries in the region a negative correlation was identified between the level of coverage of pension systems and the elderly population's participation in the labor force. According to Alós et al. (2008), in Argentina the probability of remaining active or retiring from the labor market depends on whether one meets the eligibility requirements and on the amount of the pension benefit.

The elderly population's participation in the labor market also depends on factors from the demand side. According to Dorn and Sousa-Poza (2004), in some developed countries one observes that a substantial number of early retirements are involuntary and are motivated by the employer. In a context of elevated unemployment rates, both the demand for employment as well as the state create early retirement programs with the goal of reducing the pressure on the job market.

Simultaneously, workers' health and their level of human capital at age 60 influence the demand for older workers. These factors, in fact, influence employers' perceptions of the elderly population's productivity. This appraisal, however, does not always reflect the real productivity of older workers, as has been discussed widely in the literature on the relationship between age and productivity, which is examined in detail in chapter 11.

The Dependency Ratio and Economic Participation

As mentioned in the previous section, the demographic dependency ratio can be interpreted as the proportion of the population younger than age 15 and older than age 65 as a proportion of the total population. The idea behind this definition is to understand the relative importance of those population groups that, given their stage in the life cycle, consume more than they generate in terms of income and for this reason depend on income from third parties. In general, this concept is utilized to perform international demographic comparisons.

Figure 10.1 shows the evolution of the youth, adult, and total dependency ratios between 1974 and 2012.[3] Between 1974 and 1990, the demographic dependency ratio was growing as a product of the baby boom during the 1970s and 1980s. Subsequently, while the youth dependency ratio began to fall as the baby boomers grew into adults, the dependency ratio for the elderly over age 65 began to grow. Given that the decrease in the former is greater than the increase in the latter, beginning in the 1990s the total dependency ratio began to fall, creating a window of opportunities.

The grouping of individuals is directly correlated to the ability to generate income with age. However, this ability, or its opposite, income dependence, is not just a function of age—although age is indirectly the determining factor through other characteristics. First, individuals do not systematically abandon economic activity at a certain age (in this case 65 years old). In general, advances in medicine (especially preventative care) enable one to reach adulthood in better health than in the past, which creates the conditions for one to continue working longer. In this way, the period of dependence in old age is postponed. In comparison, young people do not enter the labor market systematically at age 15. In effect, a trend toward universal participation in the formal education system, along with

Figure 10.1 Demographic Dependency Ratio, 1974–2012

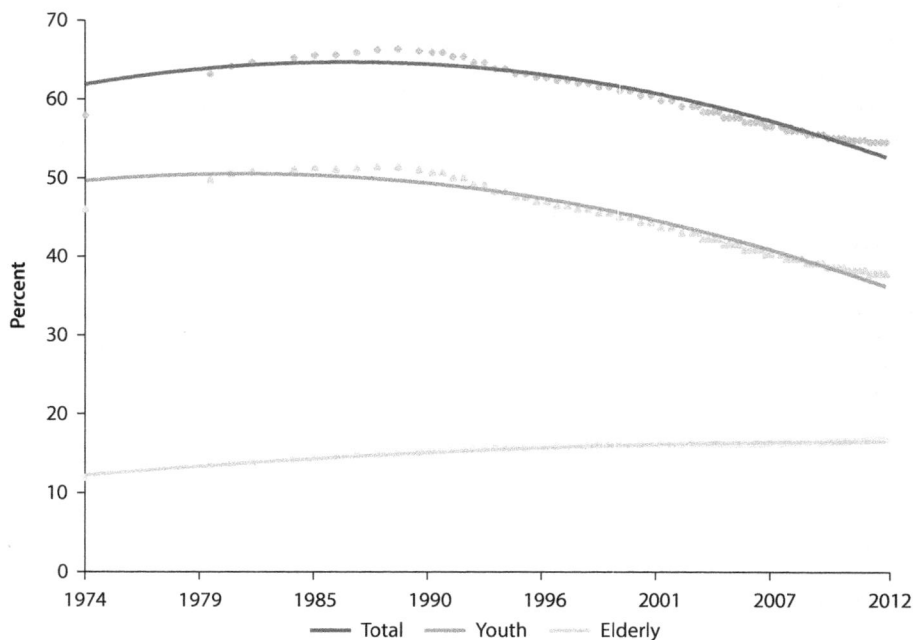

Source: Based on the EPH.

the lengthening of the system itself, incentivizes lower economic activity among this age group.

Figure 10.2 presents, for 1995 and 2012, the EAP in the labor market by ages. In general terms, the economic participation rate for men exhibits a significant increase between the ages of 14 and 34, which subsequently remains constant until exhibiting a slight decline between 35 and 55 years old. Finally, the rate decreases significantly among those ages 55–60 and above.

However, this behavior has been changing over the years. Men's participation before age 25 has fallen considerably since 1995. In particular, participation among youth between the ages of 15 and 18 fell from 36 percent in 1995 to 17 percent in 2012, reflecting the increased coverage of the education system up to the secondary level in recent years (Bertranou 2001). This behavior repeats itself among youth between the ages of 19 and 24 years old, with their participation falling from 80 percent in 1995 to 70 percent in 2012.

Figure 10.3 presents the enrollment rate among youth by age group. Even though the enrollment rate for youth between the ages of 10 and 14 years old was very high during the entire period of analysis, it still exhibited a slightly upward trend, reaching approximately 97.7 percent in 2012. Moreover, among youth between the ages of 15–19 years old and from 20 to 24 years old, the enrollment rate grew significantly, increasing 20 percentage points on average between 1974 and 2012.

Figure 10.2 Activity Rate, by Age, 1995 and 2012

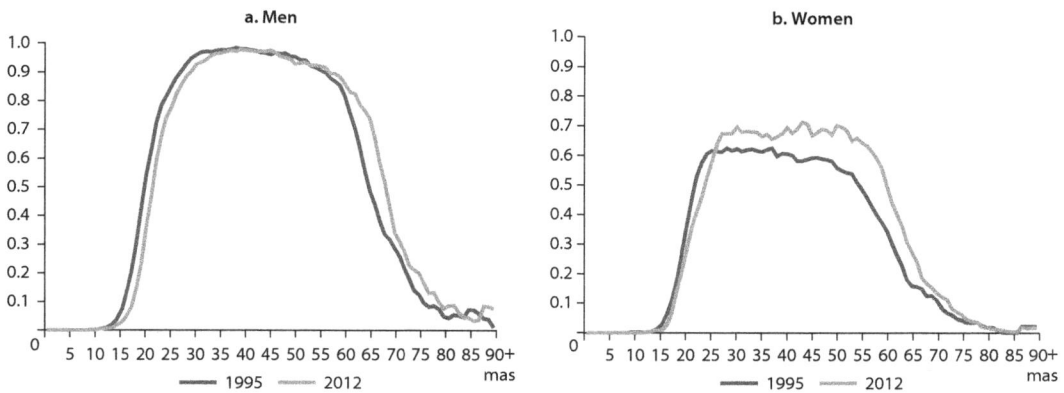

a. Men

b. Women

Source: Based on the EPH.

Figure 10.3 Enrollment Rate by Age Group, 1974–2012

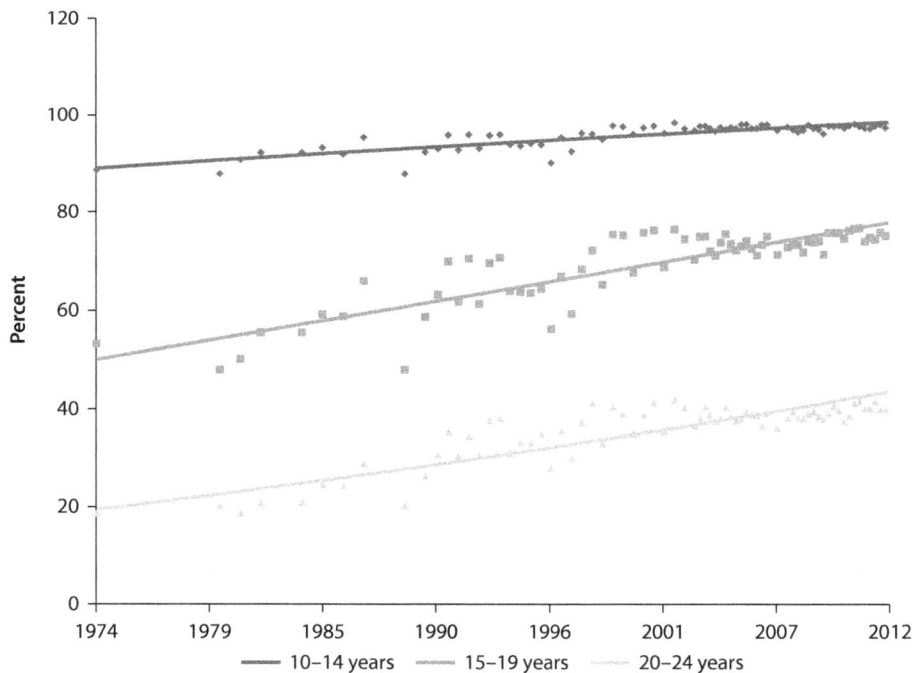

Source: Based on the EPH.

In line with the increase of the enrollment rate among youth, the activity rate for youth between ages 15 and 24 years old exhibits a downward trend between 1975 and 2012 (figure 10.4). The decrease is more pronounced among youth between the ages of 15 and 19, with the EAP falling from around 42 percent in 1974 to 22 percent in 2012. Economic participation of youth between the ages

Figure 10.4 Activity Rate among Youth, 1974–2012

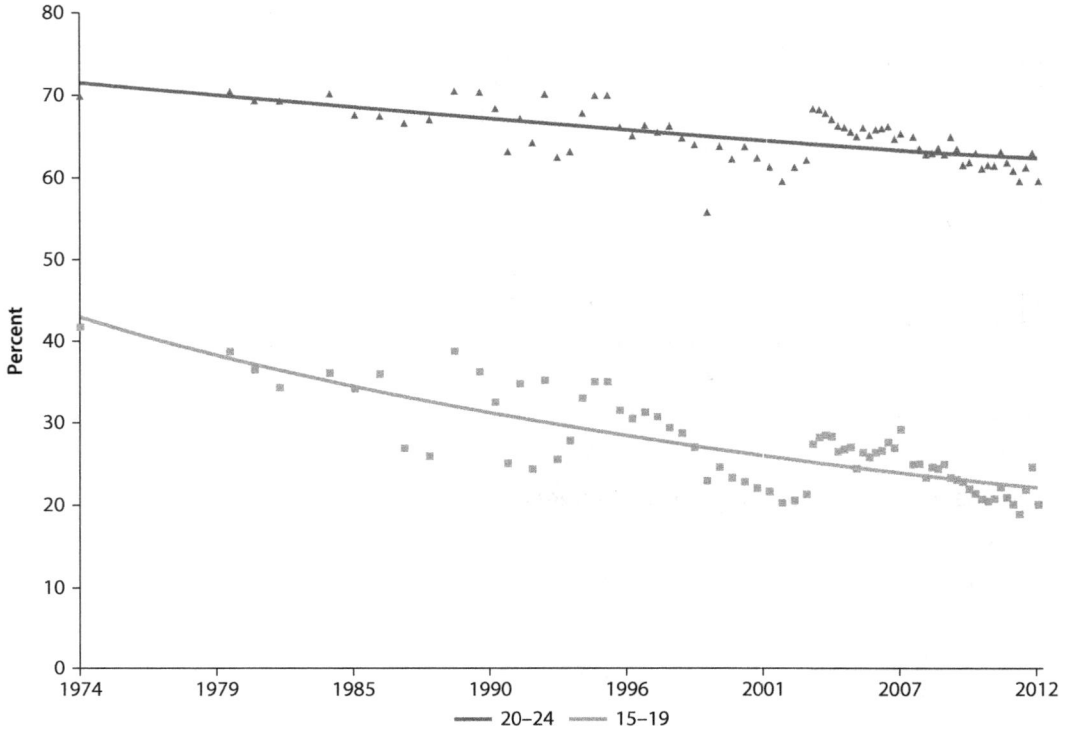

Source: Based on the EPH.

of 20 and 24 years old also fell, although at a slower pace, during the period under analysis. It fell from around 70 percent in 1974 to near 61 percent in 2012.

This phenomenon suggests that a substantial group of youth between the ages of 15 and 24 years old have begun to depend on third-party income given their inactive economic condition as a consequence of their participation in the formal education system.

Between the ages of 35 and 55 years old, participation rates have not varied significantly (figure 10.2). On the contrary, among men the differences are notable for the elderly. Participation among men near retirement age and those already past it exhibited a positive trend, growing from 27 percent in 1995 to 37 percent in 2012.

In terms of women, their behavior differs from men's. First, their participation rates are lower at all ages during the years under analysis. However, one notes a significant increase in their participation rate beginning at age 27. In 2012 their participation rate peaked between age 40 and 49 years old.

Decade after decade, the level of participation achieved and maintained until retirement has been growing. This phenomenon is associated with a general change in the composition of the EAP, especially beginning in the mid-1990s.

In particular, according to Alós et al. (2008), this acceleration of growth in female economic activity is related to the entry of women from low- and medium-income households into the labor force and is classified therefore as a strategy aimed at mitigating the effects of unemployment and precarious work among heads of household.

Among young women, even though there is evidence of a decrease in their economic participation, it is less significant than that observed among men. In this sense, although the EAP among women between the ages of 15 and 19 years old was 21 percent in 1995, this rate fell to 17 percent in 2012. Moreover, among the group between the ages of 20 and 24 years old, the EAP recorded a decrease of 16 percent (or 9.6 percentage points) between the years under analysis. Among women older than 60 years of age, the same phenomenon observed among men repeats itself, increasing their participation in economic activity.

With the goal of understanding the behavior of workers near retirement age, figure 10.5 presents the economic participation for adults between age 50 and 70 years old. Even though the legal retirement age in Argentina is 60 for women and 65 for men, it is interesting to observe workers' behavior around these ages.

Figure 10.5 Activity Rate among the Elderly, 1974–2012

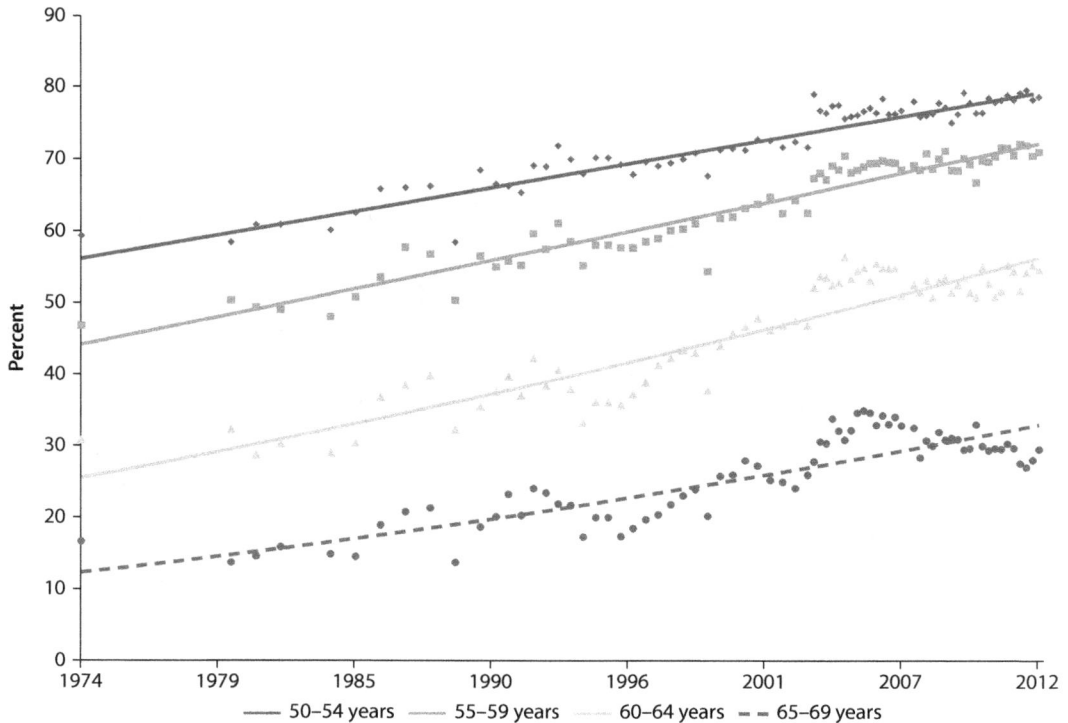

Legend: —— 50–54 years —— 55–59 years …… 60–64 years – – 65–69 years

Source: Based on the EPH.

As Time Goes By in Argentina • http://dx.doi.org/10.1596/978-1-4648-0530-1

The elderly population's economic participation trend continues to be positive and homogeneous across different age groups. Although participation among adults between the ages of 60 and 64 years old grew from around 30 percent in 1974 to 55 percent in 2012, the participation of adults between the ages of 65 and 69 years old grew from 16 percent in 1974 to 30 percent in 2012. This trend is the product of joint increases in both men's and women's participation (figure 10.2). However, the increase in female participation is substantially higher for the majority of older age groups. For the group of individuals between ages 60 and 64 years, the increase in participation among men was 38 percent, whereas for women it reached 101 percent. Among the elderly between ages 65 and 69 years old, the variation in men's economic participation was slightly higher than the increase among women, and after age 70, the increase in the female EAP was greater than for men.

The change observed in the economic activity rates by age group establishes a modification of the labor force's structure. Figure 10.6 presents the ratio between the EAP older than 60 years of age and the EAP between the ages of 15 and 59 years old.

The relative participation of the elderly exhibits slight but sustained growth between 1995 and 2012, increasing from 5 to 8 percent relative to the young

Figure 10.6 Percentage of Active Population of Adults Older Than 60 Years of Age/Active Population of Adults Younger Than 60 Years of Age, 1995–2012

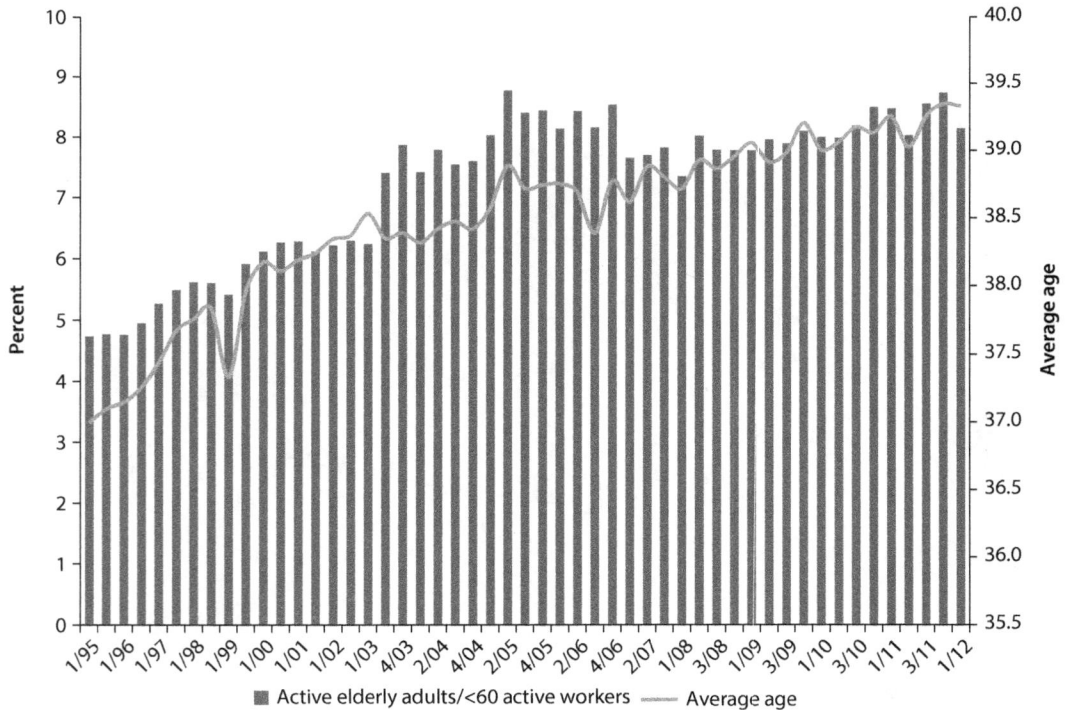

Source: Based on the EPH.

labor force. The average age of the labor force increased from 37 to 39.3 years old. These observations appear to confirm the existence of a positive relationship between the demographic transition and the aging of the labor force, with a greater percentage of active elderly adults. An analysis of these workers' individual characteristics would enable us to identify the determinants that are behind their decisions to remain in the labor force during old age.

Clearly, the composition of the population dependent on the income of others is changing over time, and for this reason, the use of the traditional dependency ratio presents some limitations. For this reason, the economic dependency ratio is suggested as an indicator that enables a better approximation, although incomplete, of the concept of the population dependent on third-party income. It is defined as follows:

$$TdE_t = \frac{N_{<15,t} + N^i_{15-24,t} + N^i_{55-75,t} + N_{>75}}{N^a_{15-24,t} + N_{25-54} + N^a_{55-75}},$$

where

$N_{<15,t}$ is the population less than 15 years old;

$N^i_{15-24,t}$ is the inactive population between the ages of 15 and 24 years;

$N^i_{55-75,t}$ is the inactive population between the ages of 55 and 75 years;

$N_{>75,t}$ is the population older than age 75 years;

$N^a_{15-24,t}$ is the active population between the ages of 15 and 24 years;

$N_{25-54,t}$ is the population between the ages of 25 and 54 years; and

$N^a_{55-75,t}$ is the active population between the ages of 55 and 75 years.

In contrast to the commonly used dependency ratio, the numerator of this ratio could be greater, inasmuch as it does not contemplate just youth younger than 15 years old, but also all youth between the ages of 15 and 24 years old who are economically inactive. In addition, with the goal of including all adults near the legal retirement age, it includes inactive adults between the ages of 55 and 75 years old and those older than 75 years old. In addition, the denominator is different. On the one hand, in terms of the active population, it does not just contemplate youth between the ages of 15 and 24, but rather those who are actively participating in the labor market. On the other hand, active elderly adults are included. Figure 10.7 presents the evolution of this indicator between 1974 and 2012 for each age group and the total. Upon refining the dependency ratio concept, we can see that it increased in quantitative terms during this period. For example, in 1974 for each active worker, there were 1.8 inactive persons. However, the trend over time is different. While the demographic dependency ratio exhibits a parabolic shape, the economic dependency ratio maintains a more profound decreasing trend.

The following sections will analyze in detail the determinants of economic participation for the populations belonging to the two reference age groups, youth and the elderly.

Figure 10.7 Economic Dependency Ratio, 1974–2012

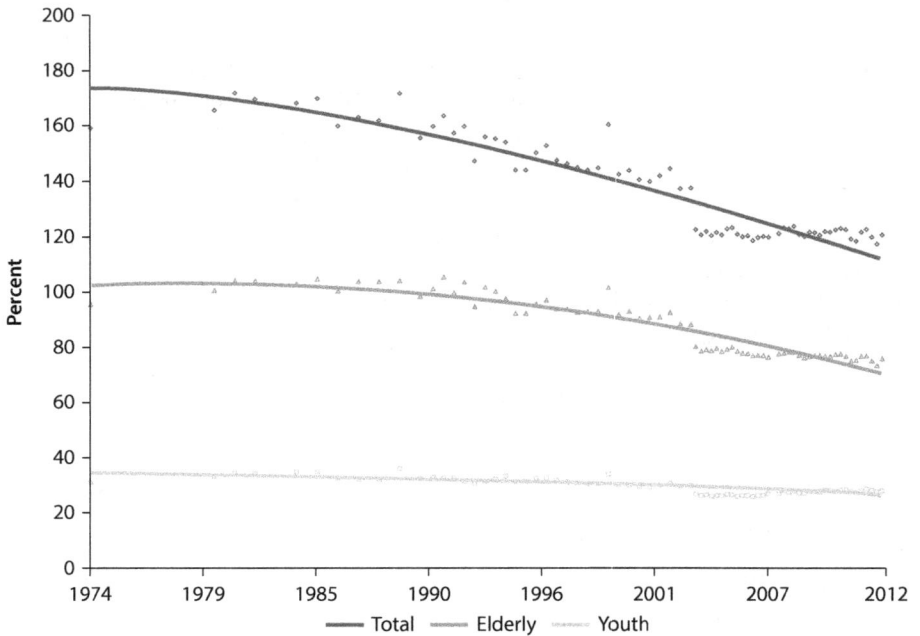

Source: Based on the EPH.

Economic Participation among Young People in Argentina

As has been observed in the previous section, entry into the labor market has been postponed to older ages throughout the years under analysis (1974–2012). However, this change appears to be much less pronounced than the postponement of the retirement age observed among the elderly.

Table 10.1 presents the activity rate among young people by age and five-year period. One observes that the activity rate has decreased mostly among the younger age groups and to a lesser extent among the older age groups. No substantial differences were recorded among the 24-year-old population in particular.

Among individuals between the ages of 14 and 18 years old, one identifies large differences in the rate of decrease of the EAP depending on the period under analysis. The decline in the activity rate is significant until the mid-1980s, it slows until the end of the 1990s, and it is stagnant between 2000 and 2005. A substantial jump is observed beginning in 2006–10 relative to the previous five-year period, and in an even larger way in the last two years (2011–12). Nonetheless, these wide differences between periods are not observed among young people over 20 years of age.

Table 10.2 presents some characteristics of active youth between the ages of 15 and 24 years old for some selected years. The group of active young people

Table 10.1 Activity Rate among Young People, by Age and Five-Year Period
Percent

Age	1974–80	1981–85	1986–90	1991–95	1996–2000	2001–05	2006–10	2011–12
14–15	16	15	13	12	11	11	9	5
16–17	32	29	27	27	25	25	22	16
18–19	49	46	43	44	45	44	41	35
20–21	63	60	59	61	61	59	57	55
22–23	72	73	72	72	71	69	69	69
24–25	74	74	75	75	72	72	72	74

Source: Based on the EPH.

exhibits a moderate aging phenomenon. The average age of active young people increased from 20.7 years old in 1995 to 21.2 in 2012. Although the percentage of men always exceeded 58 percent, the trend over time has been volatile.

In 2012, 71.1 percent of this subgroup of young people did not attend an educational institution, and 28.7 percent were enrolled in formal studies. Over time, on the one hand we have observed an increase in the participation of active young people who attend an educational institution; between 1995 and 2012, this proportion increased by eight percentage points. Simultaneously, we observed a reduction in the percentage of active young people who were not studying. This enables us to suggest that part of the young labor force chose to continue their formal studies despite dedicating some of their time to either working or looking for work.

Regarding the maximum education level reached by active young people, it is not possible to establish a defined behavior pattern. Although in 1995 more than half of active youth achieved full primary education or partial secondary education, in 2012 the situation was different. The majority of young people who were employed or looking for a job had achieved partial secondary education or full secondary education and partial university education. These results, together with the decrease of the young EAP, suggest the existence of a process of prolonging formal education among active youth.

The employment situation for active young people shows significant improvements in recent years. Their unemployment rate fell from 32.2 percent in 2001 to 16.5 percent in 2012 as a result of the recovery following the exchange-rate and economic crisis of 2001–02. Even so, this age group's unemployment rate is still more than double the national average, as is the case in many countries in the region. Finally, following the same pattern observed for the population as a whole (Alós et al. 2008), the economic sector that employs the largest quantity of workers is services and commerce.

Table 10.3 presents some of the characteristics of inactive youth between ages 15 and 24 years old. In general terms, the average age does not show a significant change, and on average 60 percent are women.

Table 10.2 Characteristics of Active Young People, 1995–2012

Characteristics	1995	1998	2001	2004	2007	2010	2012
Age (years)							
Average age	20.7	20.8	21.2	21.1	20.9	21.2	21.2
Gender (%)							
Woman	38.9	39.7	41.6	40.6	41.1	39.3	37.7
Man	61.1	60.3	58.4	59.4	58.9	60.7	62.3
Attends an educational institution (%)							
Attends	20.5	24.1	24	28.3	26.5	28.9	28.7
Does not attend, but has attended	79.0	75.7	76	71.7	73.5	71.1	71.1
Never attended	0.4	0.2	0.1	0.0	0.0	0.0	0.1
Education level (%)							
No education	0.4	0.0	0.0	0.1	0.0	0.0	0.1
Primary incomplete	3.9	3.9	3.5	3.6	4.2	3.5	3.2
Primary completed	24.4	21.3	19.2	15.2	9.9	10.8	9.3
Secondary incomplete	31.7	33.4	28.1	29.1	28.6	31.2	31.1
Secondary completed	18.6	17.9	22.9	24.9	29.6	26.4	28.8
University incomplete	14.6	17.2	17.5	23.8	22.8	23.3	23.8
University completed	6.4	6.3	8.8	3.3	4.8	4.8	3.6
Income quintile (%)							
I	17.1	16.7	19.1	20.0	17.5	17.1	17.8
II	17.9	18.6	21.3	22.7	19.3	22.1	20.4
I + II quintiles	35.0	35.3	40.4	42.7	36.7	39.2	38.2
III	22.3	22.2	20.9	20.2	22.5	19.6	21.7
IV	22.7	22.5	21.0	20.0	21.9	22.0	22.3
V	20.0	20.0	17.8	17.1	18.9	19.3	17.8
Status of activity (%)							
Employed	70.4	76.5	67.8	73.5	83.4	80.9	83.4
Formal	43.5	34.3	36.4	30.9	40.9	44.1	46.7
Unemployed	29.6	23.5	32.2	26.5	16.6	19.1	16.6
Sector of activity (%)							
Agriculture	1.2	0.7	0.9	1.3	1.0	1.8	0.9
Manufacturing	19.3	17.9	14.5	16.2	15.8	14.2	14.1
Construction	8.2	9.8	7.9	9.0	11.1	11.0	13.6
Commerce	22.8	24.3	24.6	26.6	25.6	25.7	23.7
Services	48.5	47.2	52.0	46.9	46.5	47.3	47.8

Source: Based on the EPH.

On average, during the entire period under analysis, 79.7 percent of inactive youth had achieved an incomplete maximum level of education (secondary or university). At the same time, 73 percent are attending an educational institution. These results, along with the increase in the inactivity rate among youth in recent decades, reinforces the evidence of the process of growing universal access and extension of formal education.

Table 10.3 Characteristics of Inactive Young People, 1995–2012

Characteristics	1995	1998	2001	2004	2007	2010	2012
Age (years)							
Average age	18.9	18.9	19.1	18.9	18.9	19.0	19.0
Gender (%)							
Woman	60.4	60.5	58.6	60.7	56.9	58.9	60.1
Man	39.6	39.5	41.4	39.3	43.1	41.1	39.9
Attends an educational institution (%)							
Attends	72.7	74.4	77.6	72.5	71.4	70.9	73.9
Does not attend, but has attended	26.7	24.9	22.0	27.2	28.4	28.9	25.9
Never attended	0.6	0.6	0.4	0.3	0.2	0.2	0.2
Education level (%)							
No education	0.6	0.0	0.0	0.4	0.2	0.2	0.2
Primary incomplete	3.6	3.1	3.0	4.3	4.2	4.3	3.6
Primary completed	11.3	9.5	6.9	6.3	4.6	4.6	4.5
Secondary incomplete	54.3	54.5	54.5	46.6	51.3	53.8	52.9
Secondary completed	4.1	3.9	4.9	8.5	9.1	8.9	8.3
University incomplete	20.8	23.9	25.3	33	29.8	27.6	29.8
University completed	5.2	5.0	5.4	1.0	0.8	0.5	0.7
Income quintile (%)							
I	19.4	19.9	21.0	21.0	24.8	28.4	28.5
II	19.8	21.8	21.3	22.1	24.7	24.5	24.4
I + II quintiles	39.2	41.7	42.3	43.1	49.4	52.9	52.9
III	21.0	20.1	19.9	21.3	19.4	19.6	21.2
IV	22.3	21	20.1	20.4	17.2	16.6	17.4
V	17.4	17.1	17.7	15.2	13.9	11.0	8.5

Source: Based on the EPH.

The Active Elderly Population in Argentina

With the goal of identifying the factors that are potential determinants of elderly adults' decisions to retire from or remain active in the labor market, table 10.4 presents the distribution of active elderly adults by various specific characteristics, such as social security coverage, education level, occupational category, and type of activity.

As previously mentioned, men's economic participation is higher than that observed for women among the elderly population during the entire period under analysis. Nonetheless, during the last 17 years a continuous increase in female economic participation has been confirmed, which has reduced the participation gap between genders. In effect, whereas the female EAP was 31 percent of the total in 1995, by 2012 this percentage had increased to 39.5 percent. This trend could continue deepening, enabling a convergence of activity rates by gender.

Regarding the social security coverage of active elderly adults, although 57.2 percent of the active elderly population did not have pension coverage in

Table 10.4 Characteristics of Active Adults Older Than 60 Years of Age

Percent

Characteristic/Year	1995	1998	2001	2004	2007	2010	2012
Gender							
Men	68.7	69	68.4	65.4	59.8	63.1	60.5
Women	31.3	31.0	31.6	34.6	40.2	36.9	39.5
Without social security coverage	57.2	61.4	65.1	64.5	51.5	36.0	33.9
Education level							
No education	2.5	n.a.	n.a.	1.5	1.4	0.8	1.2
Primary incomplete	19.5	22.9	20.1	19.8	16.1	11.8	13.0
Primary completed	32.9	33.5	38.2	34.3	31.6	34.5	31.4
Secondary incomplete	13.0	14.5	12.5	11.6	11.9	10.0	13.0
Secondary completed	19.2	12.9	15.2	16.3	17.4	18.5	17.2
University incomplete	3.0	4.2	3.5	5.9	3.8	5.1	4.7
University completed	9.9	12.0	10.6	10.6	17.9	19.4	19.6
Occupational category (employed)							
Employer	10.8	9.9	10.3	5.7	9.2	9	7
Self-employed	39.7	36.8	38.8	36.3	34.3	33.7	33.6
Worker/employee	48.1	51.2	49.4	55.7	55.3	56.2	59
Family work	1.3	2.0	1.4	2.3	1.2	1.1	0.3
Not sure/no response	0.2	0.0	0.0	0.0	0.0	0.0	0.0
Sector of activity (employed)							
Primary sector	1.9	1.7	1.1	2.5	1.7	2.9	1.3
Manufacturing	11.7	12.8	12.7	12.9	12.2	13.9	14.7
Construction	5.1	6.2	6.3	6.4	7.2	7.0	9.5
Commerce	19.8	17.3	15.0	21.5	19.6	19.2	17.8
Services	61.6	62.1	64.9	56.7	59.3	57.1	56.7
Formality (employed)	42.6	43.8	47.01	51.4	59.4	62.6	63.5

Source: Based on the EPH.
Note: n.a. = not applicable.

1995, this percentage had increased to 64.5 percent in 2004. These results suggest the importance of the pension system's performance, in terms of its reach, on workers' decisions to remain in the labor market.

However, since the first quarter of 2006 a continuous decrease in the number of active elderly adults without social security coverage has been recorded, falling to 33.9 percent in 2012. This result is the product of a change in the elderly population's behavior: Despite an increase in social security coverage, the elderly remain active in the labor market.

Workers' status in the labor market is an important characteristic to evaluate. Even though they are active, a portion of these elderly adults are unemployed, and a more substantial percentage is employed in the informal sector. In effect, labor informality among the elderly continues to be much higher relative to the total labor force. Workers older than 60 years of age exhibit, on average, an informality rate almost 10 percentage points higher compared with workers in the 10-year age group before retirement age (50–60-year-olds). The gap becomes almost 20 percentage points when we examine the elderly population over age 65, suggesting that some workers migrate from the formal sector to the informal sector to receive retirement benefits without giving up their labor income.

Between 1995 and 2012, an increase of three percentage points in the proportion of the elderly relative to the total EAP was observed. Nonetheless, during the same period the unemployment rate among this group fell from 13 to 3.6 percent. Moreover, informality among workers older than 60 years of age fell by 21 percentage points (Figure 10.8). These results support the hypothesis that population aging is accompanied by an increase of the demand for this type of worker.

An argument in favor of remaining economically active is associated with the opportunity cost of accumulated human capital that a person must face upon retiring, suggesting that the higher one's level of education, the greater the probability that one will remain in the labor market after the minimum retirement age. In other words, the more capital a person has invested in his or her education, the greater the individual interest in continuing to receive a return on this capital.

The structure of the elderly labor force shows some sign of duality. In 2012, 45.5 percent of active elderly adults had not completed more than the primary

Figure 10.8 Percentage of Individuals Older Than 60 Years of Age Employed in the Informal Sector, by Social Security Coverage, 1995–2012

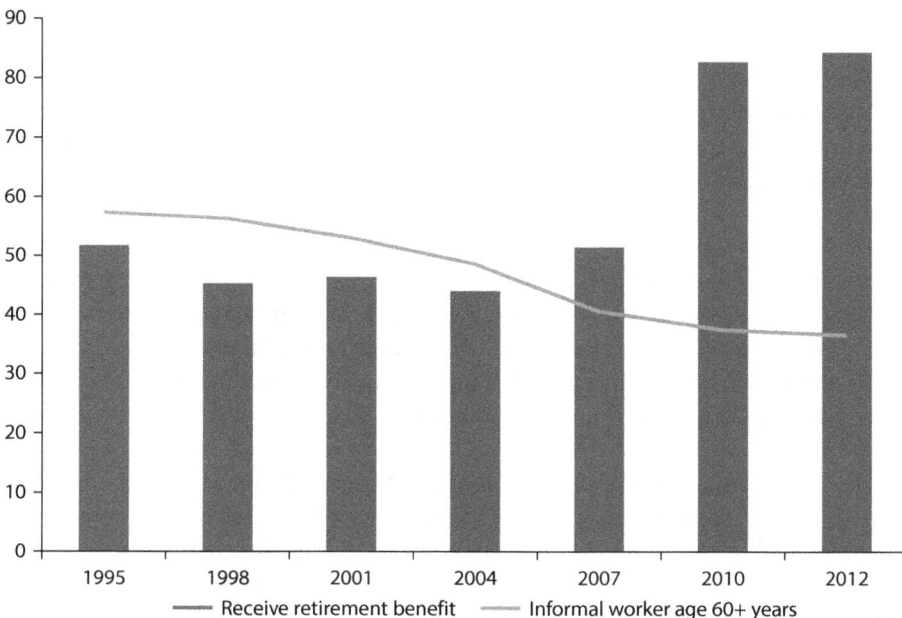

Receive retirement benefit   Informal worker age 60+ years

Source: Based on the EPH.

cycle of education (complete and incomplete), whereas 41.5 percent had completed the second/intermediate cycle. This would suggest the existence of two groups of elderly workers. The first is composed of those workers with a low level of education who remain in the labor market because they need to maintain their consumption power, and the second group is composed of those that prefer to remain in the labor market to obtain the returns they receive on their investment in human capital.

This distribution pattern of active elderly adults has experienced changes over time. Between 1995 and 2012, the participation of workers with just the primary cycle of education increased. Concurrently, a decrease of the group that had completed the intermediate education cycle was observed, from 32.1 to 29.1 percent. In terms of the types of jobs that elderly adults have in the labor market, two main groups were identified: independent businesses (self-employed) and salaried laborers with the characteristics of this age group. On average, 53.7 percent of active elderly adults were salaried workers (59 percent in 2012), and 33.3 percent decided to work independently (33.6 percent in 2012), which remained relatively constant for the entire period of analysis. Finally, 8.4 percent were employers (7 percent in 2012).

This phenomenon shows its importance when employment policies are designed to pursue the goal of improving the well-being of this population group, focusing attention on the productive sectors that demand labor.

Finally, in 2012, 56.7 percent of the active elderly population was working in the service sector, followed by 17.8 percent in commerce, and 14.7 percent in manufacturing. According to Alós et al. (2008), this pattern of distribution by sector of activity is no different than the pattern for young adults. These results are not correlated with the individual characteristics of each age group, but rather with the country's productive structure, which during the 1990s experienced significant growth in the service sector.

Next, we outline an econometric exercise using a *probit* model with the goal of estimating the probability of participating actively in the labor market for adults older than 60 years of age based on the following specification:

$$Pr\ (active)_i = \alpha_0 + \alpha_1 \cdot coverage_i + X_i \phi_i + \epsilon_i,$$

where *coverage*$_i$ is equal to 1 if the individual is covered by the pension system, the vector X_i contemplates various individual and household characteristics, such as *male* (equal to 1 if the individual is a man), *age* and *age-squared*, *married* (with a value of 1 if the individual is married or living with a partner), *head of household*, and a set of dummy variables for each maximum education level reached.

The results obtained are presented in the second column of table 10.5. With a good linear regression explaining 75.8 percent of the cases in the sample, the *coverage* variable is significant at the 1 percent confidence level with the expected negative sign. This means that not receiving a benefit from the pension system imposes a restriction on retirement that has an impact on the probability of remaining in the labor market.

Table 10.5 Probit Model: Probability of Participating in the Labor Market for Retired Adults and Pensioners Older Than 60 Years of Age

	Active elderly adults		Active pensioners	
	Coefficient	Marginal effect[a]	Coefficient	Marginal effect[a]
Male	0.3759382***	0.0292175	0.3856722***	0.0291788
	(0.0603857)		(0.0673796)	
Age	−0.1681218*	−0.0178206	0.0097234	0.0010132
	(0.0942258)		(0.12551)	
Age^2	0.0006421	0.0000681	−0.0005578	−0.0000581
	(0.0006351)		(0.0008526)	
Married	−0.0658213	−0.007359	−0.125116*	−0.0144308
	(0.059243)		(0.0663973)	
Head of household	0.3924394***	0.0565385	0.3237092***	0.043627
	(0.0685638)		(0.0773334)	
Primary completed	0.0086736	0.0009259	−0.0209422	−0.0021451
	(0.0736815)		(0.0786634)	
Secondary incomplete	0.3417388***	0.047405	0.2575719**	0.0329884
	(0.0967536)		(0.105907)	
Secondary completed	0.1764126**	0.0161757	0.1452403	0.0134242
	(0.0838238)		(0.091161)	
University incomplete	0.2301555	0.0293119	0.1608526	0.0190903
	(0.1516441)		(0.1728251)	
University completed	0.5036269***	0.0786517	0.4740116***	0.0714475
	(0.0881578)		(0.1009231)	
Pension coverage	−1.320539***	−0.3274495		
	(−0.0717413)			
Pension income			−0.0000534***	−0.00000557
			(0.0000185)	
Constant	8.108196**		0.4682709	
	−3,467,378		−4,599,504	
Hit ratio	75.8		61.2	
Log likelihood	−15,343,336		−12,769,453	
Observations	5,766		5,296	
LR χ^2	1,094.81		375.92	
Prob > χ^2	0.000		0.000	
Pseudo- R^2	0.263		0.1283	

a. The marginal effect is calculated for a married man who completed secondary school and has coverage from the pension system.
Significance level: * = 10 percent, ** = 5 percent, *** = 1 percent.

Completing a university education maintains a positive and significant effect on the probability of participating in the labor market. This suggests two complementary hypotheses about behavior: On the one hand, the existence of an opportunity cost, which suggests that a higher level of education means greater human capital accumulation and retirement from the labor market, creates a foregone return on that capital. For this reason, the elderly with higher levels of human capital postpone their retirement from the labor market with the goal of obtaining the return from their capital over a longer period.

An alternative hypothesis references the positive relationship between the education level and the quality of work throughout one's working life, such that improved job quality obtained by the most qualified elderly adults—in terms of working conditions—enables this group of workers to remain in better health than their peers with lower education levels and potentially lower quality jobs. Consequently, better health increases the probability that a worker will continue participating in the labor market.

In addition, having reached an intermediate level of education (complete or incomplete) increases the probability of remaining in the labor market. However, this does not appear to be associated with rent-seeking behavior on the invested capital, but rather a restriction created by work history. Finally, the age *dummy* variable is significant with a negative sign when men have a greater probability of participating in the labor market.

In contrast to developed countries, in developing societies the principal problem that pension systems currently face is coverage. In Argentina, this was strengthened not so much by the structural reform to the system carried out in 1994, but rather by the complementary parametric changes that made the requirements to access benefits more rigid.

The coverage problem means that workers cannot choose between retirement or remaining in the labor force as a function of their judgment based on various relevant variables. On the contrary, remaining in the labor market for those workers older than 60 years of age is a function of whether or not they meet the legal eligibility requirement for the pension system given their work history.

With the goal of enabling individuals to choose to be active or not and establishing an intensity effect, we performed a second exercise intended to identify the factors that determine the probability of remaining in or retiring from the labor market for those individuals who obtain a social security benefit (retirement or pension). To do this, we took the subgroup of elderly adults who are retired or receiving a pension and estimated the probability that they were active.

In this exercise, the dependent variable was equal to 1 if the beneficiary of a pension works or is seeking work, while incorporating the same independent variables. In addition, the amount of the social security benefit was included as an explanatory variable. The results are presented in the third column of table 10.5.

With a moderate linear regression explaining 61.2 percent of the cases in the sample, the results are as expected. Just as in the previous exercise, the condition of being male is significant with a positive sign. Age is not individually significant to explain probability, while the condition of being head of household is.

Reaching university-level education is significant and positive, indicating that favorable labor supply characteristics have an impact on the probability of remaining in the market.

The amount of the social security benefit is significant and negative. This result shows the importance of the degree of adequacy of pension system coverage, insomuch as the resources obtained from social security benefits act strongly as a budget restriction.

Final Reflections

The perception of the impact that the process of demographic transition will have on the labor market, and through it on the level of GDP and the social well-being of the population, has been one of skepticism. In general, it is assumed that the window of opportunities, or first dividend, provided by the period with the lower dependency ratio is defined by the age distribution of the population and that this period should be taken advantage of by society to grow rich before growing old, basically through the accumulation of physical and human capital that will enable an increase in productivity, also known as the second dividend.

This argument is based on the traditional age-based definition of the dependency ratio, which designates those younger than 15 or older than 65 as the dependent population, while individuals between the ages of 15 and 64 years old make up the portion of the active population that supports the others. In this conception of the dependency ratio, the upper and lower boundaries of the active population group are defined by age, and therefore the definition of this group is completely static.

It is possible to assume that the conventional definition of these age limits is based on persons' traditional behavior in the labor market, the savings profile by age, and regulations on legal retirement ages.

However, as discussed in this chapter, dependence on third-party income is not linked to age in and of itself, but rather to the role played by different age groups in the labor market. In effect, an updated definition of the dependency ratio is the economic dependency ratio, defined as the ratio between the inactive population and the group of active individuals. The first group includes those younger than age 15 years, inactive youth between the ages of 15 and 24 years old, inactive adults between the ages of 55 and 75 years old, and those older than 75 years. The second group comprises 15–24-year-olds who belong to the EAP, individuals between the ages of 25 and 54 years old, and active adults between the ages of 55 and 75 years old.

On the basis of this redefinition of the dependency concept, the limits are no longer determined exogenously by demographic movements, but rather along with these movements; the decisions that individuals make in each moment of their lives related to their participation in the labor market are what modifies the limits. Consequently, we observe two types of events according to their impact on the economic dependency ratio: those that increase it and those that reduce it.

The former includes young people's continually postponed entry into the labor market, which drives the decrease in the activity rate within this population group. The observed trend between 1974 and 2012 suggests relatively constant growth in the enrollment rate for youth of all age groups. The results appear to indicate not just an expansion of formal education, but also the lengthening of the number of years of study.

The second group of factors, those that lower the economic dependency ratio, includes the increased economic participation of adult women and the postponement of retirement from the labor market by the elderly. The first of these phenomena is associated with the entry of women from low- and middle-income households in to the labor force and is framed as a strategy aimed at mitigating the effects of unemployment and job precariousness among heads of households.

Meanwhile, both the incentives created by the pension system itself as well as the levels of human capital accumulated during working life determine retirement from the labor market for a significant group of the elderly. In this sense, the absence of social security coverage, or in the case of those who do have a pension, the low intensity of said pension, limits retirement from economic activity because individuals require an additional source of income to sustain their consumption. From another perspective, the greater one's accumulation of human capital, the greater the probability of participating actively in the labor market. This could be both as a result of the opportunity cost of retirement as well as the increased "health capital" achieved.

The results discovered suggest that even though demographic behavior is what establishes the limits of the window of opportunities in the end, the behavior of economic agents in terms of entry into and exit from the labor market and income generation gives it a certain amount of flexibility. However, the first dividend is a phenomenon characterized by potentiality, insomuch as taking advantage of it is dependent on whether labor market conditions enable maximum utilization of the labor force, not just in terms of the quantity of jobs created, but also in terms of quality.

Argentina is currently at a very opportune stage of its demographic transition, with both demographic as well as economic dependency ratios that are at their minimum values. Until the aging period commences in the 2040s, the country's principal challenge is to ensure the creation of quality jobs to ensure that the greatest portion of the active population has the ability to generate savings.

To do this, it is necessary to close the deficits for decent work, especially the one associated with informal employment. Maintaining a sustained economic growth rate, facilitating the formalization of employment, and reducing macroeconomic and labor market volatility are significantly important dimensions to keep in mind.

As an alternative to the macroeconomic and labor market conditions, creating favorable conditions for active aging is highly important—in other words, enabling conditions in which the elderly maintain their independence with reduced public health costs, as well as their level of productivity. The initiatives aimed at fomenting active aging should be defined both from a life-cycle perspective as well as from an intergenerational solidarity point of view. In this sense, current generations of youth are the elderly of tomorrow. The quality of life and level of human capital accumulated during one's youth determine the opportunities he or she will have during old age.

According to the results unearthed in the present chapter, it is possible to expect that the elderly will be more active in the future. On one hand, a trend among youth to postpone their entry into the labor market has been observed as a result of the lengthening of their participation in the formal education system. Consequently, future generations of workers will have a high educational level relative to that attained by previous cohorts of workers. On the other hand, it has been observed that workers with higher levels of education postpone their retirement from the labor market because of the quality of employment they have achieved and the returns obtained from their human capital. Thus, it is possible to suggest that a greater accumulation of human capital during younger stages of life increases the probability of participating actively in the labor market in old age.

Notes

1. ILO (2013) suggests that individuals who work but do not earn enough to exit poverty should be considered dependent as well. Doing so would increase the calculated dependency ratio considerably.

2. As was mentioned earlier in this and other chapters, by "definition" the elderly age group comprises all individuals older than 65 years of age. From this point forward, we will loosen this parameter to take into account adults older than 60 years of age with the goal of contemplating the behavior not just of retired persons, but also of those who are near retirement.

3. We chose to use information from the Continuous Household Survey to attempt to measure an alternative dependency ratio indicator as presented in the coming sections.

References

Alós, M., I. Apella, C. Grushka, and M. Muiños. 2008. "Participation of Seniors in the Argentinean Labor Market: An Option Value Model." *International Social Security Review* 61 (4): 25–49.

Bertranou, F. 2001. "Empleo, retiro y vulnerabilidad socioeconómica de la población adulta mayor en la Argentina." Documento de Investigación Universidad Empresarial Siglo 21, Buenos Aires.

———. 2005. "Envejecimiento de la población y los sistemas de protección social en América Latina." Reunión de Expertos "Implicancias Sociales y Económicas de los Cambios en la Estructura por Edad de la Población." UN Population Division and Consejo Nacional de Población, Mexico City, August 31–September 2.

Bertranou, F., and J. Mastrángelo. 2003. "Envejecimiento, trabajo, retiro y seguridad social en Chile." IV Conferencia Internacional sobre Investigaciones en seguridad Social "La seguridad social en una sociedad longeva." Antwerp, Belgium.

Dorn, D., and A. Sousa-Poza. 2004. "Motives for Early Retirement: Switzerland in an International Comparison." Discussion Paper, Research Institute for Labour Economics and Labour Law (FAA-HSG), University of St. Gallen, Switzerland.

Gruber, J., and D. Wise. 2002. "Social Security Programs and Retirement around the World: Micro Estimation." Working Paper 9407, National Bureau of Economic Research, Cambridge, MA.

ILO (International Labour Organization). 2013. *Empleo y protección social en el nuevo contexto demográfico*. Geneva: ILO.

OECD (Organisation for Economic Co-operation and Development). 1999. *Preparing Youth for the 21st Century: The Transition from Education to the Labour Market*. Paris: OECD.

Sigg, R. 2005. "A Global Overview on Social Security in the Age of Longevity." United Nations Expert Group Meeting on Social and Economic Implications of Changing Population Age Structures, UN Population Division, Department of Economic and Social Affairs. Mexico City, August 31–September 2.

Stock, J., and D. Wise. 1990. "Pension, the Option Value of Work, and Retirement." *Econometrica* 58 (5): 1151–80.

CHAPTER 11

Argentine Labor Force Productivity in a Context of Demographic Aging

Ignacio Apella and Sara Troiano

Introduction

The demographic transition to an older population poses questions associated with the impact that this transition will have on the labor market and, through this impact, on national production and the social well-being of the population. On the one hand, this phenomenon could mean there will be a lower proportion of individuals in the productive age range (15–64 years old), and that the elderly dependency ratio will increase relative to the total population. On the other hand, the effects of this transition on the economy can be difficult to estimate because the demographic transition creates endogenous change processes in the structure of the labor force, both in terms of labor market participation as well as productivity.

As discussed in chapter 10, from the labor supply point of view, an older population puts greater pressure on the social protection system to maintain consumption levels. However, given that pension systems are maturing and assuming there are no changes to eligibility criteria (retirement age, contribution rates), these systems' ability to finance more retirees' consumption could be limited, and, consequently, many workers could face an incentive to remain in the labor market. On the other hand, the demographic transition could result in an increase in demand for elderly workers to sustain a labor force reduced by the lower proportion of the younger population.[1]

The effects of these supply-and-demand trends on the labor market are usually amplified by the relative productivity of workers from different age groups. Labor forces of equal size, but composed of different age groups, are not necessarily equal in terms of the production they are capable of generating. As a result, the impact of the demographic transition on the labor market depends on the interaction between (1) the transformation of the labor force age distribution and (2) the age distribution of productivity.

In this context, the objective of the present chapter is to make progress on the development of a hypothesis about the relationship that exists between productivity and age in the specific case of Argentina as a basis for making some reflections on the potential impact of the demographic transition on the overall productivity of the economy. To do this, the chapter utilizes information from the Continuous Household Survey (Encuesta Permanente de Hogares, EPH) from 1995 to the fourth quarter of 2012, as well as from the National Transfer Accounts (NTA) system published by the National Institute of Statistics and Censuses (Instituto Nacional de Estadística y Censos, INDEC).

The analysis is organized as follows: The next section presents the theoretical framework of the analysis associated with the age profile of labor force productivity. Following that, we present and analyze the various mechanisms used in the literature to estimate workforce productivity by age. In the fourth section, we present arguments that justify the approximation used in the present work, and the fifth section discusses the results achieved, along with the simulation of future alternative scenarios. We conclude by offering some final reflections.

Theoretical Framework

According to Gragnolati et al. (2011), as the demographic transition process advances, the proportion of elderly adults in the total economically active population (EAP) begins to grow. If one assumes that workers' productivity maintains an inverse relationship with age, this phenomenon generates concerns related to the impact that this will have on the economy's overall productivity.

Previous analyses have supported this thesis, although they also stress that the effect of aging on productivity is related to the type of occupation (Skirbekk 2003) and that the productivity-age relationship is not static, but rather changes along with the requirements of the labor market (Skirbekk 2008). Essentially, the difference in workers' productivity by age depends on various factors, such as cognitive and physical abilities, health, type of occupation, and workplace turnover, among others.

In those productive sectors where physical strength has become relatively less important, cognitive ability may be the best predictor of workers' productivity (Hanushek and Kimko 2000; Tyler et al. 2000). In this sense, the young population has an advantage relative to their elderly peers. According to Skirbekk (2003), younger workers are early adopters and beneficiaries of new technologies that are probably more productive. United Nations (2007) provides evidence that the process of productive innovation is more frequent among young adults, suggesting a negative effect of the demographic transition on the growth of overall productivity.

The emphasis is on workers' ability to acquire new knowledge introduced to work environments through continuous organizational changes. According to Smith (1996), this could adversely affect workers' relative productivity, given that learning speed and ability diminish with age. In industries that have a high rate of technological change, or where technological shocks make acquired skills obsolete, early retirement becomes a regularly observed behavior (Bartel and Sicherman 1993; Ahituv and Zeira 2000), and young workers experience constant evaluation processes with the goal of improving their performance.

On the other hand, in managerial occupations and other jobs in which experience is an important criterion, older workers have a competitive advantage relative to their younger peers. Some studies suggest that as workers' ages increase, they employ strategies to accomplish their work more efficiently (Salthouse 1984). More time in a position may improve the productivity of older individuals relative to that achieved by younger workers. Ericsson and Lehmann (1996) argue that to attain significant experience in a job in which analytical skills and strategies are important, at least 10 years in the same position are necessary. In turn, Blakemore and Hoffman (1989) conducted an empirical study in the manufacturing sector and found evidence that length of service had a positive impact on productivity.

The estimate of the impact of aging on overall workforce productivity becomes even more complex if we keep a series of externalities in mind. In particular, Börsch-Supan and Weiss (2011) signal that workers' age and service have an impact not only on their productivity, but also on the remaining workers in a context of teamwork. The experience workers gain in the same job during their working life has a positive impact not just on their own productivity, but also on the efficiency of the younger workers who work with them.

In summary, the literature does not enable us to reach a definitive conclusion on the distribution of productivity by age group and the eventual effects on the entire labor force. In addition, the majority of references focus on case studies in developed countries, where the labor dynamics may exhibit features that are different from those found in developing countries. In any case, these studies suggest the most significant factors for facing the problem: the evolution of elderly adults' participation in the labor market, the high proportion of older adults in the most productive sectors of the economy, the trajectory of salaries by age, and the ratio between hours of work and total payroll. On the basis of these observations, this chapter will attempt to advance some hypotheses on the relationship between age and productivity specific to the Argentine context.

Methodologies Used to Estimate the Productivity-Age Profile

The literature suggests various strategies for approaching the task of identifying the relationship between workforce productivity and age that can be grouped in three categories: (1) relationship between labor income and productivity, (2) microestimates at the firm and individual level, and (3) aggregate measurements of productivity at the sectorial or country level. Next, we discuss the advantages and biases of each of these. A first alternative consists of utilizing workers' salary profile by age as an approximation of the productivity profile. The neoclassical theory of the firm attributes salary differences among workers to disparities in their marginal productivity. Essentially, returns to labor are equivalent to the added value that labor generates. The demographic profile of salaries follows, therefore, the demographic profile of the accumulation of human capital growing during the early stages of working life and diminishing as human capital depreciates (Mincer 1974).

However, some arguments exist—underlying assumptions—that could threaten the explanatory capacity of this theory. One of the more well known is based on the deferred compensation hypothesis, in which firms, faced with an environment of information asymmetry and limited ability to monitor workers' performance, pay them a salary that is less than their productivity when they are young and greater when they are older, as a form of aligning interests and increasing the level of effort (Lazear and Rosen 1981). On the other hand, according to the incomplete contracts theory (Hart 1995), as shown by Manning (1998), employers may utilize salary as a signal to attract or retain the best candidates, offering a bonus for experience (*seniority*), especially for specific experience with a particular firm.

Other studies have been based on efficient salary models (*efficiency wage*) to affirm the double causality between labor income and productivity, suggesting that salaries might not just be the result of productivity, but rather can also act as one of its determinants (Shapiro and Stiglitz 1984; Katz 1986). Finally, in a context of elevated rigidity in the regulatory framework of labor market—inflexibility in lowering salaries—the explanatory capacity of the neoclassical theory is weakened.

Given these limitations, various estimation methodologies based on the primary, firm-level information surveyed for this purpose emerge. The traditional measurement of the productivity-age profile is based on a comparison of qualifications that the supervisors themselves perform on their employees. In general, these studies find little or no evidence of the relationship between the scoring of the evaluation and the worker's age (Hunter and Hunter 1984; McEvoy and Cascio 1989). These results may be associated with the inflationary bias of the scores because supervisors could overscore high-ranking employees or those with more seniority as recognition of their past achievements (Salthouse and Maurer 1996).

Alternatively, workers' marginal productivity is measured by estimating the production function based on industrial surveys with data on gross production by firm and workforce participation by age group. This type of study analyzes the impact of the demographic structure of firms' labor forces on production. Haegeland and Klette (1997), Crepon et al. (2002), and Ilmakunnas et al. (2004) found a negative relationship between age and productivity. However, the difficulty of isolating the age structure from other determining factors of firm production may induce errors. In addition, these analyses are generally restricted to the industrial sector, excluding, for example, the service sector.

On the other hand, some estimates are calculated based on data from production records and tend to be more objective. The United States Department of Labor (1957) compares production among individuals of different ages using data from a group of industries. The results uncovered suggest that performance increases up to 35 years of age, at which point it begins to diminish until retirement age. However, this reduction is not equal across all economic sectors: Productivity diminishes by 14 percent in the shoemaking industry and 17 percent in the home furniture industry (United States Department of Labor 1957).

An alternative strategy is utilized by Kotlikoff and Gokhale (1992), who use information related to salary history for each worker from a specific firm included in the Fortune 500 ranking. The authors assume that, even though salary does not always equal productivity, the net present value of salary during one's working life must match the net present value of the marginal production of each employee. Thus, they make inferences about the productivity-age relationship by observing the variation in the salary offered to each worker according to the age at which he or she is hired. However, this methodology does not enable one to make generalizations based on its results and faces concerns linked to information privacy.

Finally, some studies propose alternative productivity metrics that can be estimated at the individual level. Specifically, they focus on the "typical" production of "uncommon" professionals, such as research published by scientists and writers or sports results for athletes. These studies confirm the existence of a relationship between age and productivity in an inverted-U shape, in which productivity reaches its maximum between the ages of 20 and 40 years old (Lehman 1953; Simonton 1997; Jones 2005).

Nonetheless, in these studies, the discipline analyzed, experience, and the degree of innovation are determining factors, and generalizing based on the results in terms of the whole economy is at least debatable.

The majority of the methodologies described use information with limited availability, especially in developing countries. For this reason, some authors analyze the productivity-age relationship using aggregate information, for example, each sector or country and its production (Ahituv and Zeira 2000; Feyrer 2002). Even though this is interesting from a comparative point of view, this type of analysis usually has some significant limitations in terms of endogenicity and omitting relevant variables.

In the Argentine case, the availability of information at the firm and individual levels is limited. In effect, worker-production information does not exist at the firm level, nor does employer-employee, salary history, or qualifications. Moreover, a reliable cross-sector analysis would require the availability of a historical series of capital intensity by sector. The lack of this type of information severely limits the precision of a sector-level analysis. For this reason, a possible alternative is to adopt the salary-age relationship as an approximation of the profile of productivity by age group.

Salary as an Approximation of Productivity: How Plausible Is It?

With the goal of getting some first evidence of the relationship between productivity/salary and age in Argentina, we present the average of hours worked and salary as indicators of productivity.

As Time Goes By in Argentina • http://dx.doi.org/10.1596/978-1-4648-0530-1

Figure 11.1 shows the average of hours worked by age group in 2012.[2] The average number of hours turns out to be relatively constant starting at 30 years old until age 65, varying between 4.1 and 46.4 hours per week. However, among youth and the elderly a behavior distinct from that observed in the rest of the world is identified. According to the International Labour Organization (ILO), it is possible to suggest a global trend in which the youth and elderly age groups work fewer hours than their peers between the ages of 30 and 64 years old (see Sangheon et al. 2007).

In Argentina, to the contrary, youth between the ages of 20 and 29 years old maintain a significantly higher number of average hours of work per week (48.7 hours). Similarly, the elderly work on average a greater number of hours than individuals between 30 and 64 years old. In this sense, a worker between 65 and 69 years old works up to 3.5 hours more per week than an employed person in the middle of his or her work life and between eight and nine hours more than an employed person near retirement age. This peculiar pattern could indicate greater vulnerability, associated with contractual terms or specific industries with higher burdens in terms of the number of hours worked, on the part of the youth and elderly age groups.

In turn, salaries exhibit a pattern in line with the labor productivity theory. The average salary increases until the midpoint of an individual's work life, reaching its maximum value in the 40- to 44-year-old age group and subsequently beginning to fall progressively. Also in this case, a pattern

Figure 11.1 Average of Salaries and Hours Worked, by Age Group, 2012

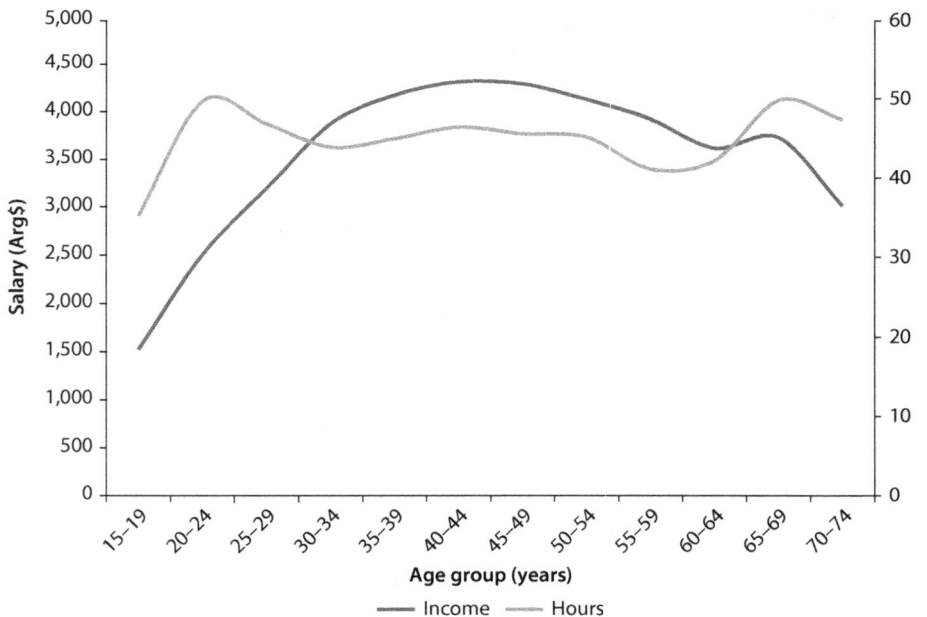

Source: Based on information from the EPH, 2012.

distinct from that observed in the wealthy Organisation for Economic Co-operation and Development (OECD) countries is observed, especially the European countries, in which once salary reaches its maximum value, the nominal salary remains constant for all age groups because of the existence of labor market rigidities (minimal movement of personnel, union power in salary negotiations, high cost of severance pay) (Boeri and van Ours 2008).

The combined effect of the elevated average of hours worked and relatively low labor income suggests a significant reduction in salary per hour among youth and the elderly. Figure 11.2 shows the average per-hour salary by age group, confirming that the inverted-U shape that labor income exhibits is not the consequence of a preference of youth or the elderly to work fewer hours.

Figure 11.3 enables us to analyze the situation from a different perspective. In this figure, the relative weight of each group in the economy is compared in terms of hours worked and total payroll. However, the same group represents just 7 percent in terms of the total payroll. The trend reverses itself after age 30, when the proportion of each group in terms of payroll becomes greater than the relative weight of the hours worked.

In this case, the Argentine situation is different relative to the wealthy OECD countries, in which the gap between total payroll and hours worked is

Figure 11.2 Average Salary per Hour, by Age Groups, 2012

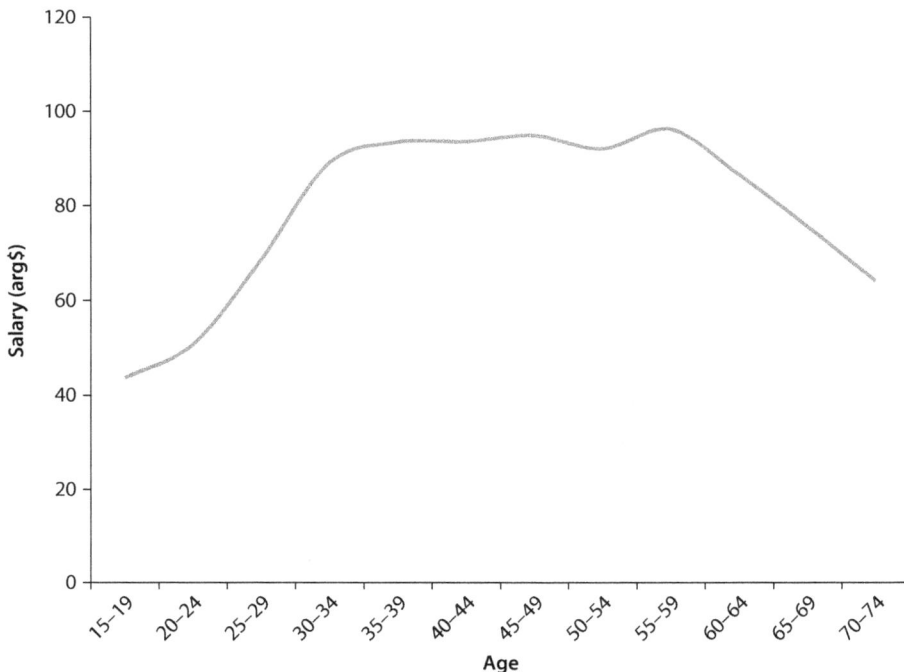

Source: Based on EPH data, 2012.

As Time Goes By in Argentina • http://dx.doi.org/10.1596/978-1-4648-0530-1

Figure 11.3 Hours of Work and Total Payroll, by Age Group, as a Percentage of the Entire Economy, 2012

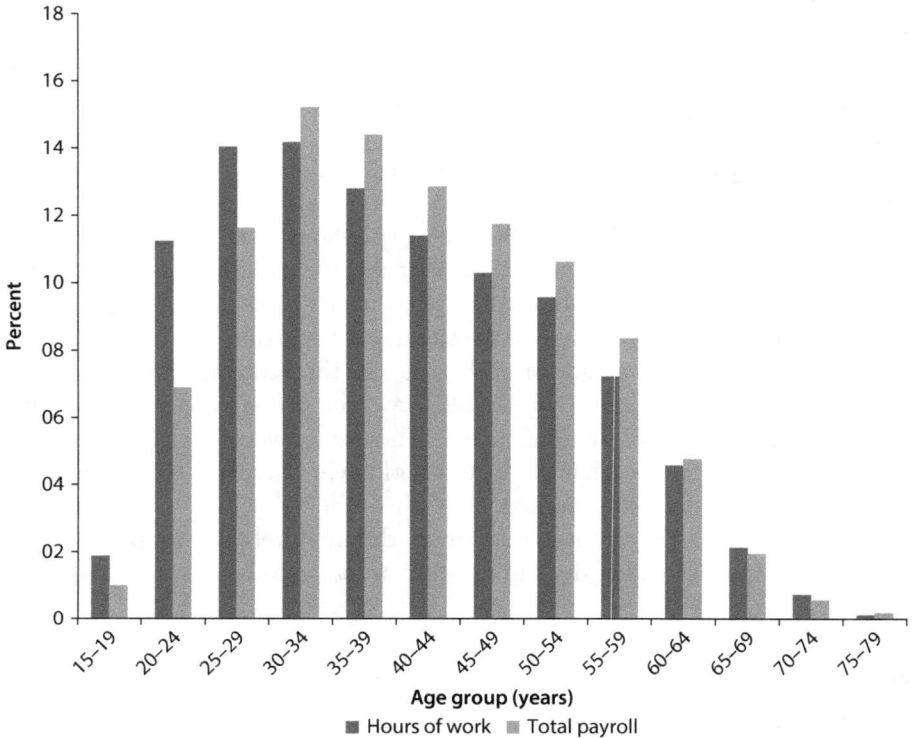

Source: Based on EPH data, 2012.

positive starting at age 35 and increases with age. To the contrary, in Argentina, the gap decreases with age and falls notably beginning at age 60, subsequently becoming negative again after age 70, indicating that the aforementioned theories of deferred compensation and incomplete contracts do not apply to this case, in which the economy as a whole pays a lower price for the elderly population's labor.

The results presented allow us to reflect on the differences observed between the trends in the more developed countries and the Argentine reality. Specifically, contrary to what happens in wealthy OECD countries, we observe the following in Argentina:

1. Youth and the elderly do not work fewer hours on average than employed persons in the middle of their work lives
2. Salaries, and to an even greater extent per-hour salaries, by age group exhibit an inverted-U shape
3. The elderly do not enjoy greater privileges in terms of the gap between the proportion of production received (total payroll) and what they contribute to the economy (hours worked).

The data would appear to indicate that employed persons older than 65 years of age supply a greater number of hours to maintain their income level. In other words, the per-hour value assigned to their work falls with age, indicating a decrease in their productivity or, at a minimum, a perception of a decrease in productivity on the part of employers. This result could suffer from a selection bias: That is, if the workers that remain in the labor market after 65 years of age are less qualified, this would contribute to a negative bias in the estimation of the productivity of active workers in this age group.

As discussed in chapter 10, the group of active elderly adults is divided, in a rather comparable way, into two groups of workers: those who exhibit better qualifications (completed secondary school, work history of formal employment) and those who are less qualified, but remain in the labor market out of necessity (low level of education, no social security coverage, etc.). However, in terms of educational achievements, the group of elderly workers does not differ significantly from the EAP as a whole. In fact, even though the active population as a whole exhibits better results (−2.6 percent who do not have more than a primary level education, +3.1 percent who finished secondary school), this could be attributed to a cohort effect, created by the evolution of the education system, which has been characterized by increased efficiency and more years of compulsory education. In summary, the evidence does not allow us to attribute the significant drop in salary (and, to a greater extent, per-hour salary) to just the self-selection effect.

The observations described serve as arguments to justify, at least partially, the use of the neoclassical theory in the estimation of the profile of productivity by age group. Regardless of the technical or cognitive abilities effectively associated with age, the evidence shows that in the Argentine case, young people who have recently entered the job market, as well as the elderly, exhibit lower productivity, whether as a result of the type of work they are able to obtain or employers' perceptions. In the range of methodologies available, and considering the availability of data, the relationship between salaries and productivity is defined as a plausible strategy for drafting an approximation of the age profile of workforce productivity.

Estimation of the Age Profile of Productivity

Projection of Total Workforce Productivity

As has been observed, in the Argentine case the salary profile represents a plausible approximation of productivity by age group. For this reason, we utilize this variable to construct an initial productivity index, based on the normalization of each age group's salary by the maximum salary observed in the following way:

$$l_e = \frac{W_e}{W^{max}},$$

where W_e is the average salary of each age group e and W^{max} is the maximum salary.

Applying this age productivity profile to the demographic projections estimated in chapter 2 enables us to obtain an approximation of the evolution of overall workforce productivity during the 2010–2100 period.

To do that, the NTA estimates of returns to labor are utilized, as presented in chapter 3 (see figure 11.4). It is worth remembering that this variable is adjusted by macrocontrols from the national accounts. Even though this methodology could entail a lesser degree of precision relative to the EPH, on the other hand, the use of macrocontrols ensures that we consider the totality of labor income in the country.

On the basis of this index, total workforce productivity is measurable using the following method:

$$G_t = \sum_{e=15}^{E} l_{e,t} \cdot N_{e,t} \cdot EAP_{e,t},$$

where $N_{e,t}$ is the total population at age e in year t and $EAP_{e,t}$ is the EAP of the age group e in year t.

To predict the evolution of Argentine workforce productivity, we evaluate a constant participation rate by age equivalent to that from 2012. This will enable us to show evidence of the impact of the age productivity profile and its future effect on total productivity on the economy.

Figure 11.4 Productivity Index by Age, according to NTA Estimates of Returns to Labor

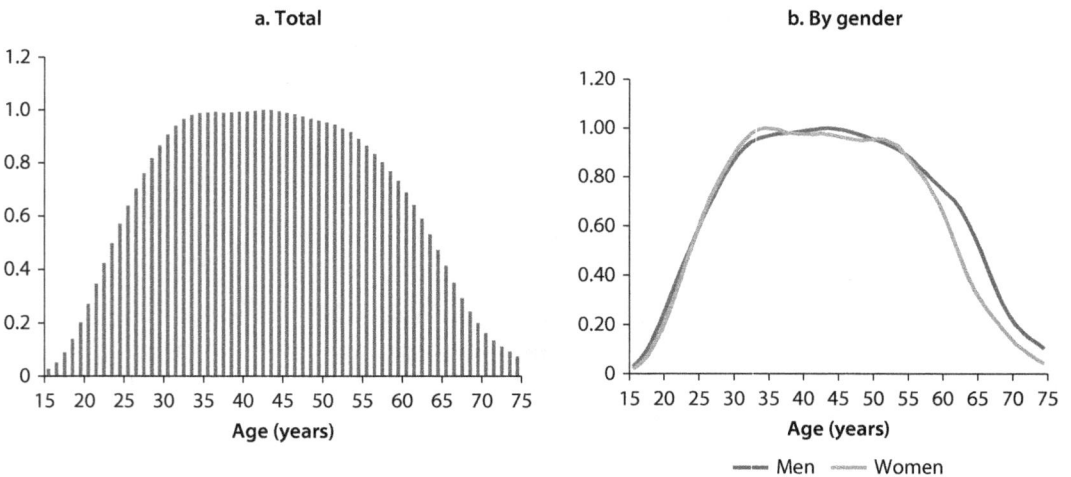

a. Total

b. By gender

Source: Based on estimates of the NTA presented in chapter 3.

Figure 11.5 presents the results obtained. Using 2010 as the base year, we observe that the demographic transition, and more specifically the demographic dividend, could enable the Argentine economy to achieve a productivity increase of approximately 29 percentage points between 2010 and 2047. This increase is associated with two joint effects. On the one hand, the growth of the population entails a larger labor force and, *ceteris paribus*, an increase in the overall economy. On the other hand, the demographic dividend enables the growth of average workforce productivity. Nonetheless, at a later stage of the demographic transition, this trend reverses itself: A greater proportion of the elderly in the makeup of the labor force entails a drop in average productivity around the year 2100. In any case, this reduction in productivity could develop slowly and in the very long term.

However, given the generality of the assumptions, the estimated magnitude of these phenomena is not definitive. Nonetheless, this exercise confirms the validity of one concern about the potential slight fall in overall workforce productivity in the long term due to the heterogeneity of the participation rate and of productivity by age.

Figure 11.5 Overall Workforce Productivity Index, 2010–2100

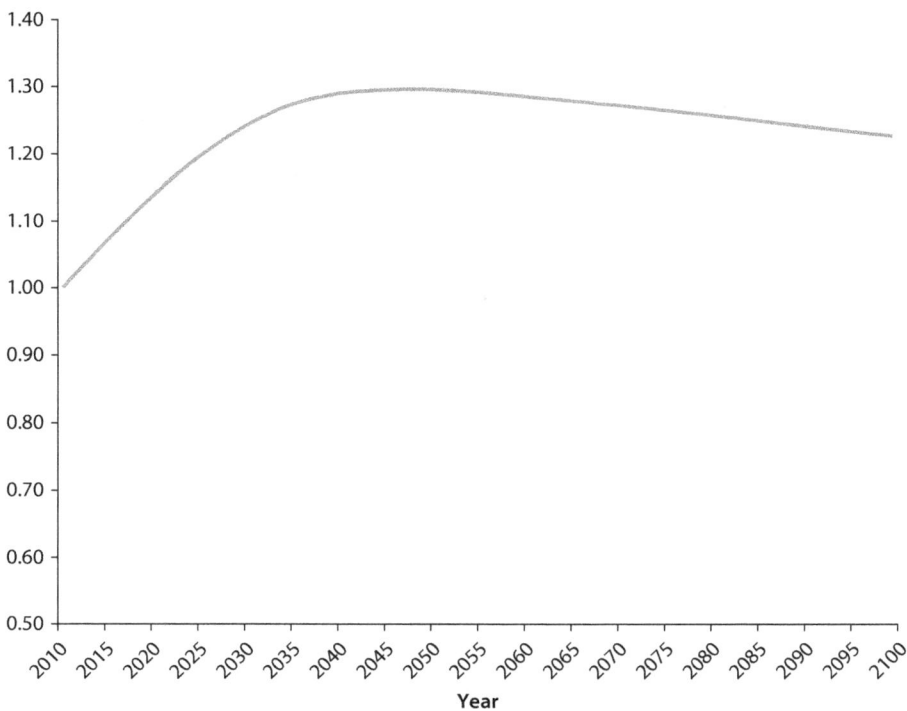

Policy Options: Taking Advantage of Heterogeneity in the EAP and Productivity

With the goal of offsetting the negative effect of demographic aging on the labor force's capacity to generate added value, one could enumerate a long list of policy options, or at least policy objectives. Two principal axes of policy could be categorized in the following way. The first group comprises initiatives aimed at generating changes in the population's participation rate. On the basis of this approach, we discuss (1) policies aimed at increasing the activity rate among women and (2) an increase in the retirement age. A second group of policies is composed of those initiatives designed to increase productivity taking economic participation as a given. Here the potential impact of ongoing education programs is analyzed.

As mentioned in the previous chapter, women's participation in the labor market shows a pattern of growth in recent decades in line with the behavior observed in the OECD countries in their earlier stage of development. Given this, the interannual rate of variation is calculated during the 1998–2012 period and applied to the female EAP beginning in 2012 until reaching the same level as the male EAP.

Figure 11.6 shows the potential impact that the expansion of the female EAP could have on workforce productivity, insomuch as this increase could enable increased exploitation of the demographic dividend. In particular, population growth entails not just a change in the population's age structure, but also a greater proportion of women in the overall population, which would entail a multiplier effect of the impact of the increase of labor participation among women. For this reason, active employment policies aimed at accelerating this process of convergence between the female and male EAP's would take place in a demographic context favorable to a positive effect on the labor market and the economy in general.

In this case, an increase of 0.5 in the annual growth rate of the EAP (from 1.02 percent to 1.52 percent) could enable the economy to reach a considerably higher workforce productivity rate in 2100 (46 percentage points) relative to the estimate that includes just demographic change.

Alternatively, the potential effect an increase in the retirement age could have on the productivity index by 2100 is evaluated. A legislative change that increases the legal retirement age by five years is assumed, increasing it to 70 years for men and 65 for women. This means that the fall in the EAP observed once minimum retirement age is reached would be transferred to the age group that follows and a hypothetical EAP for the 65–69 age group (60–64 for women) is obtained via interpolation. The results suggest that, even though a positive effect is obtained associated with greater individual permanence in the labor market—through a change in the level of the curve— this effect is much lower than the one that comes from increasing the female EAP. As a result, an increase of five years in the legal retirement age would achieve a workforce productivity increase of one percentage point relative to

Figure 11.6 Overall Workforce Productivity Index, 2010–2100: Policy Impacts, Female EAP, and Retirement Age

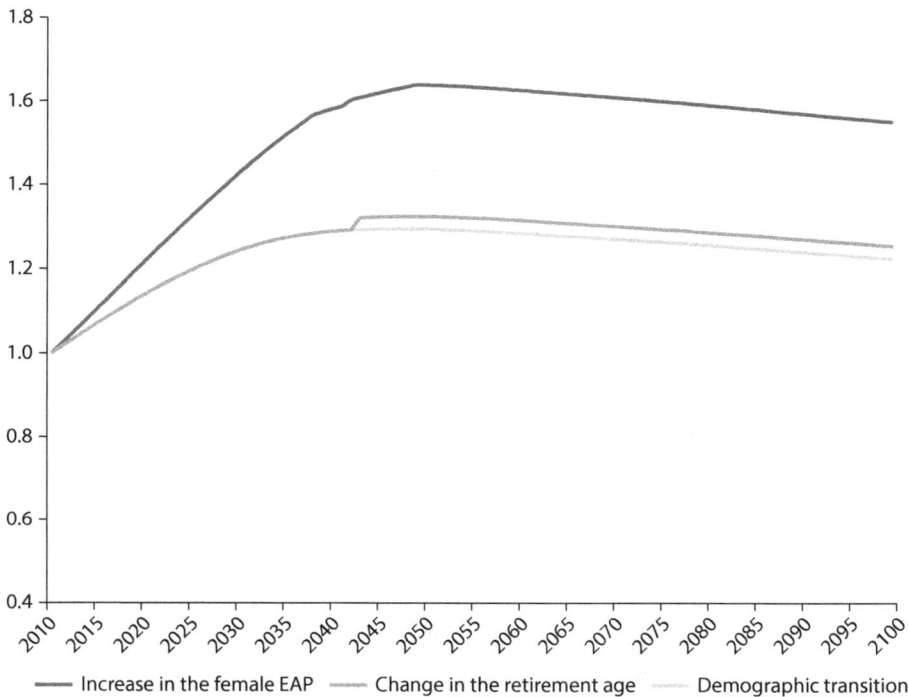

Increase in the female EAP ——— Change in the retirement age ——— Demographic transition

Source: Based on information presented in chapters 2 and 3.

the initial scenario. Even though this result is not significant, changing the minimum legal retirement age to the real retirement age facilitates an increase in productivity.[3]

Finally, we reflect on the implications of investing in ongoing education programs in the context of demographic aging. To gather evidence on the specific effect of this type of policy initiative, we evaluate the age profile of the 2012 EAP for both sexes. On the other hand, a variation of the age productivity profile is allowed.

Training the elderly as a policy to offset the drop in productivity associated with old age is growing more relevant in the debate on the participation of this group of workers in the labor market. Economies with an older age structure began to strongly promote this type of intervention in the early years of this century, to confront problems with the workforce supply and the fiscal sustainability of pension systems. In particular, countries in the European Union consolidated the experience of isolated interventions in terms of formal education, adult education, and training in and out of the workplace to move closer to a comprehensive ongoing education system, or *lifelong learning*, that contemplates all periods of an individual's life cycle.

This renewed policy interest in lifelong learning was accompanied by a vast production of literature on the empirical estimation of the impacts of education and training programs on workers' productivity measured through salary changes (Blundell et al. 1999; Carneiro and Heckman 2003; Kuckulenz and Zwick 2003, among others). Although all of these studies focus on the developed country experience, they still offer a reference point for applying changes to Argentina's age productivity profile between 2010 and 2100. On the one hand, we would expect to find a higher marginal return than in the wealthy OECD countries, given the lower initial level of human capital. On the other hand, during the period of analysis we expect a more or less rapid convergence with the patterns of educational achievement, workforce composition, and productivity observed in the more developed countries. Recent studies (Gasparini et al. 2011, among others) confirm this hypothesis and show a fall in the returns to education in Argentina in recent decades. Therefore, the literature from the OECD countries is used as a reference to infer the potential impact of ongoing education programs on productivity in Argentina.

In particular, we consider the effect that promoting ongoing education programs in the present will have on the productivity of the elderly in the future. Increased intensity of formal education, as well as professional training, is assumed to have a homogeneous effect on the productivity profile for all ages, and here we focus on programs aimed at increasing the performance of the elderly—the segment of the labor force that will have the greatest relative weight as a result of the demographic transition.

Blundell et al. (1999) suggest an average return from professional training programs of 5 percent for men and 11 percent for women over a period of 10 years. In other words, 10 years later, workers who attended these programs may have a higher salary than their peers who did not attend this type of training. In this context, these coefficients of the productivity profile outlined by Argentina are used. In this exercise, it is assumed that the objective is to extend the period during which a worker can take advantage of his or her maximum productivity, that is, delay the fall in productivity, based on increased promotion of professional training support policies at the ages when productivity declines begin to be observed—44 for men, 35 for women. Ten years later, this same cohort could obtain a salary 5 percent higher (11 percent for women) relative to what they would have received without this intervention, alleviating the speed with which this variable falls. Figure 11.7 shows the potential change of the productivity profile for the male and female groups as a consequence of this policy.

Even though the marginal impact is significant, above all for women, at the aggregate level the change is not sufficient to counter the average fall in productivity that is a result of an older demographic structure (figure 11.7). In the aggregate, this policy could increase average productivity by 0.01 percentage points during the 2050–2100 period (figure 11.8). It is worth mentioning that this exercise assumes that all of the cohorts participate in professional training courses, although it does not leave room for their cumulative effects.

Figure 11.7 Productivity Profile: Ongoing Training

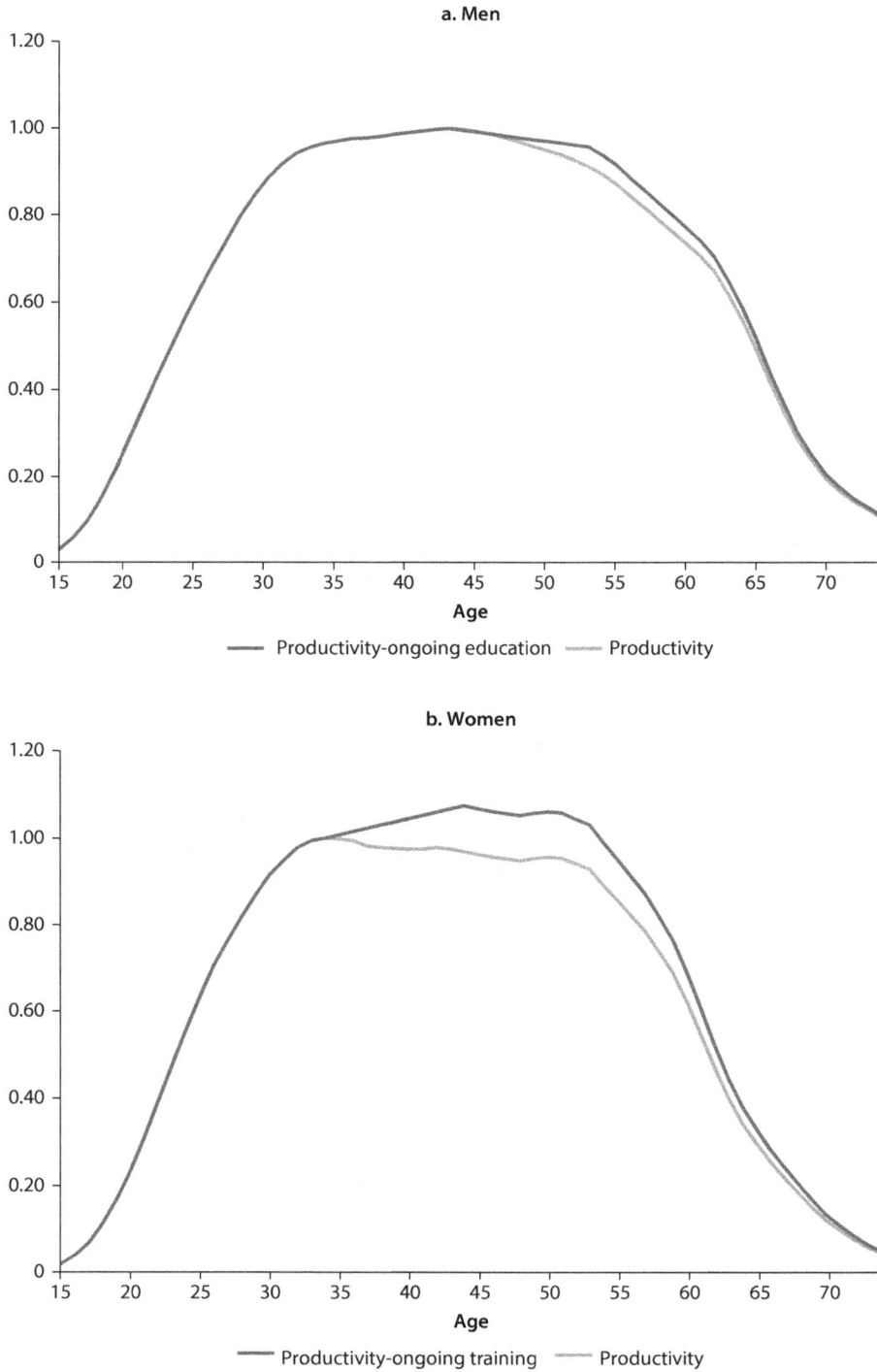

a. Men

b. Women

Source: Based on information presented in chapter 2.

Figure 11.8 Overall Workforce Productivity Index, 2010–2100: Policy Impacts, Professional Training

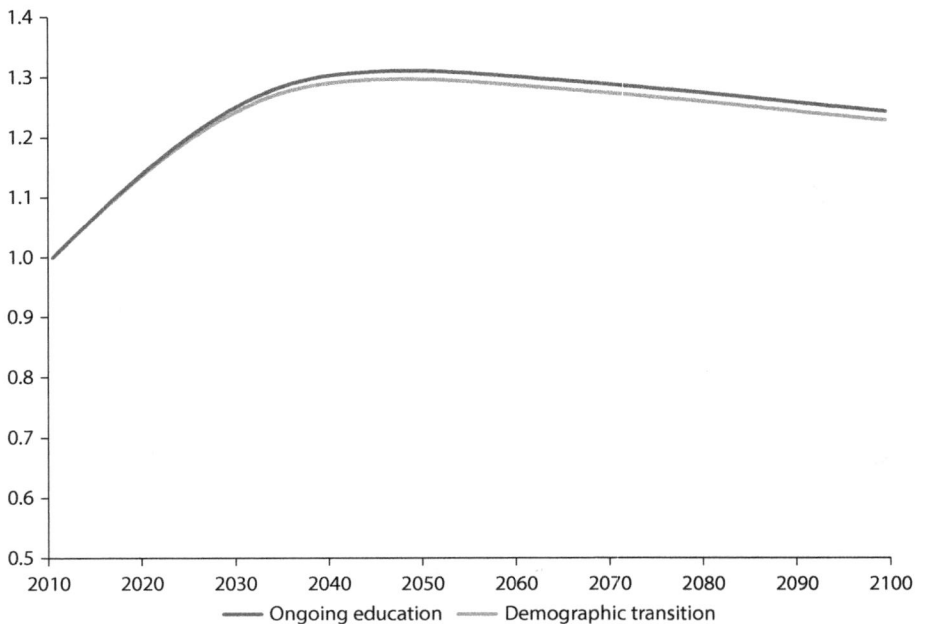

Source: Based on information presented in chapters 2 and 3.

Final Reflections

This chapter presents initial evidence on the relationship between age and productivity specific to the Argentine context. In particular, the data from the EPH suggest a productivity profile that varies with age and partially supports the affirmation that salary reflects workers' marginal productivity.

Compared with what has been observed in more developed countries, salaries exhibit an inverted-U-shaped curve, suggesting the inability of the elderly who remain in the labor market to maintain constant labor income. It is even more impactful that the reduction of income does not appear to be the result of fewer hours worked. An analysis of the profile of these economically active elderly individuals does not show evidence of a bias toward a lower educational level relative to younger workers, although there is room for a possible cohort effect. Evidence can be definitely identified that indicates lesser productivity among the elderly relative to the workforce average—or at a minimum a perception of lower productivity on the part of employers.

In a context of demographic aging, this poses some concerns about the overall productivity of the Argentine economy in the future. Essentially, the simulations proposed show some initial positive effects from the demographic dividend, with an increase in average productivity until approximately 2050, but subsequently a continuous fall as a result of the intensification of the proportion of the elderly in the total labor force.

Among the policy options considered in this study, the programs aimed at increasing female participation in the labor market would appear to be the most effective in countering the effect of the fall in average productivity. Other policies aimed at increasing the EAP, such as increasing the minimum retirement age, for example, exhibit impacts of a considerably lower magnitude. These initial conclusions suggest that, in contrast to what intuition would suggest, policy options with higher political and economic costs, as is the case with increasing the retirement age, are not necessarily the most effective.

Finally, in terms of policies aimed at increasing productivity, the simulations did not find a program sufficient to offset the aging of the labor force within the ongoing training options. It is worth pointing out that, in this case, the simulation is sensitive to the specification utilized, and thus the results could vary considerably depending on the type of training, the estimates of returns evaluated, and the age groups to which the program is applied. In particular, the interaction of ongoing education with other policies could have considerable effects. For example, the greater return that these courses generate among women, combined with the greater participation of women in the EAP in a context of demographic transition could represent an interesting option to be analyzed in greater detail.

Nonetheless, the results discussed in the present chapter will benefit from the support of future studies. In particular, the eventual availability of microdata on the composition of the labor force and production at the firm level will enable a more precise estimate of the age-productivity relationship.

Notes

1. The substitution elasticity among workers from different age groups is a topic of study that is highly debated by an expansive literature (including, among others, Fitzenberger and Kohn 2006). However, applying these arguments to Argentina requires specific research. As a result, this topic is not the subject of the present study.

2. The entire labor force is considered, both in the formal and informal sectors.

3. In any case, changing the minimum legal retirement age to the real age at which workers retire from the labor market favors a reduction in the economic dependency ratio and the sustainability rate of the social protection system. All of this occurs in a context of active aging with an increasing life expectancy.

References

Ahituv, A., and J. Zeira. 2000. "Technical Progress and Early Retirement." CEPR Discussion Paper 2614. London.

Bartel, A., and N. Sicherman. 1993. "Technological Change and Retirement Decisions of Old Workers." *Journal of Labor Economics* 11 (1): 162–83.

Blakemore, A., and D. Hoffman. 1989. "Seniority Rules and Productivity: An Empirical Test." *Economica*, n.s., 56 (223): 359–71.

Blundell, R., L. Dearden, C. Meghir, and B. Sianesi. 1999 "Human Capital Investment: The Returns from Education and Training to the Individual, the Firm and the Economy." *Fiscal Studies* 20 (1): 1–24.

Boeri, T., and J. van Ours. 2008. *The Economics of Imperfect Labor Markets.* Princeton, NJ: Princeton University Press.

Börsch-Supan, A., and M. Weiss. 2011. "Productivity and Age: Evidence from Work Teams at the Assembly Line." MEA Discussion Paper Series 07148, Munich Center for the Economics of Aging (MEA), Max Planck Institute for Social Law and Social Policy.

Carneiro, P., and J. Heckman. 2003. "Human Capital Policy." In *Inequality in America: What Role for Human Capital Policies,* edited by J. Heckman, A. Krueger, and B. Friedman. Cambridge, MA: MIT Press.

Crépon, B., N. Deniau, and S. Perez–Duarte. 2002. *Wages, Productivity and Worker Characteristics: A French Perspective.* France: Mimeo, INSEE.

Ericsson, K. A., and A. C. Lehmann. 1996. "Expert and Exceptional Performance: Evidence of Maximal Adaptation to Task Constraints." *Annual Review of Psychology* 47: 273–305.

Feyrer, J. 2002. "Demographics and Productivity." Research paper, Dartmouth College.

Fitzenberger, B., and K. Kohn. 2006. "Skill Wage Premia, Employment, and Cohort Effects: Are Workers in Germany All of the Same Type?" IZA Discussion Paper 2185, Bonn, Germany.

Gasparini, L., S. Galiani, G. Cruces, and P. Acosta. 2011. "Educational Upgrading and Returns to Skills in Latin America: Evidence from a Supply-Demand Framework, 1990–2010." Policy Research Working Paper 5921, World Bank, Washington, DC.

Gragnolati, M., O. H. Jorgensen, R. Rocha, and A. Fruttero, eds. 2011. *Growing Old in an Older Brazil: Implications of Population Aging on Growth, Poverty, Public Finance, and Service Delivery.* Washington, DC: World Bank.

Haegeland, T., and T. J. Klette. 1997. "Do Higher Wages Reflect Higher Productivity? Education, Gender and Experience Premiums in a Matched Plant-Worker Data Set." Discussion Paper 208, Statistics Norway Research Department. http://www.ssb.no/a /publikasjoner/pdf/DP/dp_208.pdf.

Hanushek, E., and D. Kimko. 2000. "Schooling, Labor-Force Quality, and the Growth of Nations." *American Economic Review* 90 (5): 1184–208.

Hart, O. 1995. *Firms, Contracts and Financial Structure.* Oxford: Oxford University Press.

Hunter, J. E., and R. F. Hunter. 1984. "Validity and Utility of Alternative Predictors of Job Performance." *Psychological Bulletin* 96: 72–98.

Ilmakunnas, P., M. Maliranta, and J. Vainiomaki. 2004. "The Role of Employer and Employee Characteristics for Plant Productivity." *Journal of Productivity Analysis* 21: 249–76.

Jones, B. 2005. "Age and Great Invention." NBER Working Paper 11359, National Bureau of Economic Research, Cambridge, MA.

Katz, L. 1986. "Efficiency Wage Theories: A Partial Evaluation." In *NBER Macroeconomics Annual, 1986,* vol. 1, edited by S. Fischer, 235–90. Cambridge, MA: MIT Press.

Kotlikoff, L., and J. Gokhale. 1992. "Estimating a Firm's Age-Productivity Profile Using the Present Value of Workers' Earnings." *Quarterly Journal of Economics* 107: 1214–43.

Kuckulenz, A., and T. Zwick. 2003. "The Impact of Training on Earnings–Differences between Participant Groups and Training Forms." ZEW Discussion Paper 03–57, The Centre for European Economic Research, Mannheim, Germany.

Lazear, E., and S. Rosen. 1981. "Rank-Order Tournaments as Optimum Labor Contracts." *Journal of Political Economy* 89 (5): 841–64.

Lehman, H. C. 1953. *Age and Achievement.* Princeton, NJ: Princeton University Press.

Manning, A. 1998. "Mighty Good Thing: The Returns to Tenure." CEP Discussion Papers dp0383, Centre for Economic Performance, London School of Economics and Political Science.

McEvoy, G. M., and W. F. Cascio. 1989. "Cumulative Evidence of the Relationship between Employee Age and Job Performance." *Journal of Applied Psychology* 74 (1): 11–17.

Mincer, J. 1974. *Schooling, Experience, and Earnings,* New York: National Bureau of Economic Research. Distributed by Columbia University Press.

Salthouse, T. 1984. "Effect of Age and Skill in Typing." *Journal of Experimental Psychology* 113: 345–71.

Salthouse, T., and T. Maurer. 1996. "Aging, Job Performance, and Career Development." In *Handbook of the Psychology of Aging,* 4th ed., edited by J. Birren and K. Schaie, 353–64. New York: Kluwer Academic.

Sangheon, L., D. McCann, and J. Messenger. 2007. *Working Time around the World: Trends in Working Hours, Laws and Policies in a Global Comparative Perspective.* Geneva: International Labour Organization.

Shapiro, C., and J. Stiglitz. 1984. "Equilibrium Unemployment as a Worker Discipline Device." *American Economic Review* 74 (3): 433–44.

Simonton, D. K. 1997. "Career Productivity: A Predictive and Explanatory Model of Career Trajectories and Landmarks." *Psychological Review* 104 (1): 66–89.

Skirbekk, V. 2003. "Age and Individual Productivity: A Literature Survey." MPIDR Working Paper 28, Max Planck Institute for Demographic Research, Rostock, Germany.

———. 2008. "Age and Productivity Potential: A New Approach Based on Ability Levels and Industry-Wide Task Demand." *Population and Development Review* 34: 191–207.

Smith, A. 1996. "Memory." In *Handbook of the Psychology of Aging,* 4th ed., edited by J. Birren and K. Schaie, 236–47. New York: Academic.

Tyler, J., J. Murnane, and B. Willett. 2000. "Do the Cognitive Skills of School Dropouts Matter in the Labor Market?" *Journal of Human Resources* 35 (4): 748–54.

United Nations. 2007. "Determinants of Total Factor Productivity: A Literature Review." Staff Working Paper 02, Research and Statistics Branch, Vienna, Austria.

United States Department of Labor. 1957. "Comparative Job Performance by Age: Large Plants in the Men's Footwear and Household Furniture Industries." Bulletin no. 1223, Washington, DC.

CHAPTER 12

Demographics and Macroeconomics: Opportunities and Risks in Dividend-Era Argentina

José María Fanelli

Introduction

The demographic transition is a very long-term process that affects all countries around the world. This transition consists of three major stages: the early stage, the demographic dividend, and the aging stage. An important feature is that the beginning of the process and the speed of the transition are not the same in all countries, which creates demographic asymmetries in the global economy. Argentina is currently inside the so-called demographic window of opportunity (DWO) that will be followed by the population aging stage.

Even though the demographic transition is related to variables that go beyond the economic sphere, a dimension of interaction between the economic and the demographic variables exists that is a source of both opportunities as well as challenges in terms of growth. Recent analytical developments have shown that although the demographic dividend period is characterized by a more favorable environment for economic growth, the aging period may be a source of restriction and even macroeconomic instability. From this perspective, the essential challenge that demographics poses today for the country can be summarized in the question: What must Argentina do to grow rich before growing old?

Despite the importance of this question for the process of designing public policies, the restrictions and opportunities associated with demographics are rarely at the forefront of the discussion. Demographic changes occur gradually, and, as a result, policies aimed at dealing with them are easily displaced from the public agenda by the exigencies of the moment. A representative example in this sense is that frequently governments turn to funds from the social security system—intended to pay for the future life-cycle deficit—to finance the current fiscal deficit. This is a way of obtaining financing by generating an "invisible" liability for the public accounts that is left as a legacy for future generations. An other element that has contributed to reducing the visibility of demographic issues is that only recently have data related to income and consumption at the cohort level begun to be available. Without a doubt, these developments will continue to have a greater and greater influence on the design of public policies (Mason and Lee 2011).

This chapter studies the links between macroeconomics and demographics in Argentina. Two fundamental questions are analyzed: What macroeconomic factors should be considered to take advantage of the demographic dividend period by accumulating assets and making income per inhabitant grow?[1] What macroeconomic dynamics should be taken into account to avoid an outcome whereby during the aging period demographics become a source of macroeconomic instability and/or income stagnation?

In terms of the first question, the Mason and Lee (2006) approach is utilized (see also Bloom and Williamson 1997; Bloom et al. 2003; Bloom et al. 2010; Mason 2005; Mason and Lee 2006). According to these authors, the demographic dividend is in large part a possibility and eventually materializes as a first and second "growth dividend." To be able to "collect" these dividends, the economic behavior of the different cohorts and the government's policies must be appropriate. In terms of the second question, related to aging and stability, we consider the analytical scheme and methodologies developed in Wilson and Ahmed (2010), Haldane (2010), and Albrieu and Fanelli (2013), which focus on the interaction between the life-cycle deficits, on the one hand, and the fiscal deficit, the current account, and the accumulation of assets, on the other. This scheme points out that macroeconomic imbalances associated with demographics tend to distinguish themselves for their persistence. Examples include prolonged social security deficits that transform into unsustainable public debt or risks exacerbated by the lack of financial instruments to deal with life-cycle deficits and longevity risks.[2]

In the realm of politics, the questions that motivate the work are as follows: Where should public policies focus so that the demographic growth dividends materialize? What aspects should public policy monitor to reduce the risk of persistent macroeconomic imbalances? On which factors should efforts be focused to channel the extra savings generated by the demographic dividend toward investment? What policies could facilitate achieving these objectives starting with the current macroeconomic environment and keeping in mind the experience of countries that have already passed through the demographic periods that await Argentina?

The elaboration of this chapter has enjoyed two advantages. The first is that estimates were available for the cohort income, consumption, taxes, and public sector transfers profiles that were created following the methodology proposed by the National Transfer Accounts (NTA) Project and presented in chapter 2. The second comprises the studies of the consequences of aging that appear in the other chapters of this book.

The chapter is structured as follows: Next, a set of indicators related to the demographic transition is presented. They are necessary to characterize Argentina's current stage in the process and to identify the channels through which demographics influence macroeconomics in general and the two dividends as well as the subsequent period of aging in particular. The third section advances a step further in specifying these channels and, turning to the methodologies and data provided by the NTA project,[3] evaluates the consumption and income profiles for cohorts in the Argentine case and the life-cycle deficit. On the basis of this, the consumption support ratio is defined and measured. The fourth section discusses the relationship between the life-cycle deficit and the two growth dividends. The fifth section deals with the way in which aggregate life-cycle deficits are financed and their links with savings, the current account, public debt, and external asset accumulation. It also uses this framework to quantify aggregate life-cycle wealth (LW) and transfer wealth (TW). The last section summarizes the conclusions.

Transition Demographics, Window of Opportunity, and Savings

This section discusses a set of indicators related to the population and its age structure that is necessary to analyze the links between the demographic transition, economic growth, and macroeconomic stability. The focus is on the examination of the indicators associated with the demographic dividend that is generated during the period when the DWO is open and in the subsequent period of aging. Among these indicators, those that stand out include the dependency ratio and those that identify the weight of the cohorts of "prime savers" among the total population.

The Window of Opportunity and the Dependency Ratio

United Nations (2004) defines the DWO as a transition period during which the proportion of the population that is younger than 15 years old permanently falls below 30 percent, and the proportion of individuals age 65 and above is relatively even lower (less than 15 percent). Before entering the window, a country is classified as "young" and upon exiting it is called "old." Argentina has been inside the window of opportunity since 1995 and, according to projections, will remain there until around 2035–38 (figure 12.1a).[4]

The countries that are inside the DWO exhibit a greater proportion of people in the active age range. This means that even if average productivity per worker remained constant, income per capita would increase thanks to the relative expansion of the working-age population. It is evident that income per capita will not be the same if 50 percent of the population works instead of 60 percent. This fact, as will be discussed later, is central to generating the first demographic dividend (FD). A direct way of evaluating the effect of demographics as it relates to this is to calculate the "dependency" indicator: the ratio of the population that is not in the active age range (those younger than age 15 and older than 65) to the group that is working-age (between 15 and 64 years old). Figure 12.1 presents the inverse of this indicator, which expresses how many potential workers exist for each dependent person.[5]

The figure clearly shows why Argentina is in a period that is favorable for growth: Until the DWO closes, in 2035, the potential supply of labor will be at

Figure 12.1 Inverse of the Dependency Ratio, the Fertility Rate, and Economic Participation by Age, 1950–2050

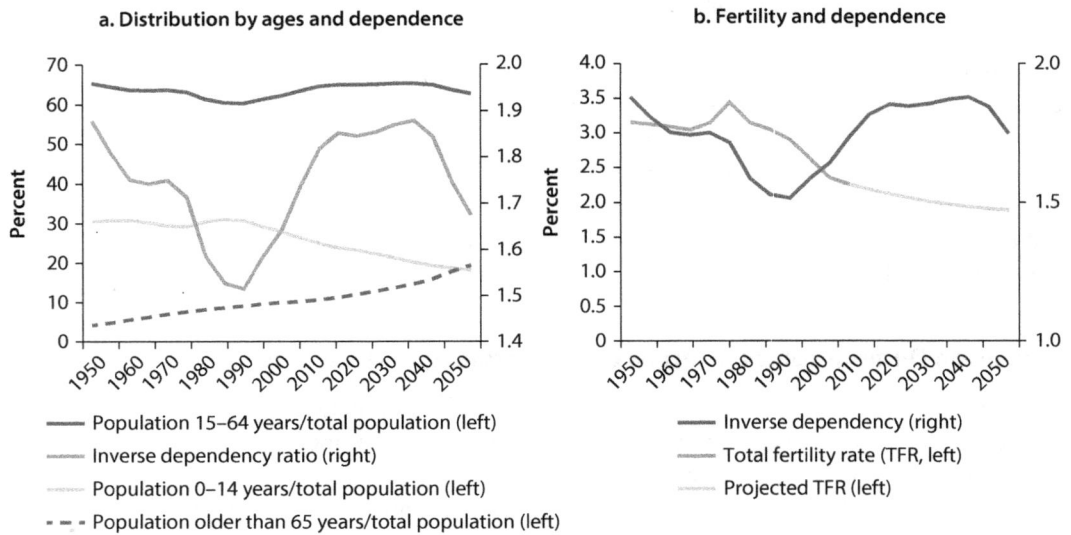

a. Distribution by ages and dependence

b. Fertility and dependence

——— Population 15–64 years/total population (left)

——— Inverse dependency ratio (right)

········· Population 0–14 years/total population (left)

- – - Population older than 65 years/total population (left)

——— Inverse dependency (right)

——— Total fertility rate (TFR, left)

········· Projected TFR (left)

Source: Elaboration based on information from United Nations 2013.

elevated levels and will reach a maximum during that year of 1.88 potential workers per dependent person. Obviously, for this potential supply to become real supply, the economy must create sufficient jobs. Thus, it is not surprising that Mason and Lee (2011) warn that the benefits of demographics are not automatic. Note, on the other hand, how the relative quantity of working-age persons falls during the aging period that follows the DWO beginning in 2040. According to projections from the United Nations, in 2050 the indicator will have a value of 1.67 potential workers per dependent person. If the economy does not prepare for this period during the demographic dividend, the burden for future genera-tions could be very significant because there will be more dependent persons per worker. It is projected that in 2050, as we can observe in figure 12.1a, the propor-tion of persons older than 65 years of age will be around 20 percent of the total population, surpassing the proportion of children.

One favorable demographic feature that Argentina exhibits is that it is projected that the duration of the DWO will be longer than in other comparable countries. In effect, whereas in Argentina the duration will be approximately 40 years, in Brazil it will be 10 years less, and in the Republic of Korea it was 15 years less.

The evolution of the fertility rate explains, to a large extent, why the DWO has a longer duration in Argentina. Figure 12.1b shows the trajectory of the fertil-ity rate. As one can observe, this rate has been falling since 1975–80 and is currently around 2.2. Although the decrease in fertility is a common characteristic of the countries in the region that are demographically similar to Argentina, the trajectory of fertility exhibits characteristics that are somewhat atypical. On the one hand, during the 1970s an increase in fertility was recorded that was uncommon and, on the other hand, the speed of the decrease is slower in Argentina. In countries such as Brazil, China, and Korea, the fall in the fertility rate has been more pronounced. For example, whereas at the beginning of the 1950s Argentina already had a fertility rate of 3.15, in Brazil the rate was 6.15. In 2010, the Brazilian rate was 1.9, and the Argentine rate was still 2.25. In Korea and China, one can observe trajectories that are even more pronounced than Brazil's. In these countries, the fertility rate was as low as 1.3 in Korea and 1.6 in China in 2010. This situation favors the potential for growth that the country has today inasmuch as the duration of the demographic dividend is extended and the beginning of aging is delayed.

During the period when the fertility indicator is lower and there are relatively more working-age people, the effort of providing for the needs of children and youth can be divided among a larger quantity of workers. This influences the growth rate for two reasons: The first is that when the number of minors in the household is reduced, women's participation in the labor market is facilitated—which causes the participation rate to grow[6]—increasing a household's disposable income and the potential for savings; the second is that parents can invest more intensively in human capital for a lower number of children.

Of course, in the countries in which the fertility rate falls more rapidly, the number of workers per dependent person tends to grow more rapidly, making it easier to sustain the household. But this benefit has a cost: The window of opportunity period is shortened, because the aging period arrives more quickly, and the dependency ratio begins to grow prematurely because of the fact that there are more elderly individuals in households, and the number joining the work force is reduced, revealing that the DWO is a temporary phenomenon. Thus, the reversion will surely be more rapid in countries such as China due to the one-child policy, but we would also expect it to be so in Brazil and Korea as a result of the rapid fall in fertility rates; in fact, these countries already exhibit fertility rates below those required to maintain the population (2.1 children per woman). In Argentina the reversion will be delayed because of the slower evolution of fertility.

The Prime Savers

When a country is inside the DWO, as the size of the working-age cohorts increases, the proportion of prime savers increases. In other words, the proportion of individuals who because of their age, are characterized by a high propensity to save because they have higher incomes and should prepare themselves for retirement. Therefore, the higher the proportion of this group, the higher the economy's the average propensity to save. In addition, if life expectancy rises, it increases the amount of assets necessary to finance a longer period of retirement, which demands more savings. These facts, as will be explained later, are what give rise to the second growth dividend (SD).

Figure 12.2 Prime Savers, 1990–2050
Percentage of total

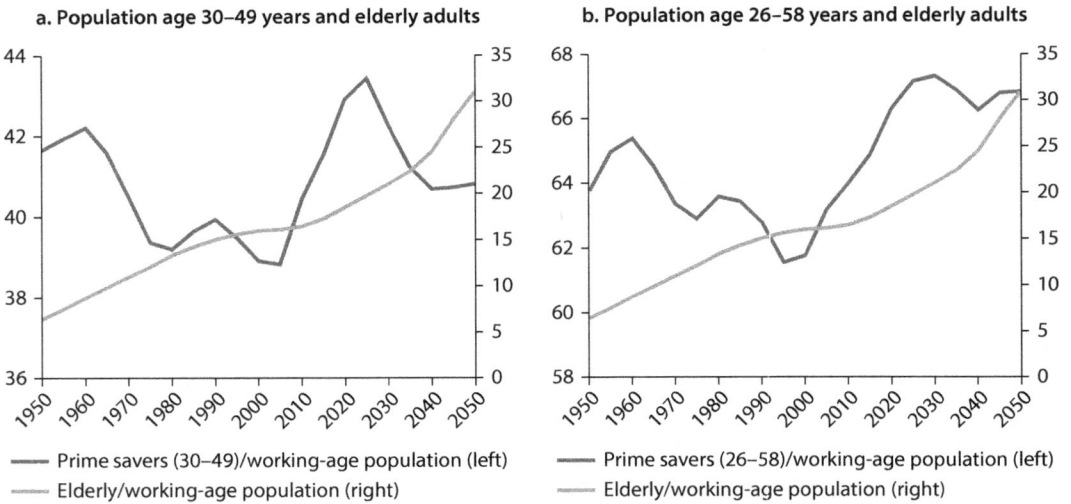

a. Population age 30–49 years and elderly adults

b. Population age 26–58 years and elderly adults

—— Prime savers (30–49)/working-age population (left)
----- Elderly/working-age population (right)

—— Prime savers (26–58)/working-age population (left)
----- Elderly/working-age population (right)

Source: Elaboration based on information from United Nations 2013.

From the preceding, one can deduce that one way of empirically evaluating the influence of demographics on savings is to examine the proportion of prime savers in the population. Figure 12.2 shows the evolution of this group of prime savers as a proportion of the working-age population. Two versions of prime saver are used. The first definition encompasses the cohorts between 30 and 49 years old, which is the group of primary workers that the NTA methodology considers for international comparisons. The second definition accounts for the ability to generate a life-cycle surplus (excess of labor income versus consumption): This version considers the cohorts between the ages of 26 and 58 years old, which, according to the examination below, are those that exhibit an excess of labor income compared to consumption in the specific case of Argentina (figure 12.3).

Figures 12.2a and 12.2b reveal that both definitions result in qualitatively similar trajectories: Hand in hand with the decrease in the dependency ratio, the proportion of savers in the work force grows until reaching its maximum values in 2025 (for the 30–49 group) and 2030 (for the 26–58 group). In turn, it is important to confirm that the maximum difference between prime savers and the elderly as a proportion of the labor force will be reached in 2020. It is reasonable to suppose, therefore, that the current stage of the demographic transition is very favorable for growth: Savings capacity is headed toward its maximum, while demands from retired workers do not yet weigh excessively on the economy.

In the figures one can clearly observe how, once the window of opportunity closes in the mid-2030s, the situation worsens substantially: While the proportion of prime savers falls, the proportion of the elderly rises, a fact that is easy to

Figure 12.3 Income and Consumption Expenditure Profiles by Cohort

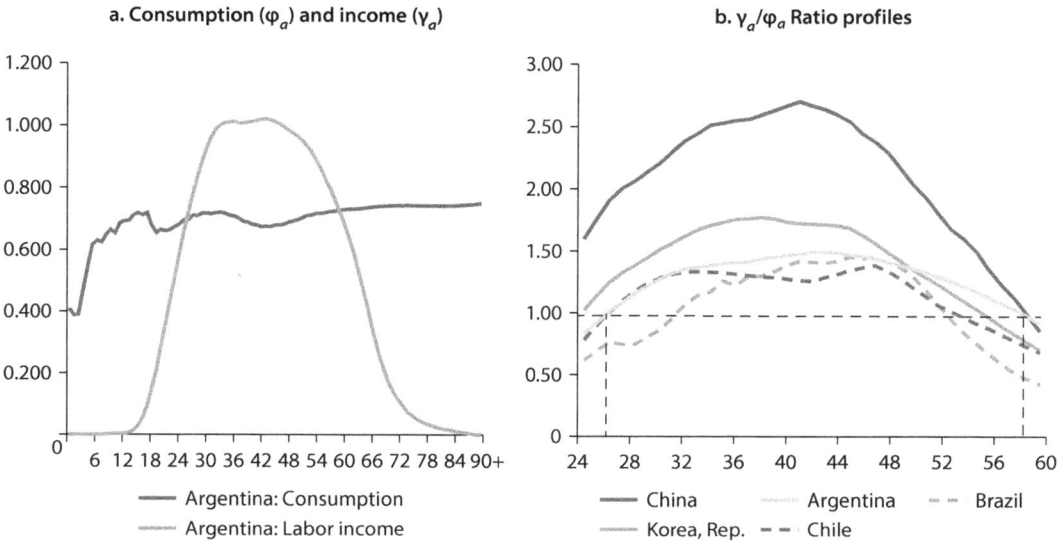

a. Consumption (φ_a) and income (γ_a)

b. γ_a/φ_a Ratio profiles

— Argentina: Consumption
— Argentina: Labor income

— China   Argentina   — — Brazil
— Korea, Rep. — — Chile

Source: Elaboration based on information from the NTA.

anticipate if one takes into account the current experience of the most aged countries, such as Japan.

A good portion of the economic effects of the dividend and aging operate through the inventory of capital that each worker possesses, the availability of fiscal space, and capital flows. The following points deserve to be highlighted in the Argentine case.

In terms of the inventory of capital, one must consider that, even though as savings fall the ability to accumulate capital also falls, it is also true that as the relative quantity of working-age persons falls, it is not necessary to accumulate as much capital because the employment needs of the new cohorts are less. In fact, if worker retirements increase, then the capital that the now-retired workers were utilizing remains available, the capital/labor ratio increases and, with it, productivity. In other words, if a society accumulated a good amount of capital during the dividend, the challenges of aging are lessened. A more negative face of aging is that it can reduce the ability of the economy to drive productivity beyond what the capital/labor ratio contributes, through risk taking and innovation. This is the case because during the period in which the working-age population is younger, it is very likely that entrepreneurial spirit will reach its peak and that this peak precedes a decline in the aging period.

The weight of the cohorts who compose the group of prime savers influences the size of the fiscal space. As the proportion of prime savers increases—likely along with their productivity and salaries because of a higher capital production ratio—the tax base also broadens and, therefore, fiscal space: *ceteris paribus*, the larger the relative size of the work force, the larger the tax base and the available fiscal room. Because the state is the entity that invests in public infrastructure works, public goods, and human capital, if the fiscal space is utilized efficiently, growth is strengthened. Note, nonetheless, that a *trade-off* exists insomuch as tax collections reduce disposable income and private savings; the SD is strengthened only if the social returns of public investment are higher than private investment, because of phenomena such as externalities, coordination advantages, and the production of public goods.

When society ages, in contrast, the fiscal space is reduced. This is due not only to the shrinking of the tax base as a result of the drop in labor income, but also because public expenditure on pensions and health care increases, as was discussed in chapters 5 and 6. This is an important reason to solidify the health of public finances during the stage before the aging period.

Capital flows enter the analysis because the uneven evolution of the global demographic transition creates differences in the balance between savings and investment in countries that are passing through different stages of the transition.[7] And, obviously, if it influences the balance between savings and investment, demographics must also contribute to determining the balance of the current account—which is just the difference between national savings and investment—and, consequently, the direction of global capital flows. In this sense, it should be expected that relatively younger countries that are entering or about to enter the DWO offer good investment opportunities and have insufficient savings, whereas the opposite occurs in countries that are aging and generating an excess of savings compared with investment, preparing themselves for the stage in which retired workers will demand resources for consumption without working themselves. This means that Argentina may not only need to insert itself into the capital markets to finance productive projects in the current stage, but also to have the ability to place a surplus from the current account in these markets.

In summary, the examination of the demographic structure indicates that in the next 25 years a favorable period for saving, investing, creating jobs with growing productivity, and increasing per capita income is taking shape for Argentina. During this period, the economy could be favored by the increase in the relative weight of the cohorts composed of working-age individuals and, within them, composed of prime savers. Because the realization of the potential benefits is not automatic and, moreover, what is a demographic advantage in one period can easily become a social (unemployment) or economic (excessive expenditure burden on the pension system) liability if the resources are poorly assigned, this means that from now until the DWO closes, errors, or delays in the implementation of policies "count double."

The Life-Cycle Deficit and Sustaining Consumption

The indicators from the previous section are based on information about the population. To deepen this analysis of the economic consequences of the demographic transition, it is necessary to incorporate data on cohort behavior provided by the NTA estimates, which will then enable us to define the life-cycle deficit and the two demographic dividends.

We begin by studying what consumption behavior and the ability to generate labor income are like, on average, for each of the a cohorts in society. The coefficient φ_a stands for the per capita consumption profile of cohort a, and per capita labor income is γ_a.[8] On the basis of the discussion presented, we expect to observe $\varphi_a > \gamma_a$ among economically dependent groups (younger than 15 years old and older than 65) and the opposite with the working-age cohorts. Figure 12.3a shows values of φ_a and γ_a corresponding to each age group for the Argentine case, providing a synthetic vision of the differences between consumption and labor income at each age. When the curve corresponding to consumption is higher than the income curve, a per capita life-cycle deficit (PCLD) is recorded because this deficit is defined as the difference between consumption and labor income for each cohort.

On the basis of what Figure 12.3a shows, one can deduce that, on the one hand, the relationship between labor income and consumption varies significantly as a function of age, and, on the other hand, the groups that tend to generate a life-cycle deficit are those that are not in the working-age range. More specifically, in Argentina the period of life in which individuals generate a life-cycle *surplus* (labor income is greater than consumption: $PCLD_a < 0$) is between the ages of 26 and 58 years old. Nonetheless, in per capita terms, the surplus generated during this period is not sufficient to compensate for the deficits ($PCLD_a > 0$) generated in the first and last parts of life, before age 26 and after age 58.

If the sum of the PCLDs throughout all of one's life is positive, this signifies that consumption expenditure exceeded labor income and, therefore, one must resort to nonlabor income (private or government transfers, income from assets, or the sale of existing assets) to finance the difference. Decisions regarding the level of the LD and its financing at the microeconomic level for cohorts have important macroeconomic consequences as we will see.

Figure 12.3b provides a synthetic way of evaluating the Argentine position relative to international parameters. The ratio between per capita labor income and per capita consumption (γ_a/φ_a) is graphed in the figure. If the indicator is greater than one, it signifies the existence of a per capita life-cycle *surplus* and means that this cohort is a net contributor, via its labor income, to aggregate savings. On the basis of the figure, we note that the high-growth Asian countries selected have a propensity to consume much less per capita than we observe in Latin America. The ratio for China and Korea is much higher than one (in China it reaches its maximum levels above 2). This evidence indicates that the group of Argentine prime savers has a lesser propensity to give up consumption (and the same occurs in Brazil and Chile). This weakness in the savings rate is not good news in terms of the ability to take advantage of the DWO.

One must not forget, however, that these figures on consumption and income are expressed in per capita terms for each cohort, and the number of inhabitants in each cohort is not the same. For example, even though the deficit for the 90-year-old cohort is very high, the number of individuals at this age is very low.

To capture this reality, the focus of the NTA works with the concepts of effective consumers (N_t) and effective producers or workers (L_t). If we call the number of inhabitants in each cohort a at time t, x_{at}, then the maximum age that can be reached is ω and is defined as

$$N_t = \sum_{a=0}^{\omega} \varphi_a x_{at}$$

$$L_t = \sum_{a=0}^{\omega} \gamma_a x_{at}.$$

In other words, the number of effective consumers to keep in mind in each cohort depends not just on the number of people who make up the cohort at each point in time x_{at}, but also the per capita consumption of each of them φ_a. The quantity of effective workers is computed the same way considering per capita income per cohort γ_a.

On the basis of these definitions, it is possible to inquire more precisely, based just on the just the dependency ratio, about what happens to the ability of the working-age population to support those who depend on them as a result of the demographic transition. With this purpose in mind, we define the consumption support ratio (SR) as the ratio between the number of effective workers and effective consumers:

$$SR_t = L_t / N_t.$$

It is evident that if the SR_t follows an upward trajectory, the ability to sustain a society's consumption will increase even keeping in mind that not all the cohorts are equally large and that each one of them generates a different PCLD. On the basis of the evidence discussed in the previous section, the SR coefficient must be increasing in Argentina as long as the country finds itself inside the DWO. Figure 12.4a shows that, effectively, this is the Argentine case.

The Argentina ratio worsened until the beginning of the DWO, in the mid-1990s, when the trajectory reversed itself and the indicator began to increase (figure 12.4a). Figure 12.4b shows that this movement, which was first decreasing and subsequently increasing, is typical of countries that after a certain point experience the demographic dividend. However, the movement of the SR in Argentina—which entered the DWO in 1995—is smoother, which corresponds to a longer duration for the demographic window and a lesser effect on the increase of the level of labor income because of the cohorts' more elevated propensity to consume, which increases the value of effective consumers (N_t). This last phenomenon is also observed in figure 12.4b in the case of Brazil, a country that saves little, but not in the Asian countries, which save more. In reality, Argentina and Brazil exhibit the most depressed SR coefficients, well below one. No country, however, reaches the value of 1, with the notable exception of China. This includes Japan, highlighting that the trajectory of the support ratio

Figure 12.4 Support Ratio, 1955–2045

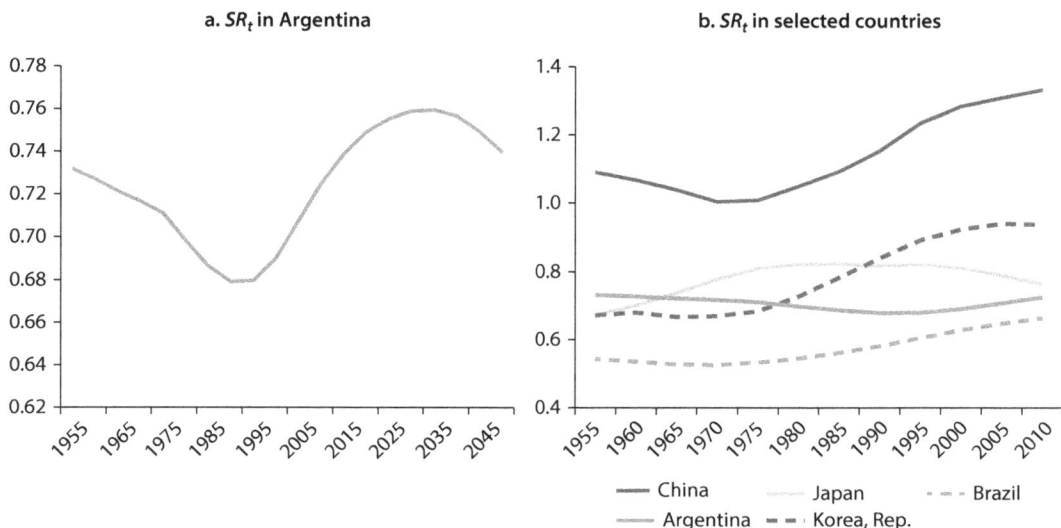

a. SR_t in Argentina

b. SR_t in selected countries

— China   Japan   - - Brazil

— Argentina   — — Korea, Rep.

Source: Elaboration based on information from the NTA and the Ministry of Economy and Public Finances.

for an aging country is decreasing, because of the growing weight of retiree expenditures.

Considering the definition of consumers and effective workers—and without forgetting that the φ_a and γ_a coefficients are normalized based on $y_m{}^9$—total aggregate consumption (C) and total labor income (YL) for the population can be expressed as

$$C_t = y_{m,t} N_t = y_{mt} \varphi_a x_{at}$$

$$YL_t = y_{m,t} L_t = y_m \gamma_a x_{at}.$$

On the basis of this, we can define, in turn, a key variable for comprehending the influence of demographics on macroeconomics, starting with the decisions of cohorts at the microeconomic level: the aggregate life-cycle deficit (LD). This variable is the difference between the total consumption of all of the cohorts and their labor income (YL):

$$LD_t = C_t - YL_t = y_{m,t}(N_t - L_t) = y_{m,t} N_t (1 - SR_t) = C_t (1 - SR_t).$$

In terms of the YL of the population,

$$LD_t/YL_t = C_t/YL_t(1 - SR_t).$$

This expression demonstrates that a direct relationship exists between the evolution of the support ratio, the propensity to consume relative to labor income, and the aggregate life-cycle deficit. Given the demographic characteristics, when *SR* rises, the aggregate deficit falls because, as figure 12.4 shows, the *SR* has values less than one.[10] This is what occurs during the dividend period, and, as a result, a lower deficit enables increased savings at the beginning because society can earmark less of its labor income for solving the deficit. The propensity to save will not increase, of course, if there are compensatory movements in the propensity to consume relative to salary (*C/YL*). For example, the φ_a coefficients could increase if the agents feel that by having a lower deficit it is not necessary to keep saving with the same intensity or if, based on greater collections during the dividend period, the government were to provide consumption goods that were previously financed by families, freeing up private resources that individuals decide to use for consumption and not savings.

The *LD* corresponding to 2010 for Argentina according to the NTA methodology exceeded labor income by 40 percent. Figure 12.5a presents the evolution of the *LD/YL* ratio during recent decades, only considering the effect of demographics (in other words, assuming that per capita income and consumption moved in unison, to control for the effects of these variables).

One can observe that the labor ratio *LD/YL* tends to rise up until the moment Argentina enters the DWO, when it reached a maximum of 46 percent of labor income and subsequently fell systematically, and the trend is expected to continue in the coming years, as we will see in the simulations below. The international comparison (figure 12.5b) indicates that the movement of the *LD* relative to labor income in Argentina follows a trajectory that is typical of countries that enjoy the demographic dividend and differentiates itself from the case of a country like Japan, which has an older population.

Figure 12.5 Life-Cycle Deficit Relative to Total Labor Income, 1955–2010

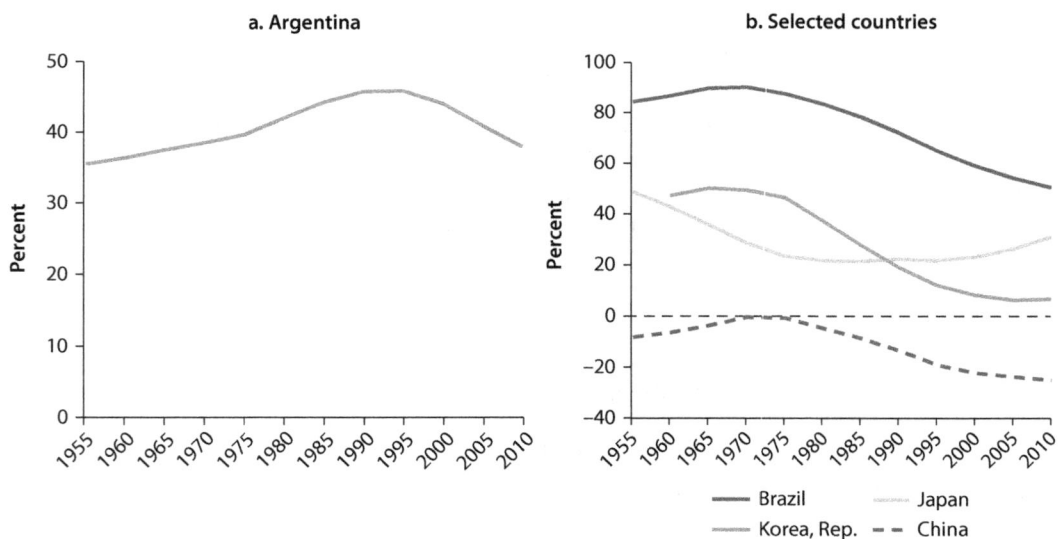

Source: Elaboration based on information from the NTA.

However, reflecting the lower propensity to save that we already mentioned, the ratio between the *LD* and labor income is higher than is the case in the Asian countries. Note that, on the other hand, all of the countries register a life-cycle deficit except for China, a country with a propensity to consume that is so low that it generates a persistent life-cycle surplus. Because the average Chinese consumer spends less than what he or she receives in labor income, workers contribute their share to capital accumulation.

Dividends and the Life-Cycle Deficit

This section utilizes the concepts and empirical evidence presented in the second section to distinguish between the FD and the SD. First, the economy's growth rate is disaggregated to be able to identify the factors associated with these dividends. Second, the FD's contribution to the growth of the economy is evaluated, showing that it is a transitory phenomenon, even though it has a long duration: During the aging period, the FD reverses itself and pulls growth down. This is because of the FD's transitory nature, which is important to keep in mind in terms of the SD.

According to Mason and Lee (2011), the SD has positive effects on growth that are associated with the period prior to aging and are not transitory. The SD essentially operates through the increase in savings and the subsequent accumulation of physical capital and foreign assets. As the capital/labor ratio increases, productivity rises, and as the stock of foreign assets increases, national income improves. The SD's contribution is, nonetheless, more difficult to identify because both productivity and income from foreign assets are affected by a good number of variables. According to the literature on the topic, experts look at the support ratio and LW to study how it is that the SD can continuously favor growth.

One point that this analysis intends to clarify is the importance of the policies that are implemented during the DWO. Both the FD and the SD are tributaries of the demographic dividend, and a key challenge is to take advantage of the increased capacity to save during the DWO with the goal of not just preparing for the reversion of the FD during aging, but also to permanently increase per capita income by making the SD a reality.

The Dividends

Now that we have introduced the ideas of effective consumers and workers that account for differences by age profile, it is advisable to express GDP per capita and productivity in terms of these concepts:

$$Y_t/N_t = (Y_t/L_t) (L_t/N_t) = (Y_t/L_t) SR_t.$$

Thus, income per consumer emerges from multiplying the productivity of effective workers (Y_t/L_t) by the support ratio. Using this expression, we can generate the following, using logarithmic growth rates to be able to disaggregate growth per effective consumer $(g^{Y/N})$ into growth contributed by the increase in productivity per effective worker $(g^{Y/L})$ and growth contributed by the growth of the SR, which is, in turn, equal to the difference between the rate of growth of effective producers (g^L) and effective consumers (g^N):

$$g^{Y/N} = g^{Y/L} + g^N - g^L = g^{Y/L} + g^{PD}.$$

On the basis of this disaggregation, it is possible to identify the FD's contribution to growth (g^{FD}) as the difference between the growth rates of effective consumers and producers. Thus, the FD is positive during the DWO because $g^N > g^L$ and reverses as the population ages because demographic forces bring about the opposite. We have already shown the evidence related to Argentina and other selected countries in figure 12.4.

The forces that give rise to a potential SD have to do with the incentives to save during the DWO and with the changes in the weight of the cohorts that save. Because the SD, unlike the FD, operates through savings and accumulation of capital, if the SD becomes a reality, it reflects the greater dynamism of labor productivity ($g^{Y/L}$). This means that the SD is achieved only if savings behaves such that the amount of capital grows more rapidly than the number of effective workers during the DWO. If this is achieved, the benefits will not be transitory because the capital stock will be permanently higher. The question that naturally emerges in this context is then, Which factors operate on aggregate savings during the demographic dividend?

First, the FD occurs automatically as the value of the SR changes, and the increased income generated by the FD can be used for both consumption and investment in assets. Only in the event that at least part of the extra per capita income that is produced by the positive result of the $g^L - g^N$ equation during the DWO is saved and is invested will the economy's capacity for growth be strengthened, contributing to the materialization of the SD.

Second, the SD can also be strengthened by the generation of extra savings associated with the growing proportion of prime savers in the population that, as we can tell from figure 12.2, is produced during the DWO. In this sense, it can be expected that the prime savers will contribute significantly to the accumulation of assets during the DWO period because the population that has completed or is near completion of their productive years is increasing and they need to save for retirement.

Third, as life expectancy increases, the number of years that one can expect to live following retirement increases, raising the amount of resources necessary to finance consumption during these extra years of life. In other words, the demand for LW necessary to sustain consumption during retirement increases.

These impulses for savings that are inherent to all demographic transitions, in turn, will have more or less strength based on microeconomic and structural factors that affect the incentives. Among the factors to keep in mind, the following should be mentioned: tax pressure on prime savers, family transfers to children and the elderly, and the generosity of the social security system, which determines what percentage of retirement needs can be expected to be covered by TW instead of using assets acquired during one's working life. These elements particularly influence the quantity of wealth accumulated by the population older than 50 years of age which usually owns the greatest portion of assets in the economy (IMF 2005). The following sections discuss the empirical evidence that is relevant for quantitatively evaluating the FD and SD in the Argentine case.

The First Dividend, Savings, and Growth

The FD's contribution to growth (g^{FD}) can be appreciated in figure 12.6, which disaggregates the growth rate using five-year averages.

During the period before the DWO, demographics' contribution to growth was negative (figure 12.6a). Between 1950 and 1995, the annual growth rate was lower on average because of this factor. On the other hand, once the window was open, the FD became positive, contributing to the growth observed in GDP per effective consumer.

The FD's contribution stands out somewhat because the growth rate of productivity has been very low. In effect, in Argentina, the evolution of income per effective worker has been slow as a reflection of the lack of dynamism of the factors that drive productivity per worker. In fact, this variable records an absolute decrease during the periods of prolonged macroeconomic imbalance associated with the debt crisis in the 1980s and with the pain of convertibility at the end of the 1990s and the beginning of the 2000s. The trajectory of the support ratio, in contrast, is more stable because it obeys demographic dynamics. It reaches a minimum at the beginning of the dividend period and later begins to contribute to growth positively and generates the FD (figure 12.6a).

Figure 12.6b records the FD's expected contribution to growth under the assumption that income per effective consumer grows at a pace of 2 percent per

Figure 12.6 First Dividend's Contribution to Growth of Income per Effective Consumer, 1950–2050

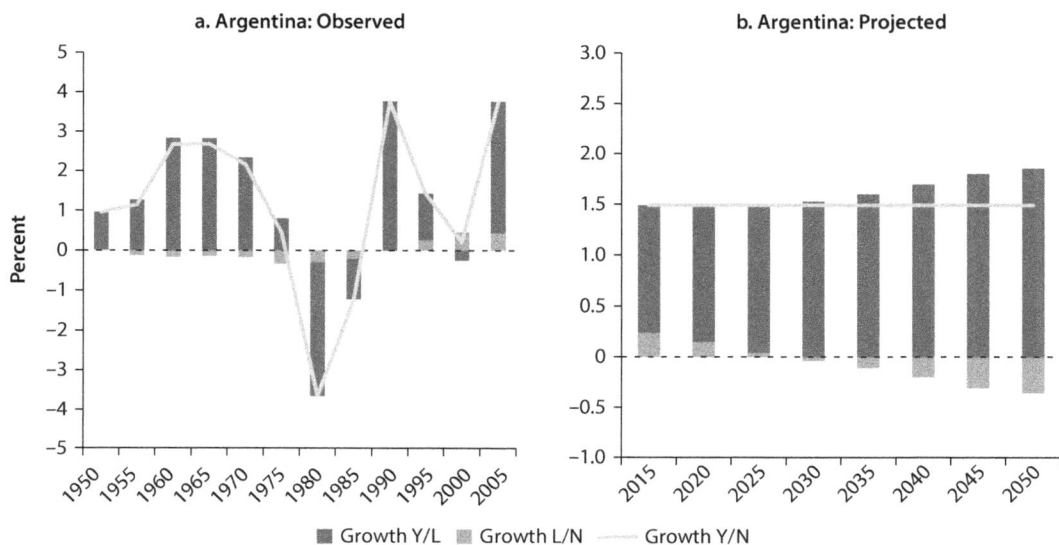

Source: Elaboration based on information from the NTA and the Ministry of Economy and Public Finances.

year, which although a modest rate, is higher than that registered in recent decades. The FD contributes positively to this objective but at a lesser scale for a relatively brief period that is exhausted by 2030. On the other hand, when the country leaves the DWO, the contribution of the FD becomes increasingly negative, concurrent with the aging process. As we evaluate the trajectory of the FD, we must keep in mind that the changes in the population structure are weighted by φ_a and γ_a, because the cohorts' average propensity to consume tends to be high, and when the dependency ratio increases, this increase is strengthened by the high level of the φ_a coefficients.

On the basis of the evidence analyzed, it is apparent that, within the DWO, the economy will tend, ceteris paribus, to generate an excess of savings on the investment as the life-cycle deficit falls as a proportion of labor income. This is a direct effect on the first demographic dividend, because it is based on the fact that income rises more rapidly than consumption because of the expansion of the labor force. A central question, from the growth point of view is, as we have stated, whether this savings surplus will be converted into a greater accumulation of assets or if, to the contrary, it will lead to an increase in consumption. In the latter case, the resources contributed by the FD will dissipate without generating growth. Figure 12.7 provides evidence that is useful for evaluating Argentina's potential for making the SD a reality.

Figure 12.7a shows the ratio of aggregate consumption by all cohorts to labor income for all cohorts in various countries. Except for Japan, which has already left the DWO, in all the cases the coefficient exhibits a decreasing trend that is driven by favorable demographics. However, beyond this dynamic, we also

Figure 12.7 Consumption and Growth in Selected Countries
Dollars from Geary-Khamis, 1960 = 100

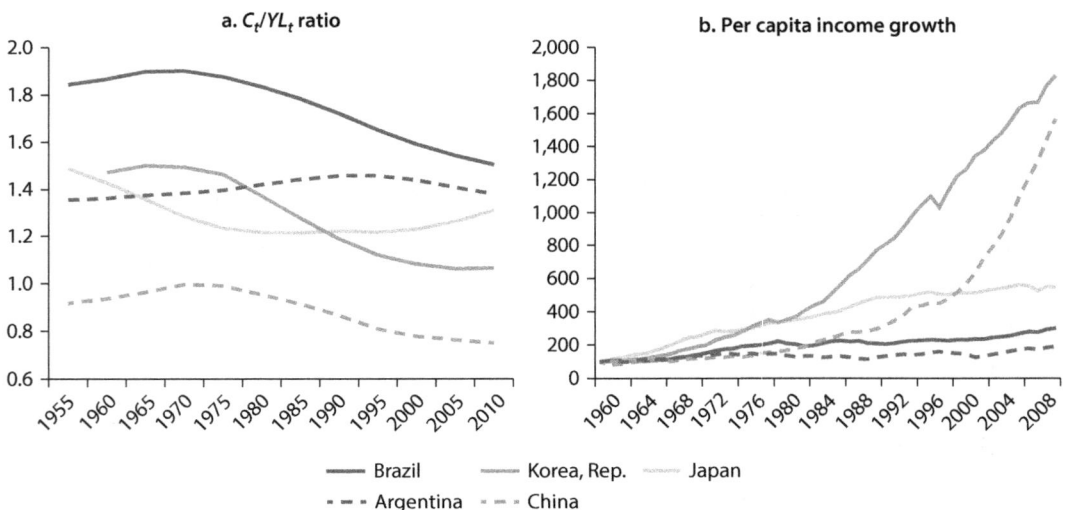

Sources: NTA, World Bank, and the National Directorate of National Accounts in the Ministry of Economy and Public Finances.

observe that the level of the *C/YL* ratio in Argentina is among the highest, exceeded only by that of Brazil.

Figure 12.7b indicates that the benefits of the dividend on growth fade when consumption, and therefore the LD, is high relative to labor income. Although the Asian countries grew significantly during the DWO, Argentina (along with Brazil) recorded the lowest increase in income per inhabitant. There is an inverse relationship in the ranking of the countries by consumption/labor income rates (which depends on the LD) in the figure on the left and by the growth rate on the right. This suggests that there could be a "threshold" effect, by which countries that save little remain prisoners in a low growth trap: The push of demographics through the growth of the SR during the DWO is not capable of generating a big push that would place the economy on a growth path that leads to higher steady state growth.[11] It is reasonable to hypothesize that this picture could change if the demographic evolution were accompanied by policies that promote savings.

It has been mentioned that identifying whether disincentives to savings exist and removing them is key to paving the way toward the SD. With this purpose in mind, we now introduce the relationship between the public sector and demographics to the picture, as well as intrahousehold transfers.

The Fiscal Support Ratio

To study the effects of the demographic transition on the available fiscal space, it is possible to define a fiscal support ratio, similar to how the consumption support ratio was defined. If β_a signifies the per capita tax burden by cohort, while α_a represents the benefits received from the government by cohort (normalized by y_m), then the effective number of taxpayers (U_t) and the effective number of beneficiaries of public spending (Q_t) can be defined as follows:

$$U_t = \sum_{a=0}^{\omega} \beta_a x_{a,t}$$

$$Q_t = \sum_{a=0}^{\omega} {}_a \alpha_a x_{a,t}.$$

Similarly, remembering that the ratios are normalized based on the average per capita income of the cohorts between the ages of 30 and 49 years old, the transfers received (G_t) and those provided (T_t) by the public sector are, respectively, $G_t = y_{mt} U_t$ and $T_t = y_{mt} Q_t$. On the basis of these definitions, the fiscal support ratio (FS) would be as follows:

$$FS_t = U_t/Q_t = G_t/T.$$

Utilizing these indicators, it is possible to identify a series of stylized facts about Argentina that may be acting as disincentives to saving. In figure 12.8, profiles of taxation and benefits by age appear.

As one can see in figure 12.8a, in Argentina the tax burden is greater than benefits in the age range from 21 to 65 years old, which signifies that the prime savers are also those who assume the responsibility of financing transfers. This is

Figure 12.8 Fiscal Benefits and Tax Burden

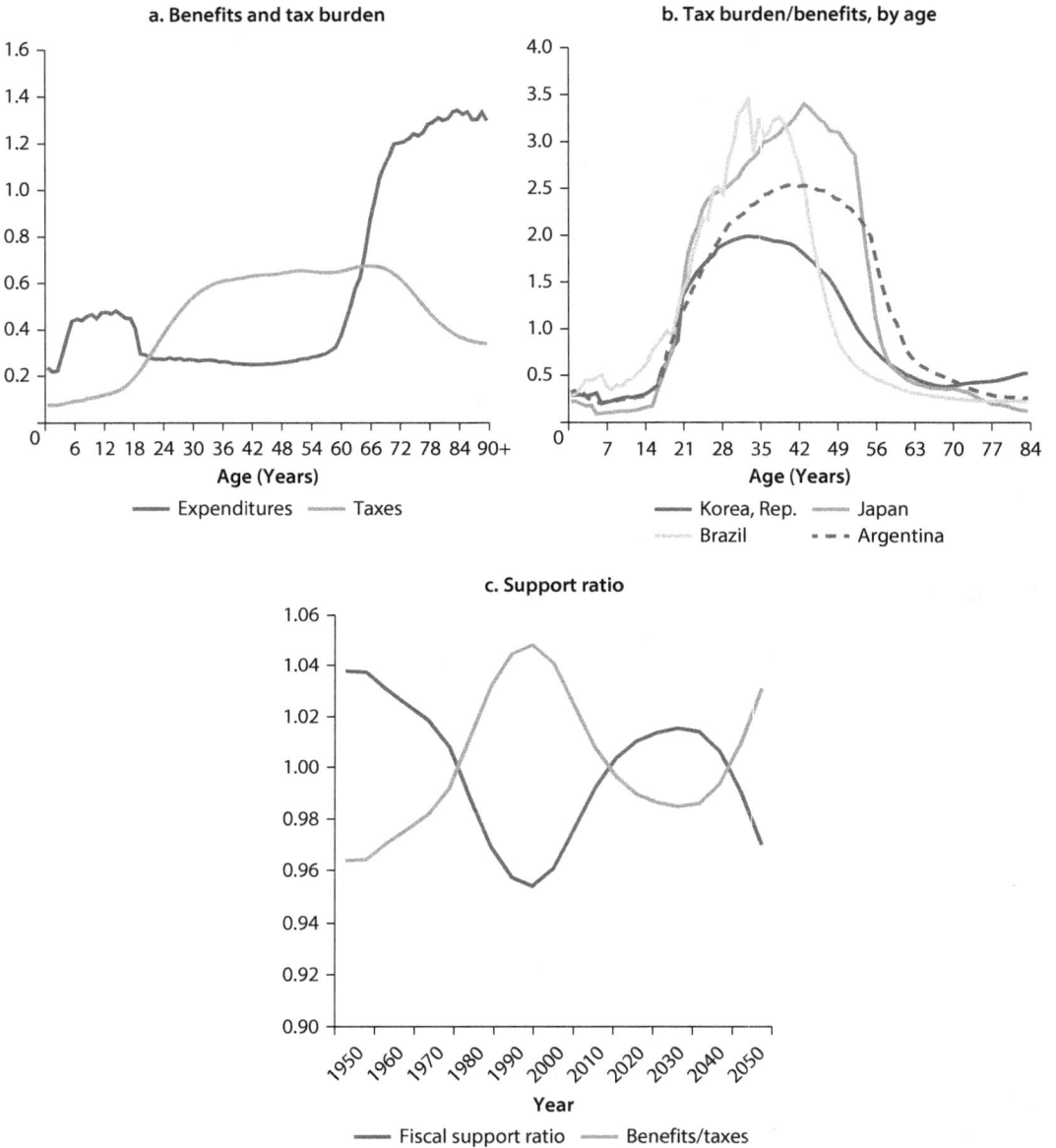

a. Benefits and tax burden

b. Tax burden/benefits, by age

c. Support ratio

Source: Based on information from the NTA.

a stylized fact common to all countries, but Argentina's profile exhibits certain negative characteristics for incentives to save.

First, benefits increase abruptly relative to taxes in the case of those cohorts older than 65 years of age (figure 12.8a). In terms of this phenomenon, one must consider that expenditure on social security has increased significantly in recent years, nearing the figures observed in Brazil, which spends nearly 10 percentage points of GDP (Turra and Queiroz 2005). A generous social security system in the dividend period can transform into an excessive burden for savings during the aging period. Moreover, during the DWO it can disincentivize private savings to finance retirement.

Second, figure 12.8b indicates that Argentina's profiles of benefits and taxes by age have a shape that places them in an intermediate spot between that which corresponds to an older country, such as Japan (with a significant deficit during old age), and that of a country that was successful in taking advantage of the dividend, like Korea. In this sense, Argentina is closer to Brazil to a certain measure, a country that despite being inside the DWO has a taxation/benefits profile similar to Japan (figure 12.8b). This is very distinct from the Korean case, which exhibits greater balance among the cohorts despite being more advanced in the demographic transition than Argentina. An excessive tax burden on the prime savers is without a doubt a dead weight on capital accumulation.

Third, the tax pressure on the prime savers is high (greater than 50 percent of the average salary for individuals between 30 and 49 years old), as one observes in figure 12.8a. This reduces available income precisely for those who are supposed to save and generate the life-cycle surplus. It appears reasonable to conjecture that these characteristics of tax pressure and benefits by age distort the incentives to save and skew the propensity to save and the SD lower.

Because of the high tax burden and demographic situation, Argentina exhibits a rather favorable FS. The ratio has increased structurally during the DWO period. The projections for the fiscal support ratio to 2050 (figure 12.8c) indicate that it will continue improving until 2030. The improvement in the ratio between benefits and salary income during the DWO has a significant weight on the favorable evolution of the fiscal support ratio. Nonetheless, one cannot lose sight of what was already mentioned based on figure 12.8b: Fiscal sustainability is based on a high tax burden on the prime savers, which depresses disposable income and pushes down savings and, therefore, growth. Thus, a situation results in which fiscal sustainability is obtained at the cost of a lower SD and reduced well-being in the long term. Beyond this situation, the projections indicate that when the country leaves the DWO the fiscal balance will worsen, concurrent with the increase in the benefits/salary income ratio that the aging of the population will provoke.

Private Transfers

When a cohort resorts to individual credit or transfers from other cohorts to fund its LD, these flows between individuals cancel each other out for the private sector as a whole because there is no debtor without a creditor and because one cohort receives what another provides. This does not mean, however, that the intrahousehold flows lack importance for savings and, therefore, for the SD. In effect, on the one hand, the credit operations influence the interest rate and, on the other, the larger the transfers—above all from parents to children—the smaller the capacity to save of those who make up the labor force, leading to a lower accumulation of physical capital and/or foreign assets. Although, obviously, we should not ignore that private transfers can result in human capital accumulation, it is true that in a context of imperfect capital markets, if transfers between individuals are significant and rationing of credit exists, then those that have projects to launch will have difficulty financing them. Thus, indirectly, a *trade-off* between investment in productive projects, investment in human capital, and consumption by children and youth is created for demographic reasons that can depress the accumulation of assets for the retirement period.

Figure 12.9 presents the difference in the life-cycle deficit for the various cohorts when transfers to children are considered and when they are not for the Argentine case (following the methodology of Mason and Lee 2007).

Figure 12.9 Life-Cycle Deficit and Private Transfers
Millions of 2010 AR$

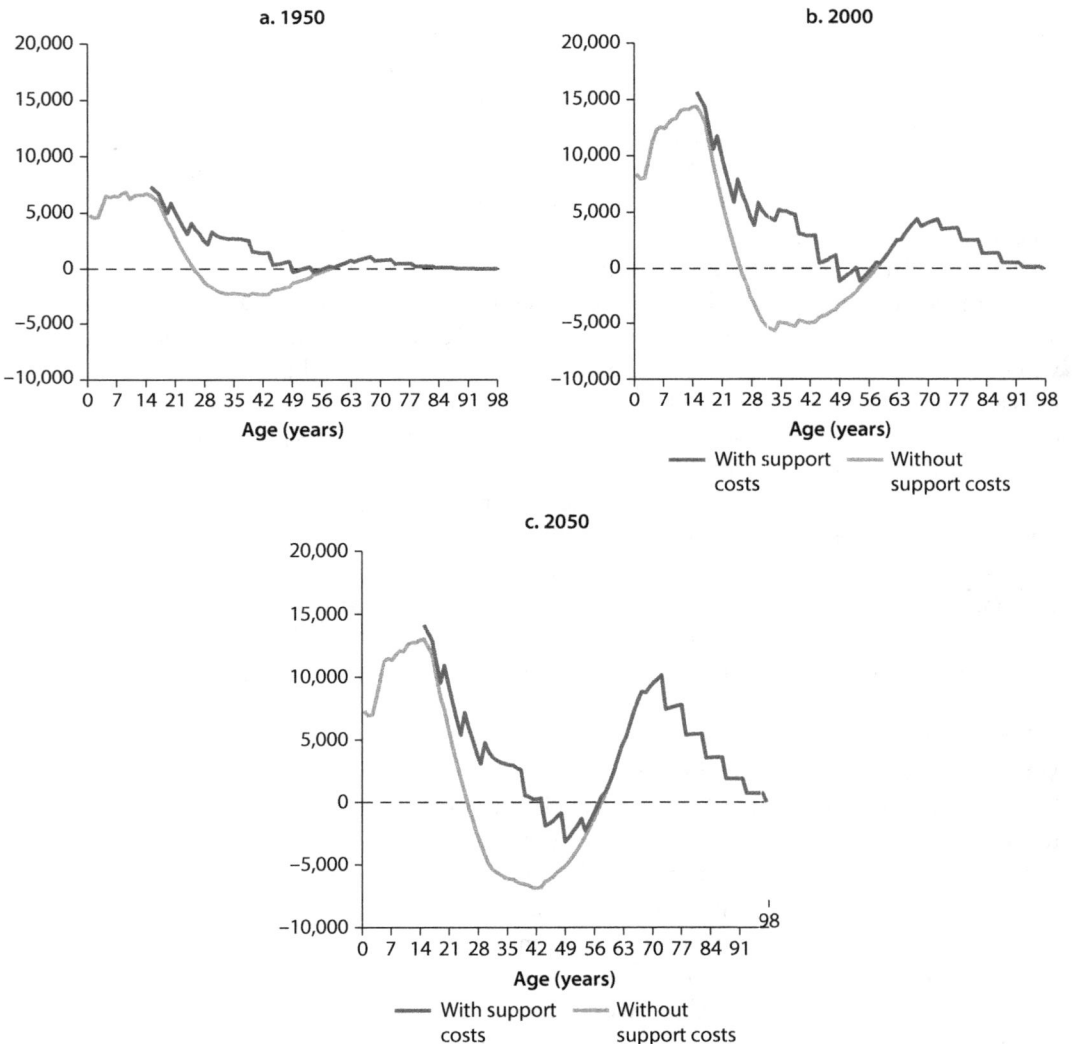

Source: Based on information from the NTA.

This evidence indicates that the portion of young people's deficit that the prime savers finance is significant and can affect the total LD differently as the demographic transition advances. In particular, before the DWO, the children's deficit is much higher than that generated by the elderly, and this situation changes significantly once the DWO ends. Note that this is not neutral for the finances nor for the organization of the economy: The transfers to the elderly are basically the responsibility of the state, which assumes that the size of the social security and health care system will grow along with the advance of the demographic transition and, therefore, must either increase the tax pressure to finance these transfers or increase public debt, which in turn assumes the existence of a developed capital market and access to international capital markets. Meanwhile, although a portion of the transfers to children and young people can be considered investment in human capital that will provide a certain rate of return in the future, transfers to the elderly are pure consumption.

The profile of both public and private transfers and income received throughout life has a direct effect on well-being and the formation of individuals' abilities and has been studied in other chapters of this book. The points that we have attempted to emphasize in this section are strictly linked to savings and the SD. To complete the picture, the following section analyzes how the financing of the LD affects the savings-investment balance.

Financing the Life-Cycle Deficit, Accumulation, and Macroeconomic Imbalances

The imbalances between aggregate savings and investment are at the essence of macroeconomic imbalances, but these imbalances usually tend to disappear in a relatively brief period of time. However, under certain circumstances, the imbalances can last over time, as occurred during the lost decade of the 1980s in Argentina or as is occurring today in some countries in Europe. In terms of the imbalances between savings and investment that are rooted in demographics, one cannot rule out that the imbalances will acquire a more permanent character, including with features of instability. One case of persistent imbalances typically related to demographics is the lack of sustainability of the public debt as aging begins due to the burden of a poorly designed social security system. Another is structural unemployment accompanied by labor informality in countries that are entering the DWO period with an economy that is incapable of generating more sustained demand for labor.

An additional problem is that if situations of multiple equilibria occur, the demographic dynamic could create initial conditions that would lead the economy to a low labor productivity growth trap.

There are two basic reasons why demographics can give rise to lasting imbalances and low-growth traps. The first is that population variables move slowly; the second is that the decisions (private and public) linked to future financing of the LD for younger cohorts have very long-term horizons as a reference point and generate a demand for wealth associated with the life cycle (LW) that strongly influences the accumulation of productive and foreign assets.

One way of studying the possibility of persistent imbalance phenomena or low-growth traps is to analyze the possible evolution of LW and the way in which the LD is financed. The LD is determined primarily by the demographic dynamics and the income and consumption profiles, which depend in turn on the labor productivity of each cohort. If the LDs that society will generate are projected as a function of demographics and income and spending profiles and the present value of these is calculated, then it is possible to have an idea of the size of the LW that it could be necessary to accumulate to satisfy this demand for wealth.

However, one must consider that a single flow of LDs can be financed in various ways. First, it may be financed by intrahousehold or state transfers as discussed in the previous section. Second, the LD may be financed based on income from assets or the disaccumulation of assets (physical or foreign) accumulated previously, or by increasing foreign debt. The financing method that is chosen is not neutral relative to the type of macroeconomic imbalance that an economy may experience or for the selection of an equilibrium in the event of multiplicity.

Public Transfers

If all the government's transfers are financed from taxes, the sum of transfers and taxes should be zero for each period $(G-T = 0)$ because the state collects with one hand while distributing with the other. If the transfers are greater than tax collections and net income from government assets, then the government generates a deficit that must be financed by placing public debt, thereby reducing the spending capacity of those that lend the money. In this way, the increased spending by the person who receives the transfer has an exact offset in the lower spending that corresponds to those that absorbed the public debt in their portfolios. Note that from the intertemporal point of view this means that the state will have to generate a surplus in the future (transfers less than the sum of collections and net income from assets) to honor the debt. Future generations of workers will have less disposable income while investors will have more. But in net terms, in the future, the restriction that states that at each point in time net transfers between inhabitants are zero is not violated either. In other words, public debt, taxes, and the social security system cannot distribute what does not exist; these mechanisms simply redistribute resources among cohorts at a point in time and commit to present and future transfers among cohorts over time.

Just because government and private transfers essentially redistribute resources does not mean that income redistribution does not have effects on growth. All redistribution that favors those who have more productive projects (in terms of physical, human, organizational, or technological capital) improves growth and, during the DWO, strengthens the SD and vice versa. The following figure shows two possible scenarios regarding public transfers in the Argentine case.

Figure 12.10 Government Transfers and Savings
Percentage of GDP

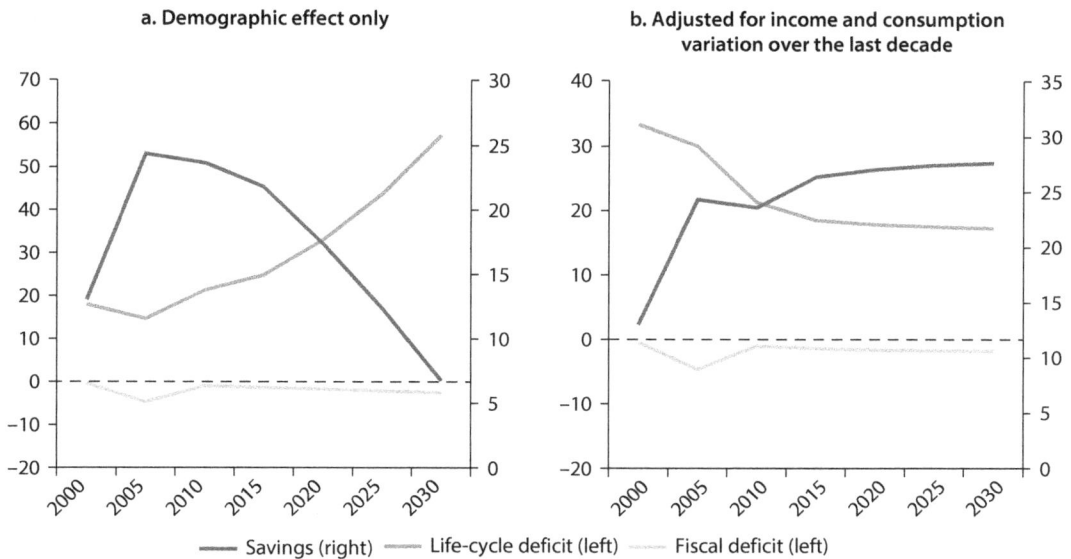

a. Demographic effect only   b. Adjusted for income and consumption variation over the last decade

— Savings (right) — Life-cycle deficit (left) ---- Fiscal deficit (left)

Source: Based on information from the NTA.

Figure 12.10a assumes that spending on consumption and income grow at similar rates, such that the trajectory is only determined by changes in demographics (the support ratio, SR). The second (figure 12.10b) assumes that spending, consumption, income, and taxation vary in addition to demographics, for reasons unconnected to it. It is assumed that they vary following the trajectory that they exhibited during the first decade of this century.

Figure 12.10a suggests that the effects of demographics in Argentina are very positive in terms of savings, even keeping in mind the transfers that the public sector must make. The savings rate tends to increase, and this opens the possibility to take advantage of the opportunities associated with the SD.

In contrast, when one assumes that consumption will continue growing faster than labor income, as has been occurring since overcoming the convertibility crisis, the situation becomes unsustainable: while the tax burden remains high to finance the elevated level that public expenditure has reached in recent years, the LD continues increasing in accordance with the fact that consumption keeps growing faster than labor income. In this scenario, taxes and the LD end up absorbing the entire economy. Note that the public sector does not face difficulties while it is not generating a greater deficit. However, if the private sector were to press to increase its disposable income, then the government would generate a larger deficit, and the problem of the lack of savings would be reflected in an increase in public debt. If the debt is placed in the domestic market, the transfers to be made among cohorts in the future increase: There will be segments of the private sector that will have to pay more taxes to enable the government to pay the public debt.

If, in contrast, the deficit is financed in international markets, it would raise the net burden of future cohorts, and this would be reflected in a net decrease in national income relative to internal income. In effect, in this case, the transfers among private agents and between them and the government would not cancel out because there is a net transfer to international markets. For this reason, in contrast to domestic debt, foreign debt is an instrument that allows society to perform transfers of an amount greater than existing resources at a point in time, at the cost of the future. When the debt is honored, the cohorts that are alive will have the responsibility of undertaking a net transfer to international markets without any domestic cohort receiving income as an offset. This net intertemporal redistribution effect that is absent in the case of domestic public debt means that the operations that increase net foreign debt should probably be monitored with greater care than those that involve domestic debt: It can be expected that the distributive conflicts among generations, and, as a result, macroeconomic imbalances associated with them will be more virulent. It is not by chance that the frequent crises associated with prolonged macroeconomic imbalances have always been closely linked to foreign indebtedness problems in Argentina.

One option with a low political cost in the short term to avoid indebtedness without reducing private disposable income is to lower public investment. In this sense, it is not surprising that in a situation in which fiscal space is significantly reduced, a typical adjustment measure in Argentina has consisted of reducing public investment to maintain social security or health care spending while avoiding exerting excessive pressure on disposable income and, as a result, on savings. The government has frequently had success in adjusting macroeconomics to avoid the instability that appears in figure 12.10b, but only at the cost of reducing investment in public infrastructure and pushing the economy toward a low-growth trap because of the lack of investment in infrastructure sectors that are usually the government's responsibility (because of market failures or those that require coordination). If this were to occur during the period in which the economy should be taking advantage of the SD, then the negative effects of the fall in investment would gain strength.

Even though the scenario of an economy with negative savings is unstable and surely has a low probability of occurring—although one must consider that a process of disinvestment in energy and infrastructure like that observed in Argentina in recent years is a form of doing just this—it is true that the simulation is very useful for illustrating the type of macroeconomic imbalance associated with the variables that we are considering. In particular, public expenditure today is much higher because of the growth in social security coverage, which has created entitlements that cannot be removed. Therefore, if an imbalance of the type that we are considering were to be generated, then it would tend to be persistent because the time associated with institutional changes is very different from the time required to avoid unsustainable macroeconomic situations.

If one observes that the increase in social security spending in Argentina (and in Brazil, which exhibits similar demographics) resulted in the situation that this expenditure is around 10 percent of GDP, that the tax burden reaches the highest levels in the region (along with Brazil), and that public investment in Argentina is around 3 percent of GDP (and 2 percent in Brazil), one arrives at the conclusion that the argument set forth at least deserves careful consideration in the design of growth policies—above all, if one considers what has already been stated regarding the low savings rate.

Financing the LD and Macroeconomic Equilibria

According to the basic identity of the national accounts, labor income (YL) plus nonlabor income (YA) and transfers abroad (YF) have as their counterpart consumption plus savings (S). Therefore, one can express the funding of the LD as follows:

$$LD_t = YA_t + YF_t - S_t = YA_t - (I_t + CA_t).$$

Thus, the LD can only increase if income from assets accumulated previously (YA + YF) is higher or if savings diminish. In this second case, this is equivalent to reducing investment (I_t) or the current account surplus (CA_t), weakening the accumulation of physical or foreign assets.[12]

With the goal of illustrating the type of macroeconomic imbalance that Argentina could face in the next 20 years as it finances the LDs, the following discussion addresses a set of simulations that show the links among savings, investment, the current account, and public debt.

Figures 12.11a and 12.11b show what would happen to investment and the current account if the savings rate were the rate that emerges from the simulation in figure 12.10a, which considers only changes in savings induced by demographics. Two scenarios are considered. In the first, the investment rate remains constant and equal to the average from the last decade.[13] In the second, the current account/GDP ratio remains constant, reflecting a Feldstein and Horioka (1980) type of scenario in which savings and investment move in unison. As can be observed, a *trade-off* exists between the result of the current account and investment as savings is determined by the level of the LD: As the LD will decrease for demographic reasons in the future, the propensity to save will increase, and if the current account/GDP ratio is fixed, investment will increase. If, in contrast, the investment rate is fixed, then the current account balance rises. The stock of public debt will increase despite the fact that the fiscal support ratio is within reasonable parameters because the government maintains a fiscal deficit during the simulation period (figure 12.11c).

This evolution of the flows is reflected in the trajectory of the levels of debt, as can be observed in figure 12.11c. In the scenario with the constant investment rate, the excess savings associated with the increase of the SR is translated into an increase in the international financial position.

Argentina would systematically increase the foreign assets in its portfolio. This scenario has similarities to what occurred during the period 2000 to 2005: As a response to the mediocre investment rate, a large portion of savings was used for the acquisition of assets abroad, with the result that today Argentina

Figure 12.11 Investment, Current Account, and Public Debt
Percent of GDP

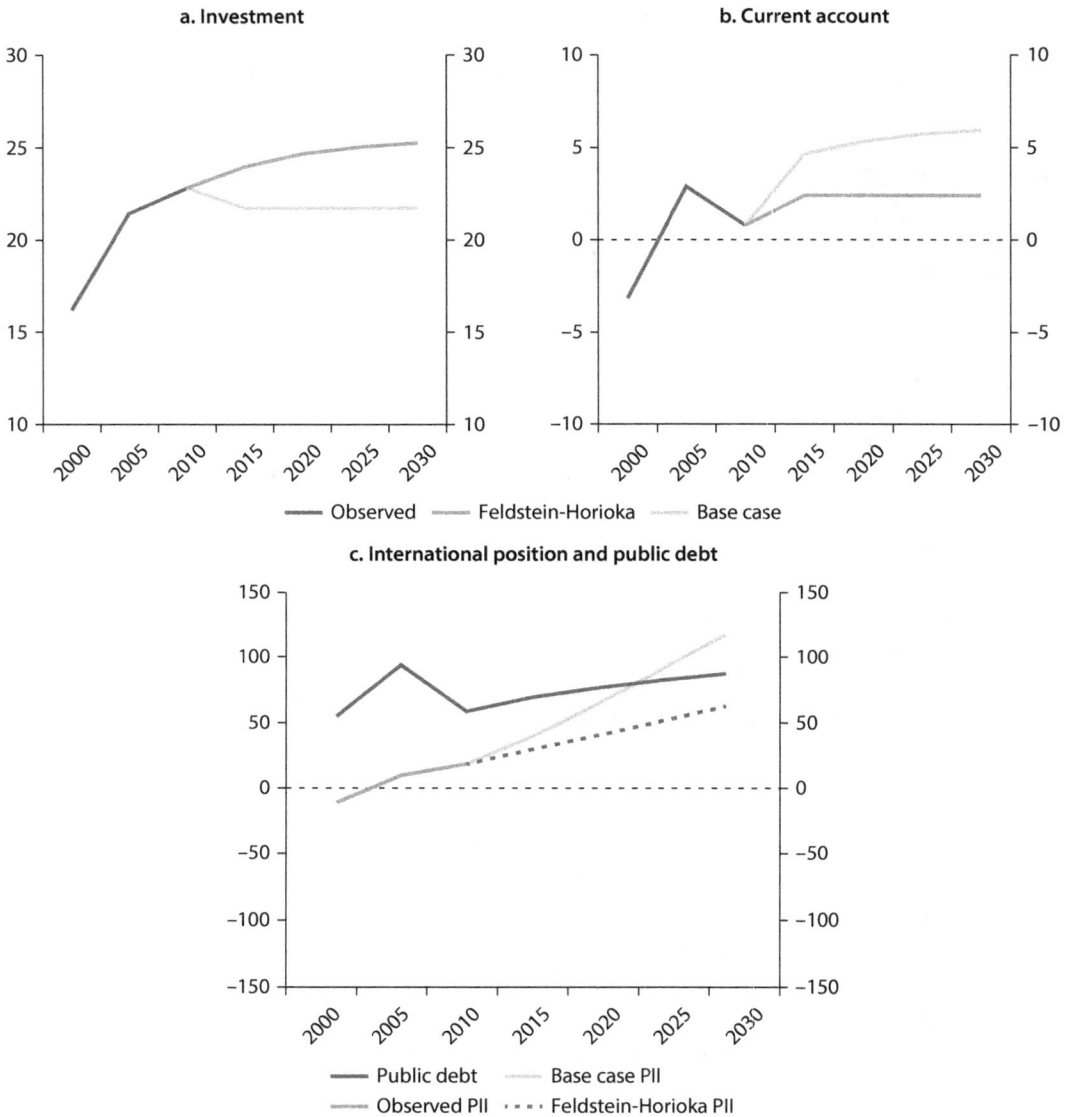

a. Investment

b. Current account

Observed —— Feldstein-Horioka —— Base case ……

c. International position and public debt

—— Public debt   …… Base case PII
—— Observed PII   ‧‧‧‧ Feldstein-Horioka PII

Source: Based on information from the NTA.

is a net creditor to the rest of the world, and the assets in private hands are estimated to exceed US$150 billion. In the Feldstein-Horioka scenario, in contrast, because the current account/GDP ratio remains fixed, productive investment absorbs a greater quantity of savings, and the external financial position increases by less.

The previous simulations assumed that SR only varied based on changes in the population. The simulations that include an increase in aggregate consumption as against salary income similar to the past decade exhibit an unsustainable evolution of the stock of debt, because of the aforementioned savings behavior in figure 12.10b.

Life-Cycle Wealth

It has been mentioned that the evolution of productive and foreign assets has to be consistent with the demand for wealth made by the various cohorts. It is necessary to consider, then, the trajectory of the demand for LW that the expected LDs create. Because the agents account for the future, the representative agent of each cohort at the private level will calculate the present value of the person's future LDs to evaluate the quantity of assets he or she must accumulate to finance the present value of excess consumption relative to salary income, once TW is discounted, which is the present value of the transfers to be received, whether from the state or other cohorts.

When one observes this problem from a macroeconomic point of view, one difficulty is identifying the planning horizon to be considered, above all in an economy as volatile as Argentina's. Fortunately, the principal interest is not in calculating what the steady state of the economy will be, but rather illustrating the type of debt level/flow ratio that it is important to monitor in the short term to evaluate if, given existing conditions, the Argentine economy could be exposed to the occurrence of lasting macroeconomic imbalances or fall into a low-growth trap. We have worked with a planning horizon of 20 years in a way that is consistent with the simulations of the current account and public debt.[14]

Figures 12.12a and 12.12b show the evolution of the present value of the LDs for 20 years—in other words, of the LW—generated by all of the generations that

Figure 12.12 Life-Cycle Wealth
Percent of labor income

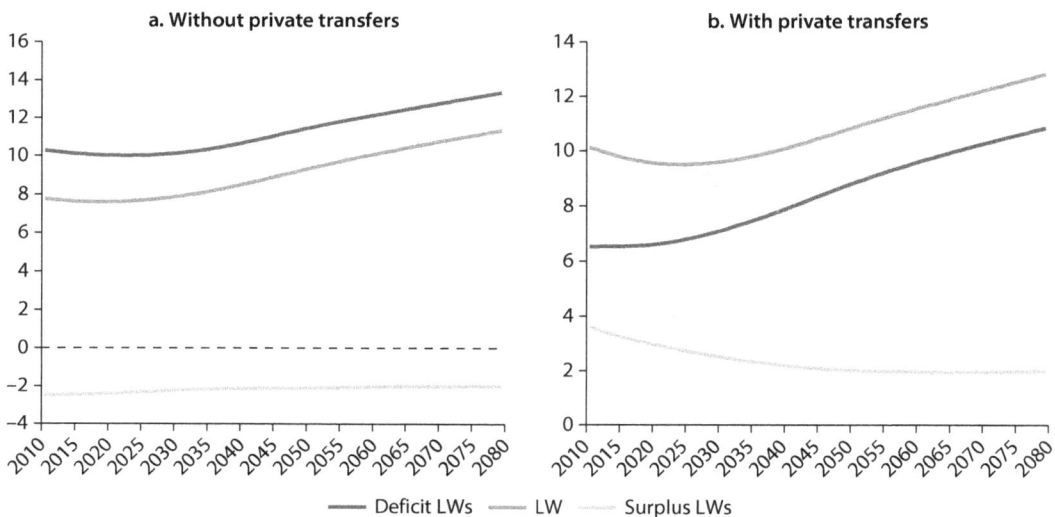

Source: Based on information from the NTA.

are alive in each of the years considered in the simulation. The variable is expressed as a percentage of labor income.

As the figures confirm, the LW is between 8 and 10 times the average salary level (figures a and b; utilizing a discount rate of 3 percent). Note how during the DWO period, the stock of wealth required remains constant, but when the window ends, demand increases accompanied by the population aging process, which expands the size of the aggregate LD.

The net demand for LW made by cohorts emerges from their expectations of expenditure and income. To meet these expectations when the moment arrives, if the LD is positive, the expenditures in excess of labor income must have as a counterpart income from previously accumulated assets, public or private transfers, or indebtedness to be paid by the cohorts that are alive once the 20 years that we are considering as a time horizon have passed. To show the quantitative significance of the intrahousehold transfers as a form of financing, Figure 12.12a records the evolution of the LW without including transfers from parents and children, and 12.12b does include them (although inheritances are absent due to a lack of information). The fundamental difference between the value of the stock of LW regardless of whether intrahousehold transfers are considered is that when these transfers are considered, we do not observe cohorts that generate a life-cycle surplus in present value terms in any portion of the simulation. This means that, when the time arrives to finance the LDs in the future, it will be necessary to utilize the revenue coming from assets because salary income will not be sufficient, and, obviously, for this revenue to be available requires that assets be accumulated during the preceding period. In other words, if the demand for LW is high, it is necessary to save today, and if that does not occur, it will be necessary to dissave (reduce physical or foreign assets) to finance the LDs in the future. Obviously, the stronger this effect is, the greater the downward pressure on savings and the lower the probability of taking advantage of the SD. This argument highlights the importance of taking advantage of the demographic dividend today to avoid problems tomorrow.

The effect of aging can be identified by showing how much LW each of the cohorts that is alive demands at a point in time as the demographic transition advances. Figure 12.13 presents the profile corresponding to four points (2010, 2020, 2030, and 2040). In both figures (with and without private transfers), one can appreciate that as the demographic transition runs its course, the deficit generated by the older cohorts (age 60 and older) increases due to aging. Moreover, if figure 12.13a is compared to 12.13b, it is clear how transfers to children affect the capacity of workers from the group of prime savers to generate a surplus.

Finally, it is possible to calculate the present value of the transfers that the public sector is expected to make in the future, which are a fundamental component of TW. Assuming constant tax and transfer policies, net transfers are determined as a function of the demographic changes that are reflected in changes to the U_t and Q_t variables over time. Figure 12.14 summarizes the simulation performed using these assumptions.

Figure 12.13 Life-Cycle Wealth, by Cohort

Millions of 2010 AR$

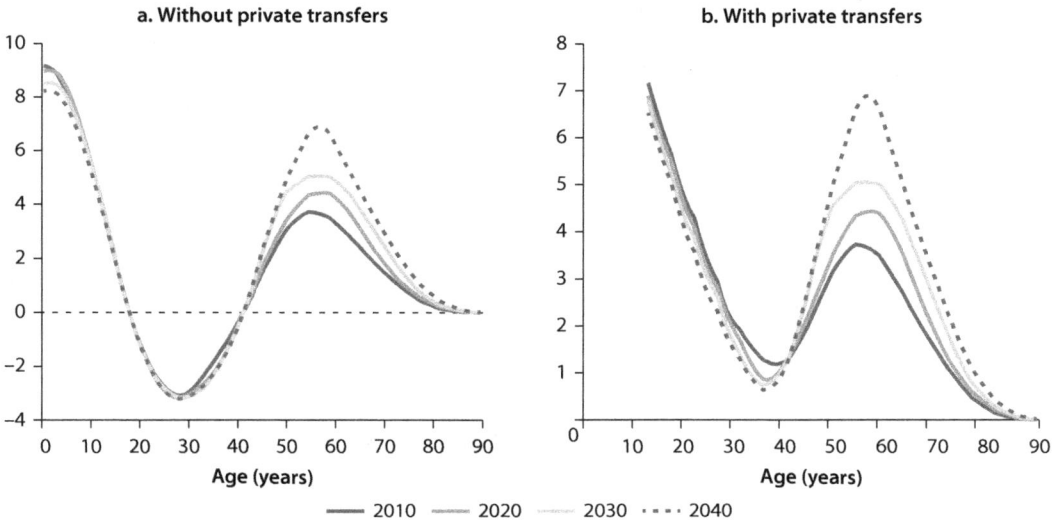

a. Without private transfers   b. With private transfers

2010   2020   2030   ···· 2040

Source: Based on information from the NTA.

Figure 12.14   Present Value of Public Transfers

Percentage of labor income

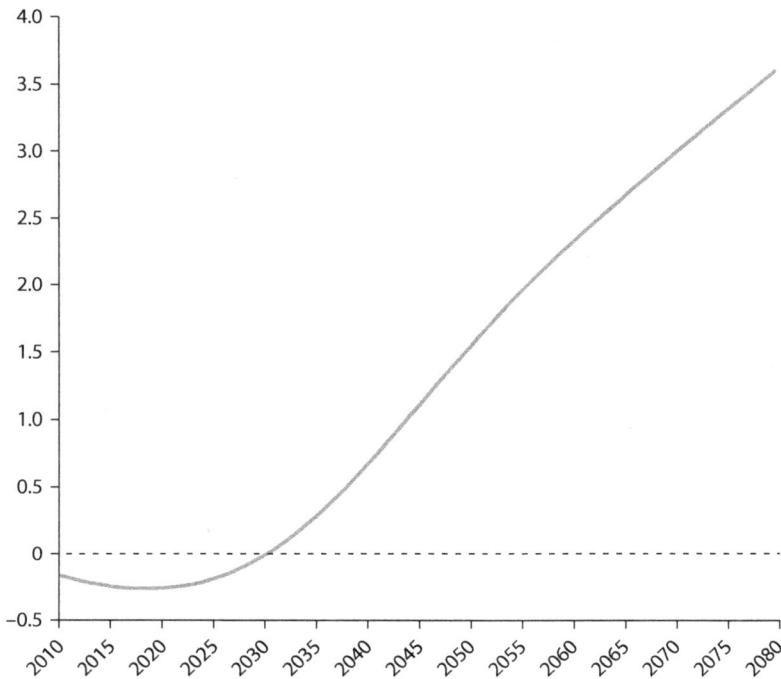

Source: Based on information from the NTA.

Transfers first fall and then increase, following the movement of the consumption support ratio. Note the strong growth expected following the end of the DWO, which means that the portion that the government must finance reaches around one-third or more of the total LW. This increase in transfers has as a counterpart the increase of public debt observed above. However, although transfers increase in relation to total salaries, the fiscal situation is not unsustainable. What is occurring is that the generations that are alive following the 20 years considered as the horizon must take responsibility for this public debt that is the counterpart to the transfers. We must clarify, however, that since the inheritance of assets that the elderly will leave behind after these 20 years is not considered, it is not clear that future generations will remain in an excessively disadvantaged position.

Final Reflections

The literature suggests that to get rich before reaching the aging period, it is vital to take advantage of the second demographic dividend, and that doing so requires appropriate policies, particularly regarding the generation of savings and channeling these resources to investment. The emphasis on this point is due to the fact that it is easy to misspend the extra resources that demographics creates during the demographic dividend period, and if this occurs the investment opportunities and policy challenges during the aging period will be very different depending on whether a society becomes rich based on the proper use of the dividends. Similarly, this chapter has called attention to the potential factors of macroeconomic instability and the persistent imbalances that operate through the imbalances between demand for LW and the accumulation of assets.

It emerges from this analysis that the threat that Argentina will grow old before growing rich is not minor. As a result, it cannot be assumed that the country will replicate the experience of developed countries such as Japan or successful emerging ones such as Korea. Regarding this situation, public policies must keep the following in mind:

a. The FD has a relatively low effect on growth and, moreover, will reverse when Argentina exits the DWO. This means that the growth policy focus should be on the SD, which has great potential to increase productivity by increasing the capital/labor ratio. The conditions for realizing the SD are created through the promotion and proper use of savings. If this is achieved, productivity will increase at a good pace during what remains of the DWO and the country will be prepared for aging.

b. During the next 25 years, mistakes "count double" because the country will enjoy an extraordinary period for growth during which the weight of the active population and, especially, of the prime savers in the population will increase.

c. Argentina exhibits a low savings rate and an excessive life-cycle deficit relative to labor income when its situation is compared to that of other countries that took advantage of the first and SDs, as in the case of Korea.

d. The evidence indicates that the country already exhibits a high tax burden on the cohorts of prime savers. This reduces disposable income and private savings capacity during the most favorable period for saving, when workers are near the completion of their period of active work.

e. During the DWO period, fiscal space enlarges because the tax base expands along with the greater weight of the active age groups. The policies linked with human capital accumulation and public investment should be favored over pure transfers. Regarding this point, it should be emphasized that transfers from the social security system already have significant weight in terms of GDP that could displace public investments that are vital for growth.

f. The way in which the aggregate LD is financed has direct effects on macroeconomic imbalances because it affects the current account and absorbs a portion of private income that originates from previously accumulated assets. If the trend of consumption growing more than productivity and income is maintained, Argentina will probably be exposed to the occurrence of situations of macroeconomic stress. This will manifest itself, above all, as a fall in savings and the accumulation of assets. A development of this type could lead the economy into a low-growth trap.

g. Financing net public transfers to various cohorts through the use of external indebtedness may be particularly harmful because it exacerbates the distributive conflicts and increases the probability that persistent economic imbalances associated with the debt crisis will occur. These crises occur when the generations that come after those that took on the debt refuse reductions to their transfers or when taxes are increased for the purpose of repaying foreign debt.

h. TW has an important role above all after the end of the DWO and will reach one-third of the demand for LW among the living cohorts. This fact could disincentivize savings. In any case, if the tax burden is maintained, the fiscal support ratio will evolve reasonably during the coming decades because of the increase of the consumption support ratio.

Finally, from a political economy point of view, the demographic transition is, above all, a process of structural change and, as such, requires appropriate changes in organizations and institutions. When one observes the challenges that the country faces from this perspective, there is a clear need to understand certain institutional aspects that have an essential role in the dividend and aging periods.

First, as a reflection of its institutional weaknesses, Argentina does not have sufficient financial development, and this will, without a doubt, be an obstacle to efficiently resolving the intermediation problems that managing the LD and LW present. Financial development is intensive in terms of requirements for clear and consistent rules of the game. In the growth models applied to demographics, sometimes sufficient attention is not paid to the mechanisms through which the economy assigns excess savings because these models usually adopt the assumption that saving is equal to investment and the imbalance between savings and investment is a "short-term" problem. Similarly, it is rarely specified how the financial structure allocates savings. When one admits that persistent macroeconomic imbalances may exist and that, moreover, macroeconomic volatility and financial underdevelopment affect growth, it follows that it is essential to pay attention to the type of institutional and organizational framework that would be most favorable for financial development.

Second, the institutional framework matters because institutions model incentives, and the literature emphasizes the disincentives associated with the social security system. If the rules of the game for this system are not consistent, it depresses savings and increases the risk of the sustainability of public debt.

Finally, it is necessary to call our attention to the *path dependence* phenomena that affect savings. In the case of Argentina and of countries such as Brazil that have suffered crises and have grown slowly following these debt crises at the beginning of the 1980s (Bacha and Bonelli 2012), it is also necessary to consider the hypothesis that an inconsistency could exist between, on the one hand, the rate of increase of consumption desired by the population, which is reflected not just in private consumption, but also in public policies, and, on the other hand, the slow rate of increase in productivity observed, above all, during the decades that followed the 1980s debt crisis. Thus, the expansion of the coverage of the social security system and spending on education could be driven by the inertia of demographic, cultural, and political economy factors that are not changing rapidly and are not necessarily fully adapted to the break in the growth trend. In the case of high-growth economies, the exact opposite is probably occurring: Consumption and institutions could be lagging in their adaptation to the speedy increase in income and productivity, as the slowness in the development of the social security system in China suggests and the "exaggerated" level of savings among workers. Because the errors might be the result of excess or defect, designing an institutional framework that appropriately accompanies the demographic transition is far from being a solved problem.

Notes

1. In this chapter, "demographic window of opportunity period" and "demographic dividend period" are used interchangeably.

2. For more on these questions, see Kent et al. (2006) and IMF (2012).

3. One advantage of the database and methodology provided by the NTA project is that it makes international comparisons possible, which enables us to have reference patterns to evaluate the evidence corresponding to Argentina. The present chapter frequently uses the cases of the Republic of Korea, because it is a country that was successful in taking advantage of the demographic dividend period; Brazil, because it is a Latin American country that is also passing through the dividend period; and Japan, as an example of a country in the advanced stage of the transition that is aging. Occasionally, the cases of Chile and China are also used to highlight specific features.

4. If we consider the alternative definition that the DWO extends during the entire period during which the total dependency ratio is less than 60 percent, the window would be longer: It would reach 2050.

5. The inverse of the dependency ratio is defined as $IDR = XA/(XY + XV)$, where XY, XV, and XA are the following populations, respectively: $Y = 0$–14 years old (children); $A = 15$–64 years old (adults); and $V = 65+$ (elderly).

6. As was discussed in chapter 10.

7. For more on this point, see Higgins and Williamson (1997), Bryant (2006), Higgins (1998), and Fanelli and Albrieu (2012).

8. According to the NTA methodology, cohort consumption includes consumption financed by the government and in-kind transfers (see Mason and Lee 2011). Also, consistent with this methodology, the variables φ_a and γ_a are expressed utilizing per capita income for workers between the ages of 30 and 49 years old (ym) as the denominator. In other words, if ca and yla are, respectively, consumption and per capita labor income for cohort a, we have $\varphi_a = ca/ym$ and, also, $\gamma_a = yla/ym$. The values of the profiles φ_a and γ_a remained fixed at the base year (2010) because information is only available for this year. For a justification of why it is possible to maintain the coefficients fixed as a reasonable approximation, see Mason and Lee (2011).

9. Note the following:

$$ym_t = \sum_{a=30}^{49} YL_{a,t} \bigg/ \sum_{a=30}^{49} x_{at}.$$

In other words, the average per capita income for salaried workers between the ages of 30 and 49 years old is equal to the total salary income of these salaried workers divided by the number of members of these age cohorts.

10. If $SR>1$, as is the case in China, the economy generates a surplus. Thus, as SR increases, the surplus increases.

11. See Ros (2000) for more about growth traps.

12. It is worth noting that YA and YL are defined as national income—in other words, net of payments or income from factors abroad. In the NTA literature, this is called asset-based reallocations in contrast to the difference between income from domestic and foreign assets and national savings (SN_t).

13. This scenario is consistent with the fact that investigators have not found a clear relationship between the investment rate and demographics from an econometric point of view (see Speller et al. 2011).

14. The LD demand for the next 20 years includes the present value of the LD for cohorts that have not yet been born. The hypothesis used here is that these LDs should be kept in mind because they either appear in the calculations of the stock of wealth of the cohorts living today or in the state's budgets, which should ensure that these LDs are financed in some way. A more precise analysis of these difficulties exceeds the limits of this chapter. The point that interests us here is evaluating how demand varies for life-cycle wealth who could be designated "notional" that which would emerge if we keep in mind all of the LDs that must be financed over the next 20 years, independent of whether those who will make these demands have been born yet and evaluate the macroeconomic consequences.

References

Albrieu, R., and J. M. Fanelli. 2013. "On the Macroeconomic and Financial Implications of the Demographic Transition." Paper presented at the IX Meeting of the Working Group on Macroeconomic Aspects of Intergenerational Transfers, Faculty of Economics, University of Barcelona, June 3–8.

Bacha, E., and R. Bonelli. 2012. "Accounting for the Rise and Fall of Post-WW-II Brazil's Growth." Draft.

Bloom, D., and J. Williamson. 1997. "Demographic Transitions and Economic Miracles in Emerging Asia." NBER Working Paper Series6268, Cambridge, MA.

Bloom, D., D. Canning, and F. Gunther. 2010. "Population Aging and Economic Growth." In *Globalization and Growth*, edited by M. Spence and D. Leipziger, 297–328. Cambridge, MA: MIT Press.

Bloom, D., D. Canning, and J. Sevilla. 2003. *The Demographic Dividend: A New Perspective on the Economic Consequences of Population Change*. RAND Monograph Report 1274, Los Angeles.

Bryant, R. C. 2006. "Asymmetric Demographic Transitions and North-South Capital Flows." Brookings Discussion Paper 170, Brookings Institution, Washington, DC.

Fanelli, J. M. 2011. "Domestic Financial Development in Latin America." In *The Oxford Handbook of Latin American Economics*, edited by J. Ocampo and J. Ros, 241–65. Oxford: Oxford University Press.

Fanelli, J. M., and R. Albrieu. 2012. "Asymmetric Demography, Global Savings, and Financial Development." Background paper for the CEDES-IDRC project Asymmetric Demography and Global Financial Governance: In Search of Growth and Common Interests in the Post-Crisis World, Buenos Aires.

Feldstein, M., and H. C. Horioka. 1980. "Domestic Savings and International Capital Flows." *Economic Journal* 90: 314–29.

Haldane, A. 2010. *Global Imbalances in Retrospect and Prospect*. http://www.bis.org/review/r101223f.pdf. Bank of England, London.

Higgins, M. 1998. "Demography, National Savings, and International Capital Flows." *International Economic Review* 39: 343–69.

Higgins, M., and J. Williamson. 1997. "Age Structure Dynamics in Asia and Dependence on Foreign Capital." *Population and Development Review* 23: 261– 93.

IMF (International Monetary Fund). 2005. "Households Balance Sheets." In *Global Financial Stability Report*. Washington DC.

———. 2012. "The Financial Impact of Longevity Risk." In *Global Financial Stability Report*, Washington DC.

Kent, C., A. Park, and D. Rees. 2006. "Demography and Financial Markets." Reserve Bank of Australia, Canberra.

Mason, A. 2005. "Demographic Transition and Demographic Dividends in Developed and Developing Countries." United Nations Expert Group Meeting on Social and Economic Implications of Changing Population Age Structure, Mexico City, August 31–September 2.

Mason, A., and R. Lee. 2006. "Back to Basics: What Is the Demographic Dividend." *Finance and Development* 43 (3):, 16–17.

———. 2007. "Transfers, Capital, and Consumption over the Demographic Transition in Population Aging." In *Intergenerational Transfers and the Macroeconomy*, edited by R. Clark, N. Ogawa, and A. Mason, 128–62. Cheltenham, UK: Edward Elgar.

———. 2011. *Population Aging and the Generational Economy: A Global Perspective*. Cheltenham, UK: Edward Elgar.

Ros, J. 2000. *Development Theory and the Economics of Growth*. Ann Arbor: University of Michigan Press.

Speller, W., G. Thwaites, and M. Wright. 2011. "The Future of International Capital Flows." Bank of England Financial Stability Paper 12, London.

Turra, C., and B. Queiroz. 2005. "Before It's Too Late: Demographic Transition, Labour Supply and Social Security Problems in Brazil." United Nations Expert Group Meeting on Social and Economic Implications of Changing Population Age Structure, United Nations, Mexico City, August 31–September 2.

United Nations. 2004. *World Population to 2300*. New York: United Nations. http://www .un.org/esa/population/publications/longrange2/WorldPop2300final.pdf.

———. 2013. *World Population Prospects: The 2012 Revision*. New York: Population Division, Department of Economic and Social Affairs, United Nations Secretariat.

Wilson, D., and S. Ahmed. 2010. "Current Accounts and Demographics: The Road Ahead." Goldman Sachs Global Economics Paper 202, Goldman Sachs, New York.

CHAPTER 13

As Time Goes By in Argentina: Economic Opportunities and Challenges of the Demographic Transition

The process of demographic transition through which Argentina is passing is a window of both opportunities and challenges in economic and social terms. Argentina is still a young country in which the working-age population represents the largest proportion of its total population. Currently, the country just began a 30-year period with the most advantageous age structure of its population, which could favor greater economic growth. This situation, a demographic window of opportunity, will last until the beginning of the 2040s. The dynamics of the fertility and mortality rates signify a gradual aging of the population, with implications for various dimensions of the economy, the social protection system, public policies, and society in general.

This book examines the opportunities and challenges that the demographic transition poses for the Argentine economy, its most important social sectors—health care, education, and social protection systems—and the potential fiscal trade-offs that must be dealt with. The study shows that even though Argentina is moving through its demographic transition, it just recently began to enjoy the window of opportunity, and this constitutes a great opportunity to achieve an accumulation of capital and future economic growth. Once the window of opportunity has passed, population aging will have a significant impact on the level of expenditure, especially spending on the social protection system. This signifies a challenge from a fiscal policy point of view, because if long-term reforms are not undertaken to mediate these effects, the demographic transition will put pressure on the reallocation of fiscal resources among social sectors. Finally, population aging poses concerns related to sustaining the rate of economic growth with a smaller working-age population. Taking advantage of the current window of opportunities, increasing savings that will finance the accumulation of capital, and increasing future labor force productivity in this way all pose a challenge for the Argentine economy.

The main goal of this book is to take the first step in the study of the potential impact that a slow but steady phenomenon such as demographic transition will have on the Argentine economy, showing the importance that the current discussion of future reforms deserves, with the goal of mitigating the adverse effects of aging. The impact on the level of spending on social protection, health care, and education systems, based on a consideration of the various possible scenarios of public policy as well as the fiscal space and spending dilemmas and their challenges, and the macroeconomic context and medium- and long-term perspectives in terms of economic growth are presented in independent chapters with the goal of covering what we understand to be a significant gap in the literature, thus contributing to the public policy debate in the areas analyzed.

Environmental Benefits Statement

The World Bank Group is committed to reducing its environmental footprint. In support of this commitment, the Publishing and Knowledge Division leverages electronic publishing options and print-on-demand technology, which is located in regional hubs worldwide. Together, these initiatives enable print runs to be lowered and shipping distances decreased, resulting in reduced paper consumption, chemical use, greenhouse gas emissions, and waste.

The Publishing and Knowledge Division follows the recommended standards for paper use set by the Green Press Initiative. Whenever possible, books are printed on 50 percent to 100 percent postconsumer recycled paper, and at least 50 percent of the fiber in our book paper is either unbleached or bleached using Totally Chlorine Free (TCF), Processed Chlorine Free (PCF), or Enhanced Elemental Chlorine Free (EECF) processes.

More information about the Bank's environmental philosophy can be found at http://crinfo.worldbank.org/wbcrinfo/node/4.

green
press
INITIATIVE